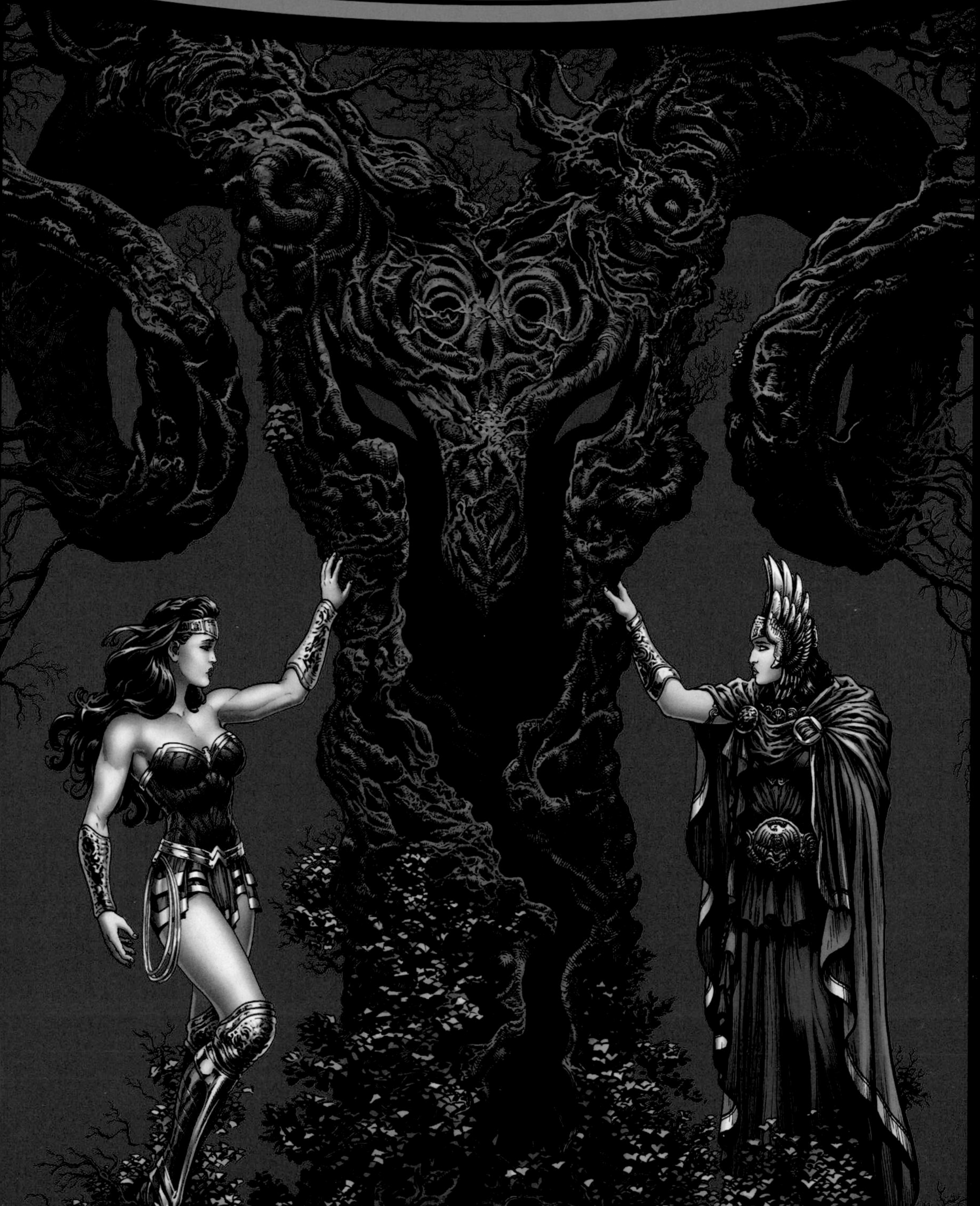

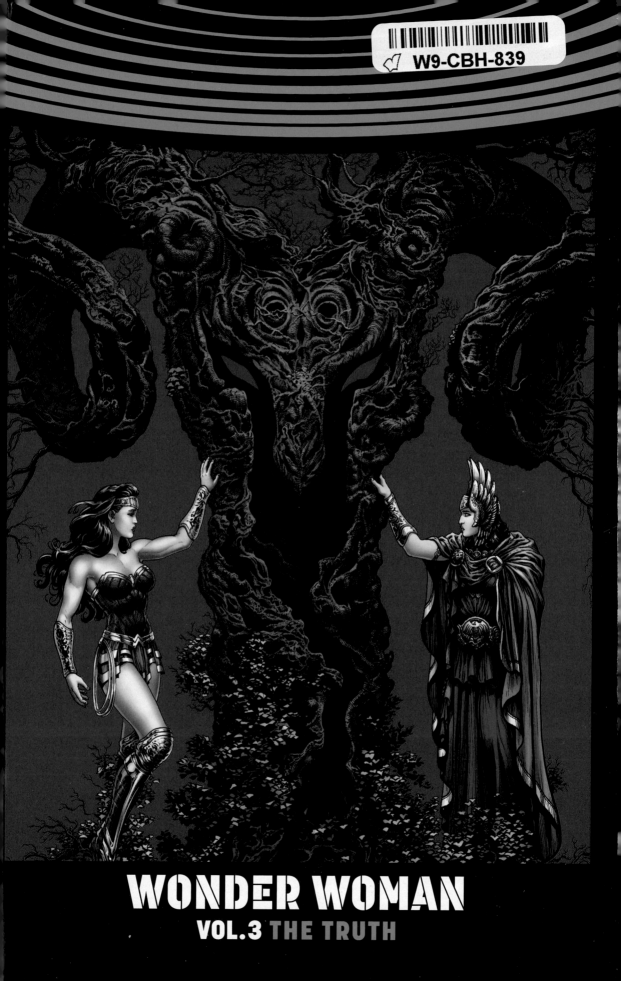

WONDER WOMAN

VOL.3 THE TRUTH

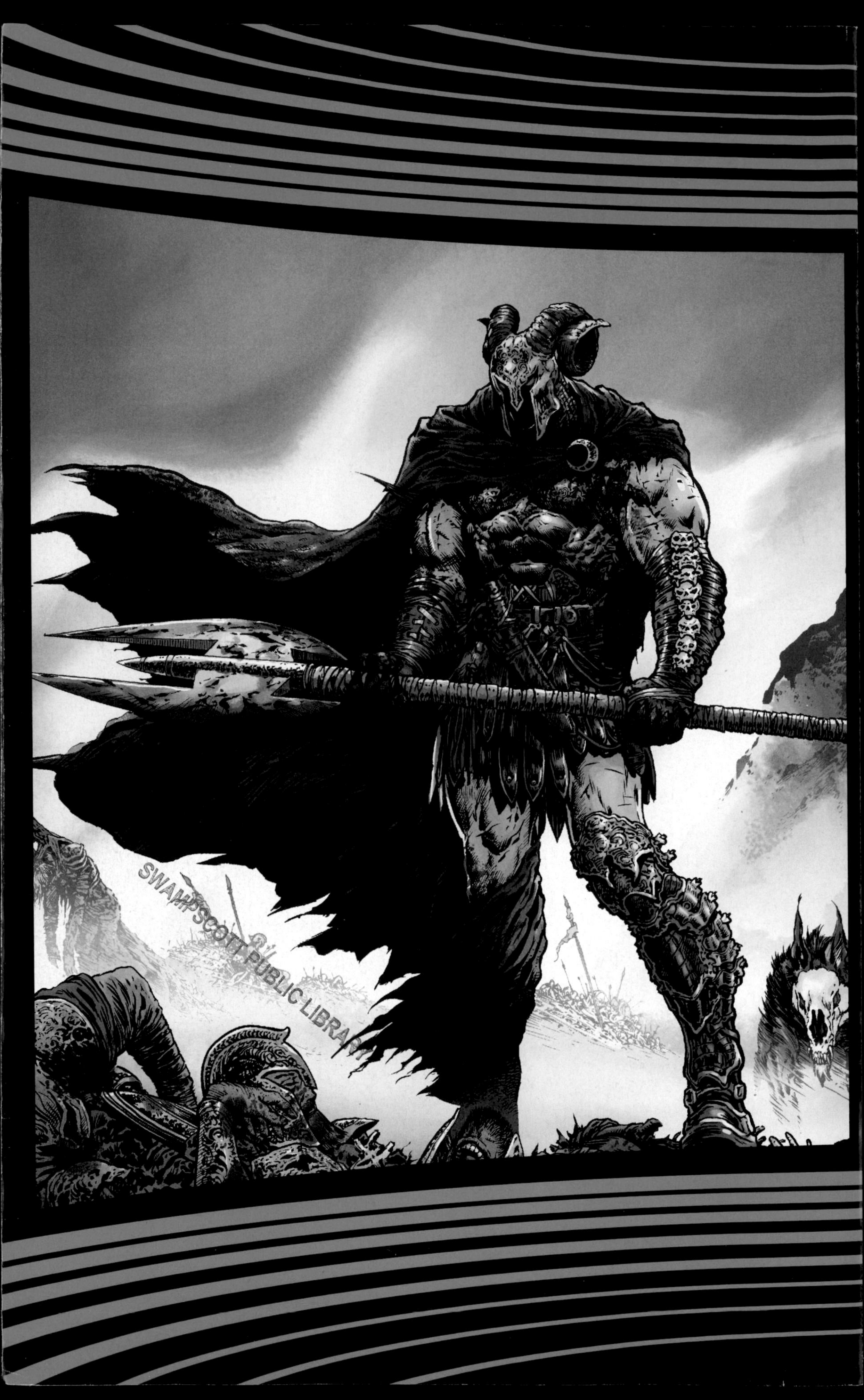

WONDER WOMAN
VOL.3 THE TRUTH

GREG RUCKA
writer

LIAM SHARP
artist
RENATO GUEDES
artist ("Angel Down")
BILQUIS EVELY
additional art ("Perfect")

LAURA MARTIN
ROMULO FAJARDO JR. * **HI-FI**
colorists

JODI WYNNE
letterer

LIAM SHARP & LAURA MARTIN
collection cover artists

WONDER WOMAN created by WILLIAM MOULTON MARSTON

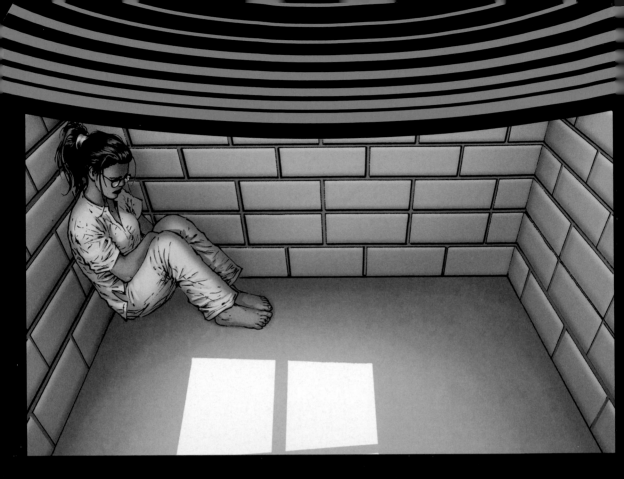

CHRIS CONROY MARK DOYLE Editors - Original Series * **DAVE WIELGOSZ** Assistant Editor - Original Series
JEB WOODARD Group Editor - Collected Editions * **ROBIN WILDMAN** Editor - Collected Edition
STEVE COOK Design Director - Books * **MONIQUE GRUSPE** Publication Design

BOB HARRAS Senior VP - Editor-in-Chief, DC Comics

DIANE NELSON President * **DAN DiDIO** Publisher * **JIM LEE** Publisher * **GEOFF JOHNS** President & Chief Creative Officer
AMIT DESAI Executive VP - Business & Marketing Strategy, Direct to Consumer & Global Franchise Management * **SAM ADES** Senior VP - Direct to Consumer
BOBBIE CHASE VP - Talent Development * **MARK CHIARELLO** Senior VP - Art, Design & Collected Editions
JOHN CUNNINGHAM Senior VP - Sales & Trade Marketing * **ANNE DePIES** Senior VP - Business Strategy, Finance & Administration
DON FALLETTI VP - Manufacturing Operations * **LAWRENCE GANEM** VP - Editorial Administration & Talent Relations
ALISON GILL Senior VP - Manufacturing & Operations * **HANK KANALZ** Senior VP - Editorial Strategy & Administration
JAY KOGAN VP - Legal Affairs * **THOMAS LOFTUS** VP - Business Affairs
JACK MAHAN VP - Business Affairs * **NICK J. NAPOLITANO** VP - Manufacturing Administration
EDDIE SCANNELL VP - Consumer Marketing * **COURTNEY SIMMONS** Senior VP - Publicity & Communications
JIM (SKI) SOKOLOWSKI VP - Comic Book Specialty Sales & Trade Marketing * **NANCY SPEARS** VP - Mass, Book, Digital Sales & Trade Marketing

WONDER WOMAN VOLUME 3: THE TRUTH

DC Comics, 2900 West Alameda Ave., Burbank, CA 91505.
Printed by LSC Communications, Salem, VA, USA. 7/21/17.
First Printing. ISBN: 978-1-4012-7141-1

Library of Congress Cataloging-in-Publication Data is available.

PEFC Certified
Printed on paper from sustainably managed forests, controlled sources
PEFC/29-31-337
www.pefc.org

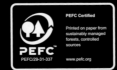

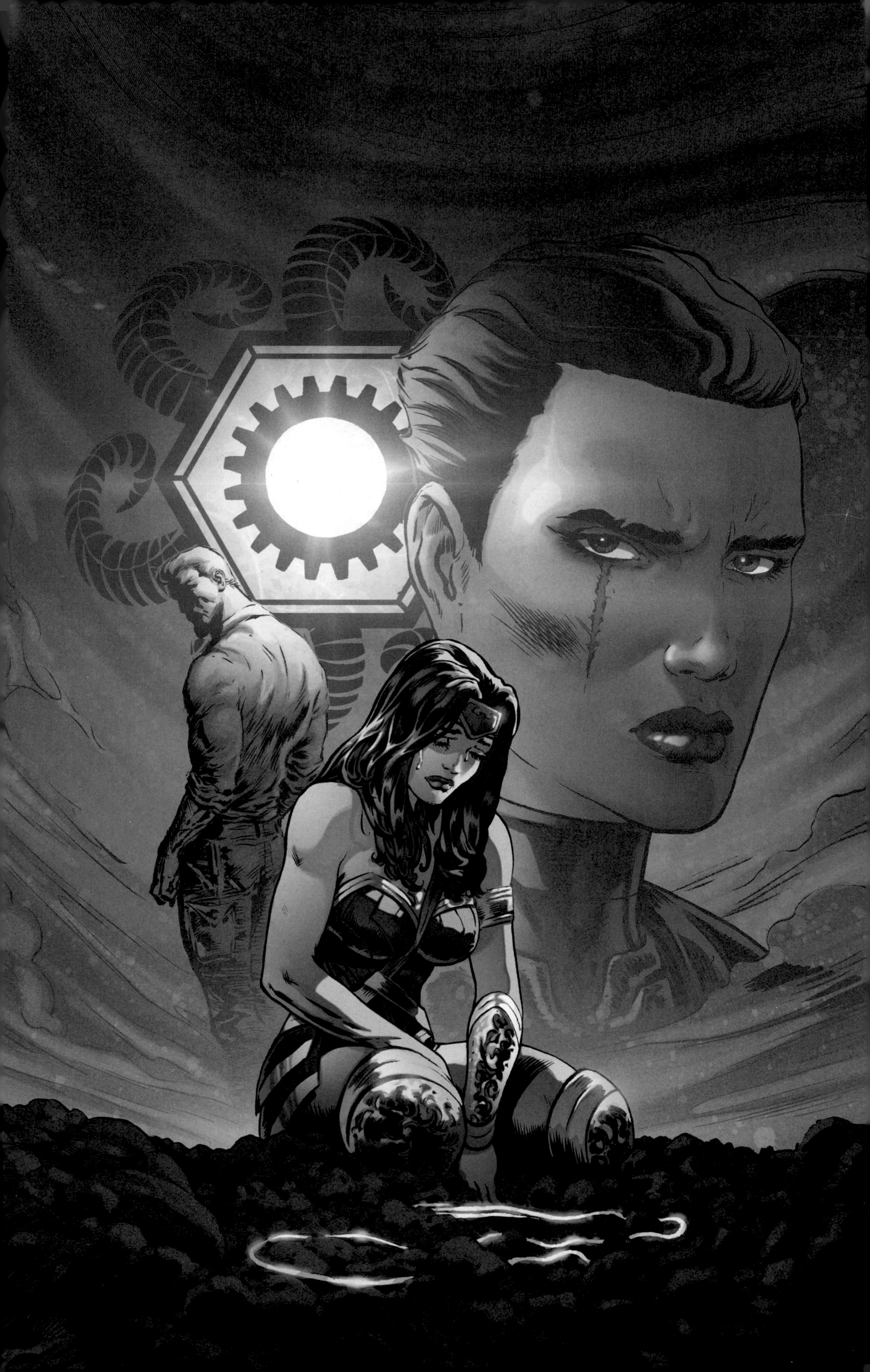

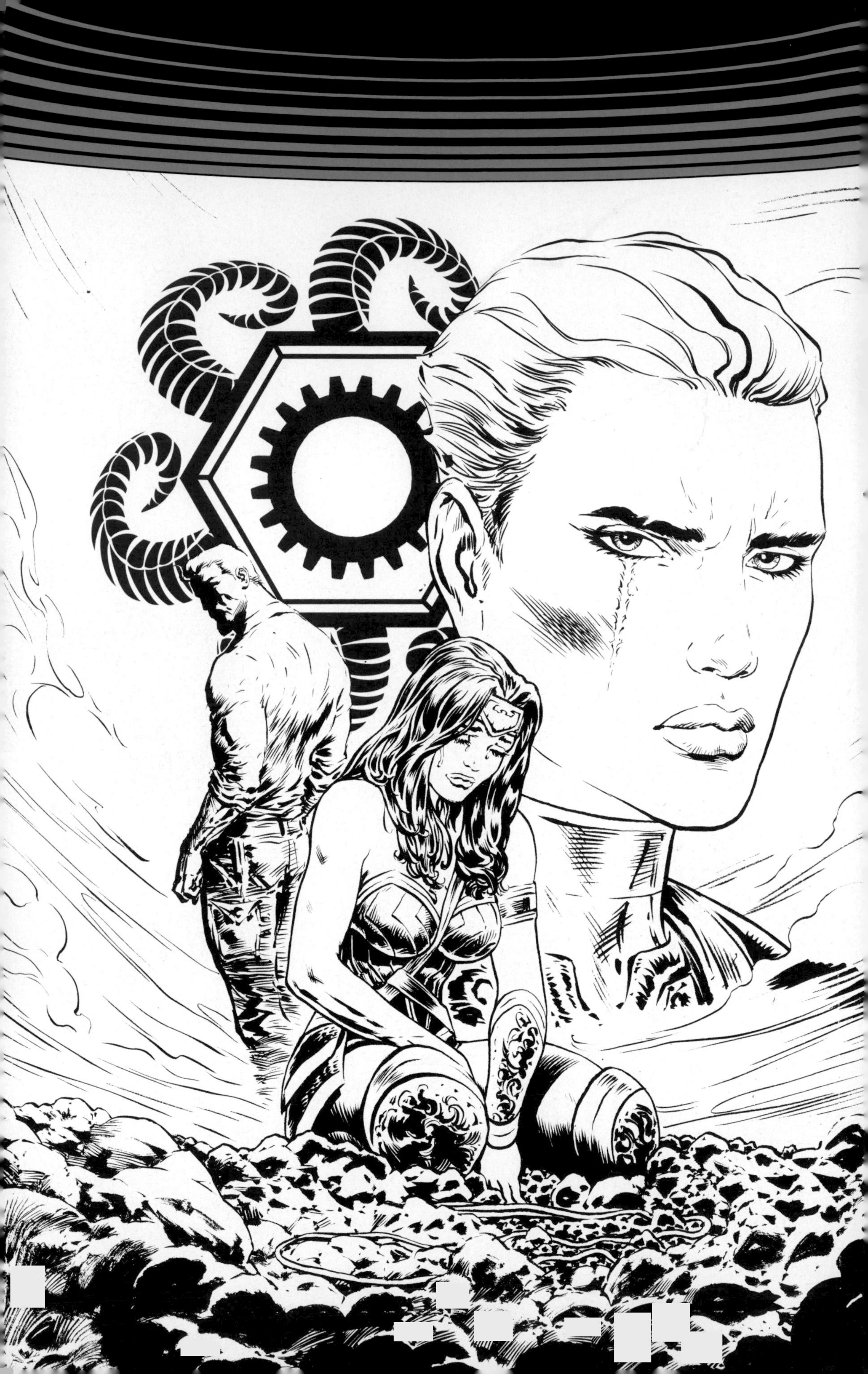

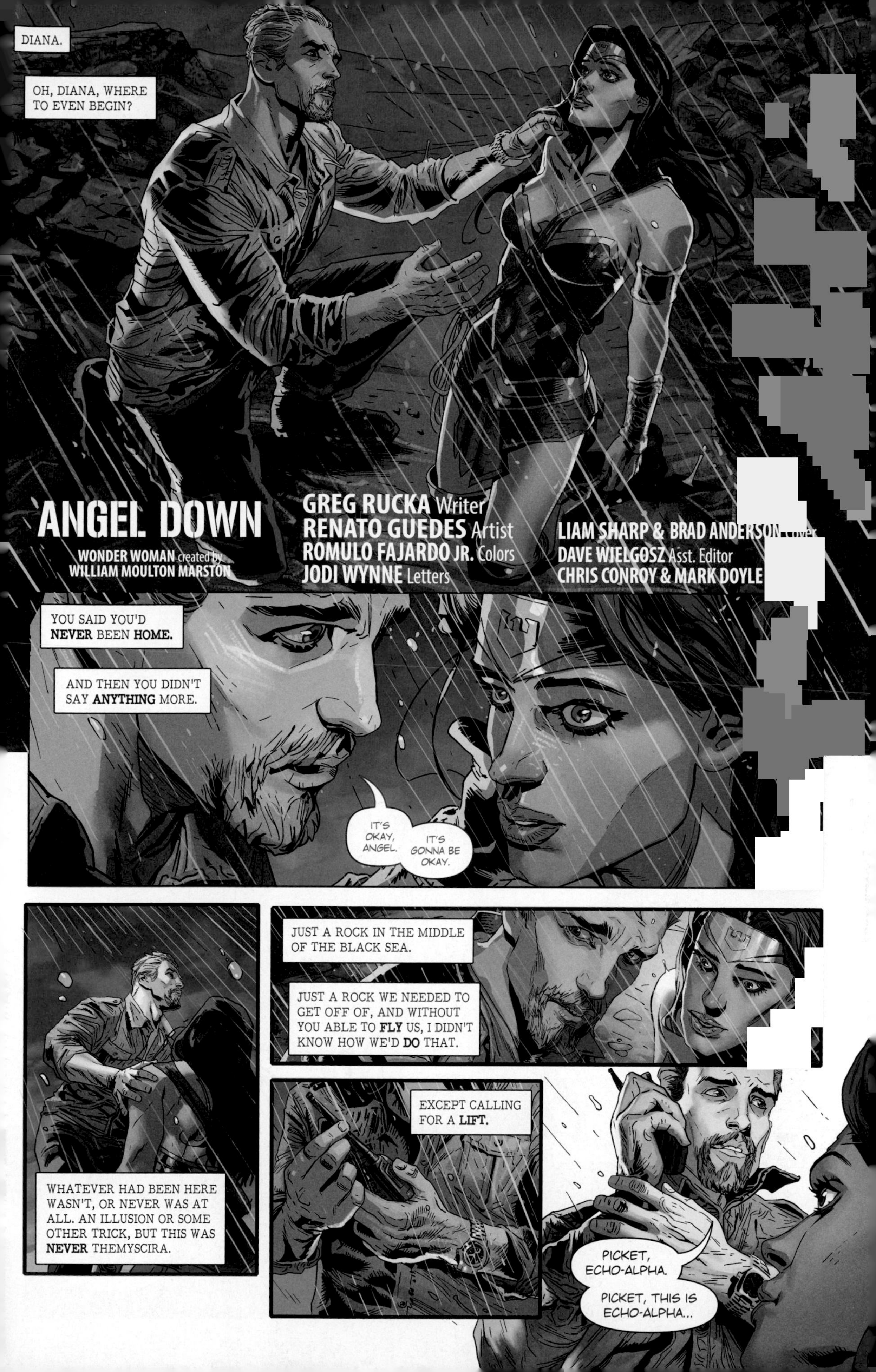

DIANA.
OH, DIANA, WHERE TO EVEN BEGIN?
ANGEL DOWN
WONDER WOMAN created by WILLIAM MOULTON MARSTON
GREG RUCKA Writer
RENATO GUEDES Artist
ROMULO FAJARDO JR. Colors
JODI WYNNE Letters
LIAM SHARP & BRAD ANDERSON
DAVE WIELGOSZ Asst. Editor
CHRIS CONROY & MARK DOYLE
YOU SAID YOU'D NEVER BEEN HOME.
AND THEN YOU DIDN'T SAY ANYTHING MORE.
IT'S OKAY, ANGEL.
IT'S GONNA BE OKAY.
WHATEVER HAD BEEN HERE WASN'T, OR NEVER WAS AT ALL. AN ILLUSION OR SOME OTHER TRICK, BUT THIS WAS NEVER THEMYSCIRA.
JUST A ROCK IN THE MIDDLE OF THE BLACK SEA.
JUST A ROCK WE NEEDED TO GET OFF OF, AND WITHOUT YOU ABLE TO FLY US, I DIDN'T KNOW HOW WE'D DO THAT.
EXCEPT CALLING FOR A LIFT.
PICKET, ECHO-ALPHA.
PICKET, THIS IS ECHO-ALPHA...

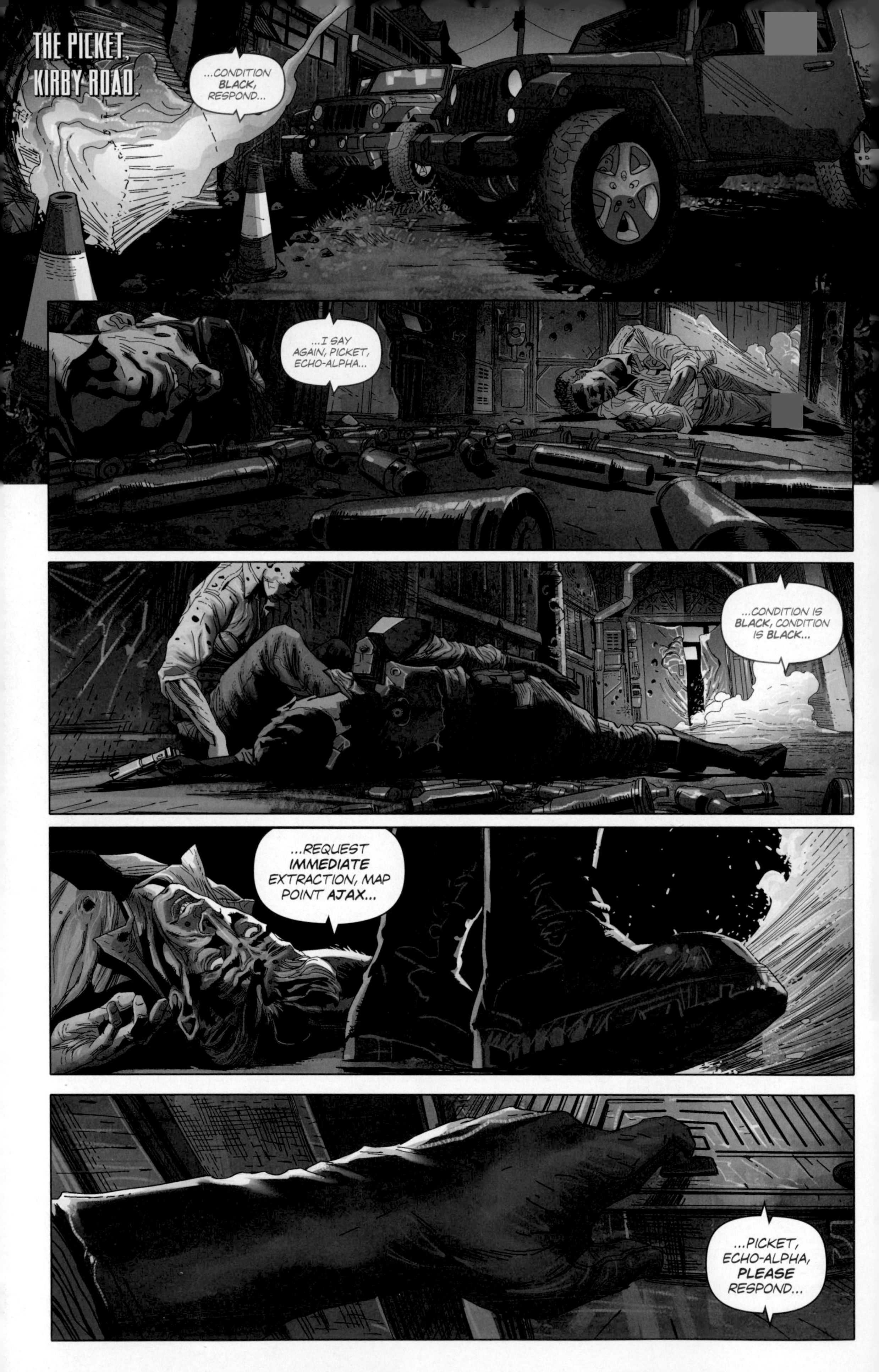
THE PICKET, KIRBY ROAD.
...CONDITION BLACK, RESPOND...
...I SAY AGAIN, PICKET, ECHO-ALPHA...
...CONDITION IS BLACK, CONDITION IS BLACK...
...REQUEST IMMEDIATE EXTRACTION, MAP POINT AJAX...
...PICKET, ECHO-ALPHA, PLEASE RESPOND...

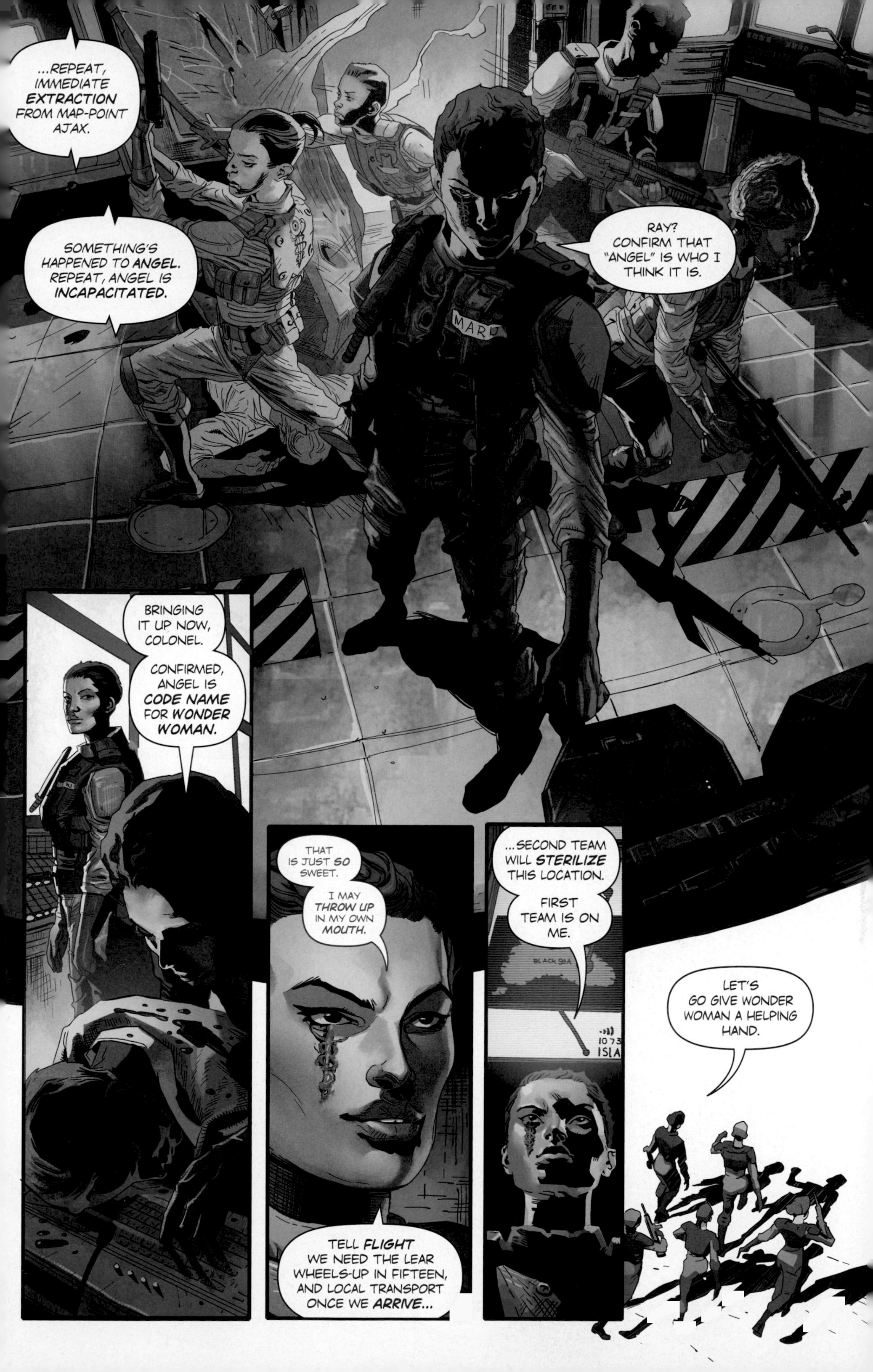
...REPEAT, IMMEDIATE EXTRACTION FROM MAP-POINT AJAX.
SOMETHING'S HAPPENED TO ANGEL. REPEAT, ANGEL IS INCAPACITATED.
RAY? CONFIRM THAT "ANGEL" IS WHO I THINK IT IS.
MARU
BRINGING IT UP NOW, COLONEL.
CONFIRMED, ANGEL IS CODE NAME FOR WONDER WOMAN.
THAT IS JUST SO SWEET.
I MAY THROW UP IN MY OWN MOUTH.
TELL FLIGHT WE NEED THE LEAR WHEELS-UP IN FIFTEEN, AND LOCAL TRANSPORT ONCE WE ARRIVE...
...SECOND TEAM WILL STERILIZE THIS LOCATION.
FIRST TEAM IS ON ME.
BLACK SEA
LET'S GO GIVE WONDER WOMAN A HELPING HAND.

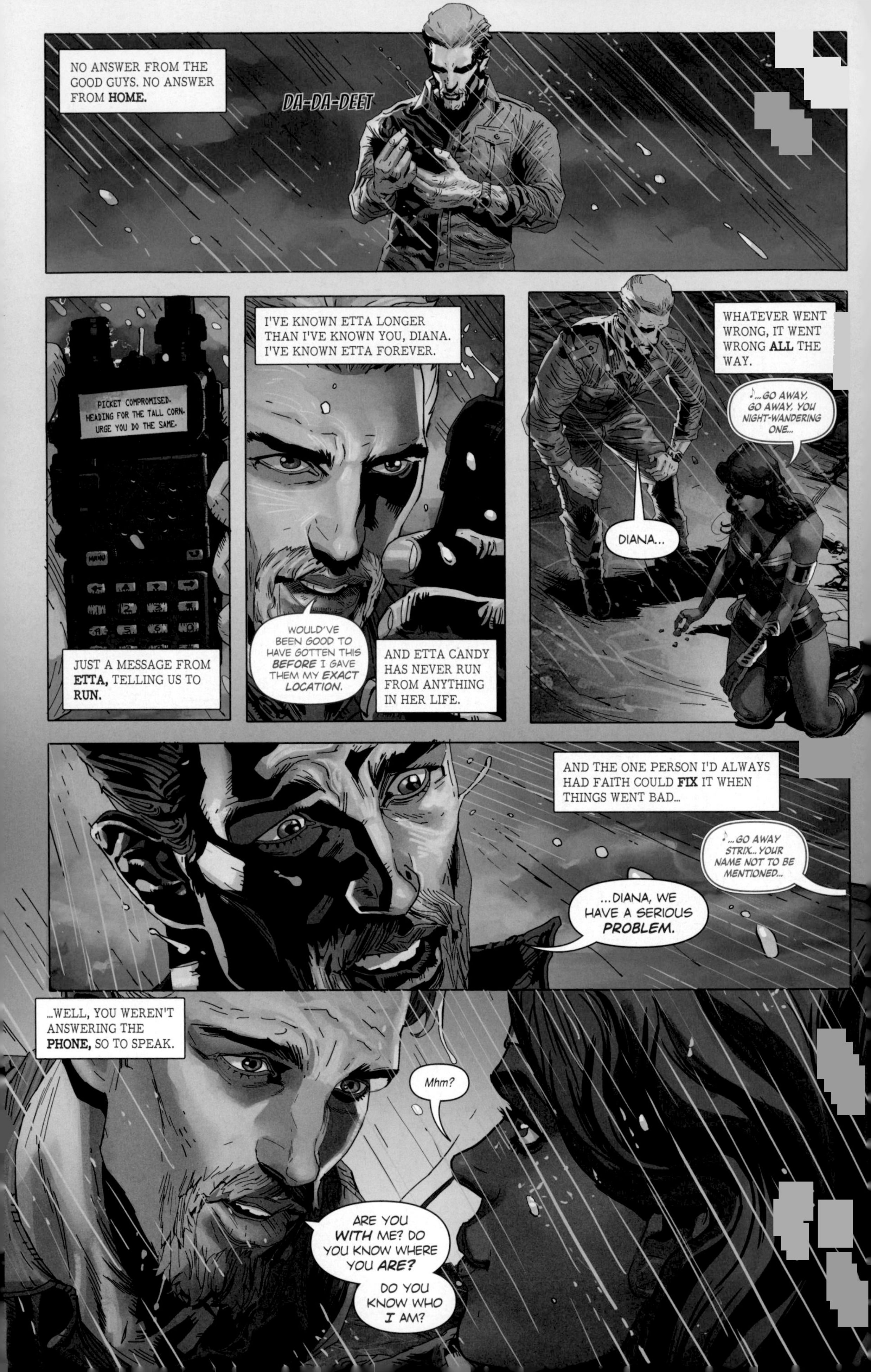

NO ANSWER FROM THE GOOD GUYS. NO ANSWER FROM **HOME.**
DA-DA-DEET
PICKET COMPROMISED. HEADING FOR THE TALL CORN. URGE YOU DO THE SAME.
JUST A MESSAGE FROM **ETTA,** TELLING US TO **RUN.**
I'VE KNOWN ETTA LONGER THAN I'VE KNOWN YOU, DIANA. I'VE KNOWN ETTA FOREVER.
WOULD'VE BEEN GOOD TO HAVE GOTTEN THIS ***BEFORE*** I GAVE THEM MY ***EXACT LOCATION.***
AND ETTA CANDY HAS NEVER RUN FROM ANYTHING IN HER LIFE.
WHATEVER WENT WRONG, IT WENT WRONG **ALL** THE WAY.
♪...GO AWAY, GO AWAY, YOU NIGHT-WANDERING ONE...
DIANA...
AND THE ONE PERSON I'D ALWAYS HAD FAITH COULD **FIX** IT WHEN THINGS WENT BAD...
♪...GO AWAY STRIX... YOUR NAME NOT TO BE MENTIONED...
...DIANA, WE HAVE A SERIOUS ***PROBLEM.***
...WELL, YOU WEREN'T ANSWERING THE **PHONE,** SO TO SPEAK.
Mhm?
ARE YOU ***WITH*** ME? DO YOU KNOW WHERE YOU ***ARE?***
DO YOU KNOW WHO ***I*** AM?

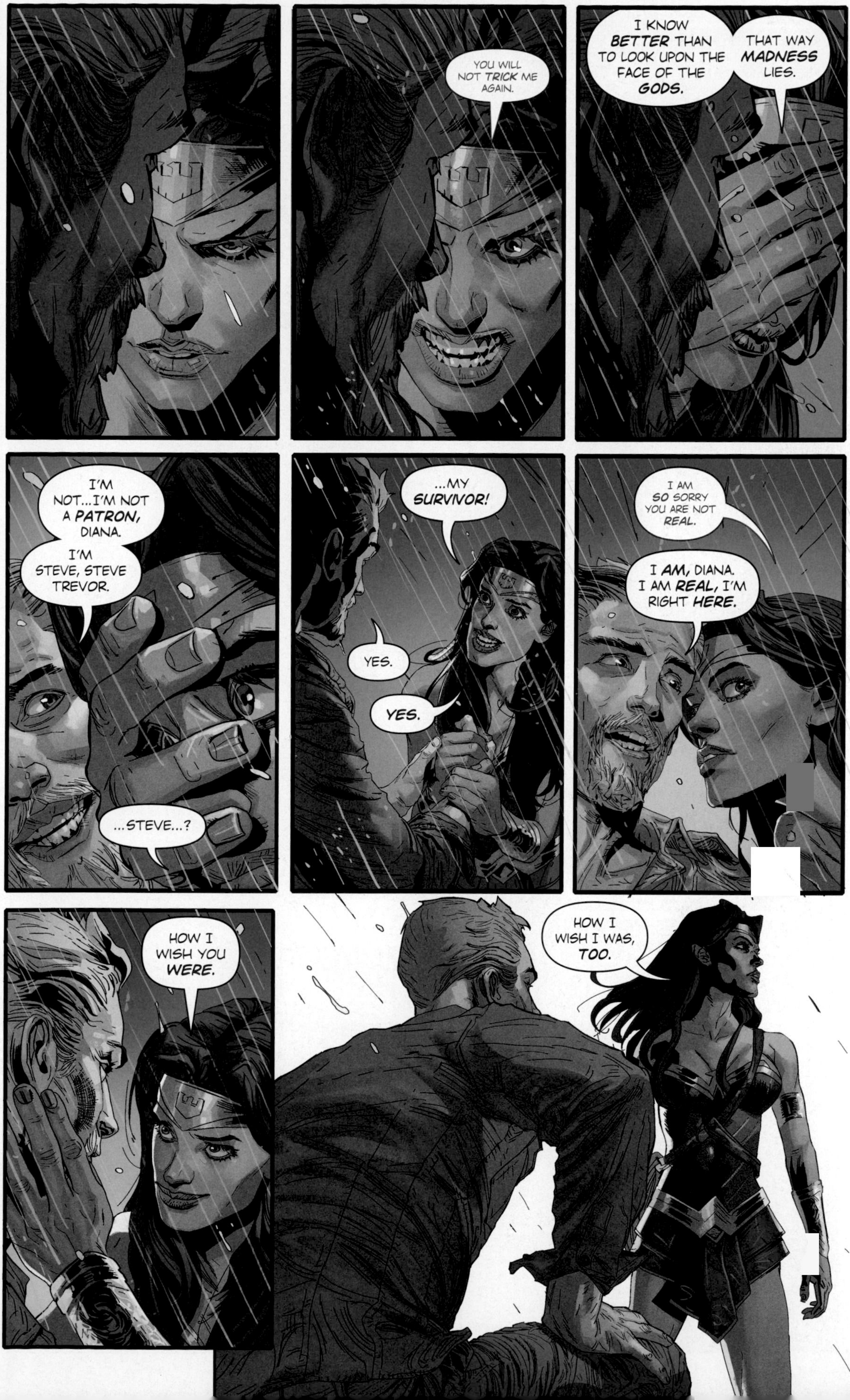
YOU WILL NOT TRICK ME AGAIN.
I KNOW BETTER THAN TO LOOK UPON THE FACE OF THE GODS.
THAT WAY MADNESS LIES.
I'M NOT...I'M NOT A PATRON, DIANA.
I'M STEVE, STEVE TREVOR.
...STEVE...?
...MY SURVIVOR!
YES.
YES.
I AM SO SORRY YOU ARE NOT REAL.
I AM, DIANA. I AM REAL, I'M RIGHT HERE.
HOW I WISH YOU WERE.
HOW I WISH I WAS, TOO.

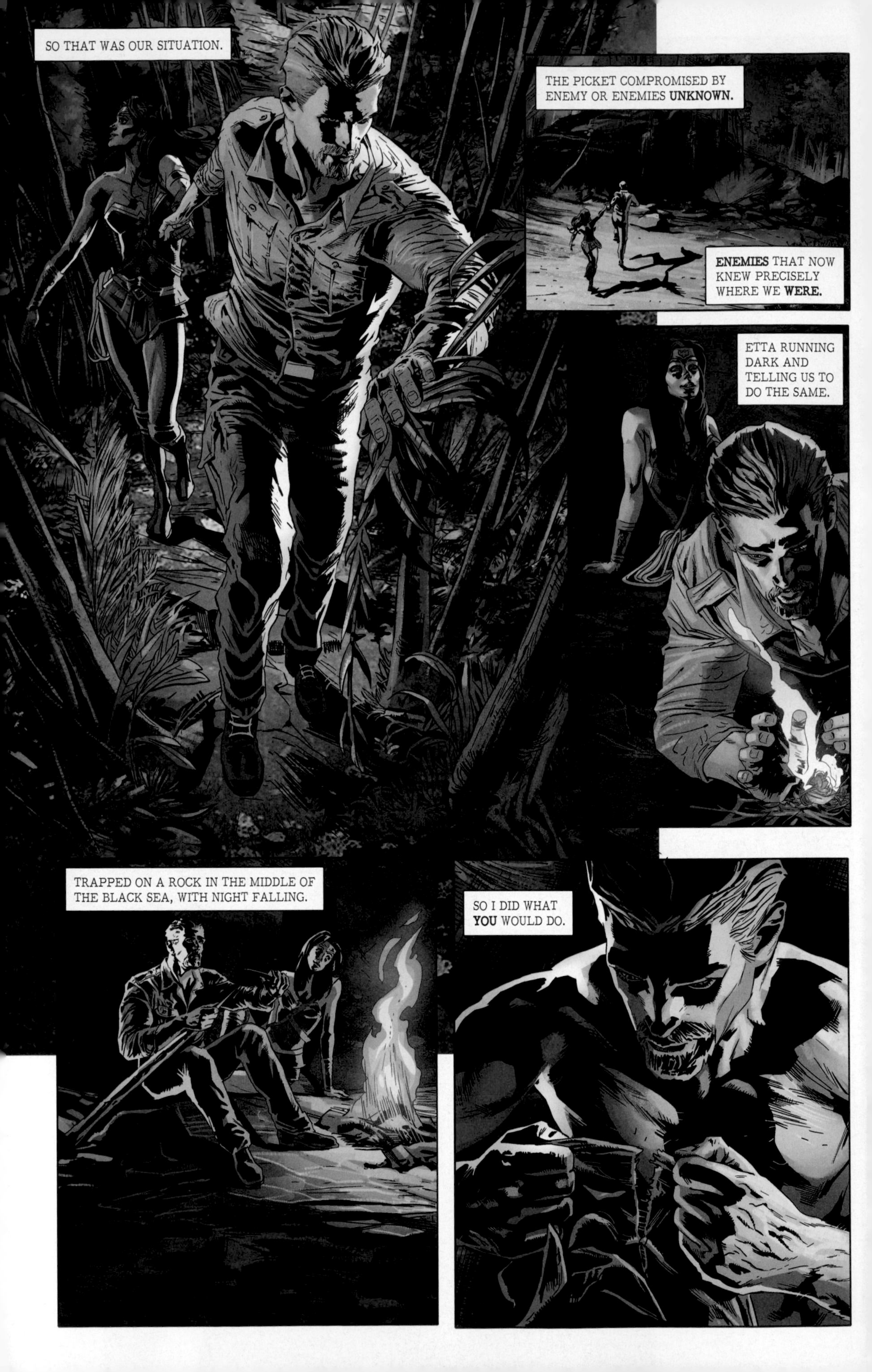
SO THAT WAS OUR SITUATION.
THE PICKET COMPROMISED BY ENEMY OR ENEMIES UNKNOWN.
ENEMIES THAT NOW KNEW PRECISELY WHERE WE WERE.
ETTA RUNNING DARK AND TELLING US TO DO THE SAME.
TRAPPED ON A ROCK IN THE MIDDLE OF THE BLACK SEA, WITH NIGHT FALLING.
SO I DID WHAT YOU WOULD DO.

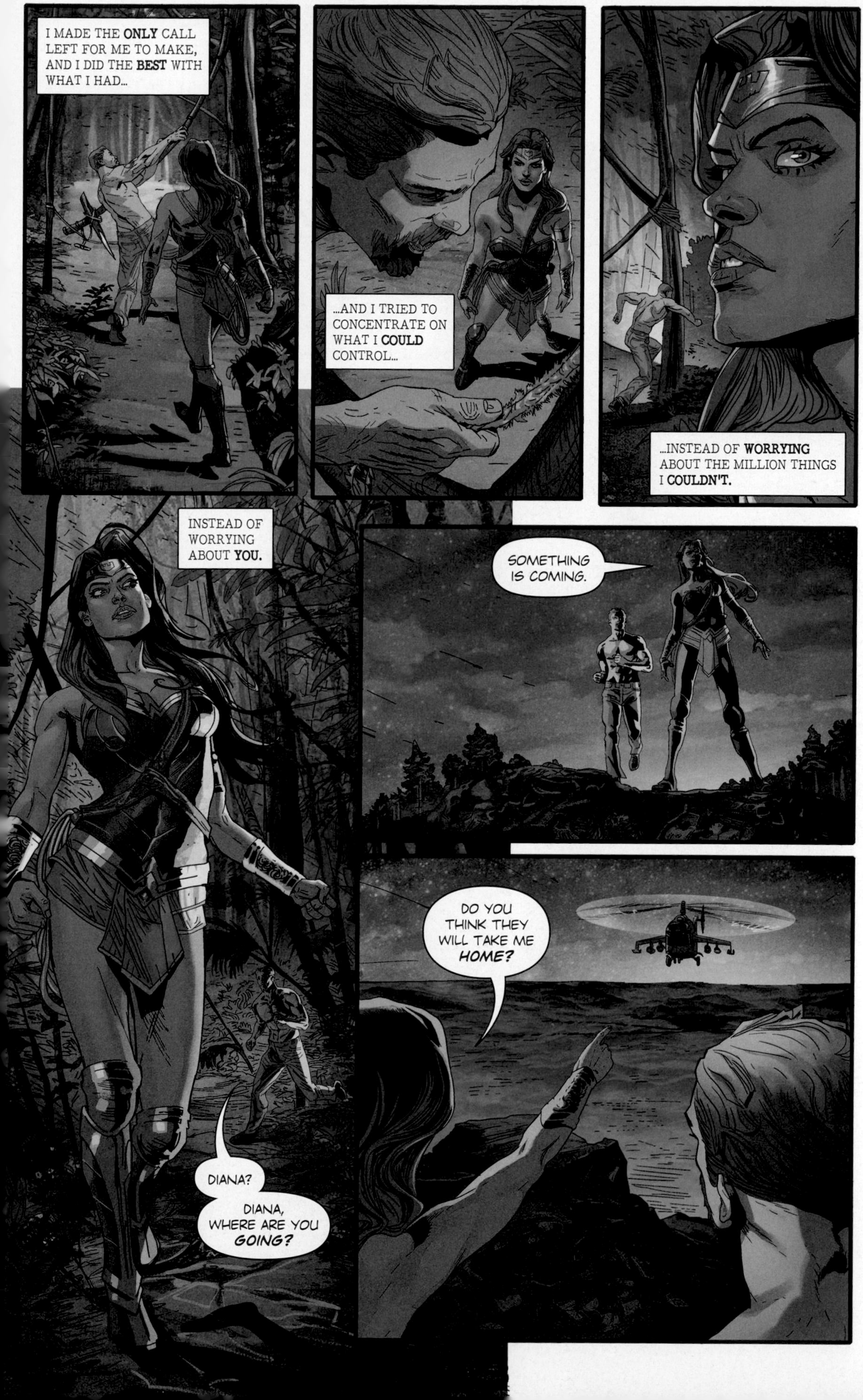
I MADE THE ONLY CALL LEFT FOR ME TO MAKE, AND I DID THE BEST WITH WHAT I HAD...
...AND I TRIED TO CONCENTRATE ON WHAT I COULD CONTROL...
...INSTEAD OF WORRYING ABOUT THE MILLION THINGS I COULDN'T.
INSTEAD OF WORRYING ABOUT YOU.
DIANA?
DIANA, WHERE ARE YOU GOING?
SOMETHING IS COMING.
DO YOU THINK THEY WILL TAKE ME HOME?

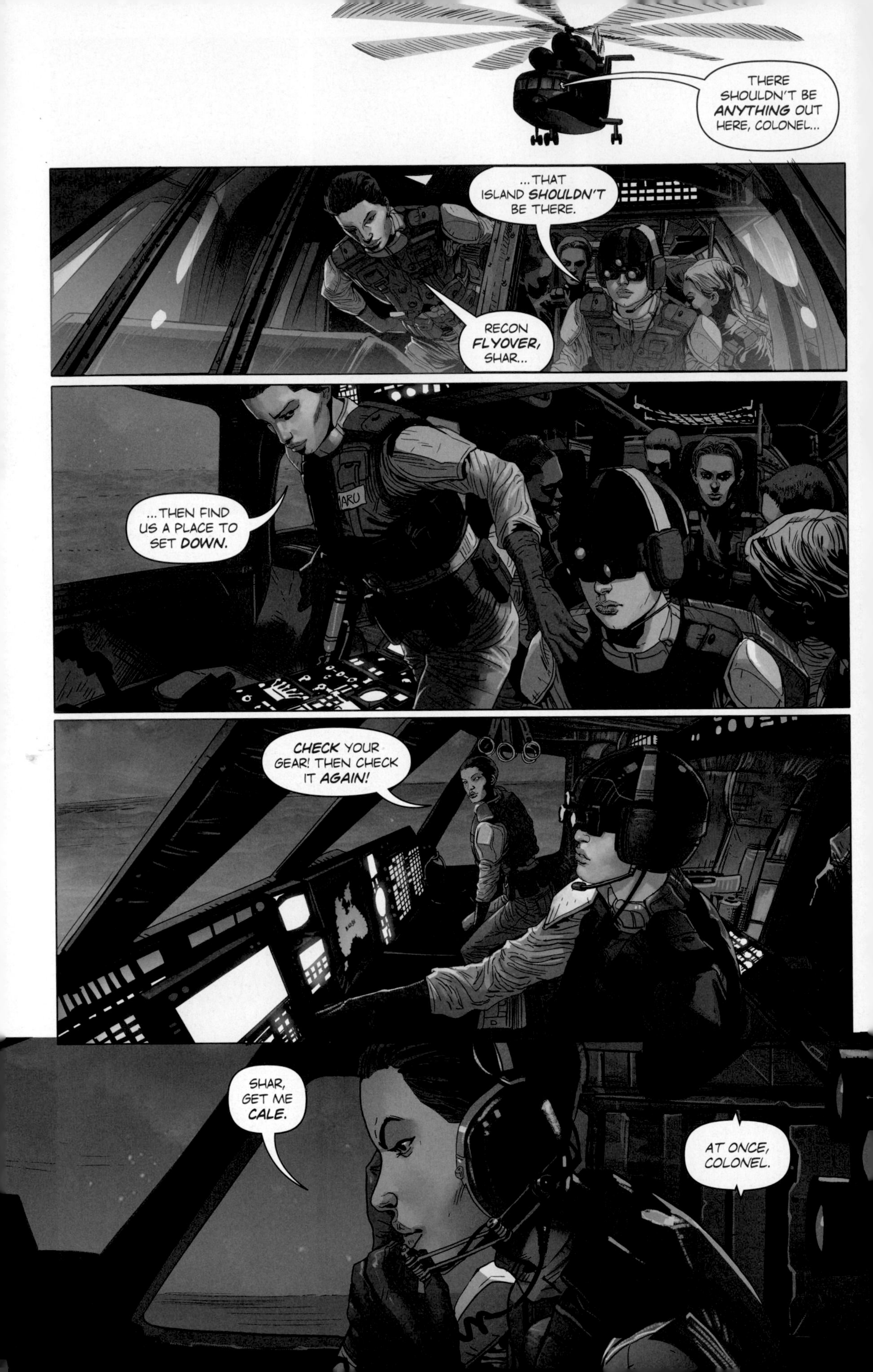
THERE SHOULDN'T BE ANYTHING OUT HERE, COLONEL...
...THAT ISLAND SHOULDN'T BE THERE.
RECON FLYOVER, SHAR...
...THEN FIND US A PLACE TO SET DOWN.
CHECK YOUR GEAR! THEN CHECK IT AGAIN!
SHAR, GET ME CALE.
AT ONCE, COLONEL.

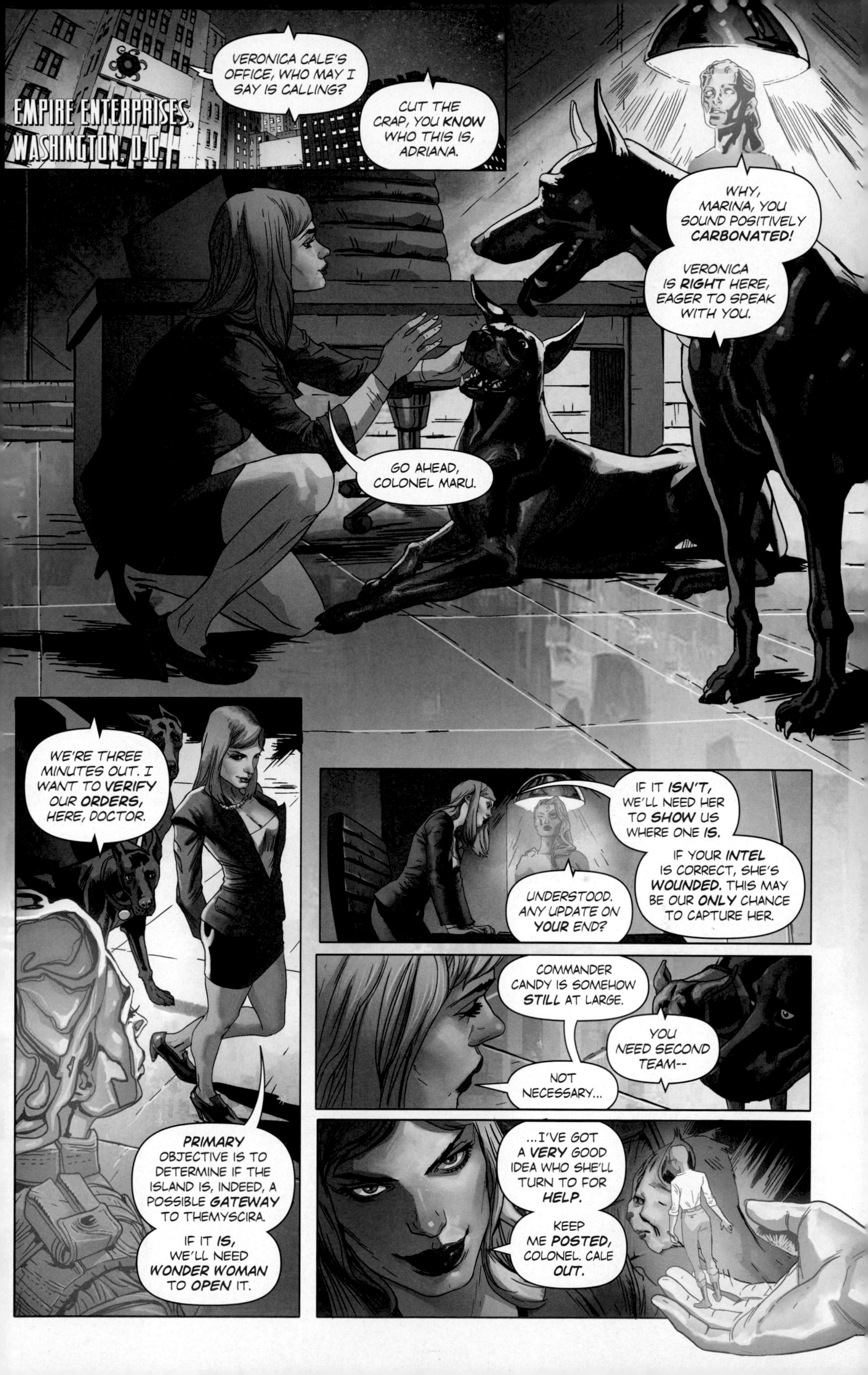
EMPIRE ENTERPRISES, WASHINGTON, D.C.
VERONICA CALE'S OFFICE, WHO MAY I SAY IS CALLING?
CUT THE CRAP, YOU KNOW WHO THIS IS, ADRIANA.
WHY, MARINA, YOU SOUND POSITIVELY CARBONATED!
VERONICA IS RIGHT HERE, EAGER TO SPEAK WITH YOU.
GO AHEAD, COLONEL MARU.
WE'RE THREE MINUTES OUT. I WANT TO VERIFY OUR ORDERS, HERE, DOCTOR.
PRIMARY OBJECTIVE IS TO DETERMINE IF THE ISLAND IS, INDEED, A POSSIBLE GATEWAY TO THEMYSCIRA.
IF IT IS, WE'LL NEED WONDER WOMAN TO OPEN IT.
IF IT ISN'T, WE'LL NEED HER TO SHOW US WHERE ONE IS.
IF YOUR INTEL IS CORRECT, SHE'S WOUNDED. THIS MAY BE OUR ONLY CHANCE TO CAPTURE HER.
UNDERSTOOD. ANY UPDATE ON YOUR END?
COMMANDER CANDY IS SOMEHOW STILL AT LARGE.
YOU NEED SECOND TEAM--
NOT NECESSARY...
...I'VE GOT A VERY GOOD IDEA WHO SHE'LL TURN TO FOR HELP.
KEEP ME POSTED, COLONEL. CALE OUT.

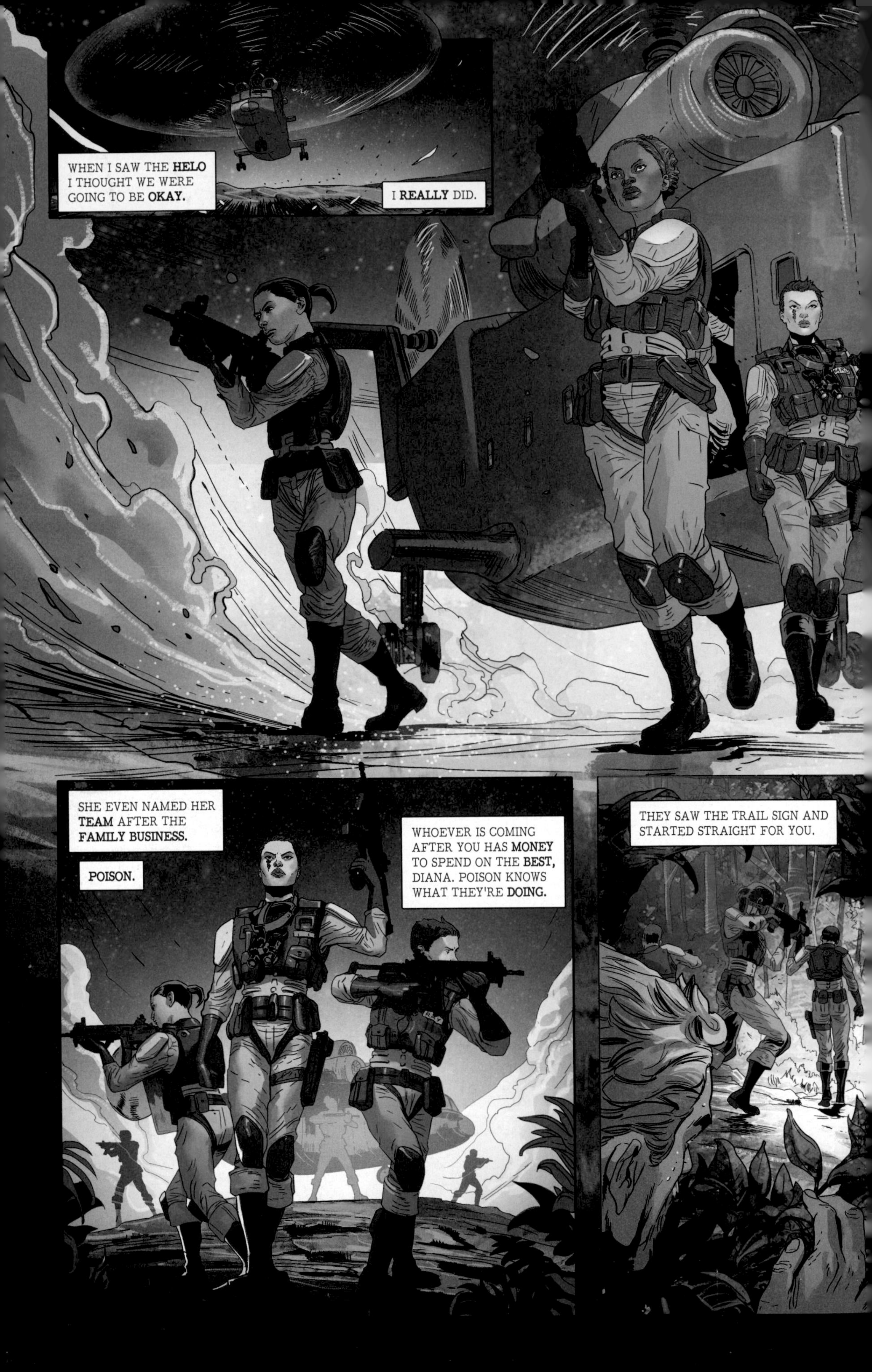

WHEN I SAW THE **HELO** I THOUGHT WE WERE GOING TO BE **OKAY.**
I **REALLY** DID.
SHE EVEN NAMED HER **TEAM** AFTER THE **FAMILY BUSINESS.**
POISON.
WHOEVER IS COMING AFTER YOU HAS **MONEY** TO SPEND ON THE **BEST,** DIANA. POISON KNOWS WHAT THEY'RE **DOING.**
THEY SAW THE TRAIL SIGN AND STARTED STRAIGHT FOR YOU.

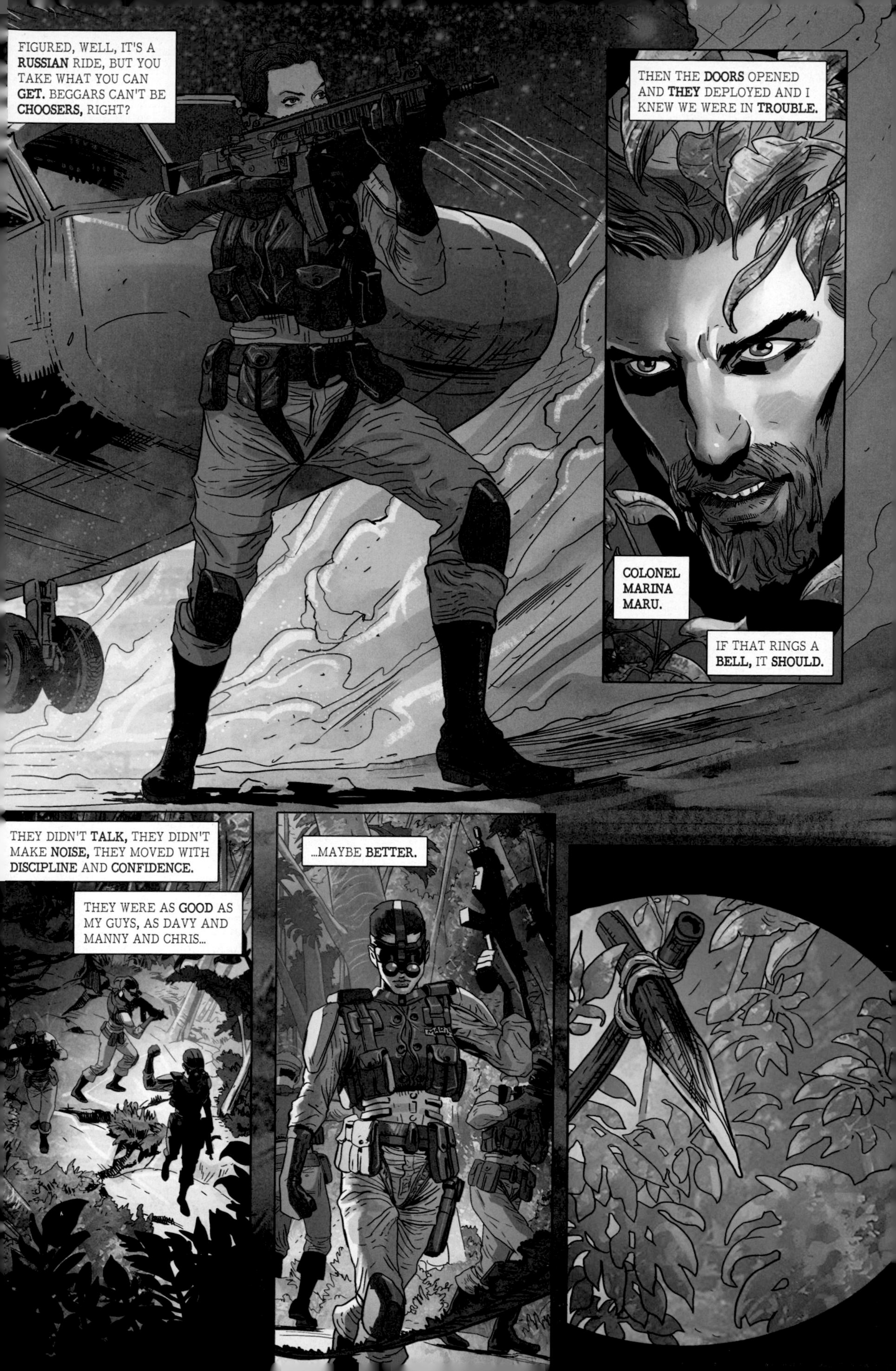
FIGURED, WELL, IT'S A RUSSIAN RIDE, BUT YOU TAKE WHAT YOU CAN GET. BEGGARS CAN'T BE CHOOSERS, RIGHT?
THEN THE DOORS OPENED AND THEY DEPLOYED AND I KNEW WE WERE IN TROUBLE.
COLONEL MARINA MARU.
IF THAT RINGS A BELL, IT SHOULD.
THEY DIDN'T TALK, THEY DIDN'T MAKE NOISE, THEY MOVED WITH DISCIPLINE AND CONFIDENCE.
THEY WERE AS GOOD AS MY GUYS, AS DAVY AND MANNY AND CHRIS...
...MAYBE BETTER.

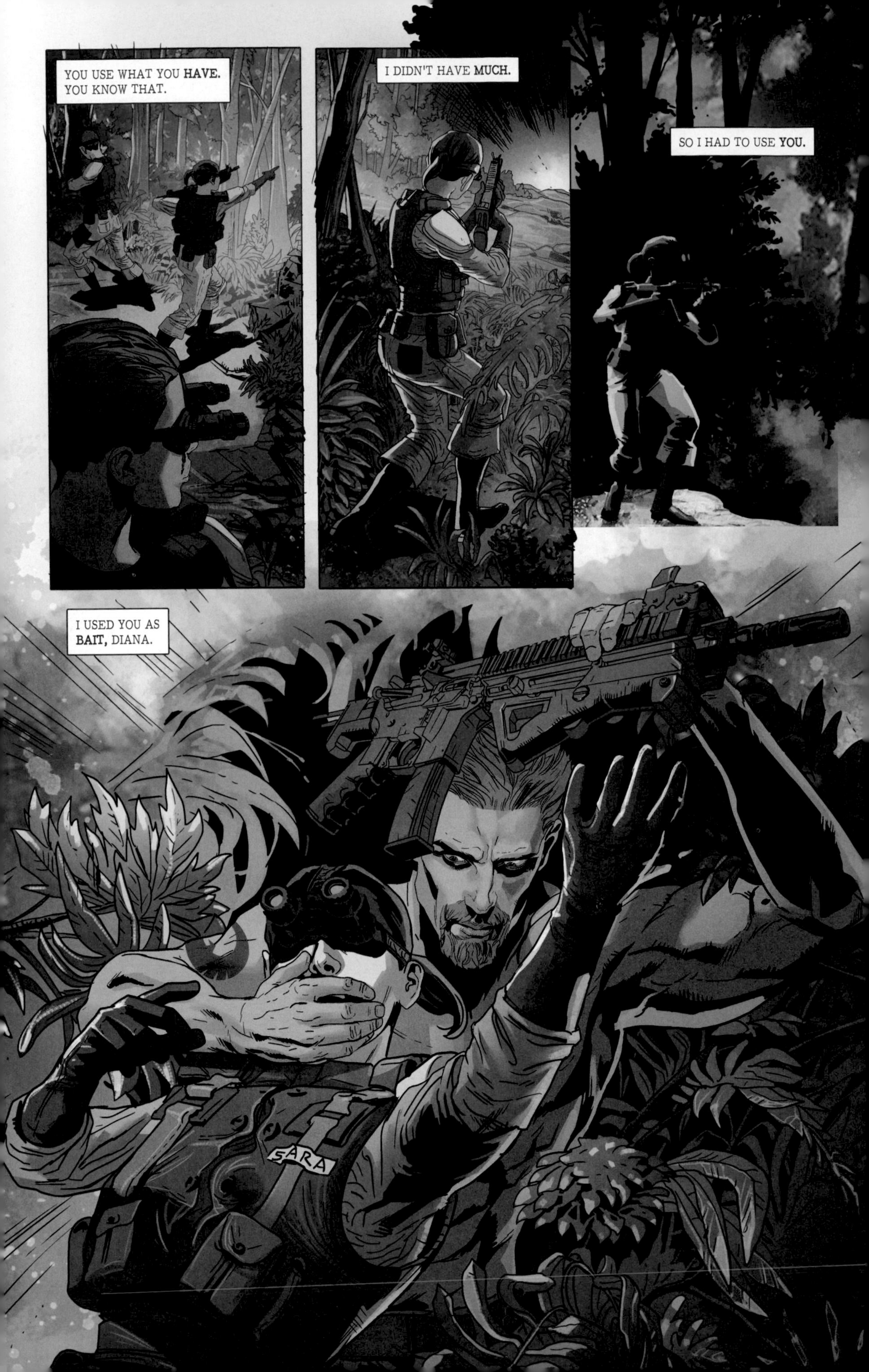
YOU USE WHAT YOU HAVE. YOU KNOW THAT.
I DIDN'T HAVE MUCH.
SO I HAD TO USE YOU.
I USED YOU AS BAIT, DIANA.
SARA

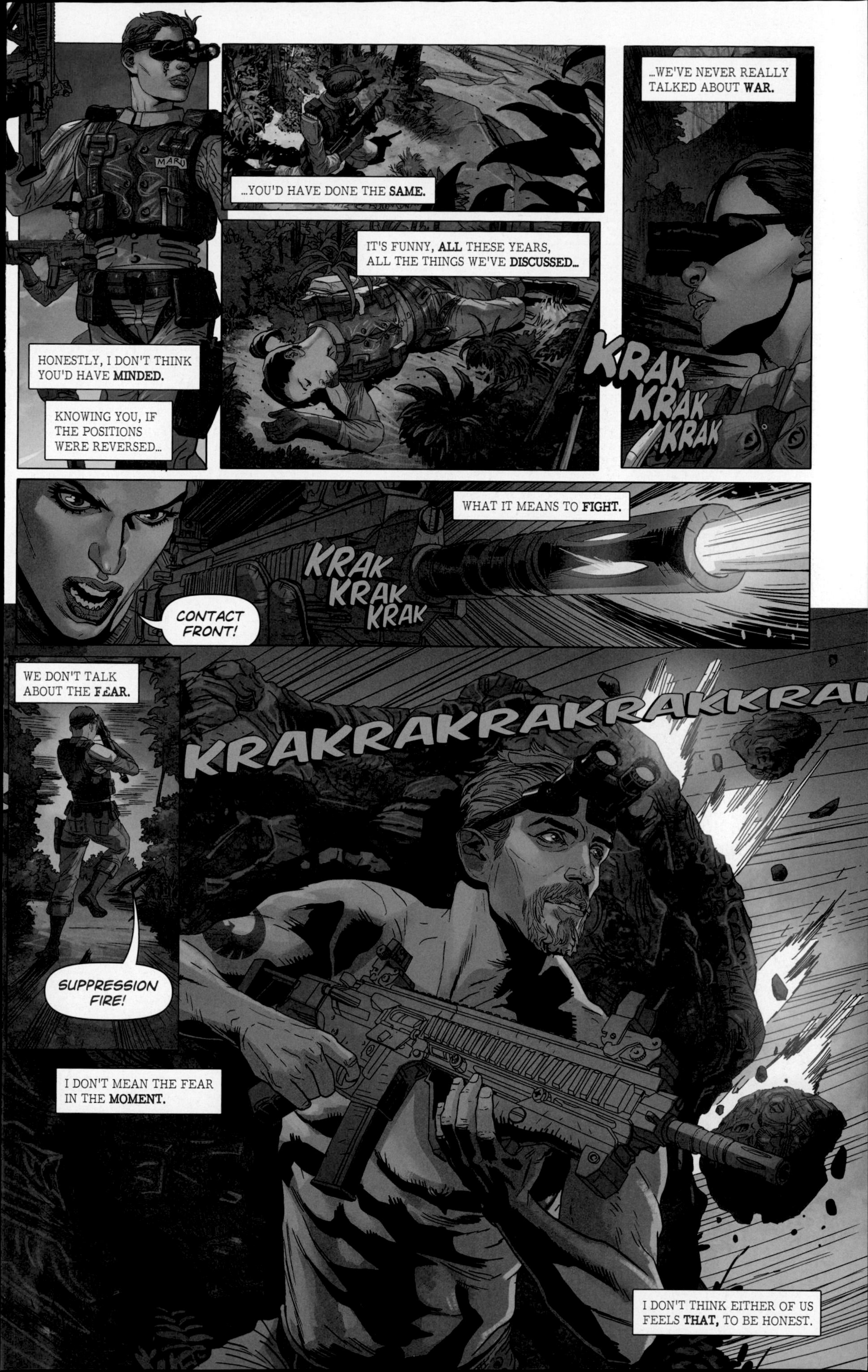
HONESTLY, I DON'T THINK YOU'D HAVE MINDED.
KNOWING YOU, IF THE POSITIONS WERE REVERSED...
...YOU'D HAVE DONE THE SAME.
IT'S FUNNY, ALL THESE YEARS, ALL THE THINGS WE'VE DISCUSSED...
...WE'VE NEVER REALLY TALKED ABOUT WAR.
KRAK KRAK KRAK
WHAT IT MEANS TO FIGHT.
KRAK KRAK KRAK
CONTACT FRONT!
WE DON'T TALK ABOUT THE FEAR.
SUPPRESSION FIRE!
KRAKRAKRAKRAKKRA
I DON'T MEAN THE FEAR IN THE MOMENT.
I DON'T THINK EITHER OF US FEELS THAT, TO BE HONEST.

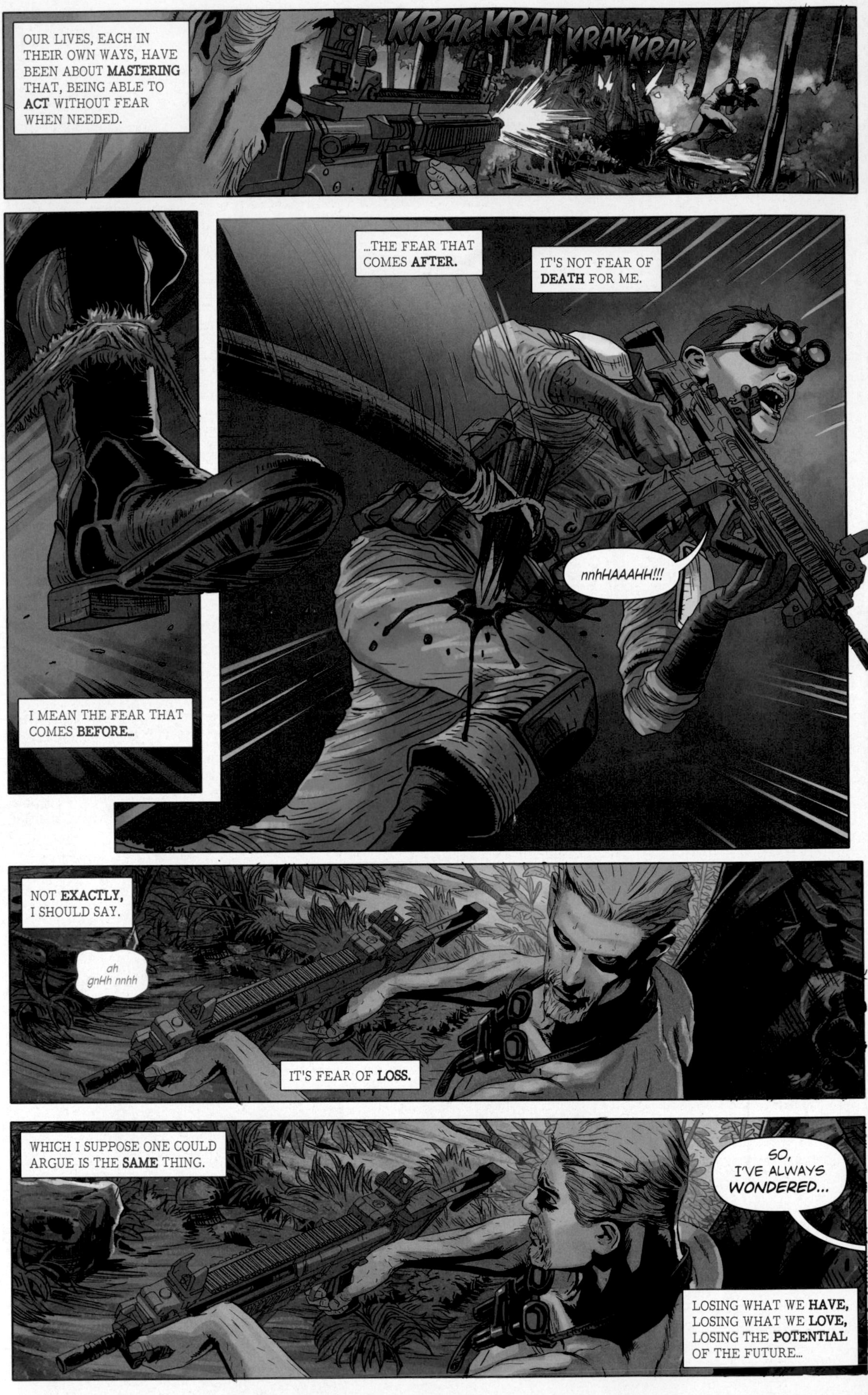
OUR LIVES, EACH IN THEIR OWN WAYS, HAVE BEEN ABOUT MASTERING THAT, BEING ABLE TO ACT WITHOUT FEAR WHEN NEEDED.
KRAK KRAK KRAK KRAK
I MEAN THE FEAR THAT COMES BEFORE...
...THE FEAR THAT COMES AFTER.
IT'S NOT FEAR OF DEATH FOR ME.
nnhHAAAHH!!!
NOT EXACTLY, I SHOULD SAY.
ah gnHh nnhh
IT'S FEAR OF LOSS.
WHICH I SUPPOSE ONE COULD ARGUE IS THE SAME THING.
SO, I'VE ALWAYS WONDERED...
LOSING WHAT WE HAVE, LOSING WHAT WE LOVE, LOSING THE POTENTIAL OF THE FUTURE...

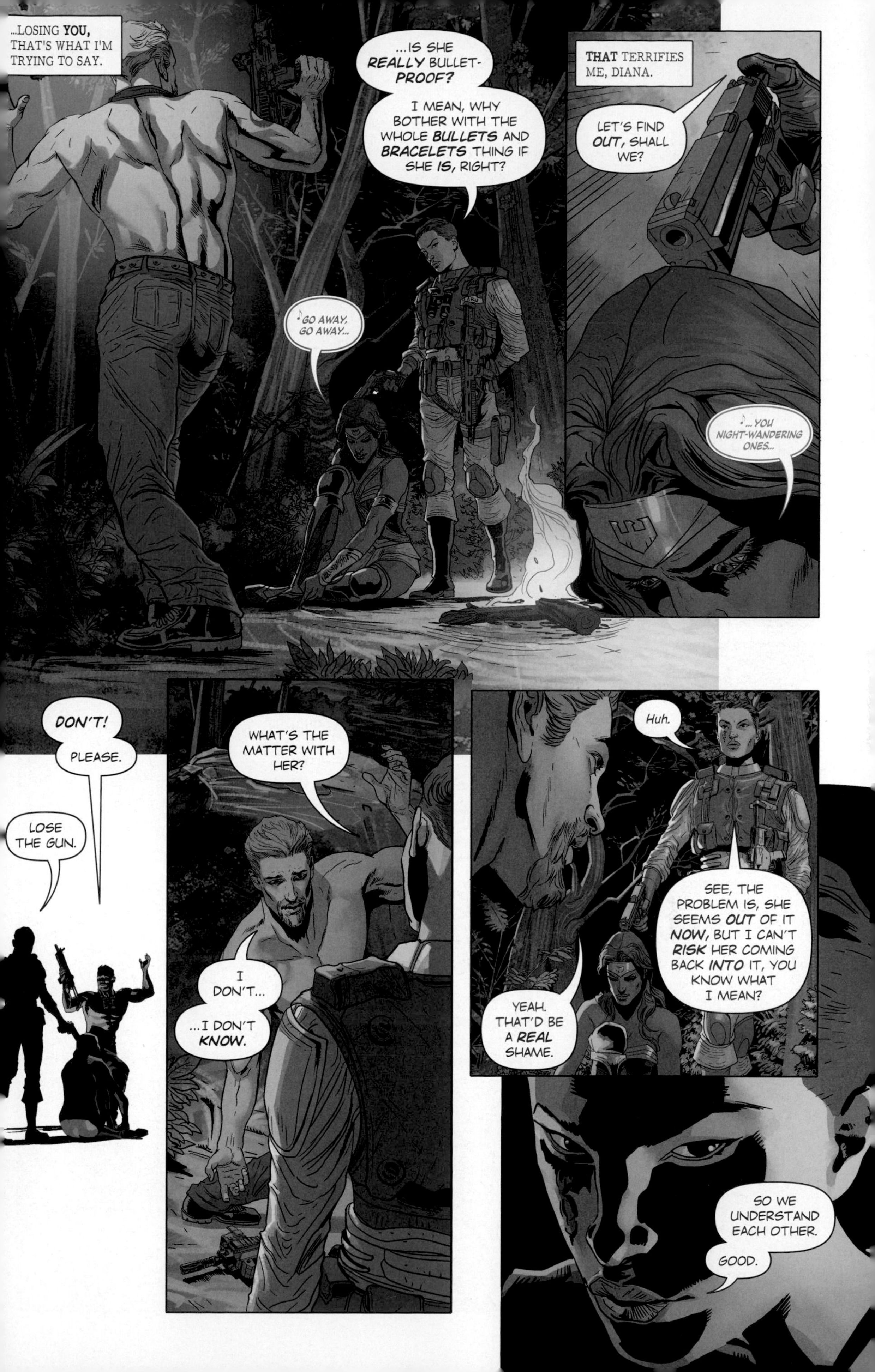
...LOSING YOU, THAT'S WHAT I'M TRYING TO SAY.
...IS SHE REALLY BULLET-PROOF?
I MEAN, WHY BOTHER WITH THE WHOLE BULLETS AND BRACELETS THING IF SHE IS, RIGHT?
♪GO AWAY, GO AWAY...
THAT TERRIFIES ME, DIANA.
LET'S FIND OUT, SHALL WE?
♪...YOU NIGHT-WANDERING ONES...
DON'T!
PLEASE.
LOSE THE GUN.
WHAT'S THE MATTER WITH HER?
I DON'T...
...I DON'T KNOW.
Huh.
SEE, THE PROBLEM IS, SHE SEEMS OUT OF IT NOW, BUT I CAN'T RISK HER COMING BACK INTO IT, YOU KNOW WHAT I MEAN?
YEAH. THAT'D BE A REAL SHAME.
SO WE UNDERSTAND EACH OTHER.
GOOD.

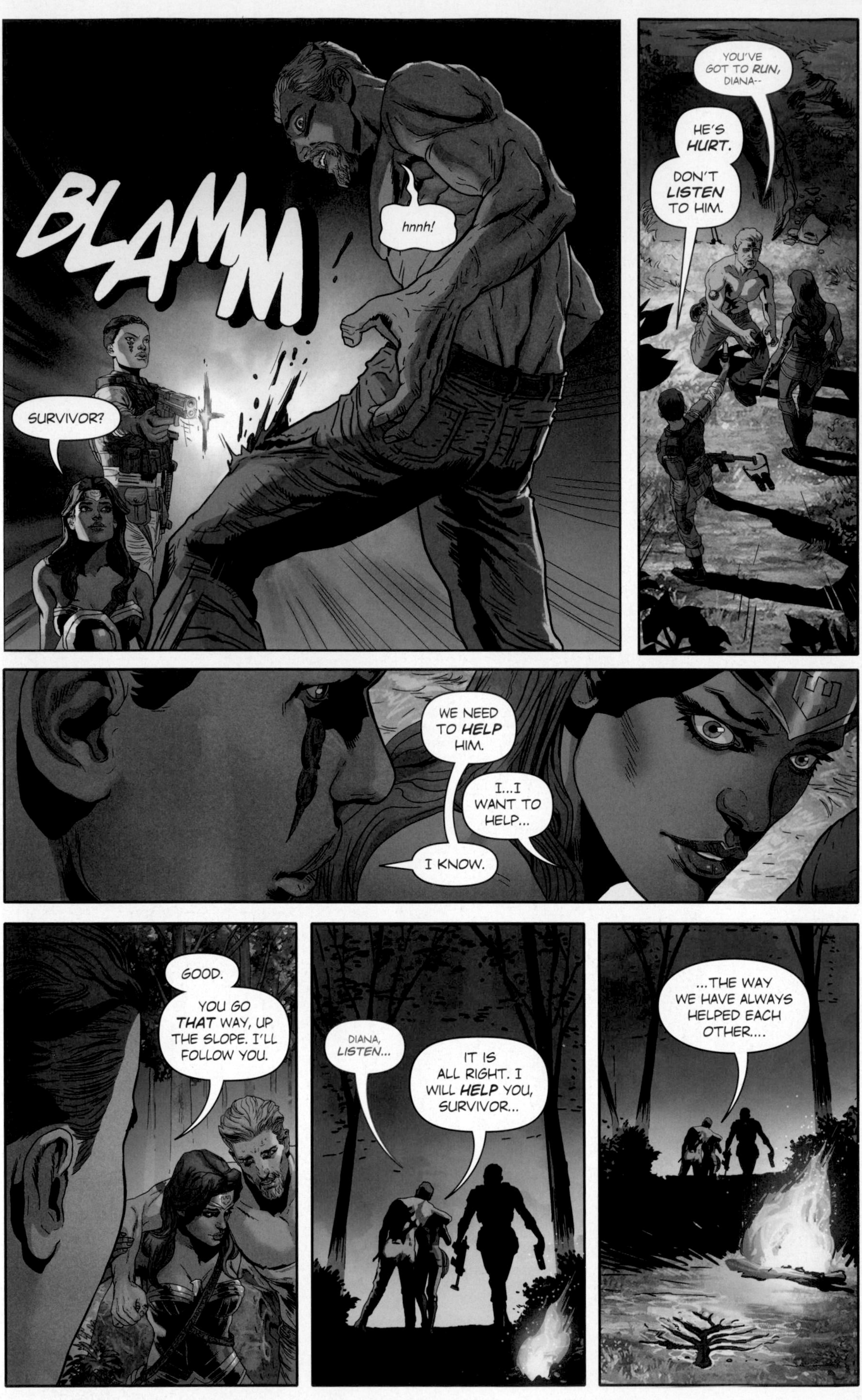
BLAMM
hnnh!
SURVIVOR?
YOU'VE GOT TO RUN, DIANA--
HE'S HURT.
DON'T LISTEN TO HIM.
WE NEED TO HELP HIM.
I...I WANT TO HELP...
I KNOW.
GOOD.
YOU GO THAT WAY, UP THE SLOPE. I'LL FOLLOW YOU.
DIANA, LISTEN...
IT IS ALL RIGHT. I WILL HELP YOU, SURVIVOR...
...THE WAY WE HAVE ALWAYS HELPED EACH OTHER....

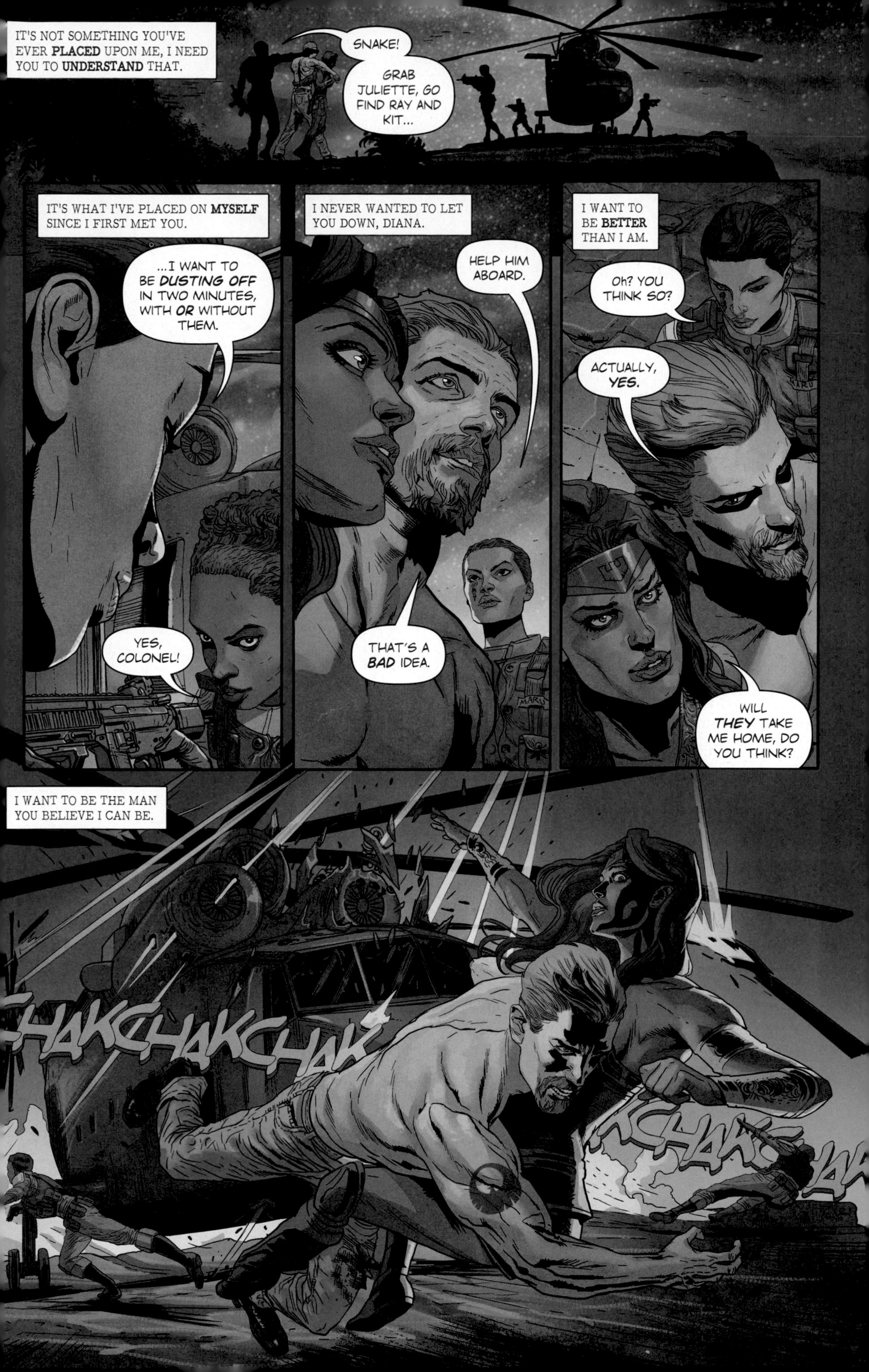
IT'S NOT SOMETHING YOU'VE EVER PLACED UPON ME, I NEED YOU TO UNDERSTAND THAT.
SNAKE!
GRAB JULIETTE, GO FIND RAY AND KIT...
IT'S WHAT I'VE PLACED ON MYSELF SINCE I FIRST MET YOU.
...I WANT TO BE DUSTING OFF IN TWO MINUTES, WITH OR WITHOUT THEM.
YES, COLONEL!
I NEVER WANTED TO LET YOU DOWN, DIANA.
HELP HIM ABOARD.
THAT'S A BAD IDEA.
MARU
I WANT TO BE BETTER THAN I AM.
Oh? YOU THINK SO?
ACTUALLY, YES.
MARU
WILL THEY TAKE ME HOME, DO YOU THINK?
I WANT TO BE THE MAN YOU BELIEVE I CAN BE.
CHAKCHAKCHAK
CHAKCHAK

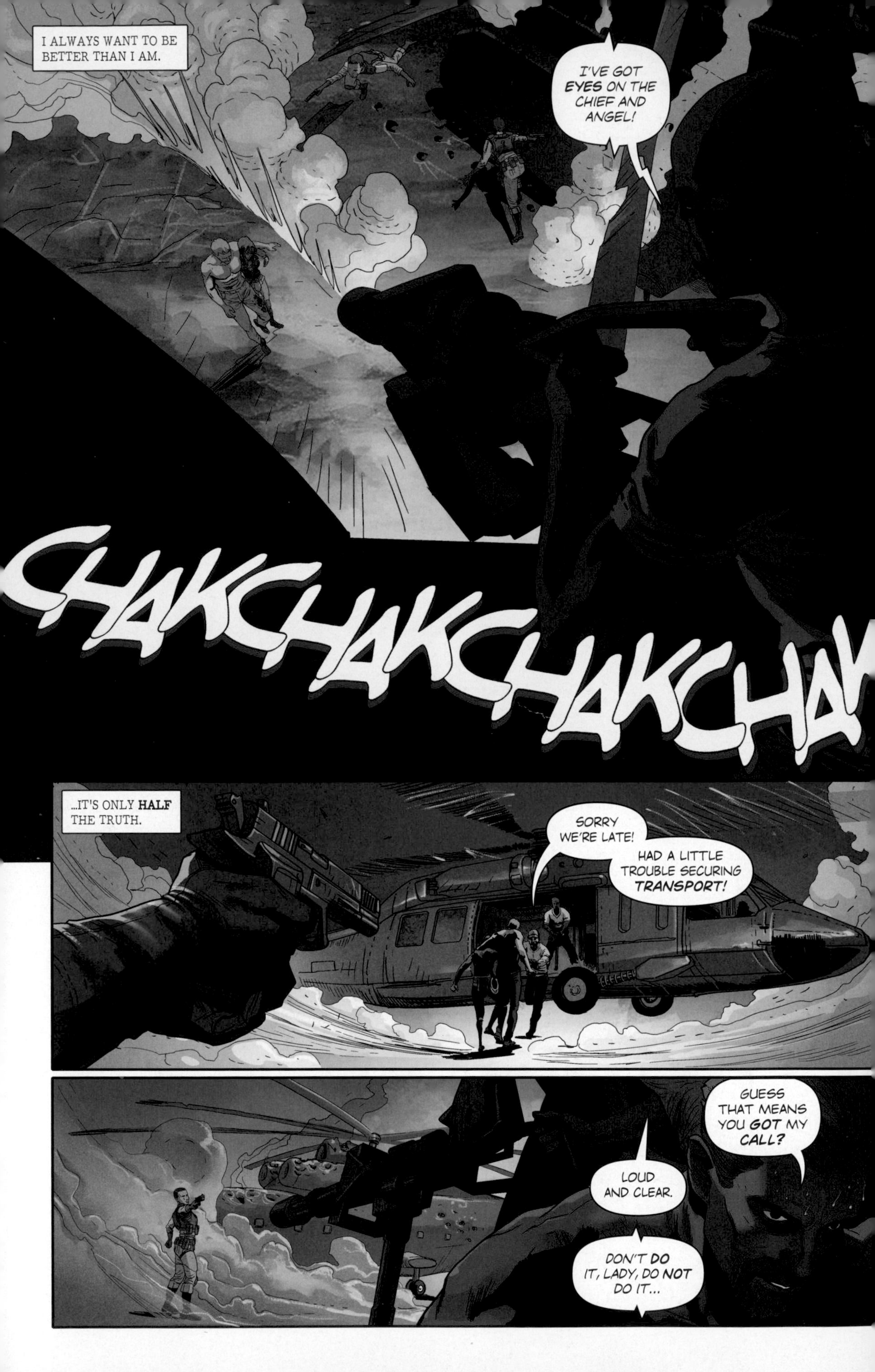
I ALWAYS WANT TO BE BETTER THAN I AM.
I'VE GOT EYES ON THE CHIEF AND ANGEL!
CHAKCHAKCHAKCHAK
...IT'S ONLY HALF THE TRUTH.
SORRY WE'RE LATE!
HAD A LITTLE TROUBLE SECURING TRANSPORT!
GUESS THAT MEANS YOU GOT MY CALL?
LOUD AND CLEAR.
DON'T DO IT, LADY, DO NOT DO IT...

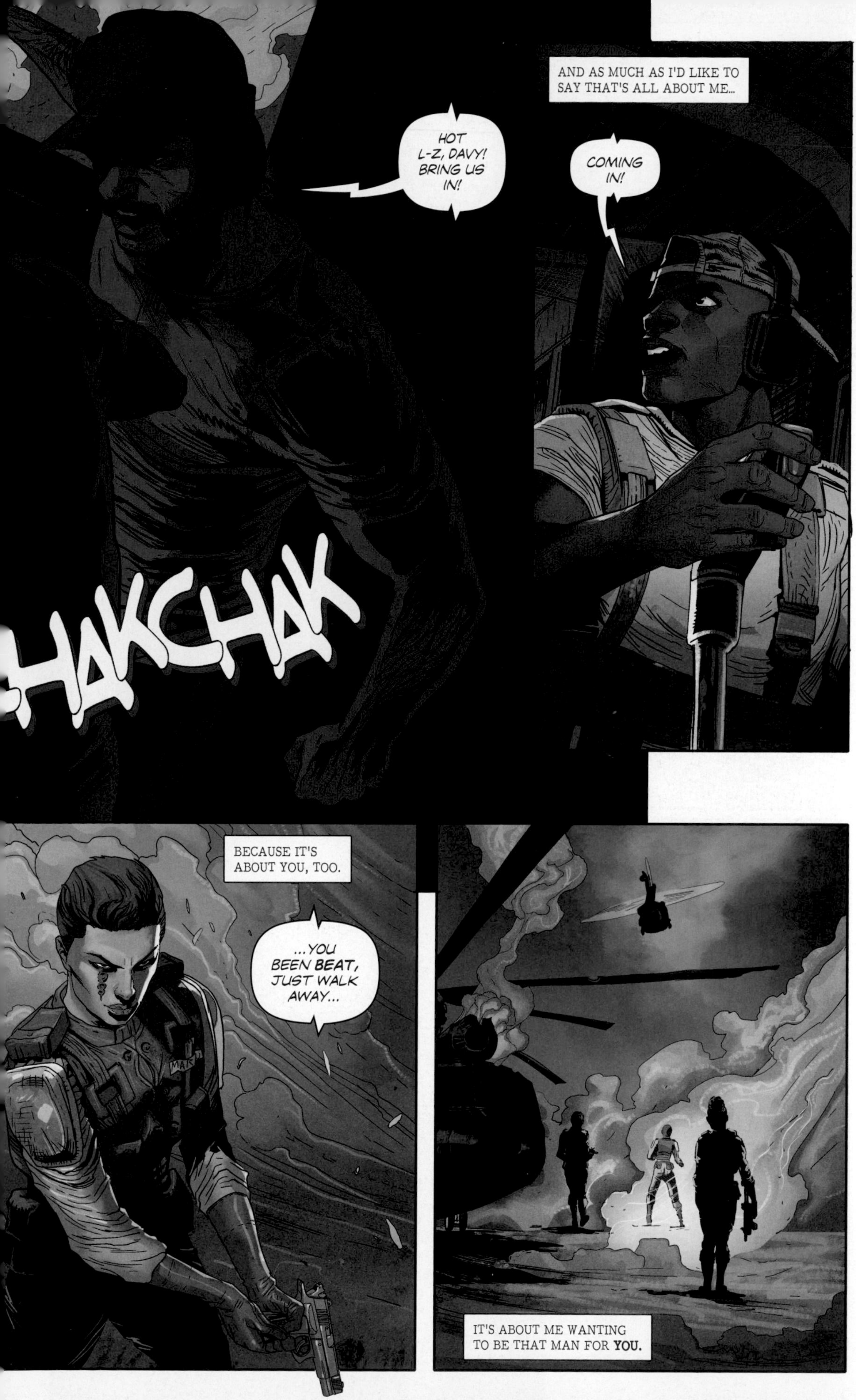
AND AS MUCH AS I'D LIKE TO SAY THAT'S ALL ABOUT ME...
HOT L-Z, DAVY! BRING US IN!
COMING IN!
HAKCHAK
BECAUSE IT'S ABOUT YOU, TOO.
...YOU BEEN BEAT, JUST WALK AWAY...
IT'S ABOUT ME WANTING TO BE THAT MAN FOR YOU.

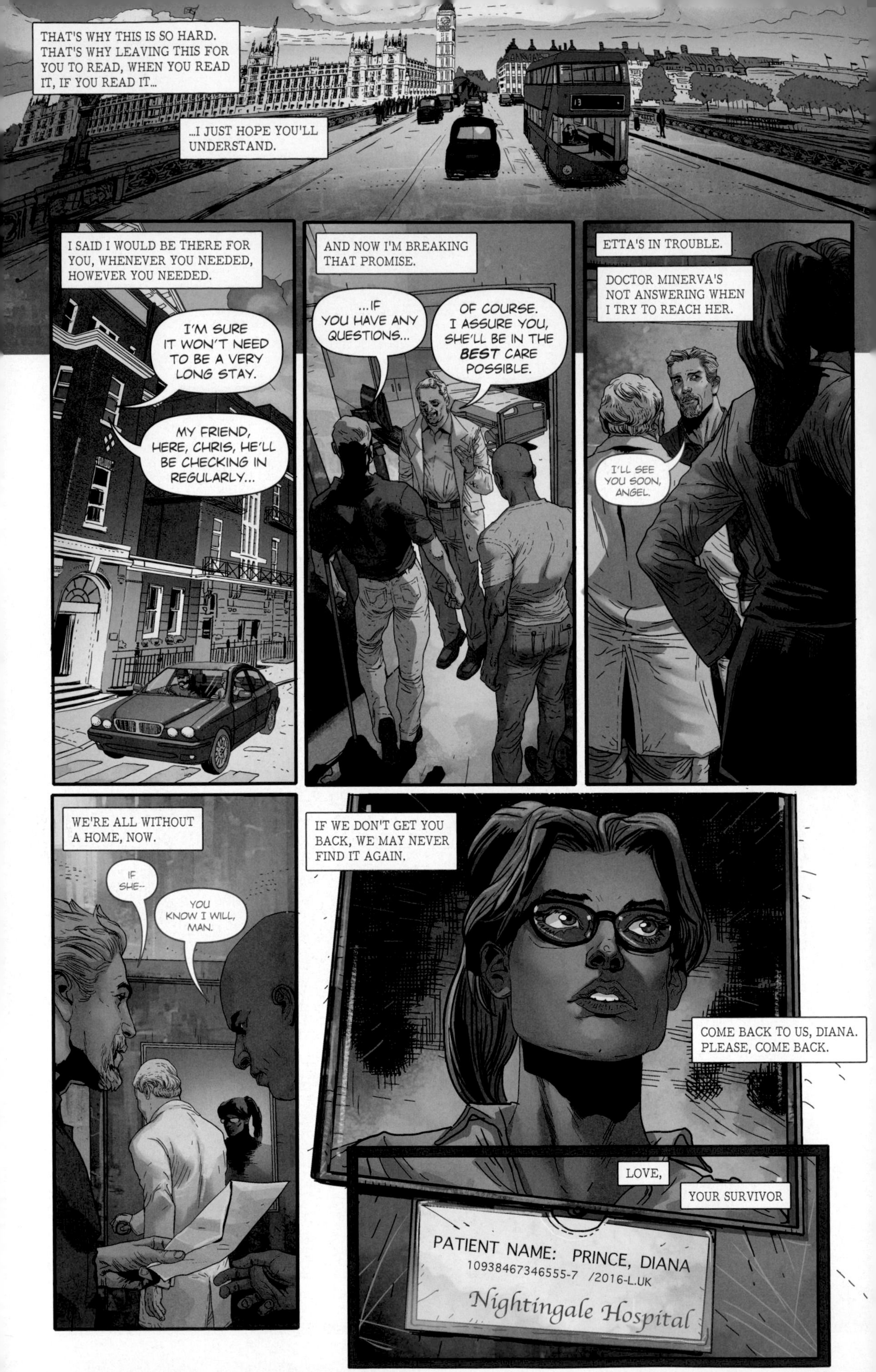
THAT'S WHY THIS IS SO HARD. THAT'S WHY LEAVING THIS FOR YOU TO READ, WHEN YOU READ IT, IF YOU READ IT...
...I JUST HOPE YOU'LL UNDERSTAND.
I SAID I WOULD BE THERE FOR YOU, WHENEVER YOU NEEDED, HOWEVER YOU NEEDED.
I'M SURE IT WON'T NEED TO BE A VERY LONG STAY.
MY FRIEND, HERE, CHRIS, HE'LL BE CHECKING IN REGULARLY...
AND NOW I'M BREAKING THAT PROMISE.
...IF YOU HAVE ANY QUESTIONS...
OF COURSE. I ASSURE YOU, SHE'LL BE IN THE BEST CARE POSSIBLE.
ETTA'S IN TROUBLE.
DOCTOR MINERVA'S NOT ANSWERING WHEN I TRY TO REACH HER.
I'LL SEE YOU SOON, ANGEL.
WE'RE ALL WITHOUT A HOME, NOW.
IF SHE--
YOU KNOW I WILL, MAN.
IF WE DON'T GET YOU BACK, WE MAY NEVER FIND IT AGAIN.
COME BACK TO US, DIANA. PLEASE, COME BACK.
LOVE,
YOUR SURVIVOR
PATIENT NAME: PRINCE, DIANA
10938467346555-7 /2016-L.UK
Nightingale Hospital

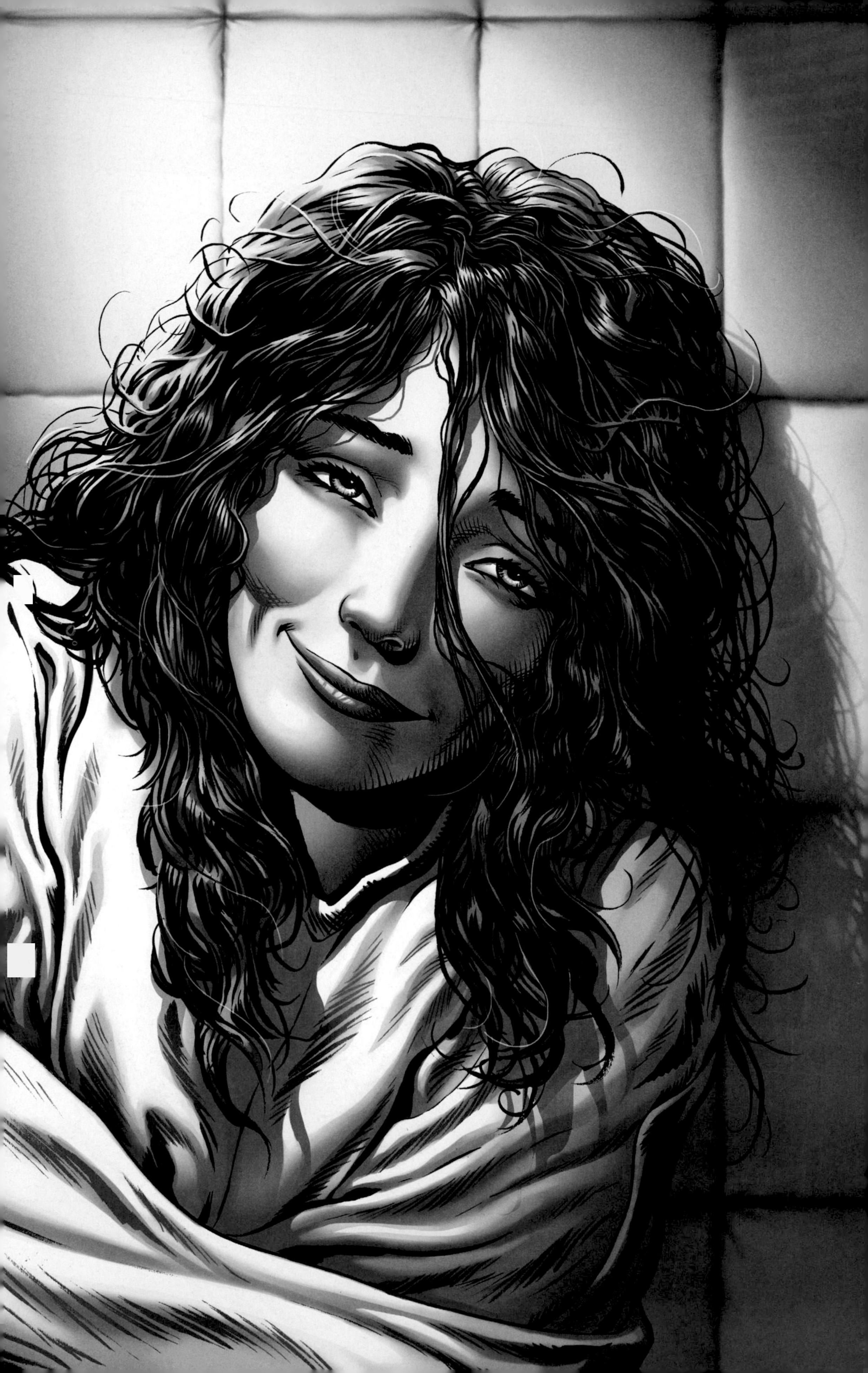

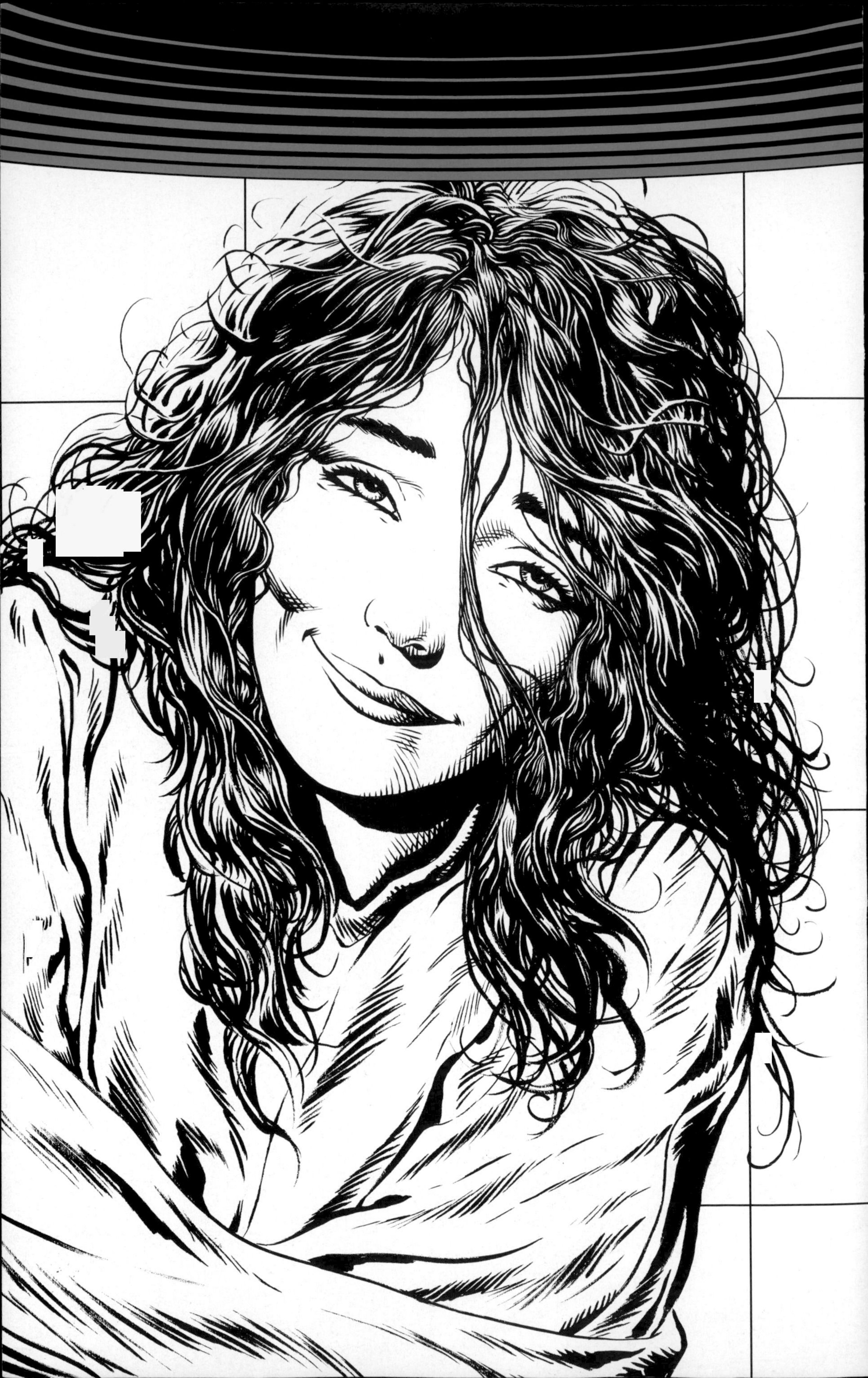

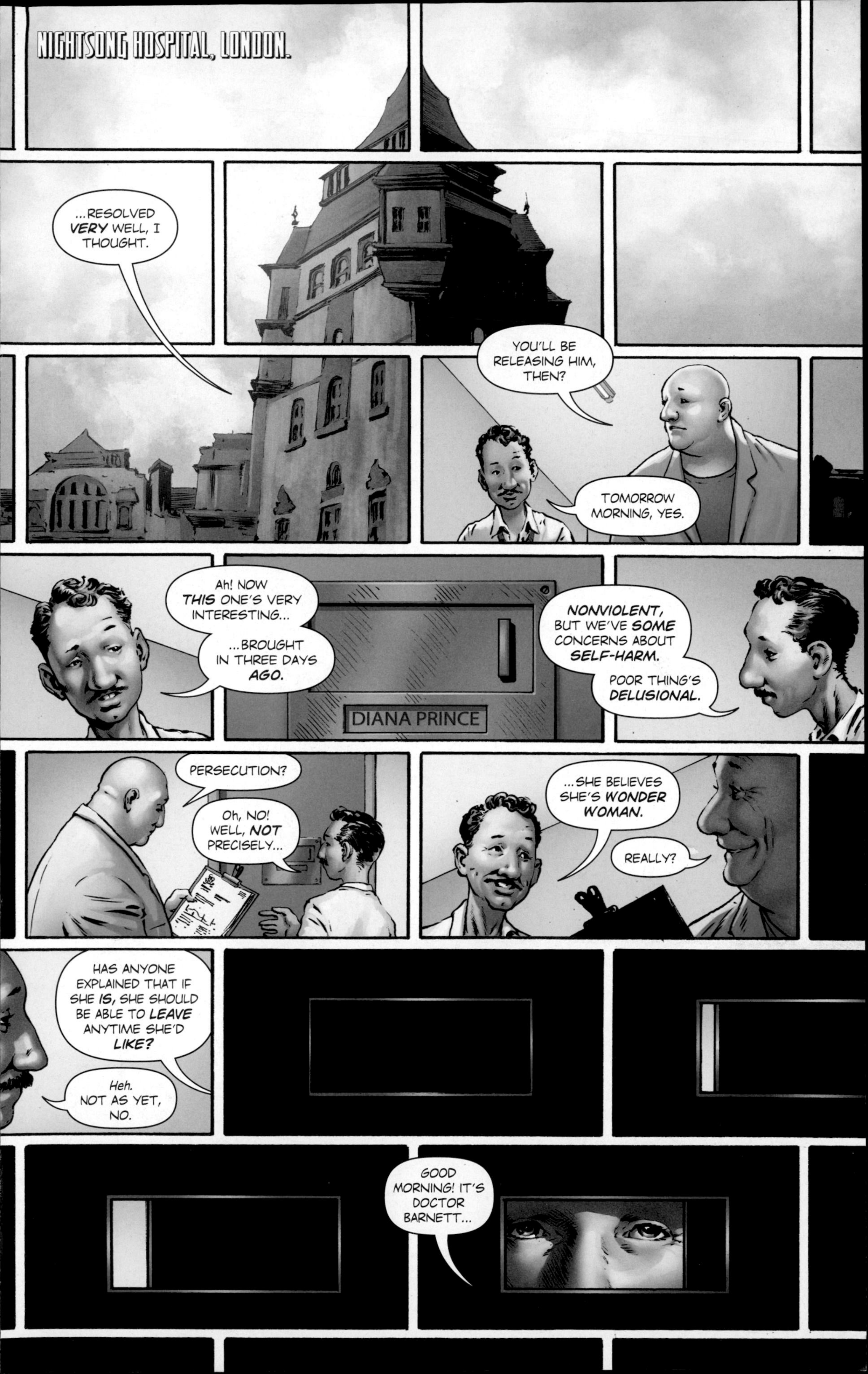
NIGHTSONG HOSPITAL, LONDON.
...RESOLVED VERY WELL, I THOUGHT.
YOU'LL BE RELEASING HIM, THEN?
TOMORROW MORNING, YES.
Ah! NOW THIS ONE'S VERY INTERESTING...
...BROUGHT IN THREE DAYS AGO.
DIANA PRINCE
NONVIOLENT, BUT WE'VE SOME CONCERNS ABOUT SELF-HARM.
POOR THING'S DELUSIONAL.
PERSECUTION?
Oh, NO! WELL, NOT PRECISELY...
...SHE BELIEVES SHE'S WONDER WOMAN.
REALLY?
HAS ANYONE EXPLAINED THAT IF SHE IS, SHE SHOULD BE ABLE TO LEAVE ANYTIME SHE'D LIKE?
Heh. NOT AS YET, NO.
GOOD MORNING! IT'S DOCTOR BARNETT...

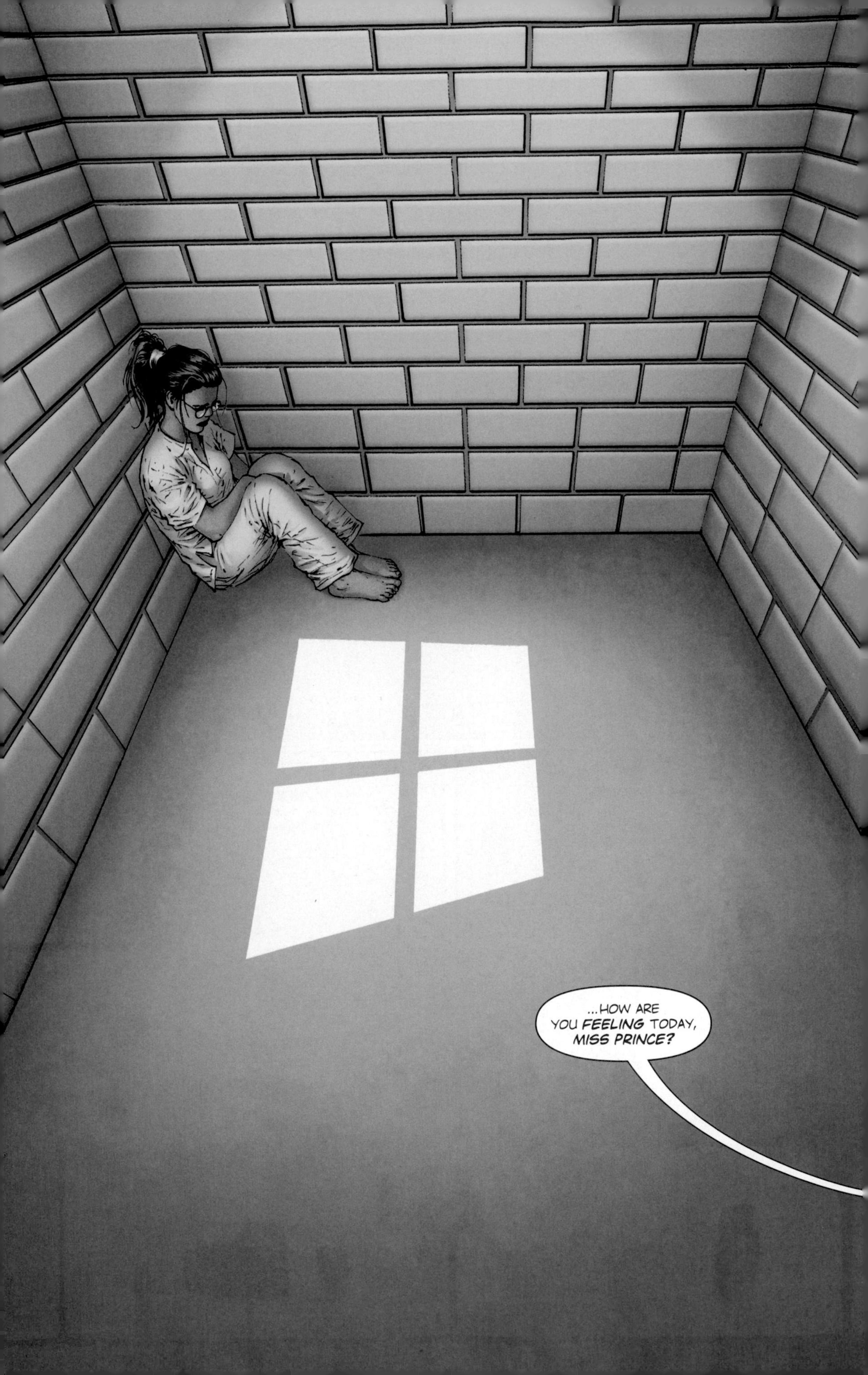
...HOW ARE YOU **FEELING** TODAY, **MISS PRINCE?**

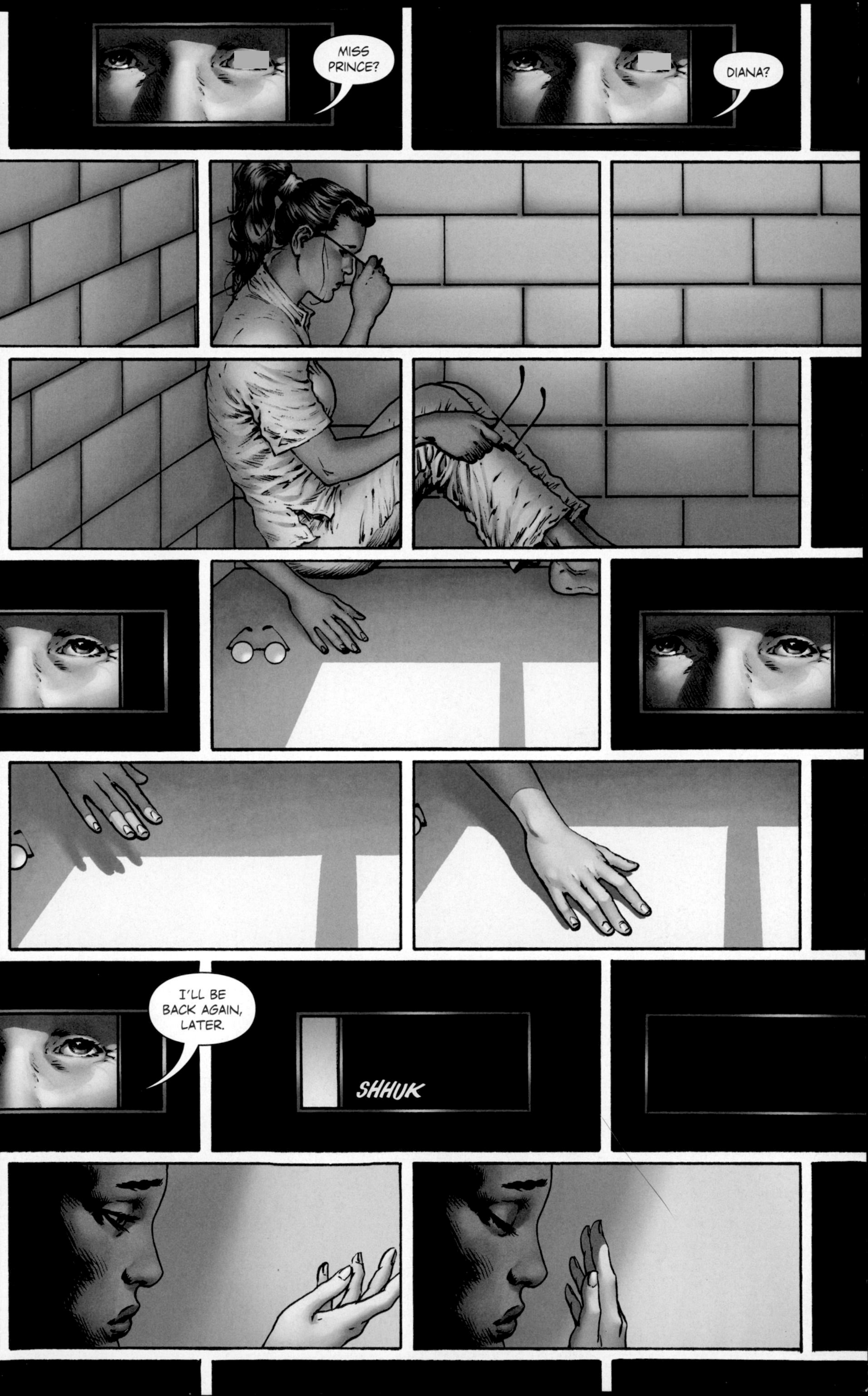
MISS PRINCE?
DIANA?
I'LL BE BACK AGAIN, LATER.
SHHUK

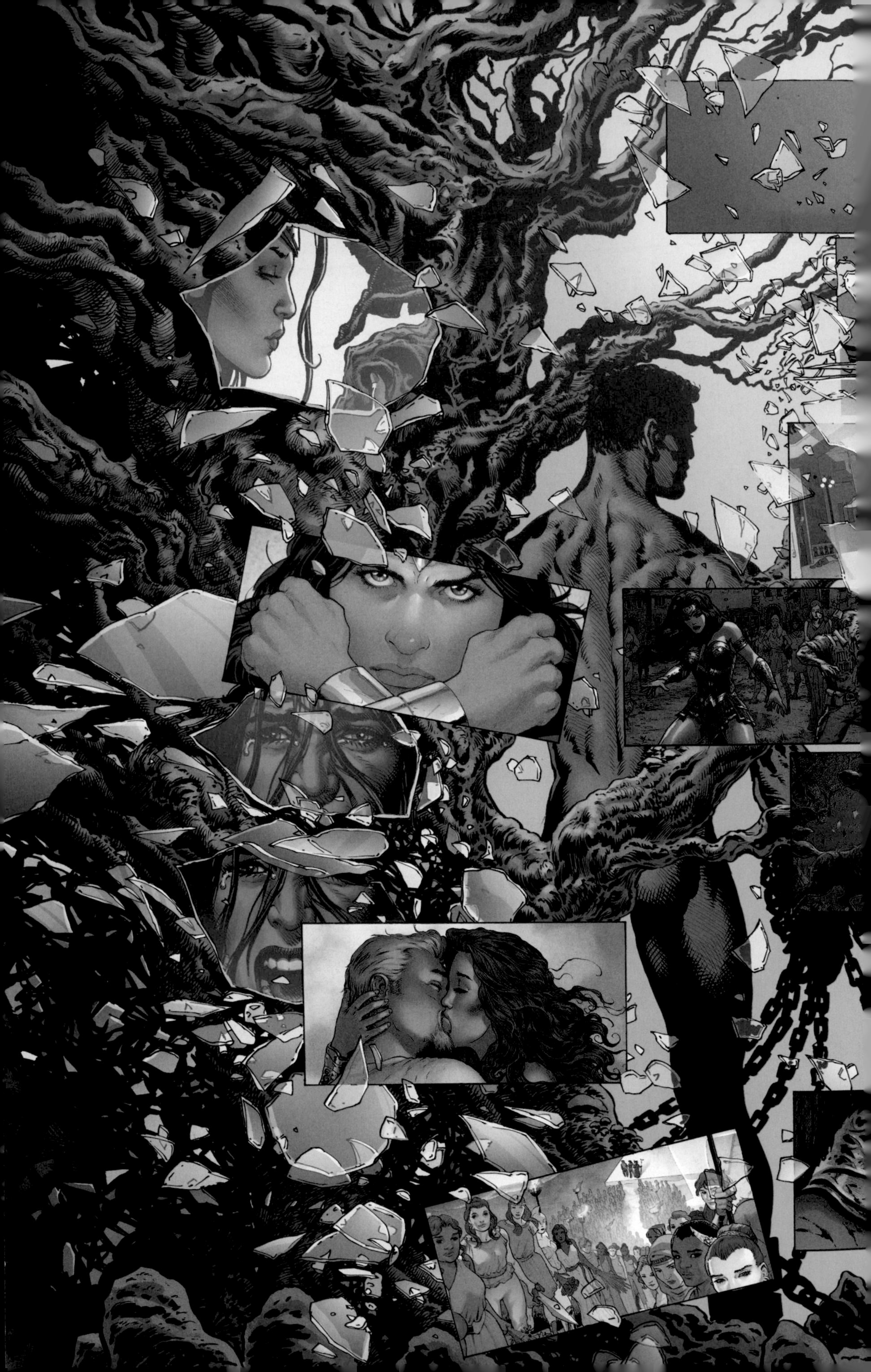

THE TRUTH Part One

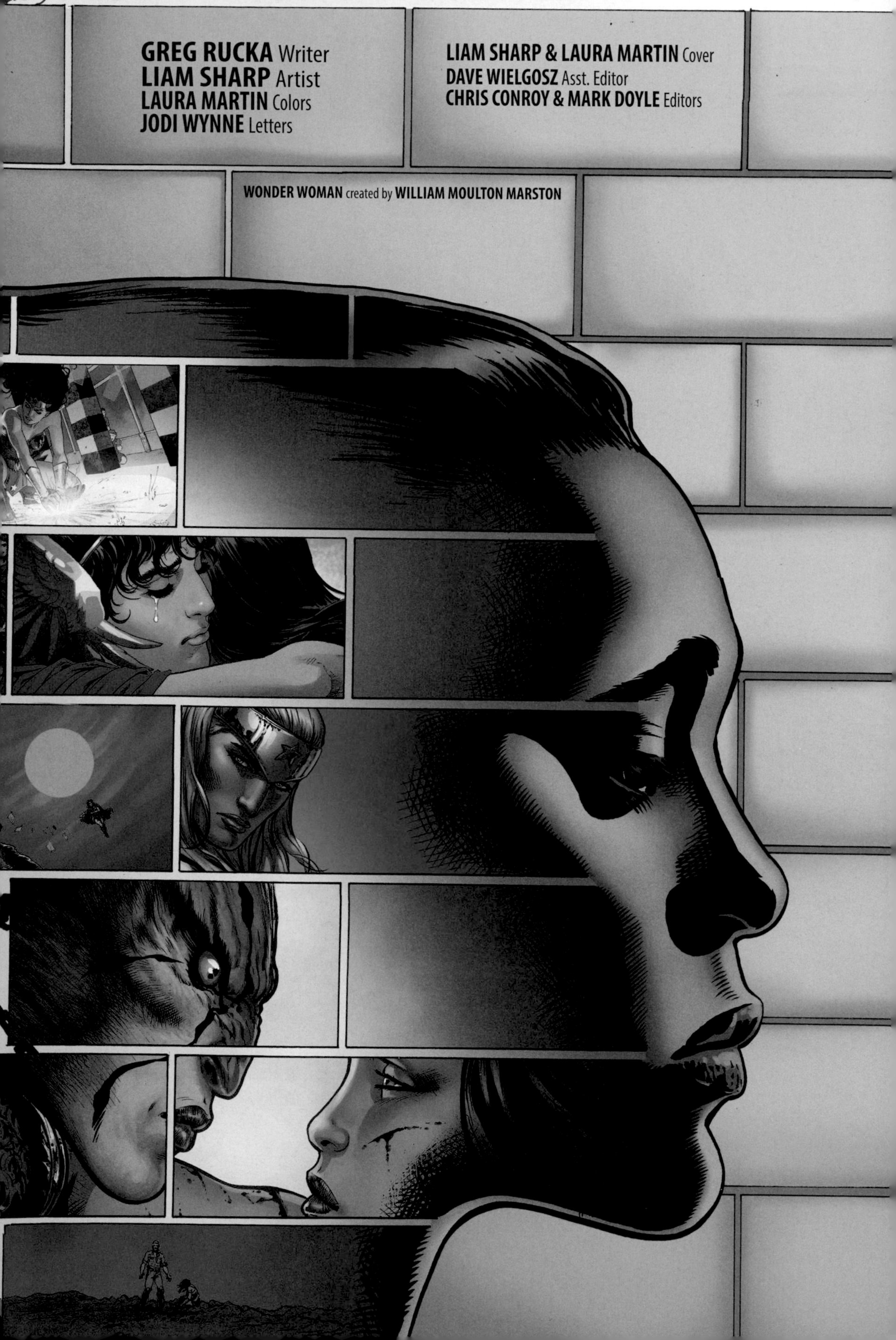

GREG RUCKA Writer
LIAM SHARP Artist
LAURA MARTIN Colors
JODI WYNNE Letters
LIAM SHARP & LAURA MARTIN Cover
DAVE WIELGOSZ Asst. Editor
CHRIS CONROY & MARK DOYLE Editors
WONDER WOMAN created by WILLIAM MOULTON MARSTON

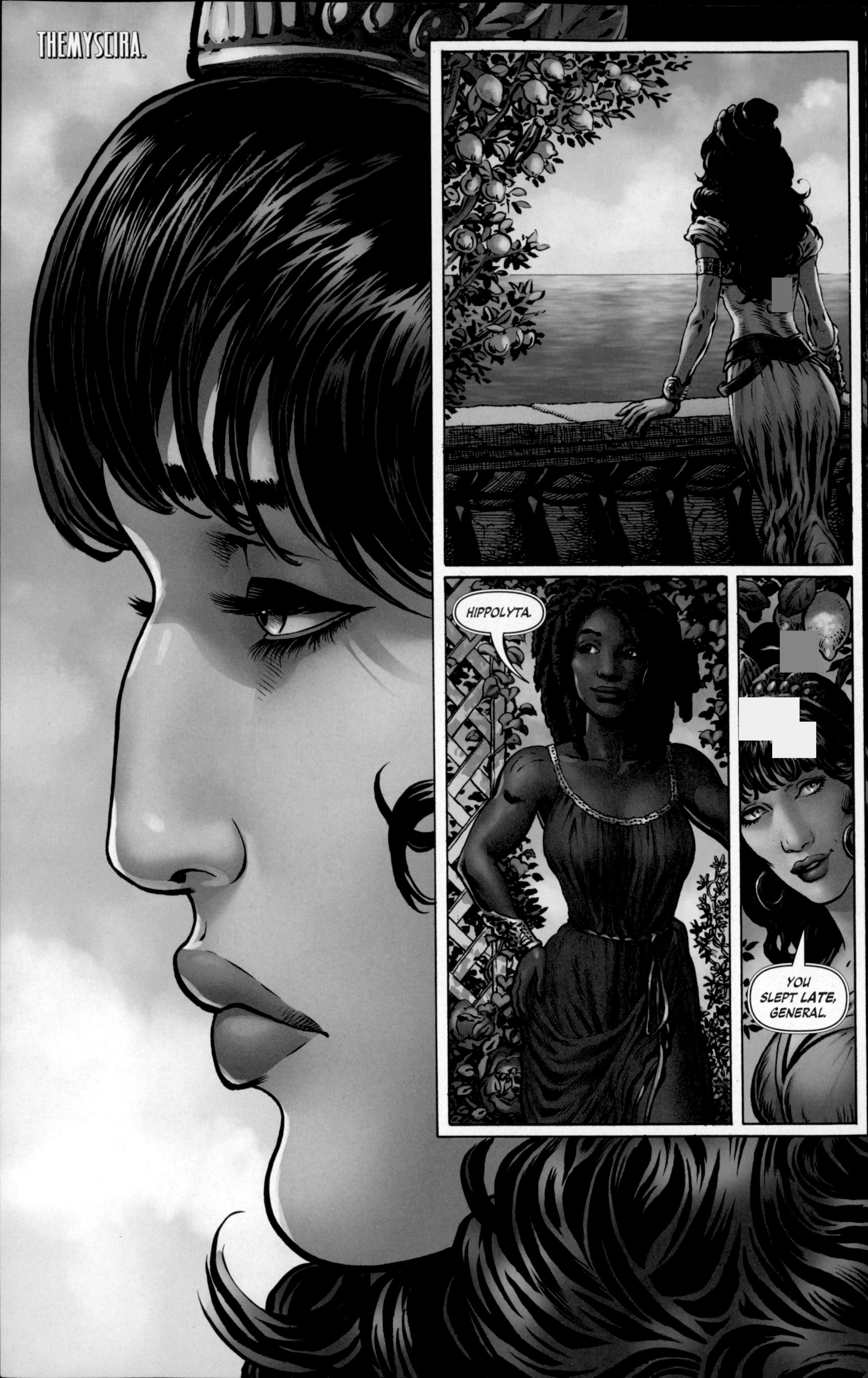
THEMYSCIRA.
HIPPOLYTA.
YOU SLEPT LATE, GENERAL.

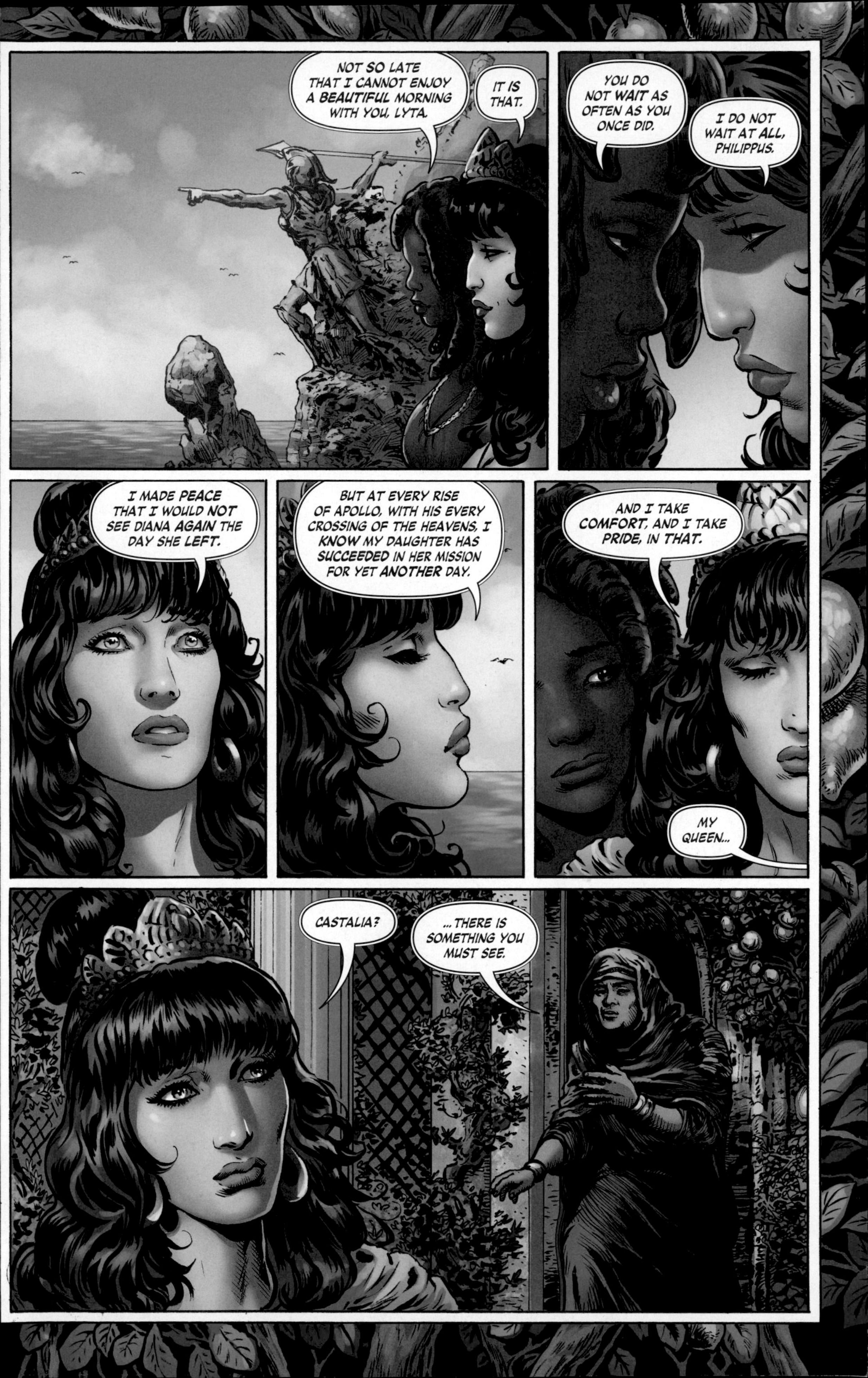
NOT SO LATE THAT I CANNOT ENJOY A BEAUTIFUL MORNING WITH YOU, LYTA.
IT IS THAT.
YOU DO NOT WAIT AS OFTEN AS YOU ONCE DID.
I DO NOT WAIT AT ALL, PHILIPPUS.
I MADE PEACE THAT I WOULD NOT SEE DIANA AGAIN THE DAY SHE LEFT.
BUT AT EVERY RISE OF APOLLO, WITH HIS EVERY CROSSING OF THE HEAVENS, I KNOW MY DAUGHTER HAS SUCCEEDED IN HER MISSION FOR YET ANOTHER DAY.
AND I TAKE COMFORT, AND I TAKE PRIDE, IN THAT.
MY QUEEN...
CASTALIA?
...THERE IS SOMETHING YOU MUST SEE.

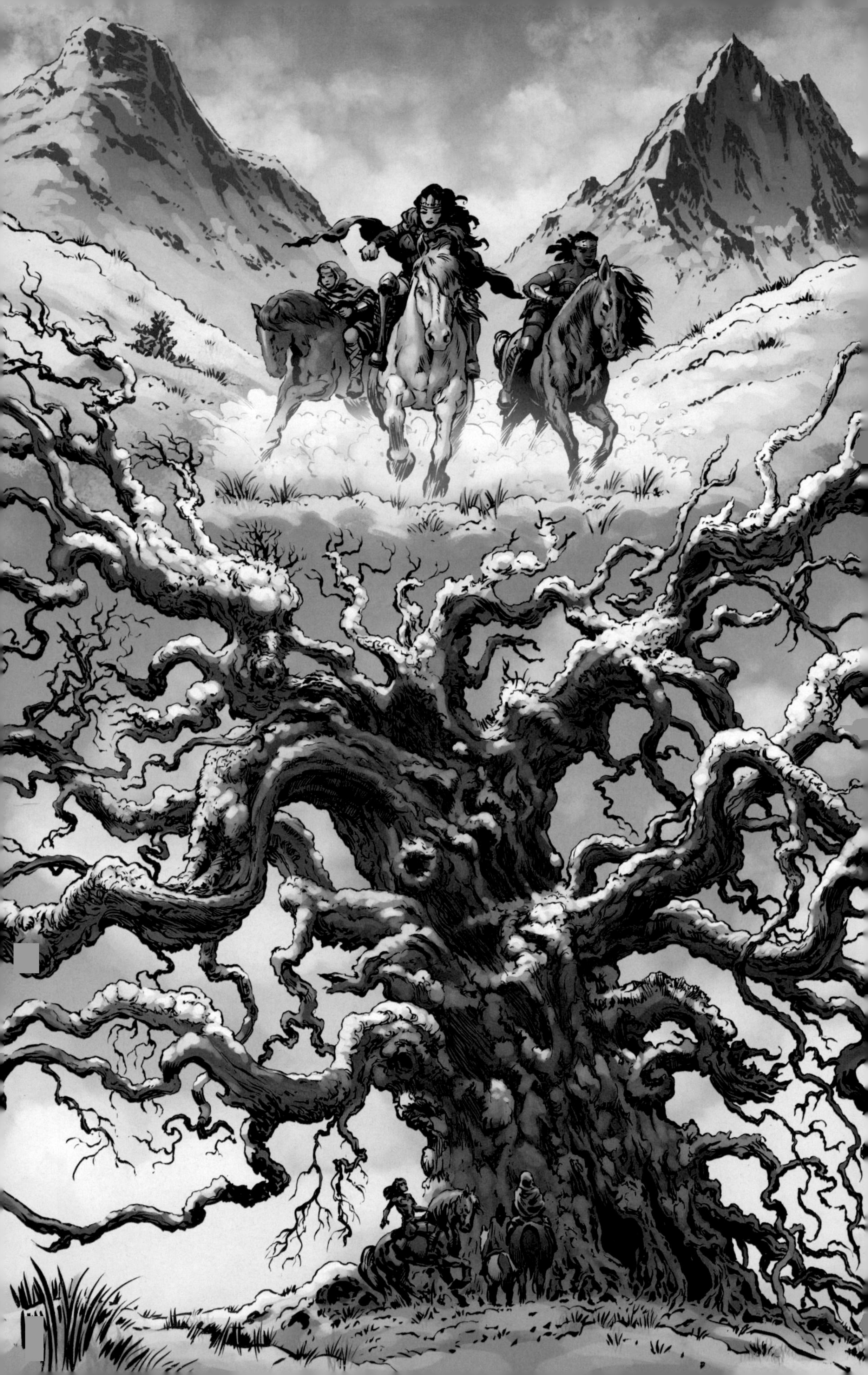

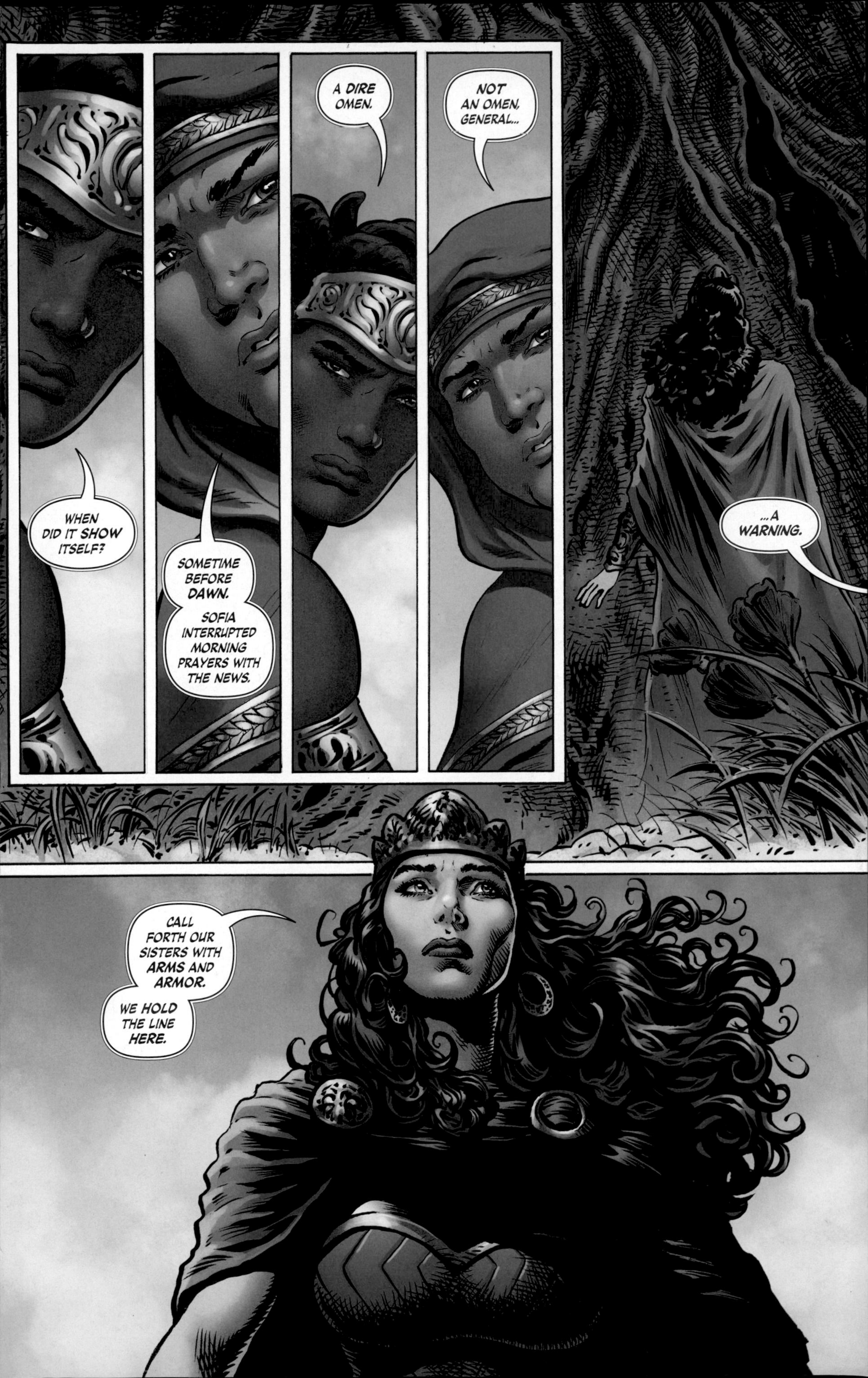
WHEN DID IT SHOW ITSELF?
SOMETIME BEFORE DAWN.
SOFIA INTERRUPTED MORNING PRAYERS WITH THE NEWS.
A DIRE OMEN.
NOT AN OMEN, GENERAL...
...A WARNING.
CALL FORTH OUR SISTERS WITH ARMS AND ARMOR.
WE HOLD THE LINE HERE.

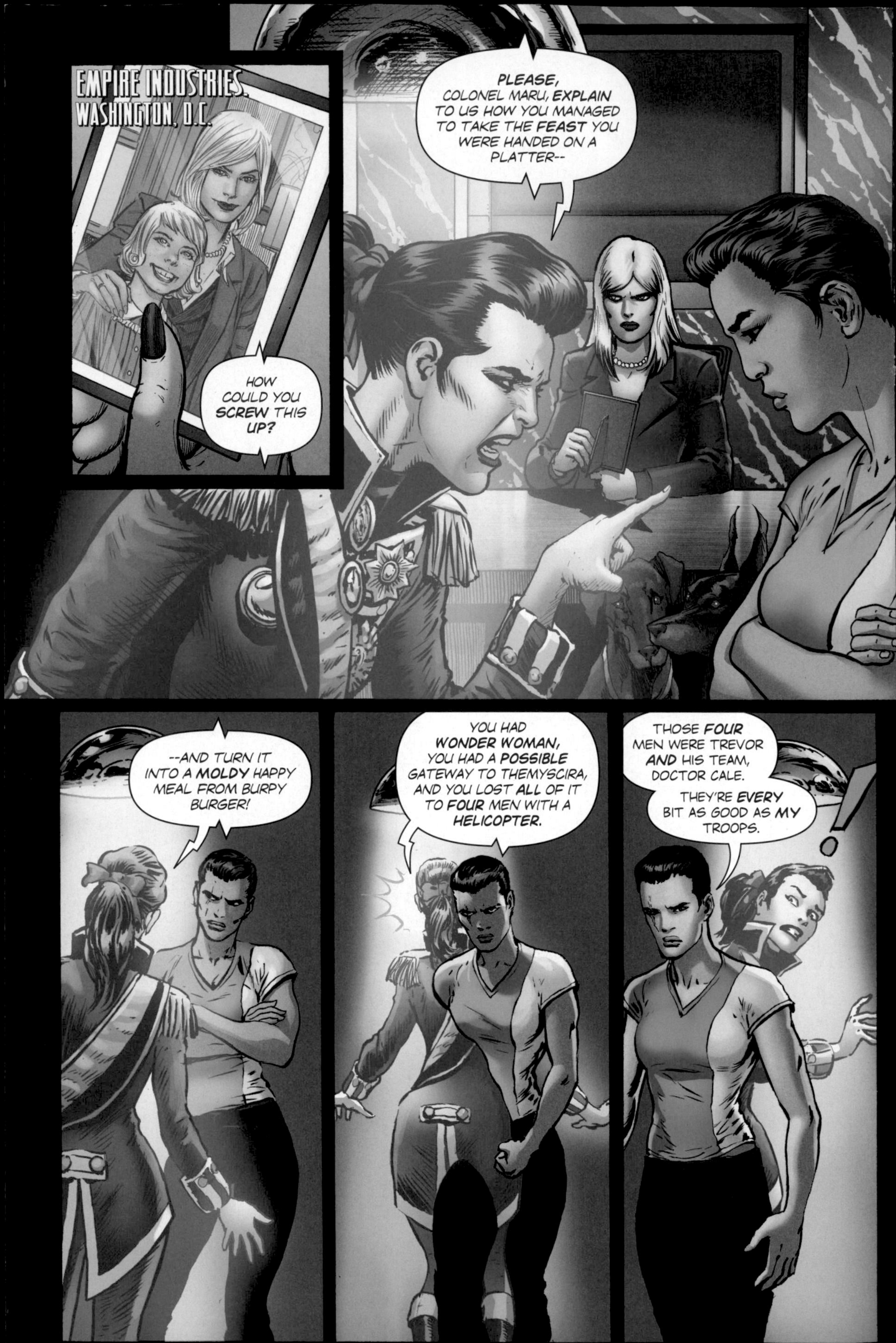
EMPIRE INDUSTRIES. WASHINGTON, D.C.
PLEASE, COLONEL MARU, EXPLAIN TO US HOW YOU MANAGED TO TAKE THE FEAST YOU WERE HANDED ON A PLATTER--
HOW COULD YOU SCREW THIS UP?
--AND TURN IT INTO A MOLDY HAPPY MEAL FROM BURPY BURGER!
YOU HAD WONDER WOMAN, YOU HAD A POSSIBLE GATEWAY TO THEMYSCIRA, AND YOU LOST ALL OF IT TO FOUR MEN WITH A HELICOPTER.
THOSE FOUR MEN WERE TREVOR AND HIS TEAM, DOCTOR CALE.
THEY'RE EVERY BIT AS GOOD AS MY TROOPS.
!

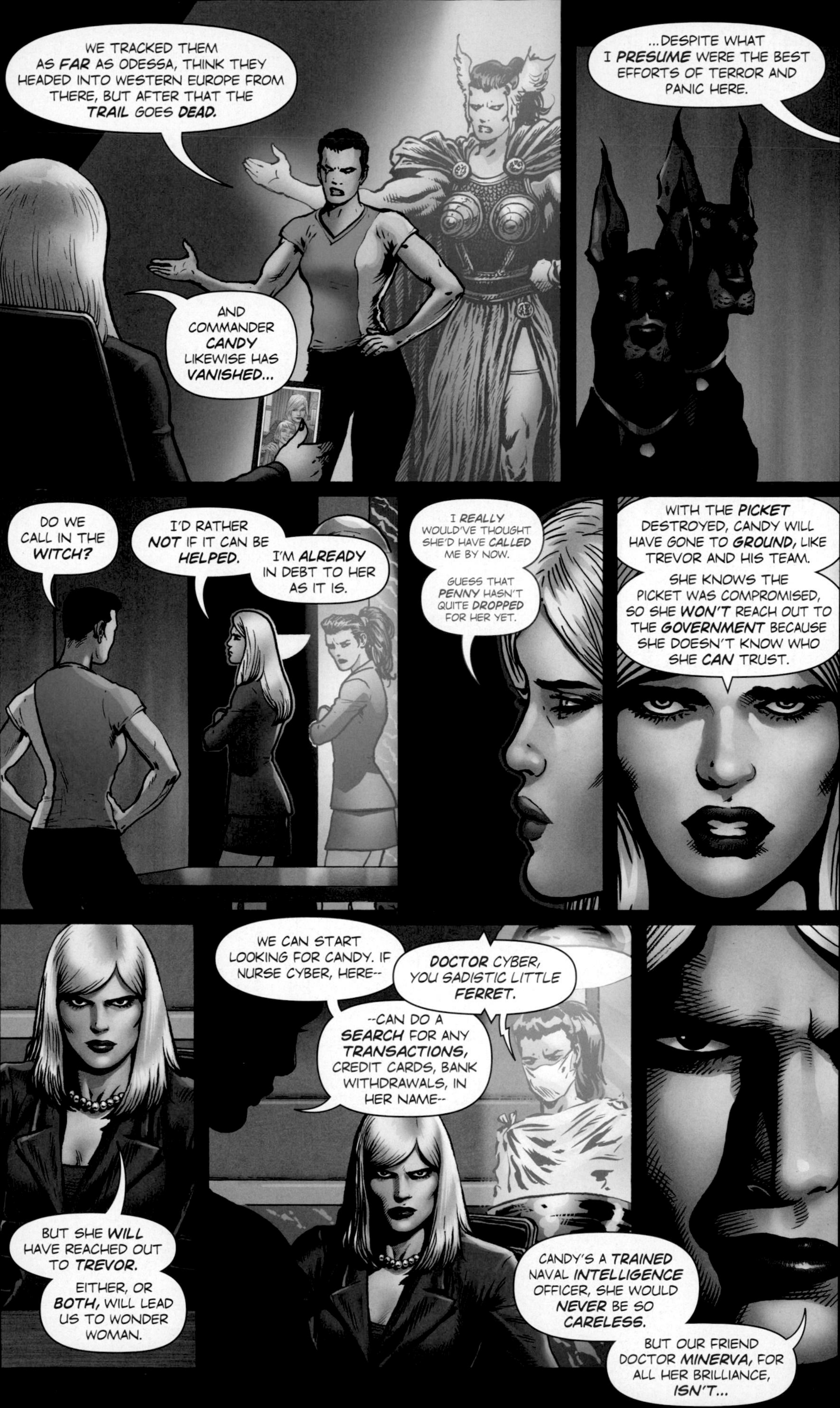
WE TRACKED THEM AS FAR AS ODESSA, THINK THEY HEADED INTO WESTERN EUROPE FROM THERE, BUT AFTER THAT THE TRAIL GOES DEAD.
AND COMMANDER CANDY LIKEWISE HAS VANISHED...
...DESPITE WHAT I PRESUME WERE THE BEST EFFORTS OF TERROR AND PANIC HERE.
DO WE CALL IN THE WITCH?
I'D RATHER NOT IF IT CAN BE HELPED.
I'M ALREADY IN DEBT TO HER AS IT IS.
I REALLY WOULD'VE THOUGHT SHE'D HAVE CALLED ME BY NOW.
GUESS THAT PENNY HASN'T QUITE DROPPED FOR HER YET.
WITH THE PICKET DESTROYED, CANDY WILL HAVE GONE TO GROUND, LIKE TREVOR AND HIS TEAM.
SHE KNOWS THE PICKET WAS COMPROMISED, SO SHE WON'T REACH OUT TO THE GOVERNMENT BECAUSE SHE DOESN'T KNOW WHO SHE CAN TRUST.
BUT SHE WILL HAVE REACHED OUT TO TREVOR.
EITHER, OR BOTH, WILL LEAD US TO WONDER WOMAN.
WE CAN START LOOKING FOR CANDY. IF NURSE CYBER, HERE--
DOCTOR CYBER, YOU SADISTIC LITTLE FERRET.
--CAN DO A SEARCH FOR ANY TRANSACTIONS, CREDIT CARDS, BANK WITHDRAWALS, IN HER NAME--
CANDY'S A TRAINED NAVAL INTELLIGENCE OFFICER, SHE WOULD NEVER BE SO CARELESS.
BUT OUR FRIEND DOCTOR MINERVA, FOR ALL HER BRILLIANCE, ISN'T...

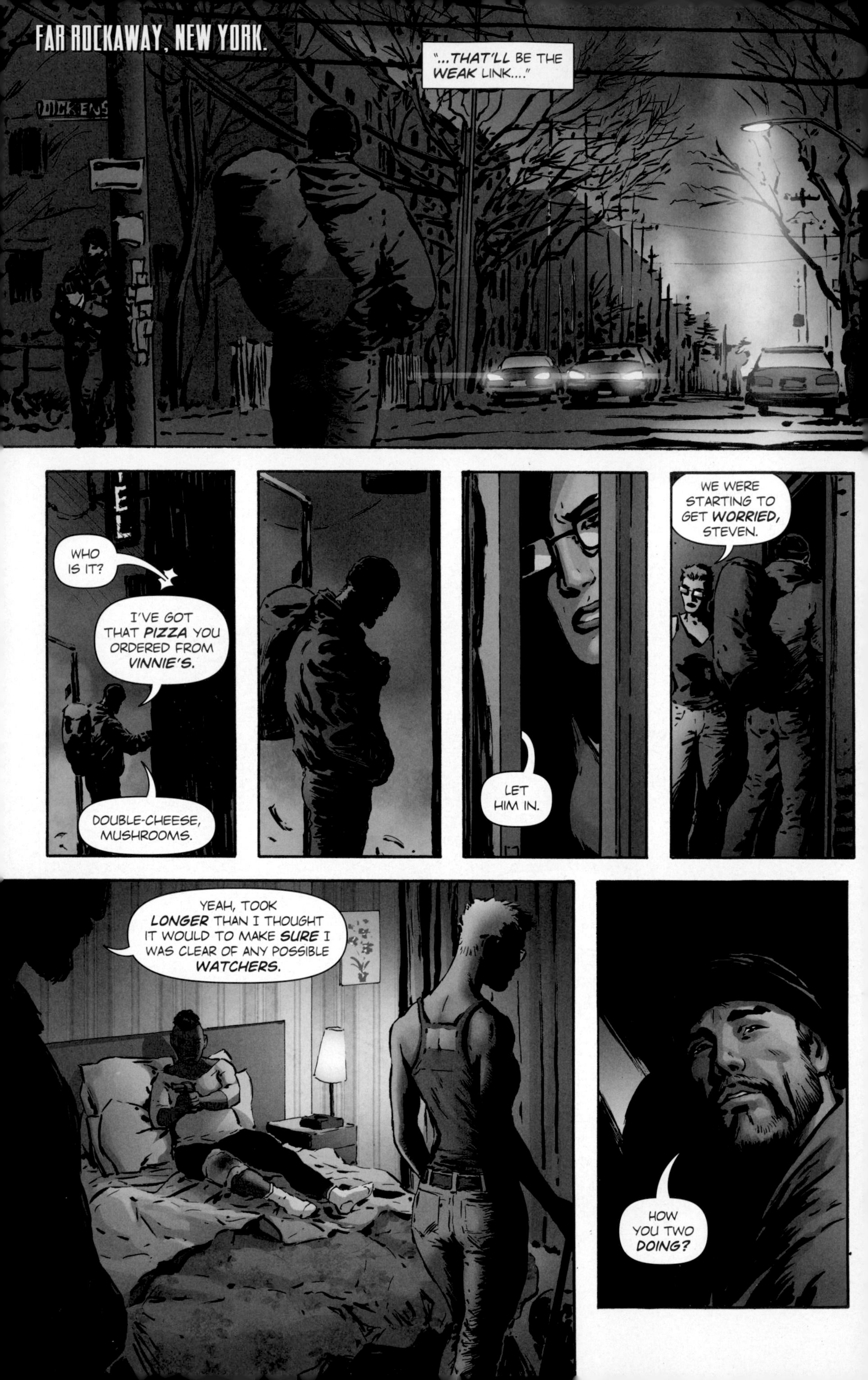
FAR ROCKAWAY, NEW YORK.
"...THAT'LL BE THE WEAK LINK...."
DICKENS
WHO IS IT?
I'VE GOT THAT PIZZA YOU ORDERED FROM VINNIE'S.
DOUBLE-CHEESE, MUSHROOMS.
LET HIM IN.
WE WERE STARTING TO GET WORRIED, STEVEN.
YEAH, TOOK LONGER THAN I THOUGHT IT WOULD TO MAKE SURE I WAS CLEAR OF ANY POSSIBLE WATCHERS.
HOW YOU TWO DOING?

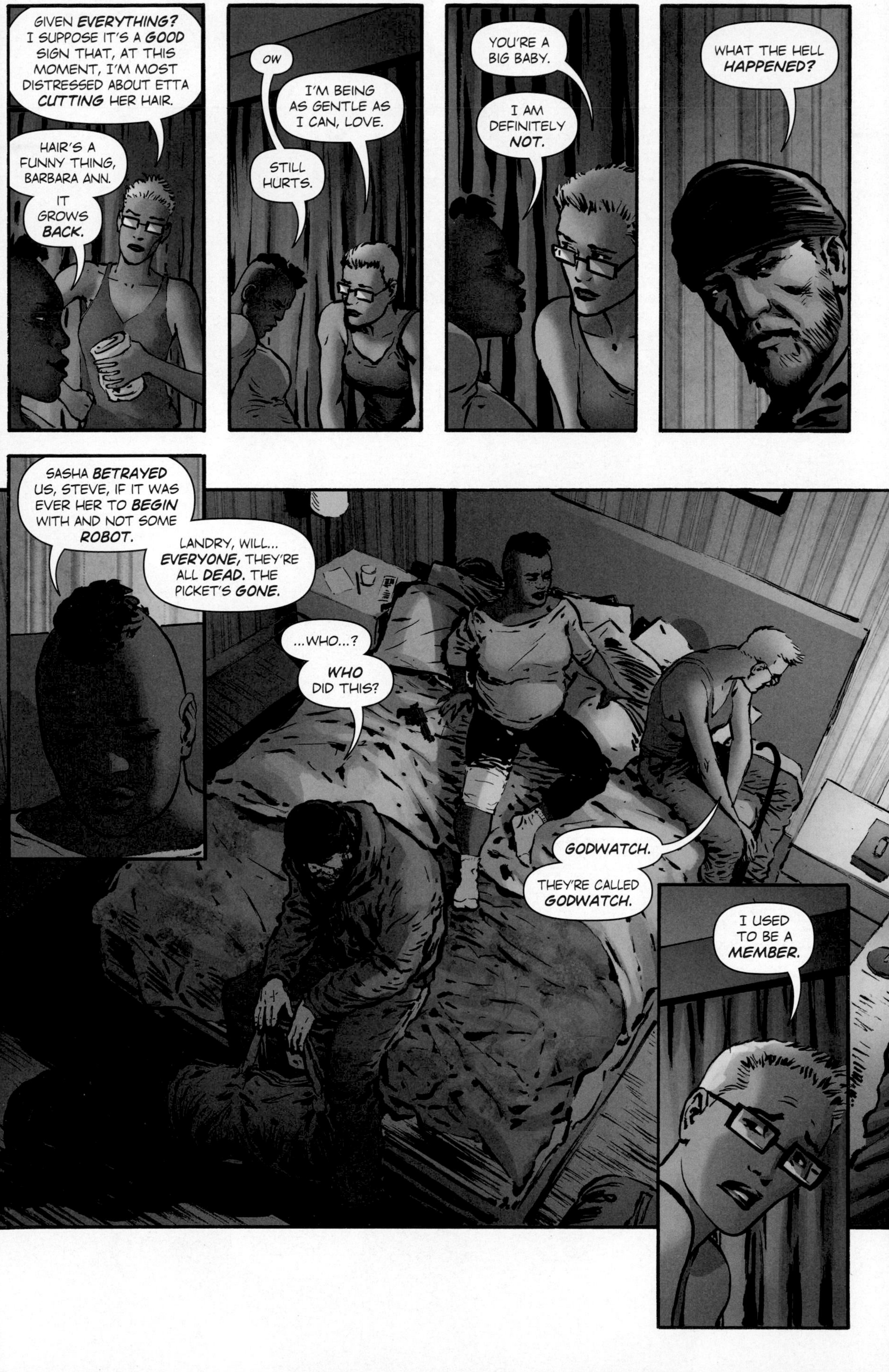
GIVEN EVERYTHING? I SUPPOSE IT'S A GOOD SIGN THAT, AT THIS MOMENT, I'M MOST DISTRESSED ABOUT ETTA CUTTING HER HAIR.
HAIR'S A FUNNY THING, BARBARA ANN.
IT GROWS BACK.
OW
I'M BEING AS GENTLE AS I CAN, LOVE.
STILL HURTS.
YOU'RE A BIG BABY.
I AM DEFINITELY NOT.
WHAT THE HELL HAPPENED?
SASHA BETRAYED US, STEVE, IF IT WAS EVER HER TO BEGIN WITH AND NOT SOME ROBOT.
LANDRY, WILL... EVERYONE, THEY'RE ALL DEAD. THE PICKET'S GONE.
...WHO...?
WHO DID THIS?
GODWATCH.
THEY'RE CALLED GODWATCH.
I USED TO BE A MEMBER.

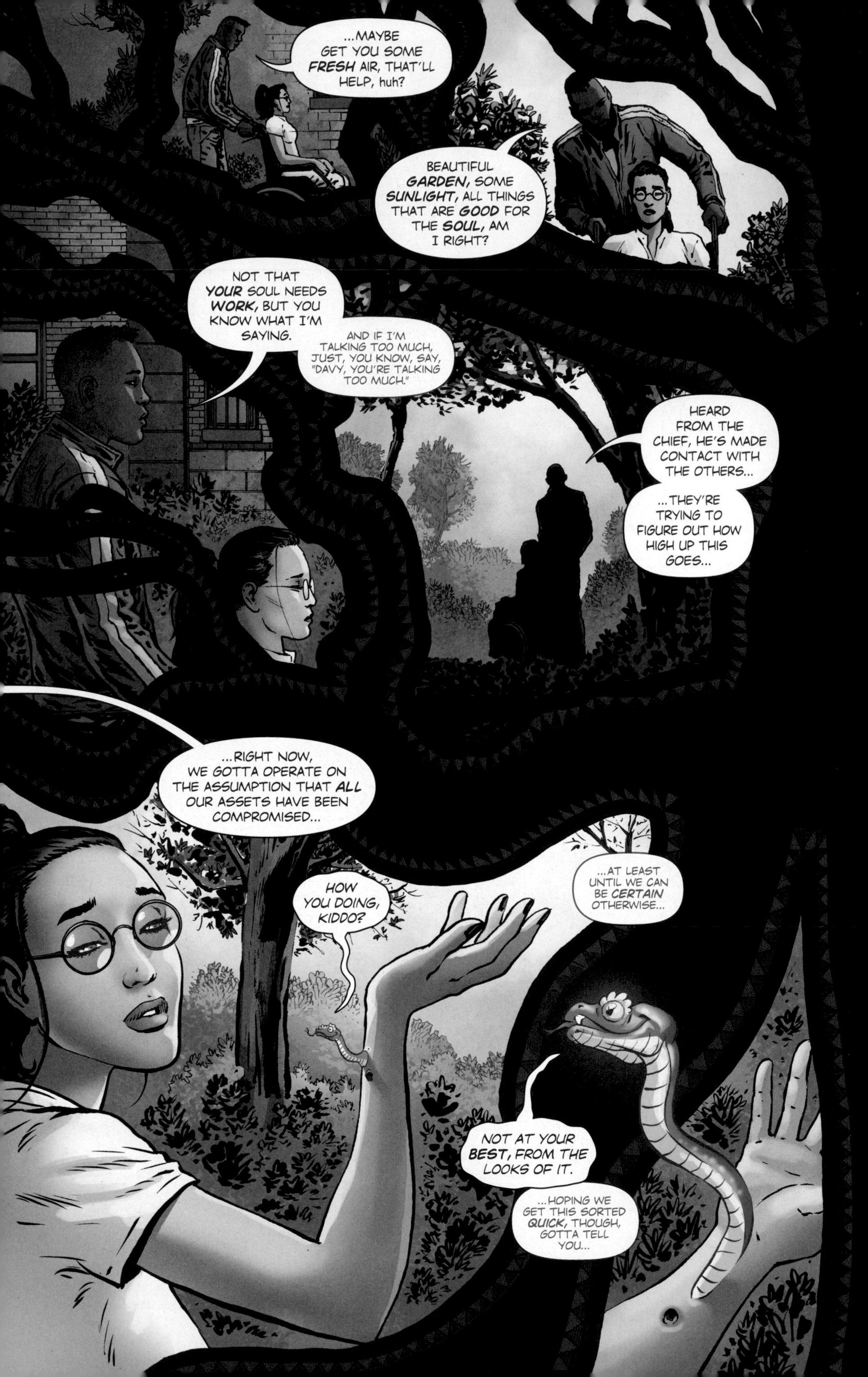
...MAYBE GET YOU SOME FRESH AIR, THAT'LL HELP, huh?
BEAUTIFUL GARDEN, SOME SUNLIGHT, ALL THINGS THAT ARE GOOD FOR THE SOUL, AM I RIGHT?
NOT THAT YOUR SOUL NEEDS WORK, BUT YOU KNOW WHAT I'M SAYING.
AND IF I'M TALKING TOO MUCH, JUST, YOU KNOW, SAY, "DAVY, YOU'RE TALKING TOO MUCH."
HEARD FROM THE CHIEF, HE'S MADE CONTACT WITH THE OTHERS...
...THEY'RE TRYING TO FIGURE OUT HOW HIGH UP THIS GOES...
...RIGHT NOW, WE GOTTA OPERATE ON THE ASSUMPTION THAT ALL OUR ASSETS HAVE BEEN COMPROMISED...
HOW YOU DOING, KIDDO?
...AT LEAST UNTIL WE CAN BE CERTAIN OTHERWISE...
NOT AT YOUR BEST, FROM THE LOOKS OF IT.
...HOPING WE GET THIS SORTED QUICK, THOUGH, GOTTA TELL YOU...

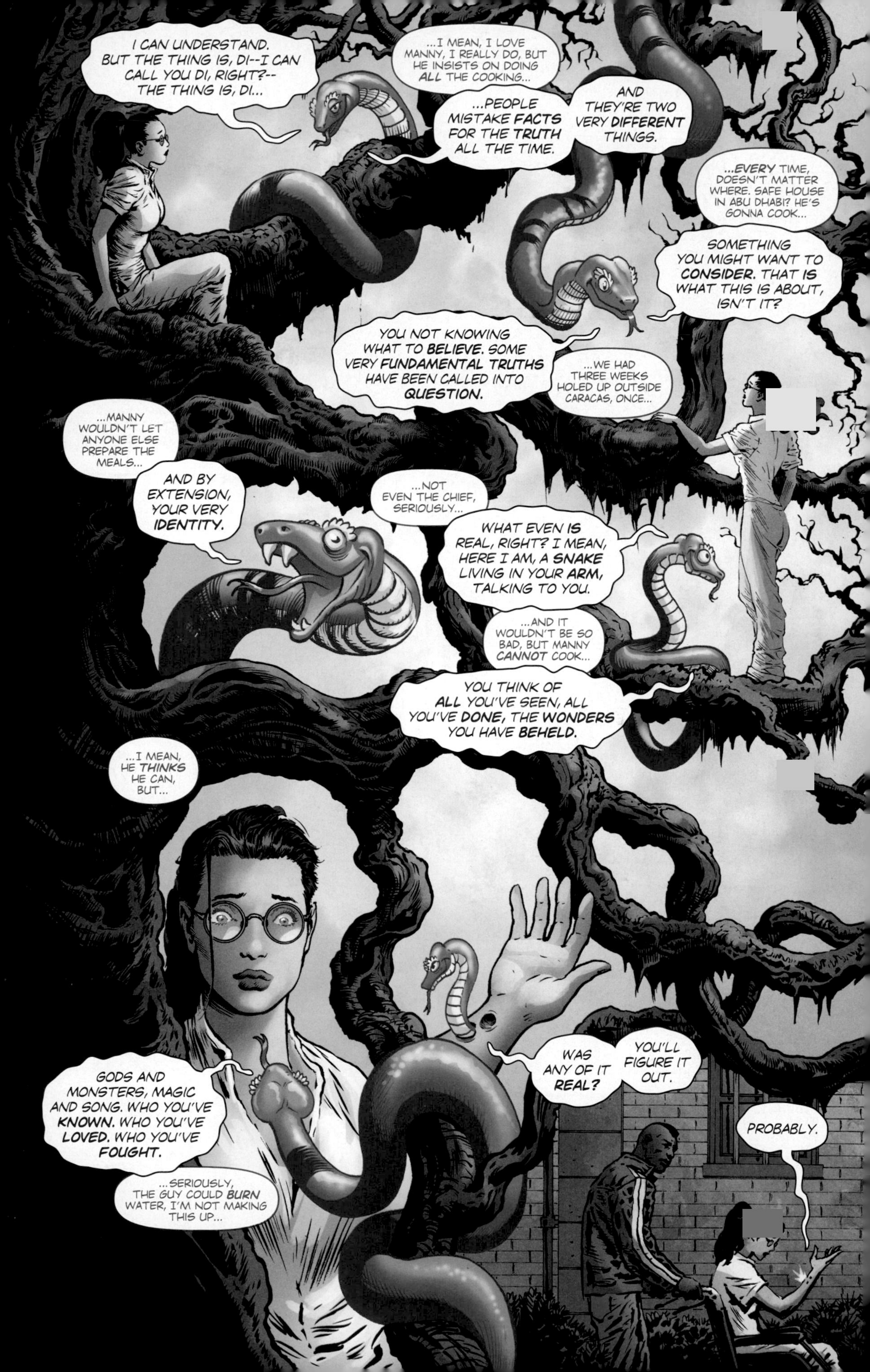
I CAN UNDERSTAND. BUT THE THING IS, DI--I CAN CALL YOU DI, RIGHT?-- THE THING IS, DI...
...I MEAN, I LOVE MANNY, I REALLY DO, BUT HE INSISTS ON DOING ALL THE COOKING...
...PEOPLE MISTAKE FACTS FOR THE TRUTH ALL THE TIME.
AND THEY'RE TWO VERY DIFFERENT THINGS.
...EVERY TIME, DOESN'T MATTER WHERE. SAFE HOUSE IN ABU DHABI? HE'S GONNA COOK...
SOMETHING YOU MIGHT WANT TO CONSIDER. THAT IS WHAT THIS IS ABOUT, ISN'T IT?
YOU NOT KNOWING WHAT TO BELIEVE. SOME VERY FUNDAMENTAL TRUTHS HAVE BEEN CALLED INTO QUESTION.
...WE HAD THREE WEEKS HOLED UP OUTSIDE CARACAS, ONCE...
...MANNY WOULDN'T LET ANYONE ELSE PREPARE THE MEALS...
AND BY EXTENSION, YOUR VERY IDENTITY.
...NOT EVEN THE CHIEF, SERIOUSLY...
WHAT EVEN IS REAL, RIGHT? I MEAN, HERE I AM, A SNAKE LIVING IN YOUR ARM, TALKING TO YOU.
...AND IT WOULDN'T BE SO BAD, BUT MANNY CANNOT COOK...
YOU THINK OF ALL YOU'VE SEEN, ALL YOU'VE DONE, THE WONDERS YOU HAVE BEHELD.
...I MEAN, HE THINKS HE CAN, BUT...
GODS AND MONSTERS, MAGIC AND SONG. WHO YOU'VE KNOWN. WHO YOU'VE LOVED. WHO YOU'VE FOUGHT.
...SERIOUSLY, THE GUY COULD BURN WATER, I'M NOT MAKING THIS UP...
WAS ANY OF IT REAL?
YOU'LL FIGURE IT OUT.
PROBABLY.

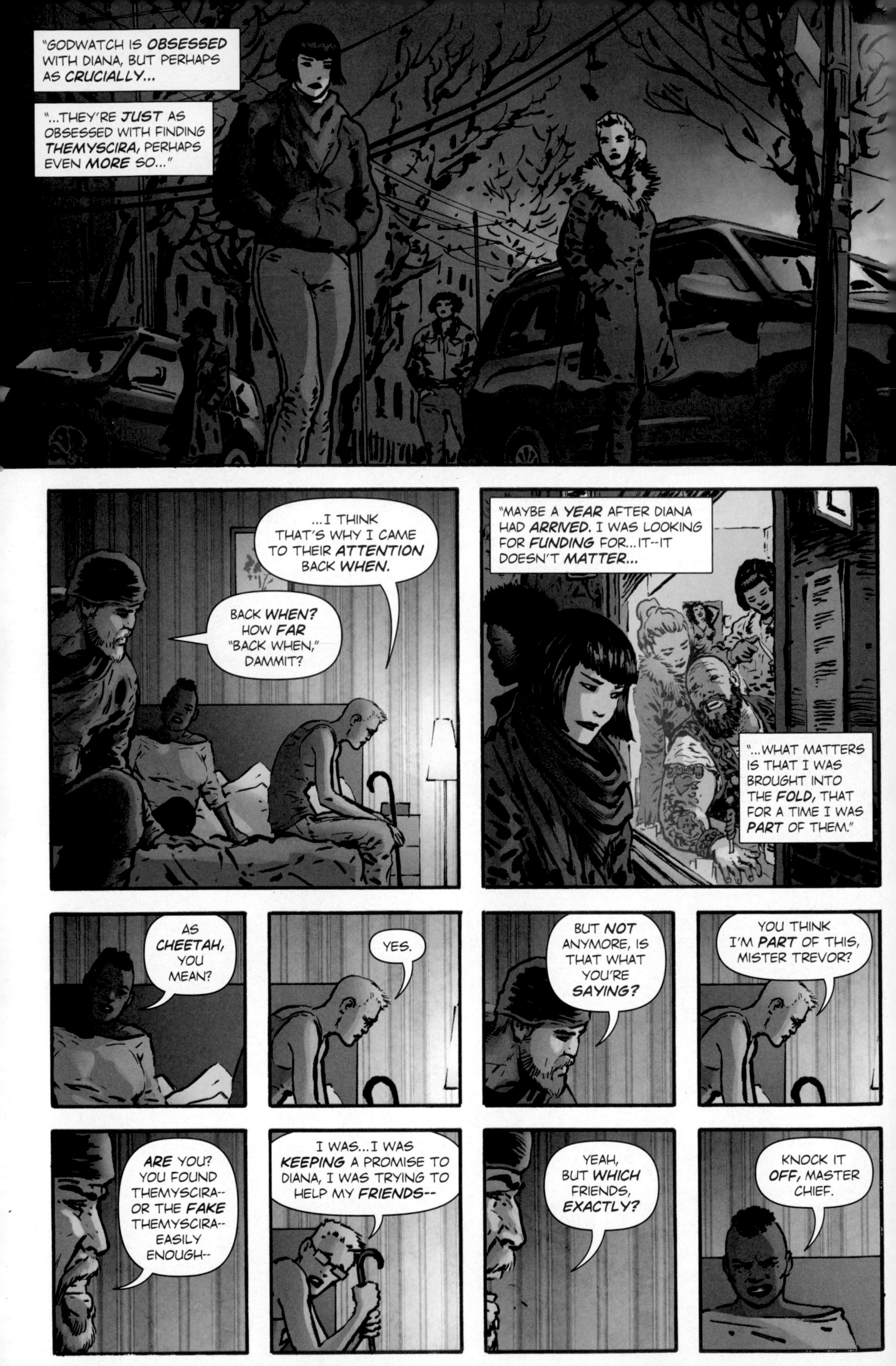
"GODWATCH IS OBSESSED WITH DIANA, BUT PERHAPS AS CRUCIALLY...
"...THEY'RE JUST AS OBSESSED WITH FINDING THEMYSCIRA, PERHAPS EVEN MORE SO..."
...I THINK THAT'S WHY I CAME TO THEIR ATTENTION BACK WHEN.
BACK WHEN? HOW FAR "BACK WHEN," DAMMIT?
"MAYBE A YEAR AFTER DIANA HAD ARRIVED. I WAS LOOKING FOR FUNDING FOR...IT--IT DOESN'T MATTER...
"...WHAT MATTERS IS THAT I WAS BROUGHT INTO THE FOLD, THAT FOR A TIME I WAS PART OF THEM."
AS CHEETAH, YOU MEAN?
YES.
BUT NOT ANYMORE, IS THAT WHAT YOU'RE SAYING?
YOU THINK I'M PART OF THIS, MISTER TREVOR?
ARE YOU? YOU FOUND THEMYSCIRA-- OR THE FAKE THEMYSCIRA-- EASILY ENOUGH--
I WAS...I WAS KEEPING A PROMISE TO DIANA, I WAS TRYING TO HELP MY FRIENDS--
YEAH, BUT WHICH FRIENDS, EXACTLY?
KNOCK IT OFF, MASTER CHIEF.

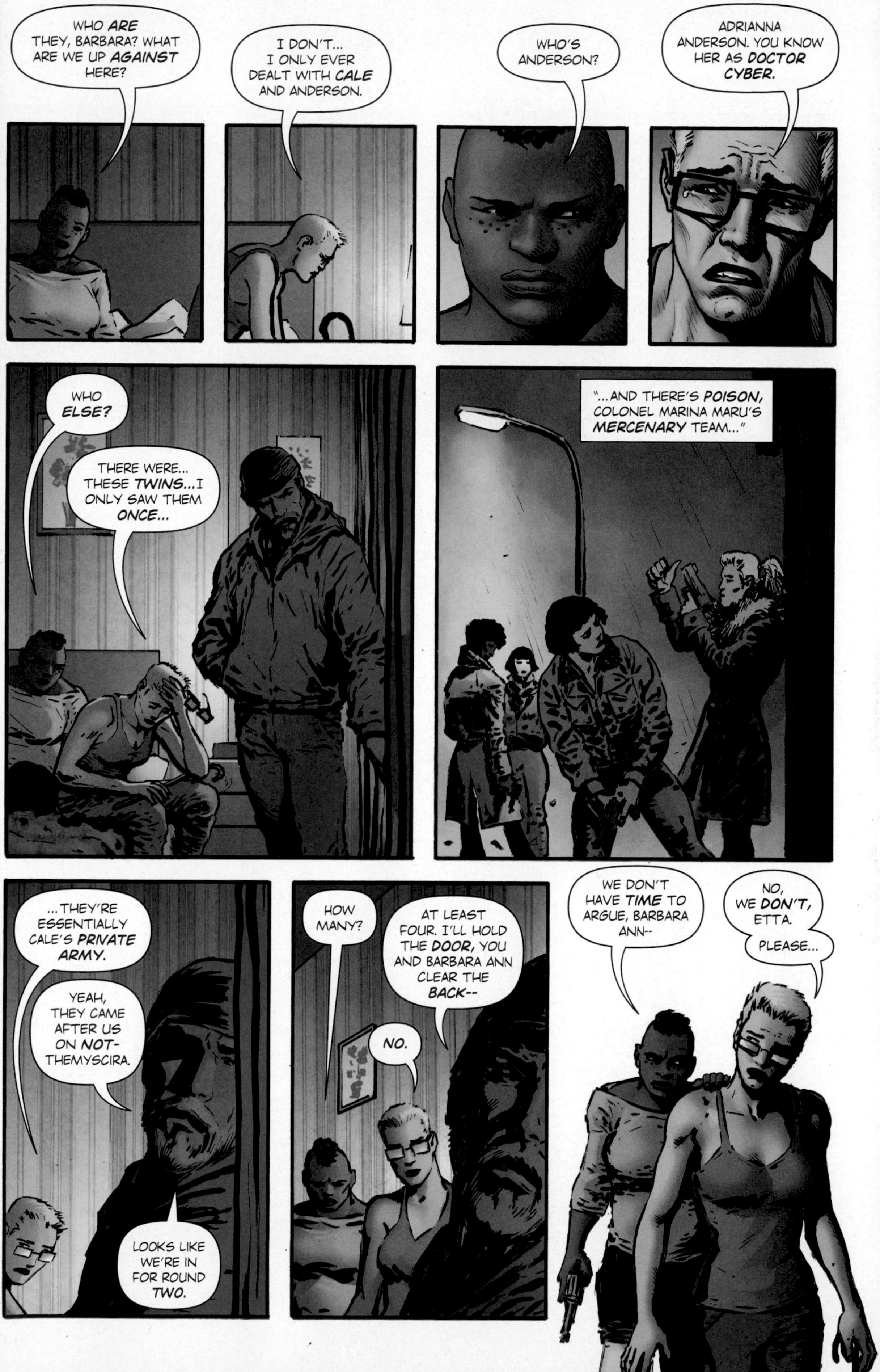
WHO ARE THEY, BARBARA? WHAT ARE WE UP AGAINST HERE?
I DON'T... I ONLY EVER DEALT WITH CALE AND ANDERSON.
WHO'S ANDERSON?
ADRIANNA ANDERSON. YOU KNOW HER AS DOCTOR CYBER.
WHO ELSE?
THERE WERE... THESE TWINS...I ONLY SAW THEM ONCE...
"...AND THERE'S POISON, COLONEL MARINA MARU'S MERCENARY TEAM..."
...THEY'RE ESSENTIALLY CALE'S PRIVATE ARMY.
YEAH, THEY CAME AFTER US ON NOT-THEMYSCIRA.
LOOKS LIKE WE'RE IN FOR ROUND TWO.
HOW MANY?
AT LEAST FOUR. I'LL HOLD THE DOOR, YOU AND BARBARA ANN CLEAR THE BACK--
NO.
WE DON'T HAVE TIME TO ARGUE, BARBARA ANN--
NO, WE DON'T, ETTA.
PLEASE...

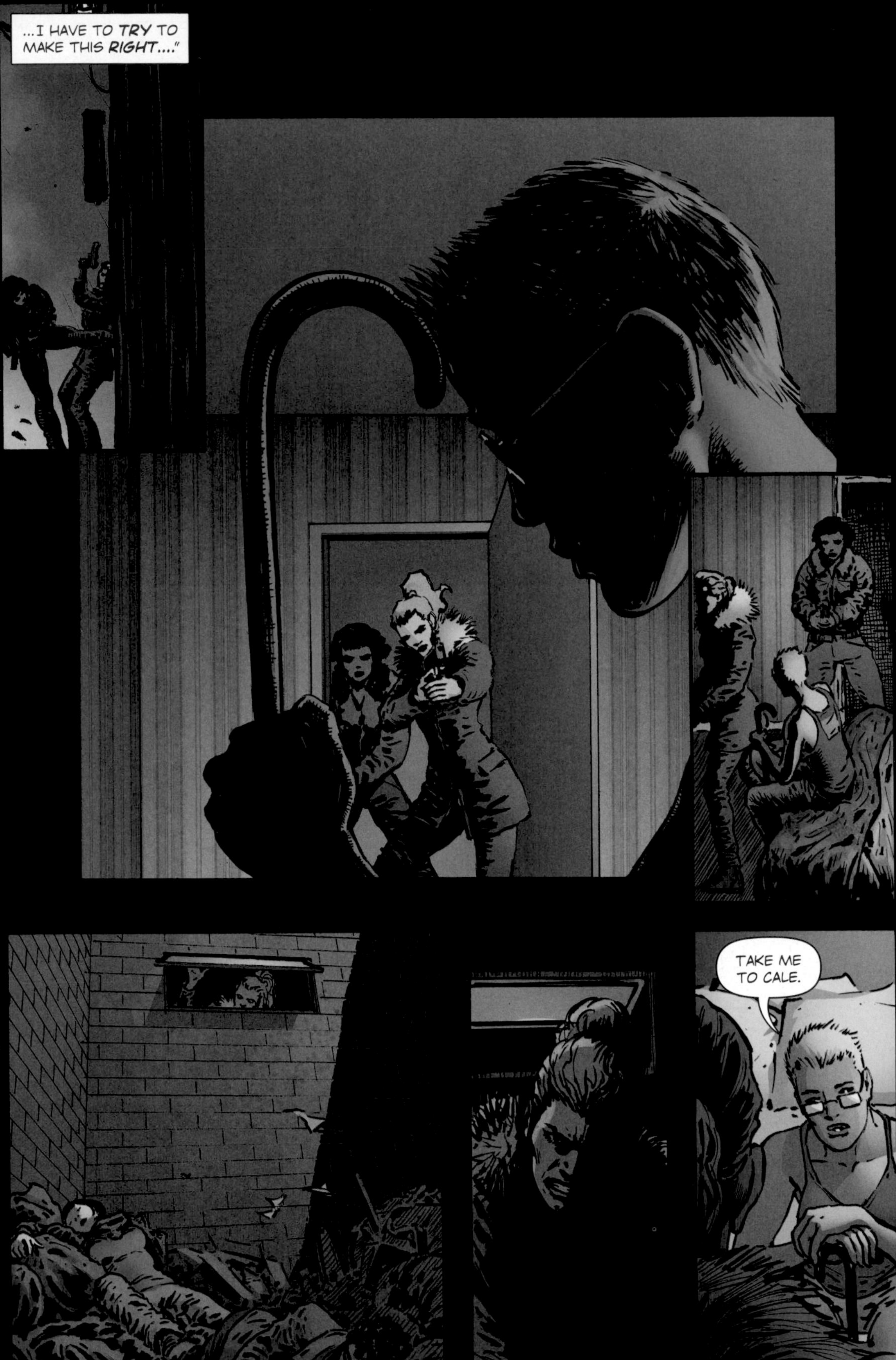
...I HAVE TO TRY TO MAKE THIS RIGHT...."
TAKE ME TO CALE.

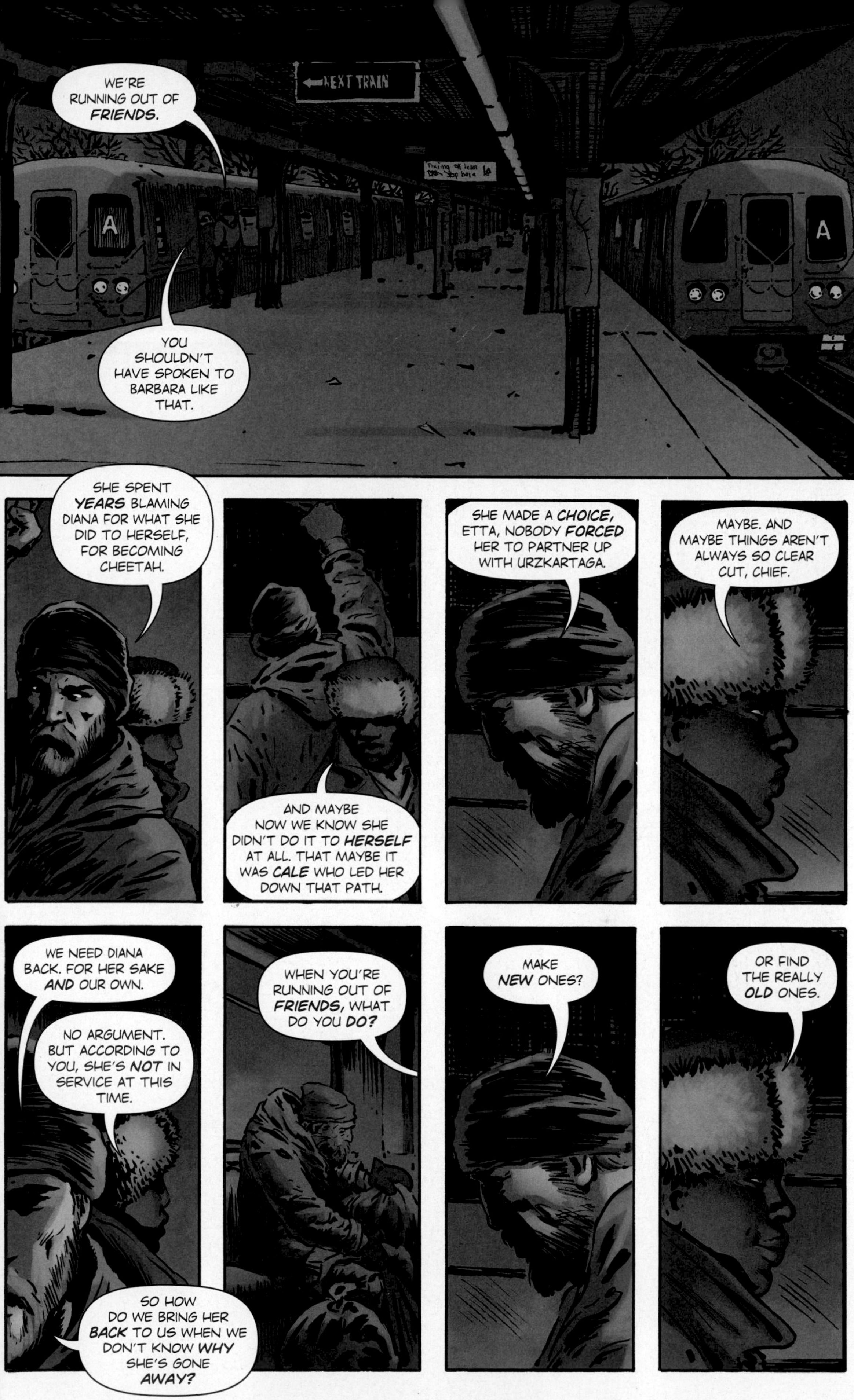
WE'RE RUNNING OUT OF FRIENDS.
YOU SHOULDN'T HAVE SPOKEN TO BARBARA LIKE THAT.
SHE SPENT YEARS BLAMING DIANA FOR WHAT SHE DID TO HERSELF, FOR BECOMING CHEETAH.
AND MAYBE NOW WE KNOW SHE DIDN'T DO IT TO HERSELF AT ALL. THAT MAYBE IT WAS CALE WHO LED HER DOWN THAT PATH.
SHE MADE A CHOICE, ETTA, NOBODY FORCED HER TO PARTNER UP WITH URZKARTAGA.
MAYBE. AND MAYBE THINGS AREN'T ALWAYS SO CLEAR CUT, CHIEF.
WE NEED DIANA BACK. FOR HER SAKE AND OUR OWN.
NO ARGUMENT. BUT ACCORDING TO YOU, SHE'S NOT IN SERVICE AT THIS TIME.
SO HOW DO WE BRING HER BACK TO US WHEN WE DON'T KNOW WHY SHE'S GONE AWAY?
WHEN YOU'RE RUNNING OUT OF FRIENDS, WHAT DO YOU DO?
MAKE NEW ONES?
OR FIND THE REALLY OLD ONES.

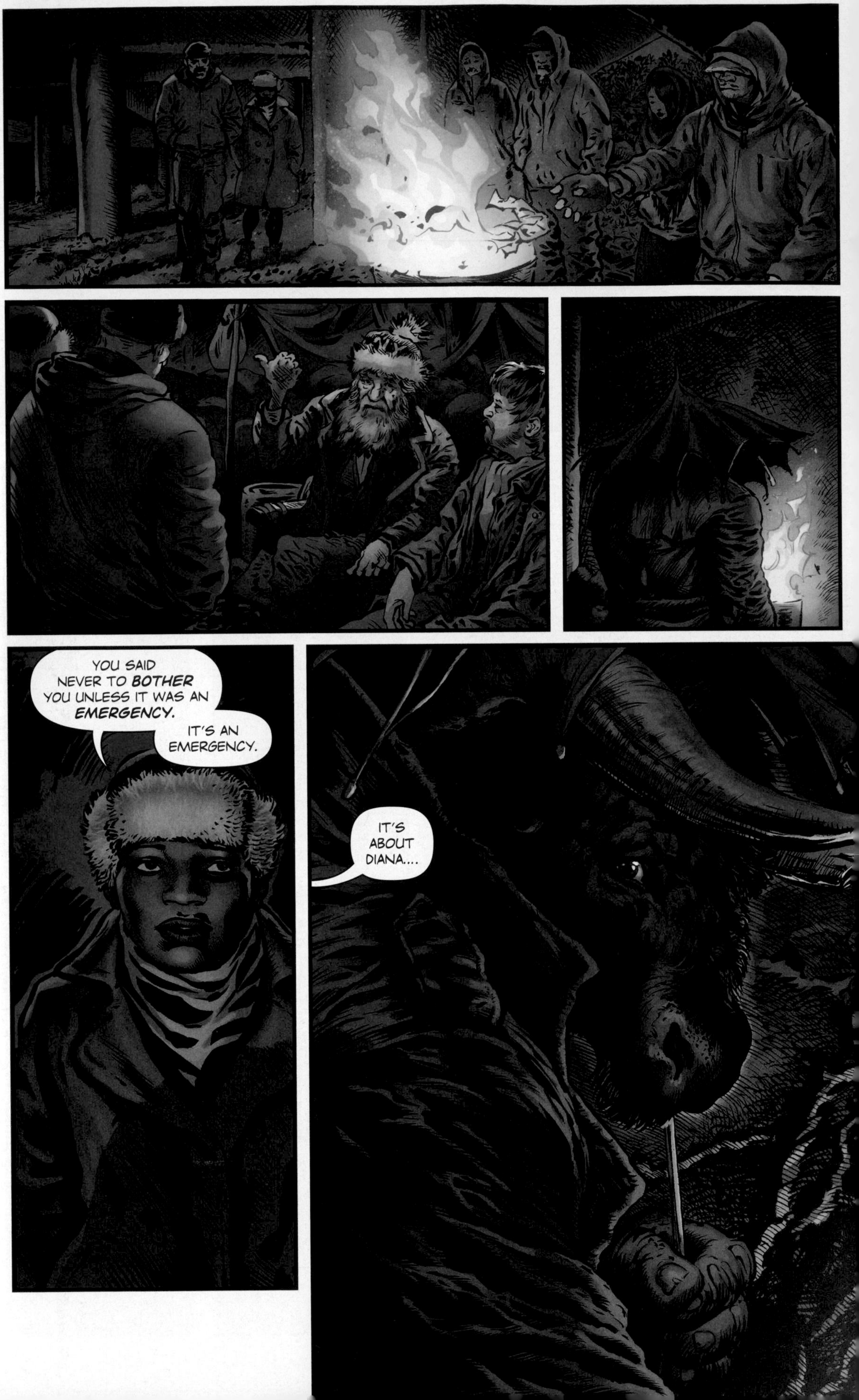
YOU SAID NEVER TO BOTHER YOU UNLESS IT WAS AN EMERGENCY.
IT'S AN EMERGENCY.
IT'S ABOUT DIANA....

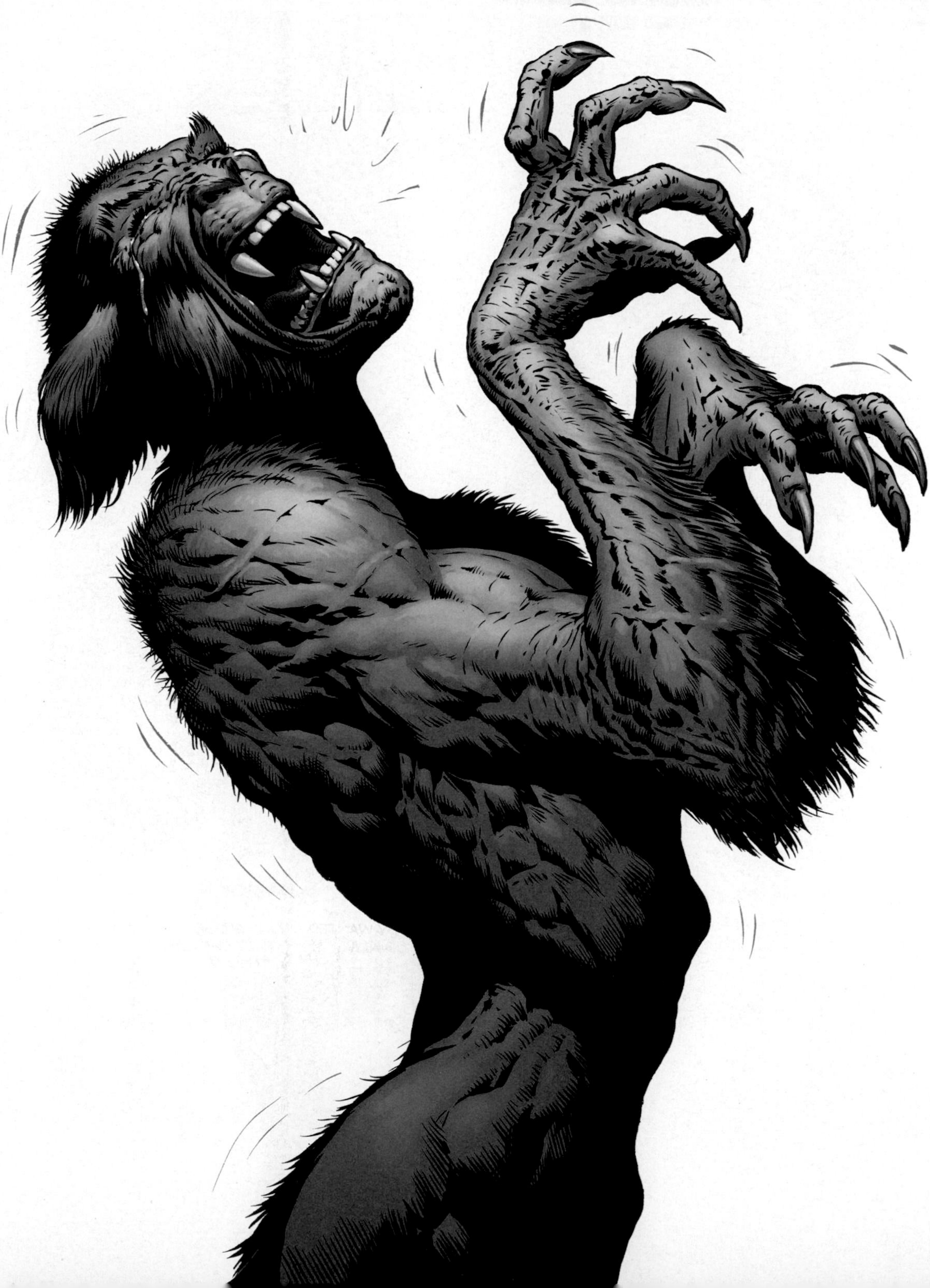

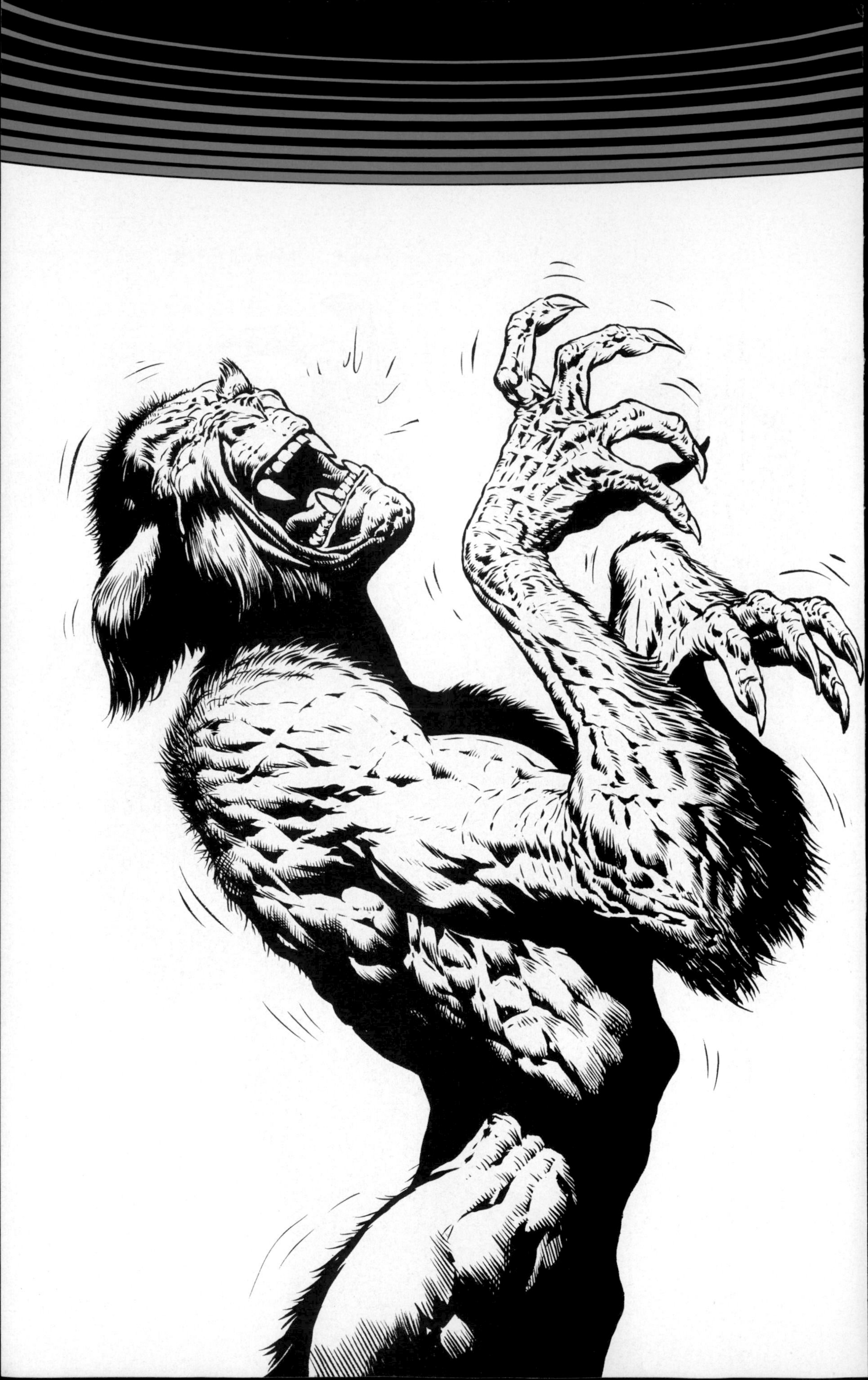

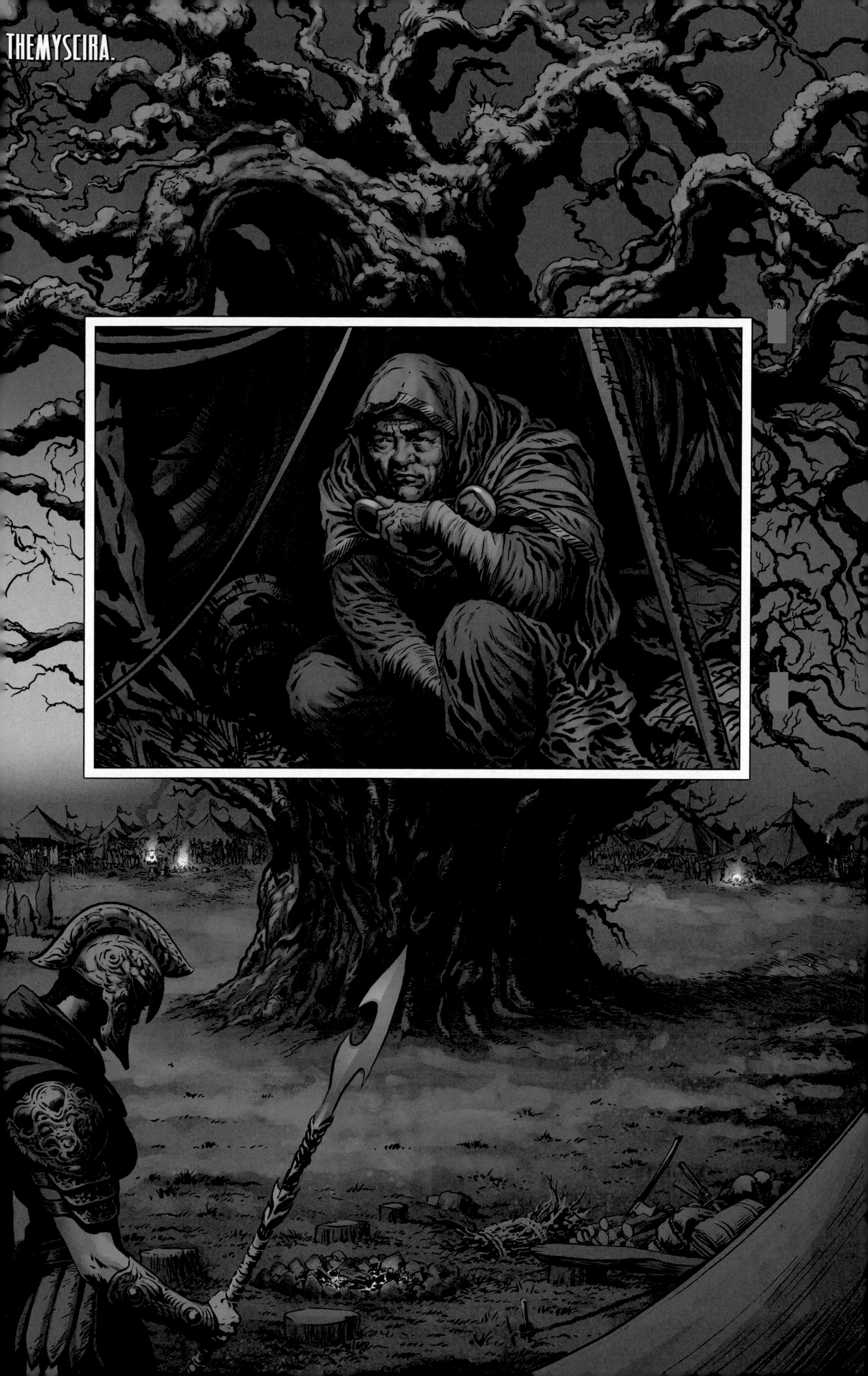
THEMYSCIRA.

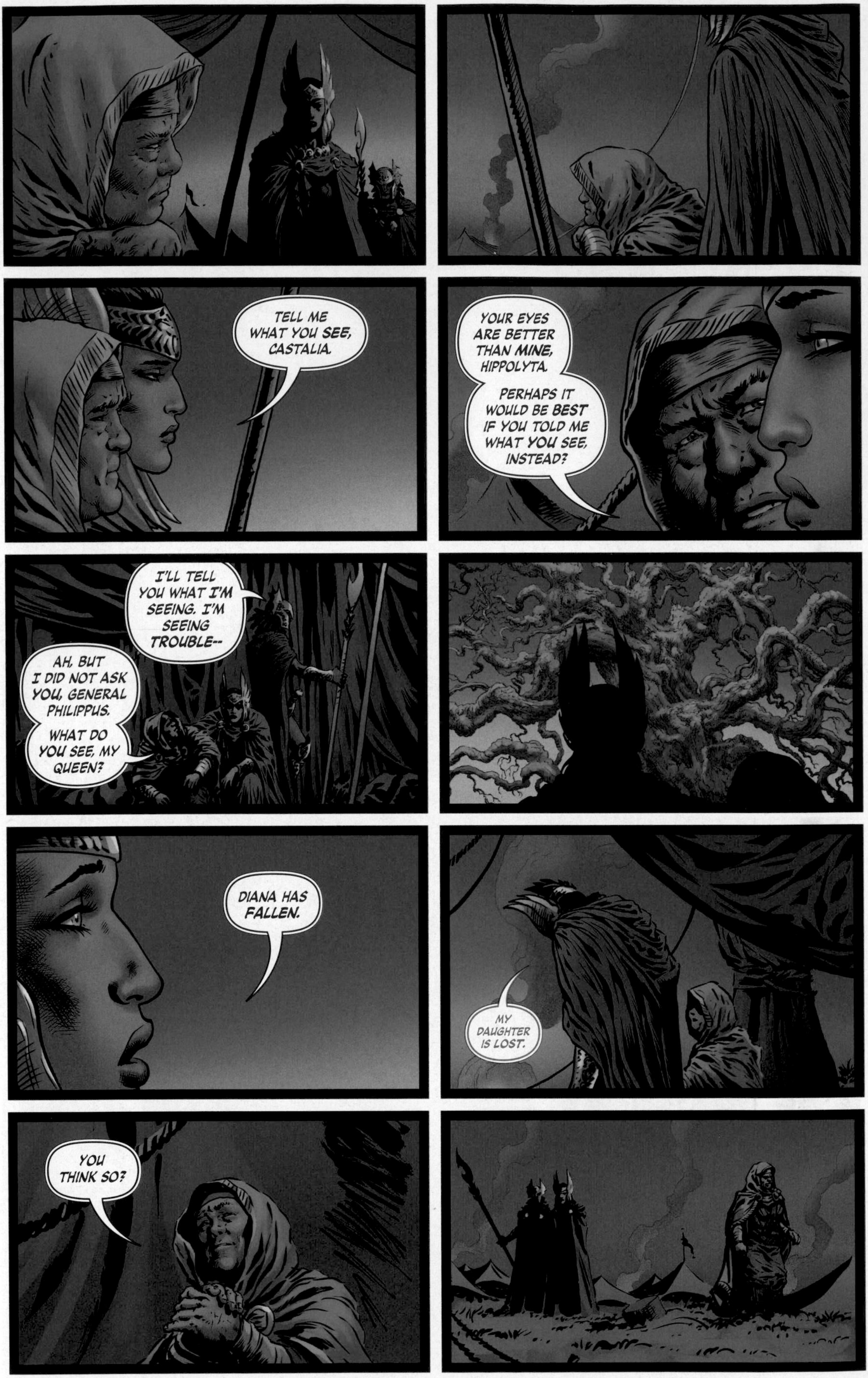
TELL ME WHAT YOU SEE, CASTALIA.
YOUR EYES ARE BETTER THAN MINE, HIPPOLYTA.
PERHAPS IT WOULD BE BEST IF YOU TOLD ME WHAT YOU SEE, INSTEAD?
I'LL TELL YOU WHAT I'M SEEING. I'M SEEING TROUBLE--
AH, BUT I DID NOT ASK YOU, GENERAL PHILIPPUS.
WHAT DO YOU SEE, MY QUEEN?
DIANA HAS FALLEN.
MY DAUGHTER IS LOST.
YOU THINK SO?

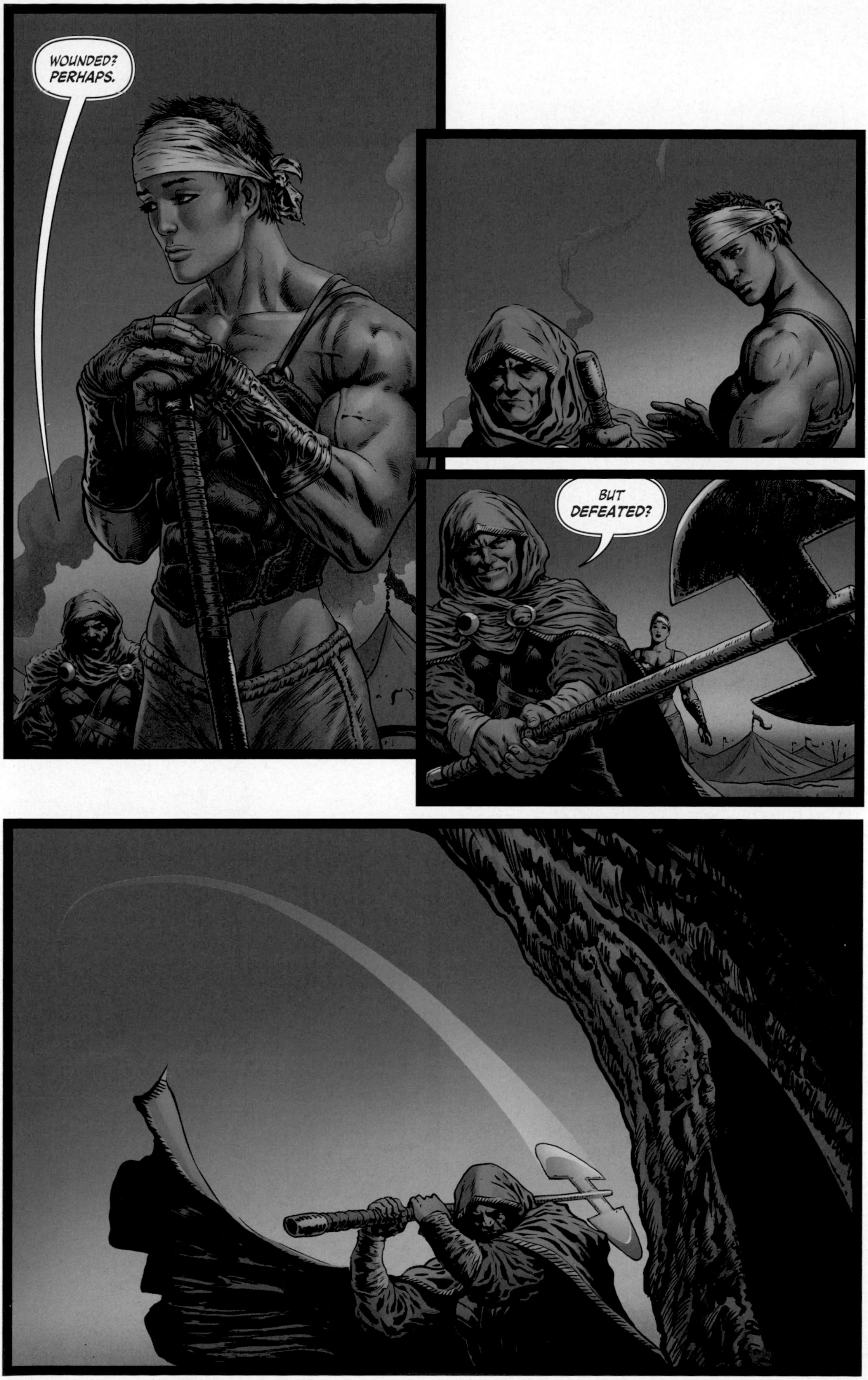
WOUNDED? PERHAPS.
BUT DEFEATED?

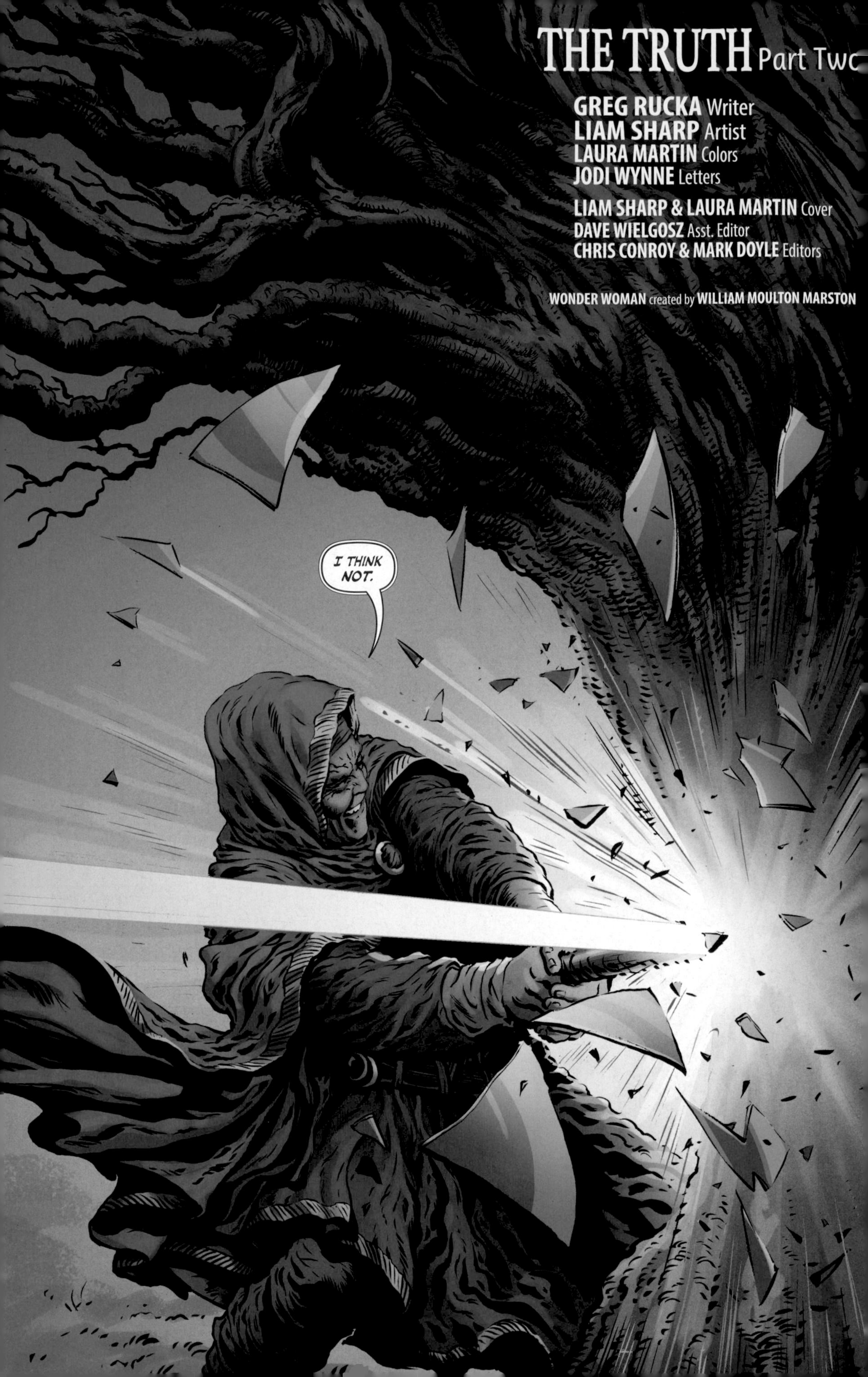
THE TRUTH Part Two
GREG RUCKA Writer
LIAM SHARP Artist
LAURA MARTIN Colors
JODI WYNNE Letters
LIAM SHARP & LAURA MARTIN Cover
DAVE WIELGOSZ Asst. Editor
CHRIS CONROY & MARK DOYLE Editors
WONDER WOMAN created by WILLIAM MOULTON MARSTON
I THINK NOT.

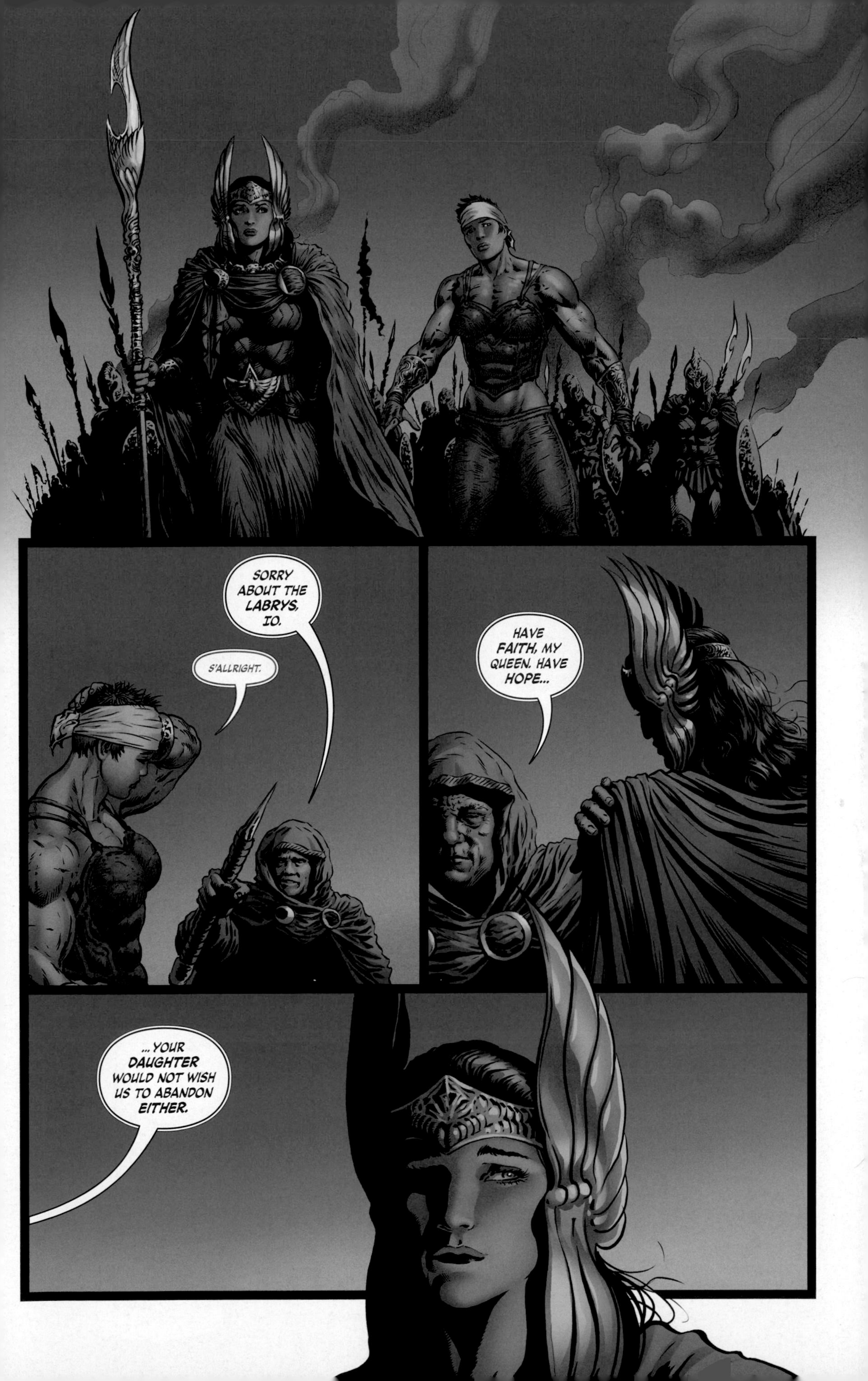
SORRY ABOUT THE LABRYS, IO.
S'ALLRIGHT.
HAVE FAITH, MY QUEEN. HAVE HOPE...
...YOUR DAUGHTER WOULD NOT WISH US TO ABANDON EITHER.

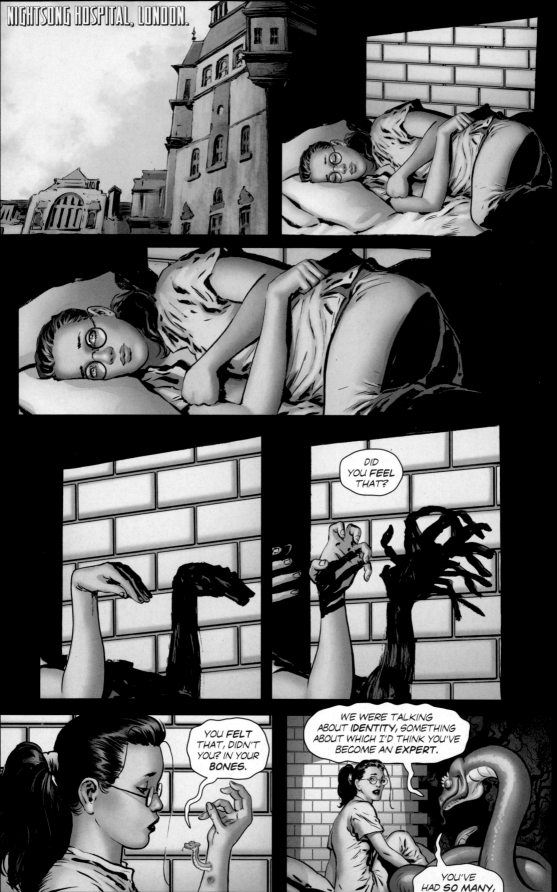

NIGHTSONG HOSPITAL, LONDON.

DID YOU FEEL THAT?

YOU FELT THAT, DIDN'T YOU? IN YOUR BONES.

WE WERE TALKING ABOUT IDENTITY, SOMETHING ABOUT WHICH I'D THINK YOU'VE BECOME AN EXPERT.

YOU'VE HAD SO MANY,

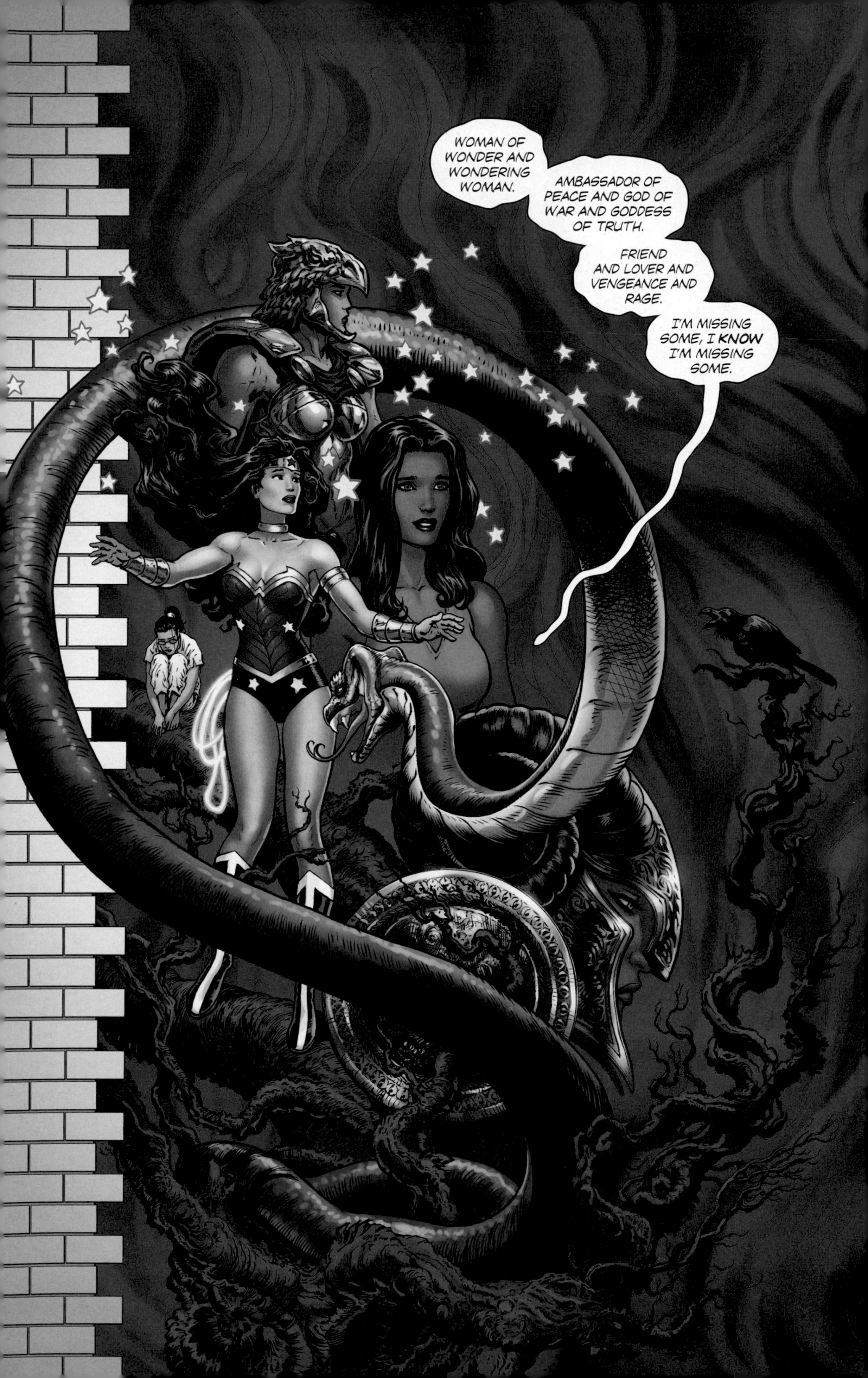
WOMAN OF WONDER AND WONDERING WOMAN.
AMBASSADOR OF PEACE AND GOD OF WAR AND GODDESS OF TRUTH.
FRIEND AND LOVER AND VENGEANCE AND RAGE.
I'M MISSING SOME, I **KNOW** I'M MISSING SOME.

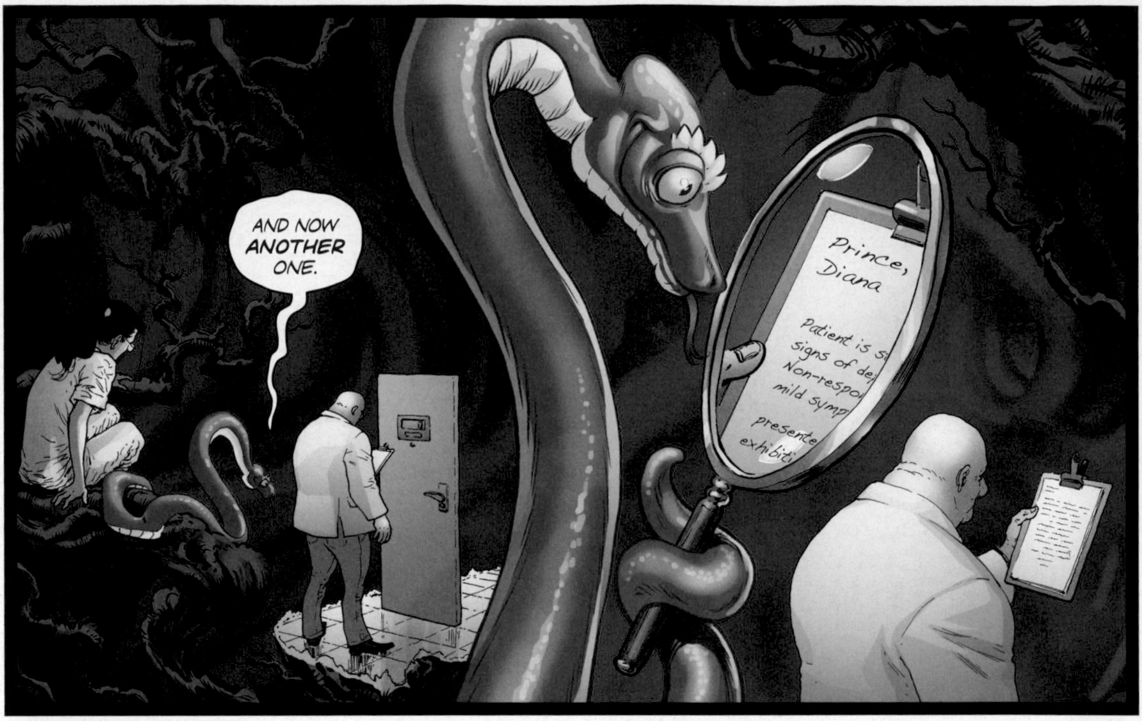
AND NOW ANOTHER ONE.
Prince, Diana

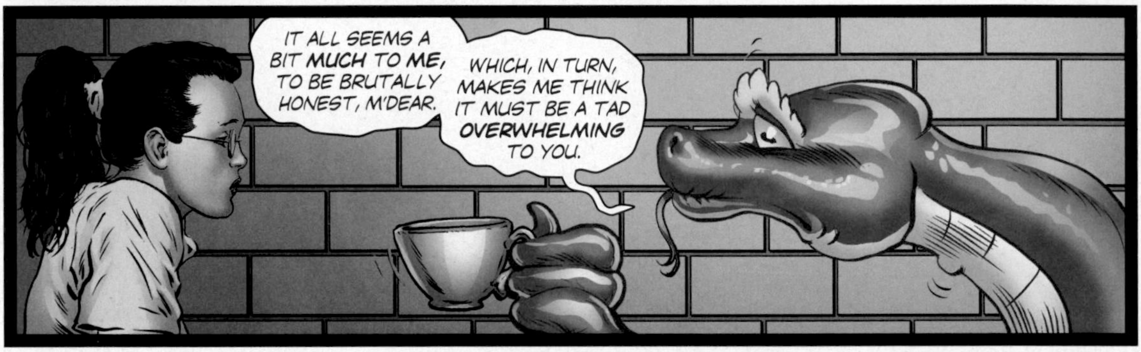
IT ALL SEEMS A BIT MUCH TO ME, TO BE BRUTALLY HONEST, M'DEAR.
WHICH, IN TURN, MAKES ME THINK IT MUST BE A TAD OVERWHELMING TO YOU.

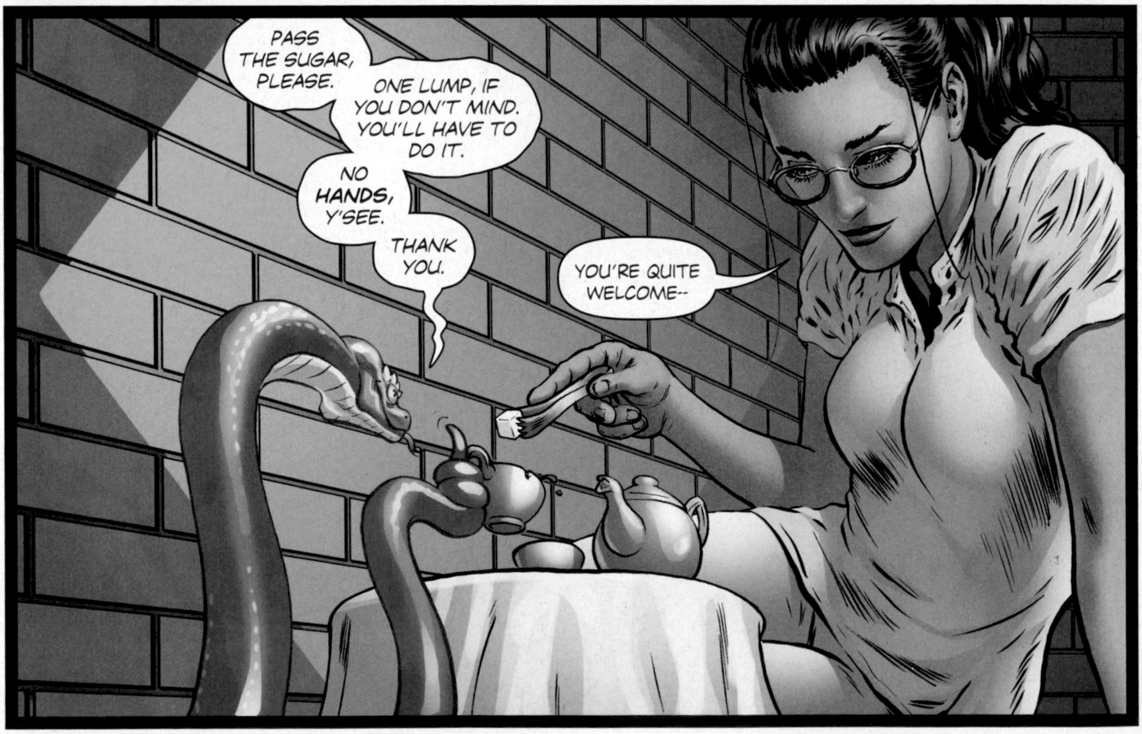
PASS THE SUGAR, PLEASE.
ONE LUMP, IF YOU DON'T MIND. YOU'LL HAVE TO DO IT.
NO HANDS, Y'SEE.
THANK YOU.
YOU'RE QUITE WELCOME--

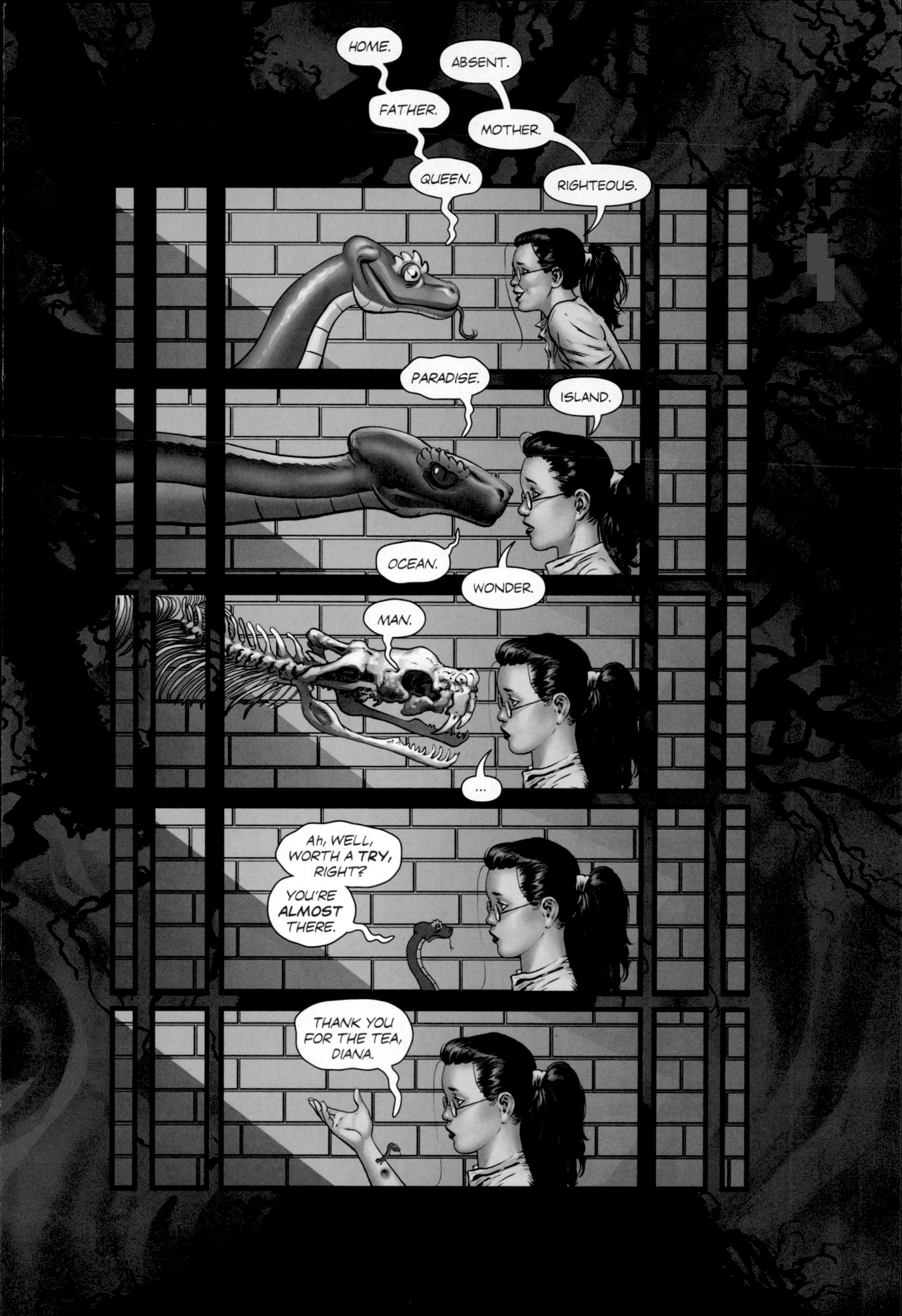

HOME.
FATHER.
QUEEN.
ABSENT.
MOTHER.
RIGHTEOUS.
PARADISE.
ISLAND.
OCEAN.
WONDER.
MAN.
...
Ah, WELL, WORTH A TRY, RIGHT?
YOU'RE ALMOST THERE.
THANK YOU FOR THE TEA, DIANA.

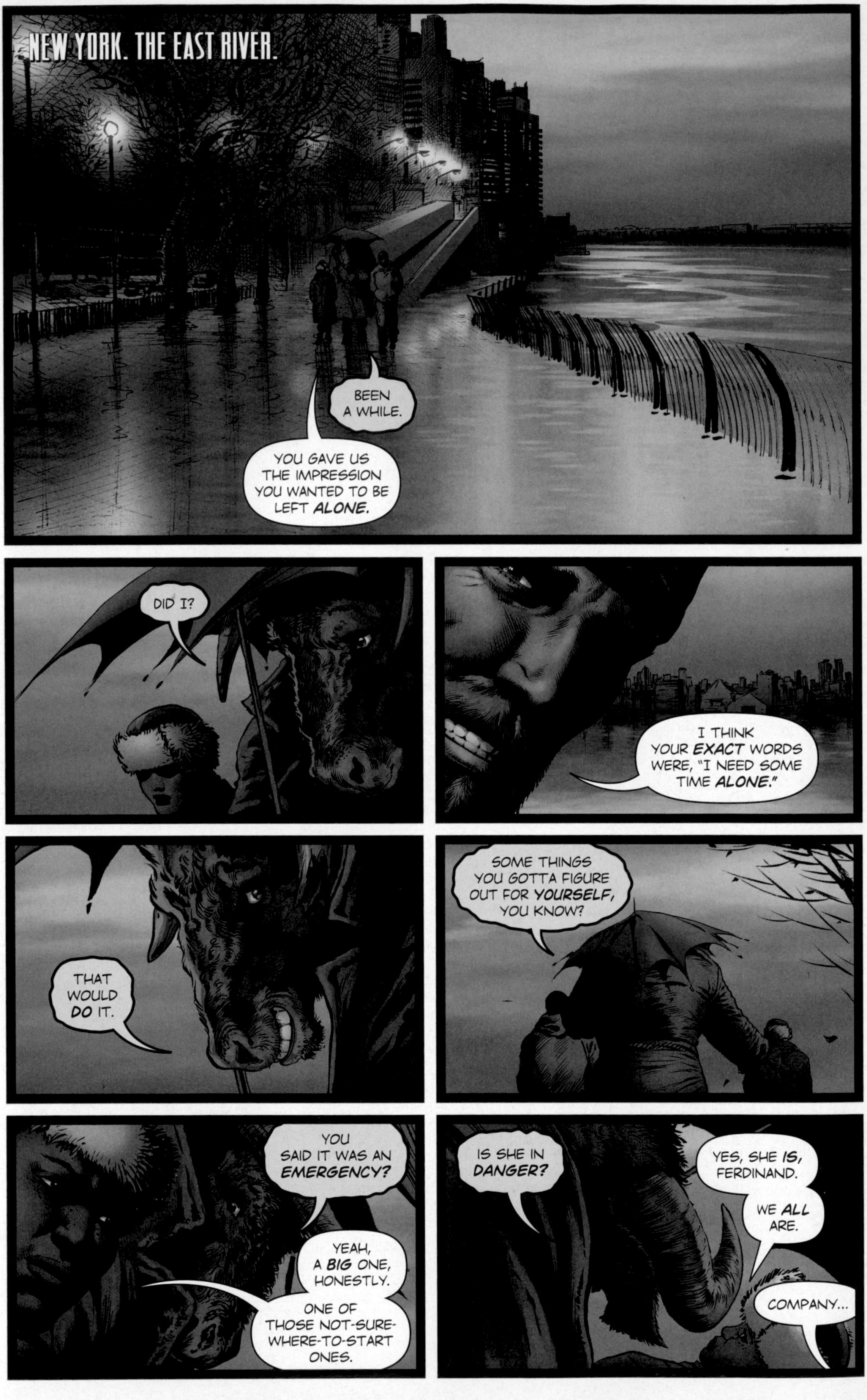
NEW YORK. THE EAST RIVER.
BEEN A WHILE.
YOU GAVE US THE IMPRESSION YOU WANTED TO BE LEFT ALONE.
DID I?
I THINK YOUR EXACT WORDS WERE, "I NEED SOME TIME ALONE."
THAT WOULD DO IT.
SOME THINGS YOU GOTTA FIGURE OUT FOR YOURSELF, YOU KNOW?
YOU SAID IT WAS AN EMERGENCY?
YEAH, A BIG ONE, HONESTLY.
ONE OF THOSE NOT-SURE-WHERE-TO-START ONES.
IS SHE IN DANGER?
YES, SHE IS, FERDINAND.
WE ALL ARE.
COMPANY...

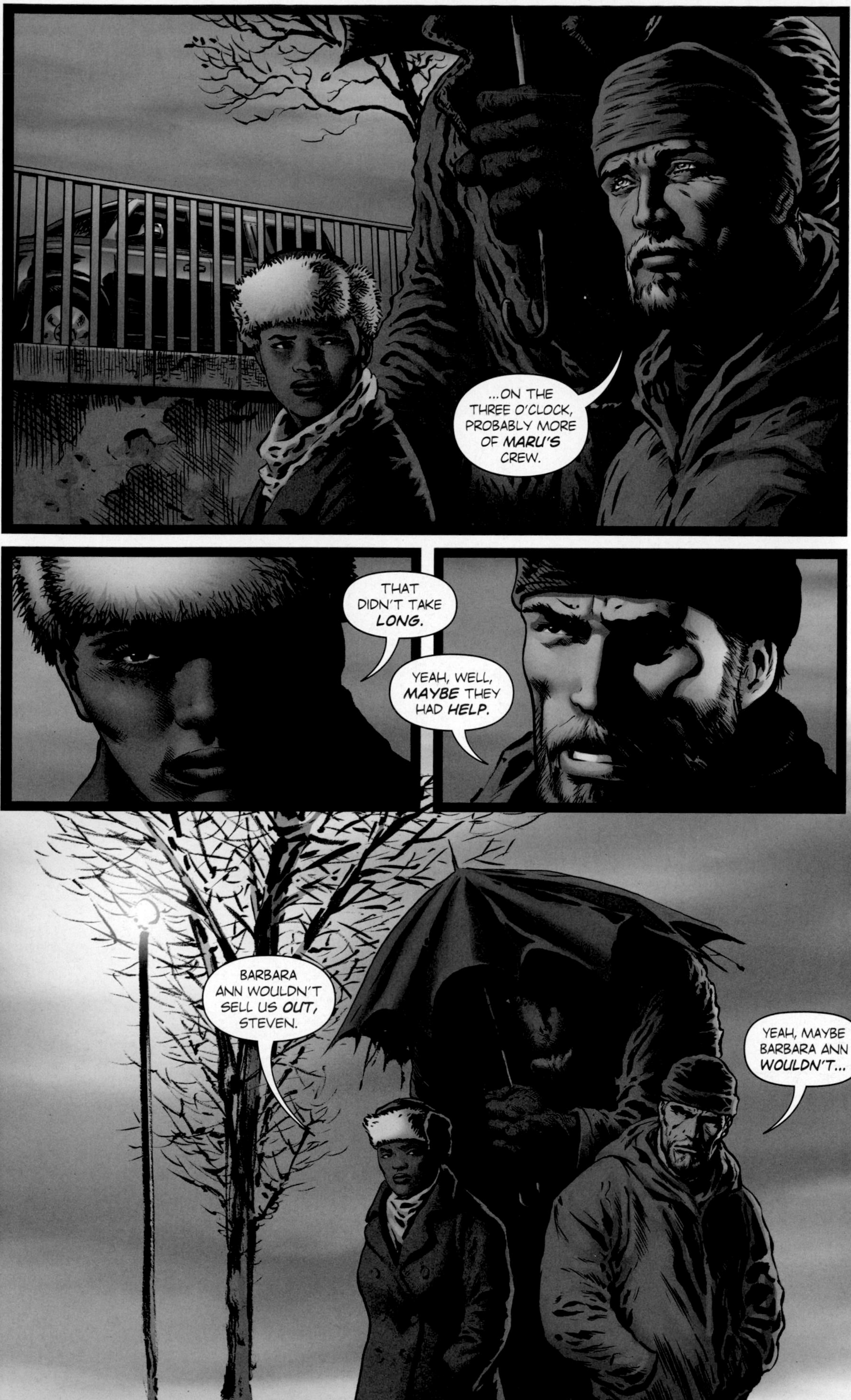
...ON THE THREE O'CLOCK, PROBABLY MORE OF MARU'S CREW.
THAT DIDN'T TAKE LONG.
YEAH, WELL, MAYBE THEY HAD HELP.
BARBARA ANN WOULDN'T SELL US OUT, STEVEN.
YEAH, MAYBE BARBARA ANN WOULDN'T...

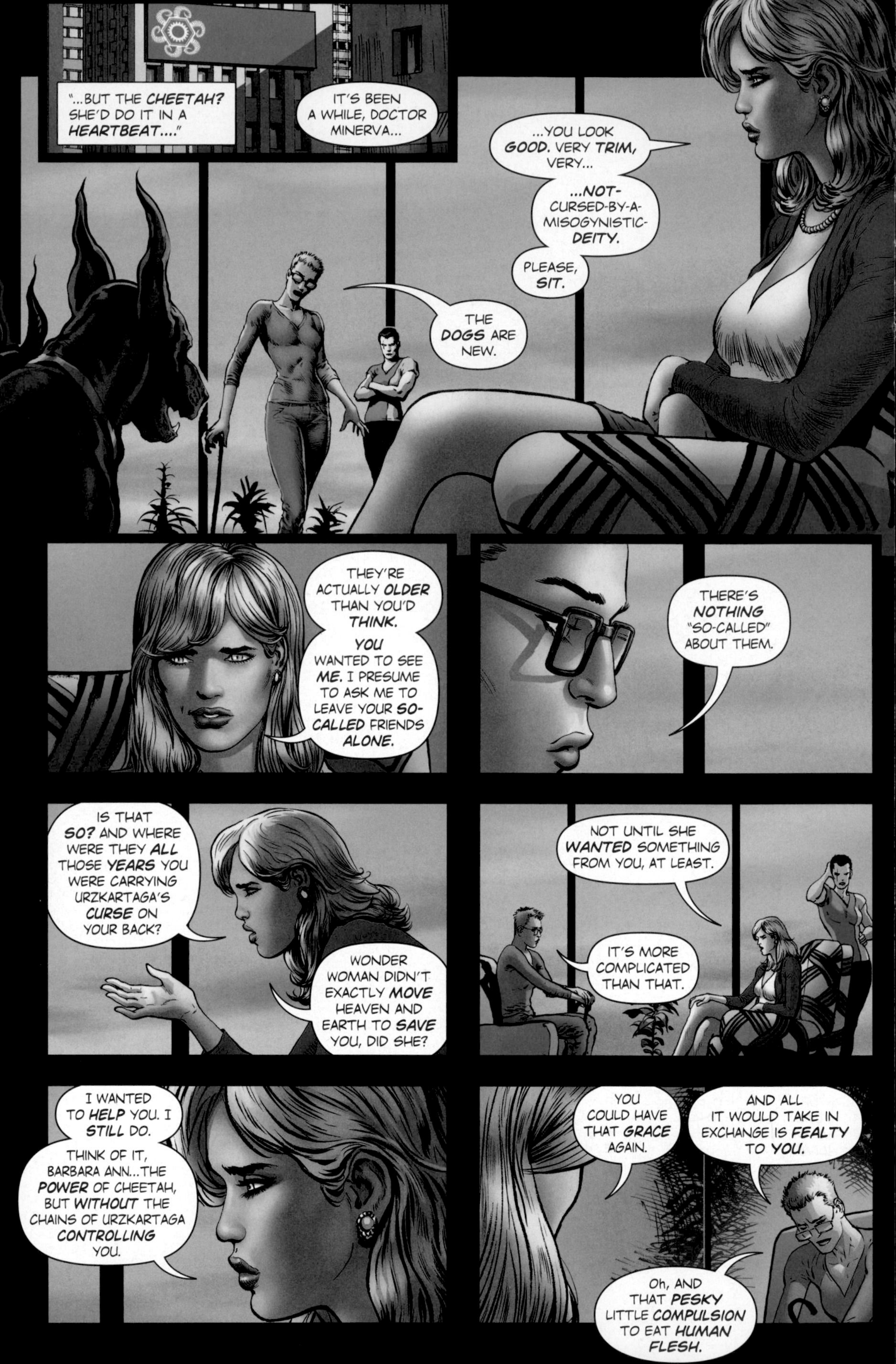

"...BUT THE CHEETAH? SHE'D DO IT IN A HEARTBEAT...."
IT'S BEEN A WHILE, DOCTOR MINERVA...
...YOU LOOK GOOD. VERY TRIM, VERY...
...NOT-CURSED-BY-A-MISOGYNISTIC-DEITY.
PLEASE, SIT.
THE DOGS ARE NEW.
THEY'RE ACTUALLY OLDER THAN YOU'D THINK.
YOU WANTED TO SEE ME. I PRESUME TO ASK ME TO LEAVE YOUR SO-CALLED FRIENDS ALONE.
THERE'S NOTHING "SO-CALLED" ABOUT THEM.
IS THAT SO? AND WHERE WERE THEY ALL THOSE YEARS YOU WERE CARRYING URZKARTAGA'S CURSE ON YOUR BACK?
WONDER WOMAN DIDN'T EXACTLY MOVE HEAVEN AND EARTH TO SAVE YOU, DID SHE?
NOT UNTIL SHE WANTED SOMETHING FROM YOU, AT LEAST.
IT'S MORE COMPLICATED THAN THAT.
I WANTED TO HELP YOU. I STILL DO.
THINK OF IT, BARBARA ANN...THE POWER OF CHEETAH, BUT WITHOUT THE CHAINS OF URZKARTAGA CONTROLLING YOU.
YOU COULD HAVE THAT GRACE AGAIN.
AND ALL IT WOULD TAKE IN EXCHANGE IS FEALTY TO YOU.
Oh, AND THAT PESKY LITTLE COMPULSION TO EAT HUMAN FLESH.

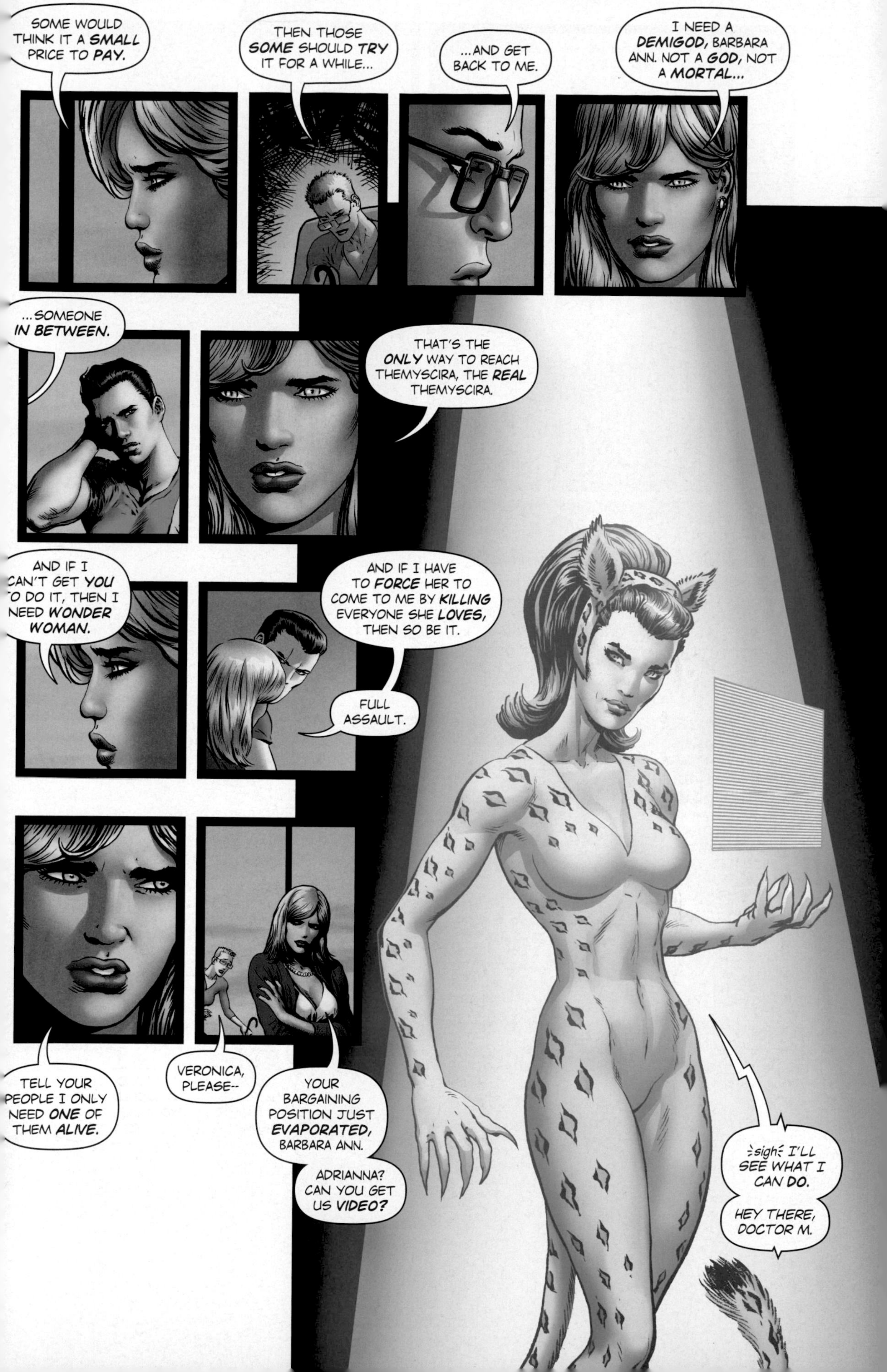
SOME WOULD THINK IT A SMALL PRICE TO PAY.
THEN THOSE SOME SHOULD TRY IT FOR A WHILE...
...AND GET BACK TO ME.
I NEED A DEMIGOD, BARBARA ANN. NOT A GOD, NOT A MORTAL...
...SOMEONE IN BETWEEN.
THAT'S THE ONLY WAY TO REACH THEMYSCIRA, THE REAL THEMYSCIRA.
AND IF I CAN'T GET YOU TO DO IT, THEN I NEED WONDER WOMAN.
AND IF I HAVE TO FORCE HER TO COME TO ME BY KILLING EVERYONE SHE LOVES, THEN SO BE IT.
FULL ASSAULT.
TELL YOUR PEOPLE I ONLY NEED ONE OF THEM ALIVE.
VERONICA, PLEASE--
YOUR BARGAINING POSITION JUST EVAPORATED, BARBARA ANN.
ADRIANNA? CAN YOU GET US VIDEO?
sigh I'LL SEE WHAT I CAN DO.
HEY THERE, DOCTOR M.

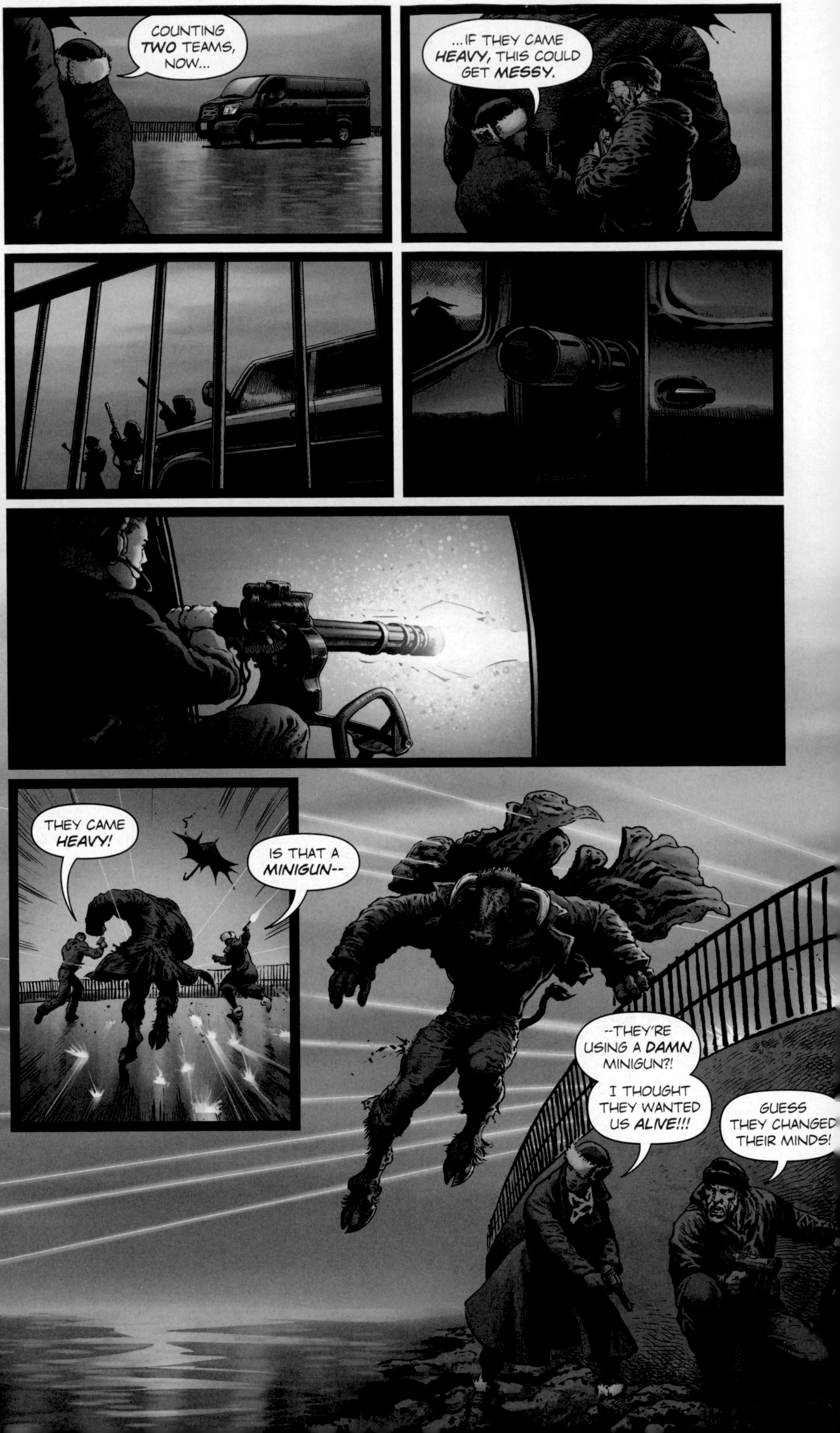
COUNTING TWO TEAMS, NOW...
...IF THEY CAME HEAVY, THIS COULD GET MESSY.
THEY CAME HEAVY!
IS THAT A MINIGUN--
--THEY'RE USING A DAMN MINIGUN?!
I THOUGHT THEY WANTED US ALIVE!!!
GUESS THEY CHANGED THEIR MINDS!

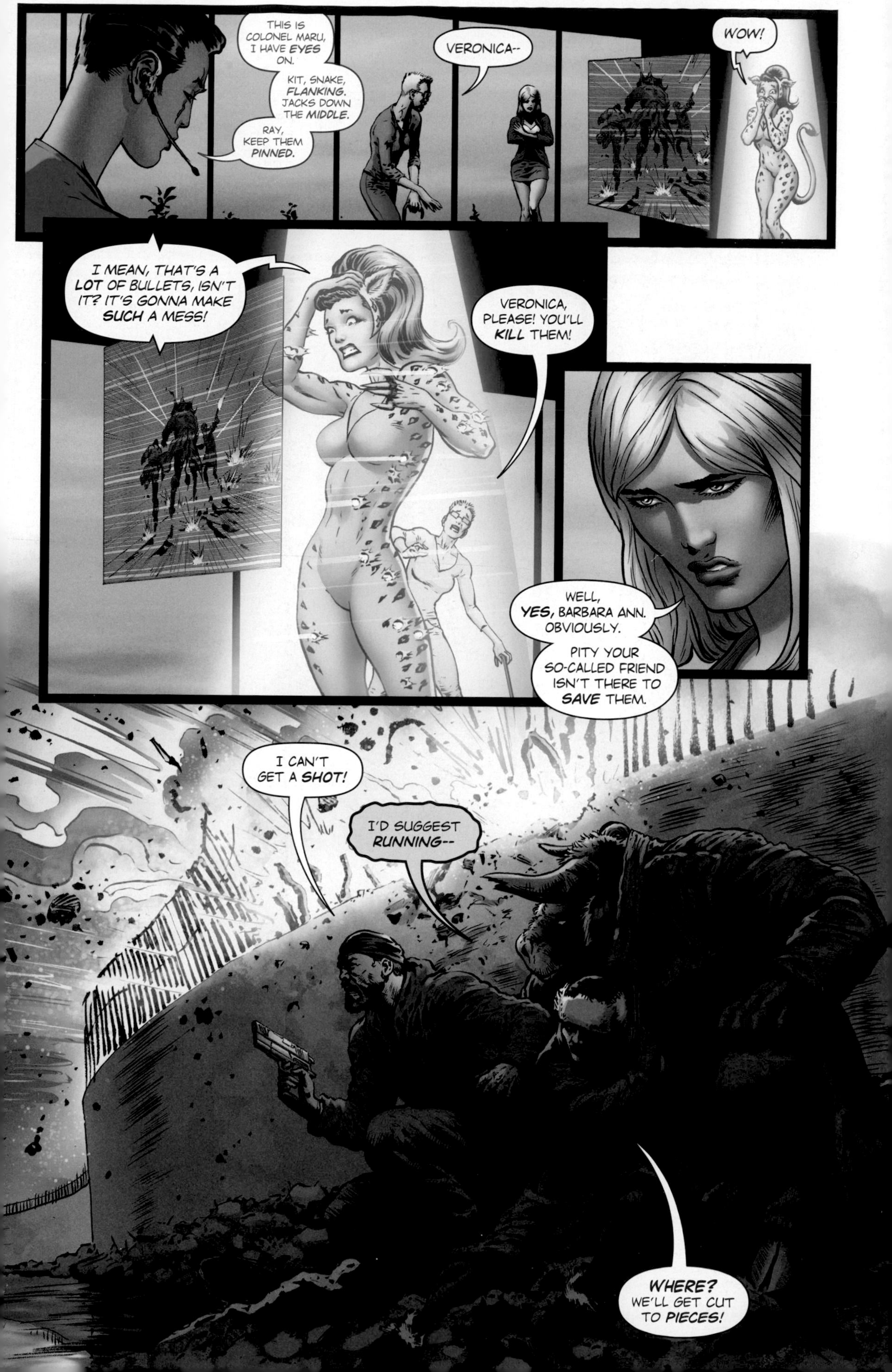
THIS IS COLONEL MARU, I HAVE EYES ON.
KIT, SNAKE, FLANKING. JACKS DOWN THE MIDDLE.
RAY, KEEP THEM PINNED.
VERONICA--
WOW!
I MEAN, THAT'S A LOT OF BULLETS, ISN'T IT? IT'S GONNA MAKE SUCH A MESS!
VERONICA, PLEASE! YOU'LL KILL THEM!
WELL, YES, BARBARA ANN. OBVIOUSLY.
PITY YOUR SO-CALLED FRIEND ISN'T THERE TO SAVE THEM.
I CAN'T GET A SHOT!
I'D SUGGEST RUNNING--
WHERE? WE'LL GET CUT TO PIECES!

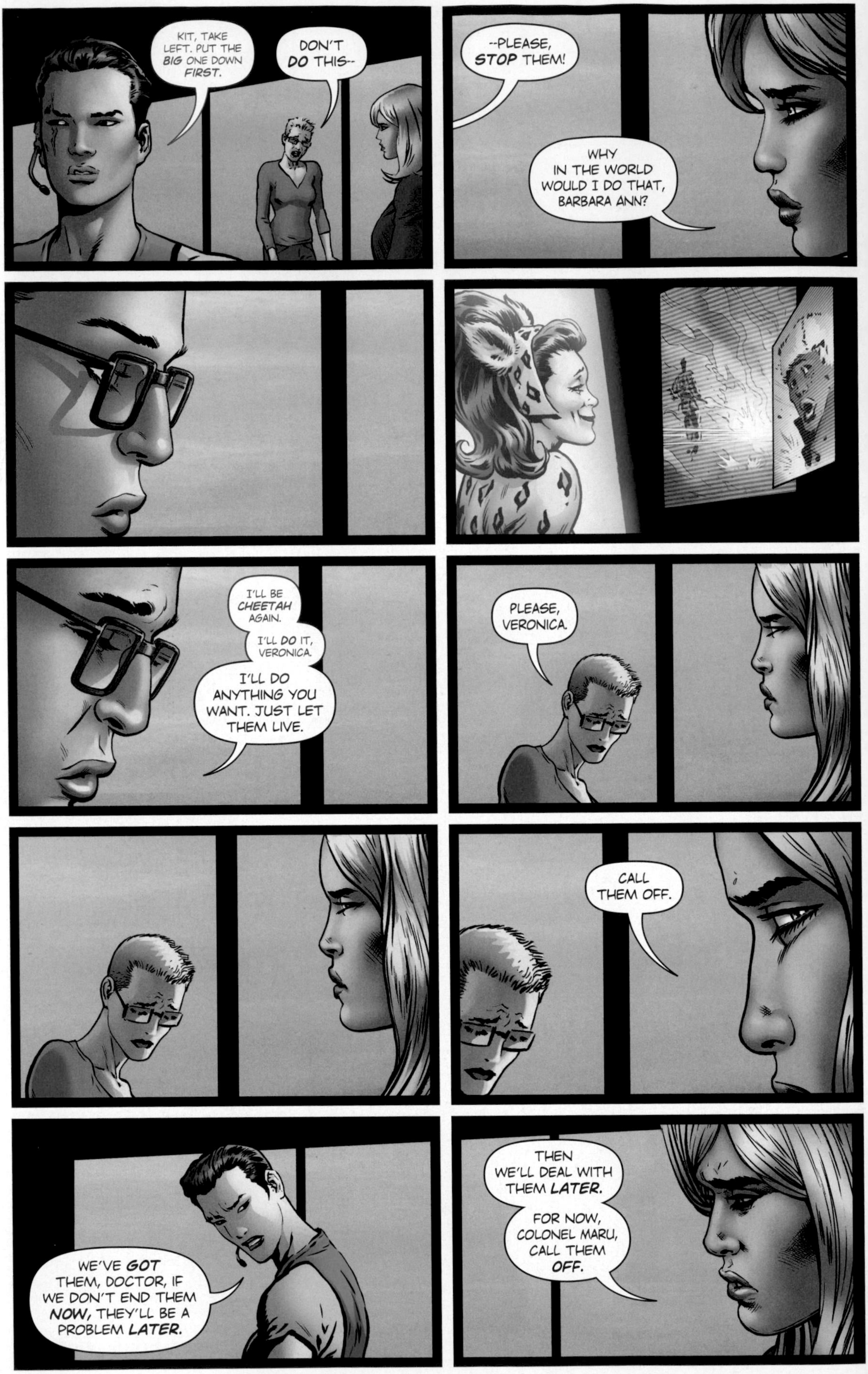
KIT, TAKE LEFT. PUT THE BIG ONE DOWN FIRST.
DON'T DO THIS--
--PLEASE, STOP THEM!
WHY IN THE WORLD WOULD I DO THAT, BARBARA ANN?
I'LL BE CHEETAH AGAIN.
I'LL DO IT, VERONICA.
I'LL DO ANYTHING YOU WANT. JUST LET THEM LIVE.
PLEASE, VERONICA.
CALL THEM OFF.
WE'VE GOT THEM, DOCTOR, IF WE DON'T END THEM NOW, THEY'LL BE A PROBLEM LATER.
THEN WE'LL DEAL WITH THEM LATER.
FOR NOW, COLONEL MARU, CALL THEM OFF.

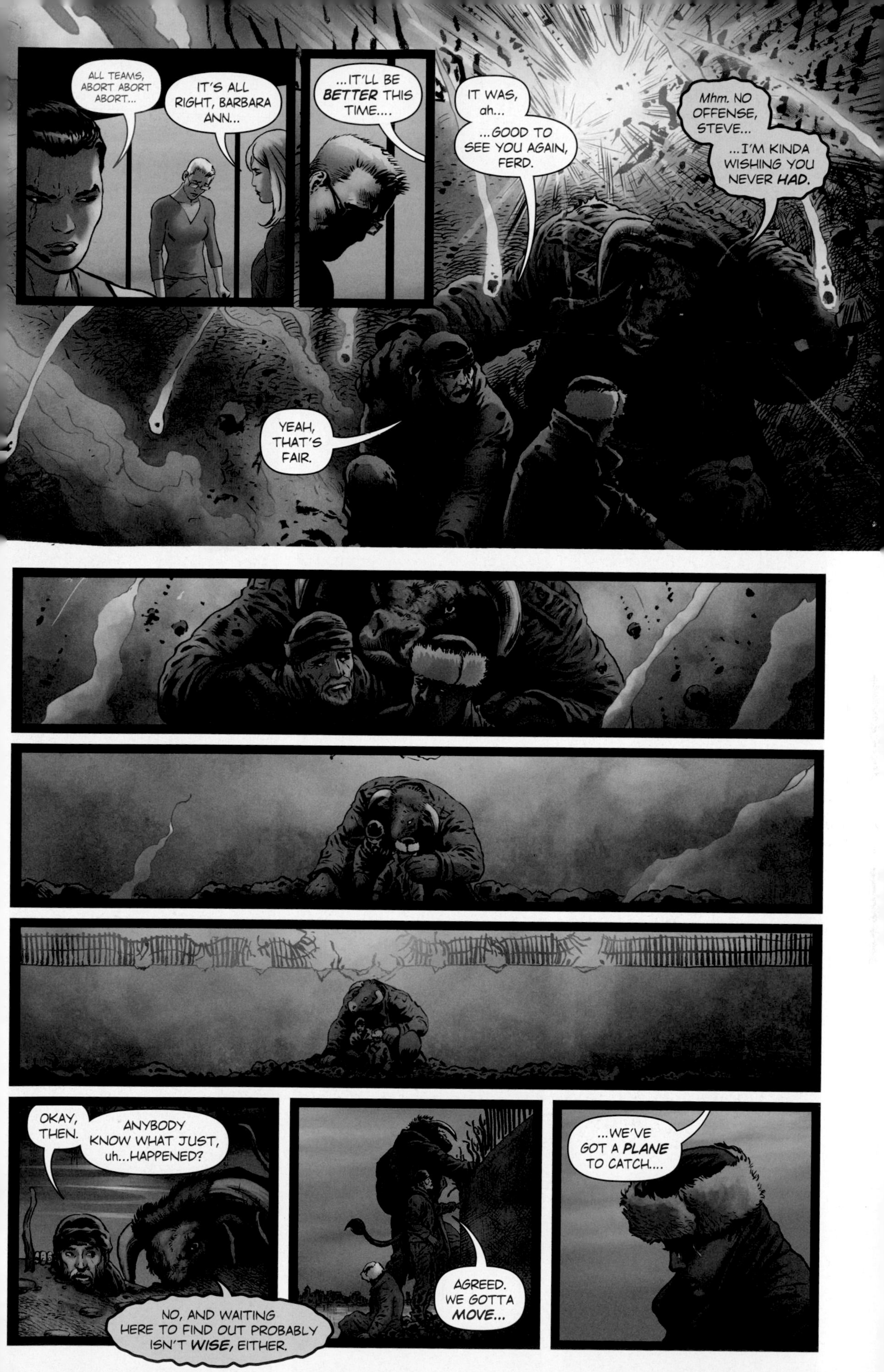
ALL TEAMS, ABORT ABORT ABORT...
IT'S ALL RIGHT, BARBARA ANN...
...IT'LL BE BETTER THIS TIME....
IT WAS, ah...
...GOOD TO SEE YOU AGAIN, FERD.
Mhm. NO OFFENSE, STEVE...
...I'M KINDA WISHING YOU NEVER HAD.
YEAH, THAT'S FAIR.
OKAY, THEN.
ANYBODY KNOW WHAT JUST, uh...HAPPENED?
NO, AND WAITING HERE TO FIND OUT PROBABLY ISN'T WISE, EITHER.
AGREED. WE GOTTA MOVE...
...WE'VE GOT A PLANE TO CATCH...

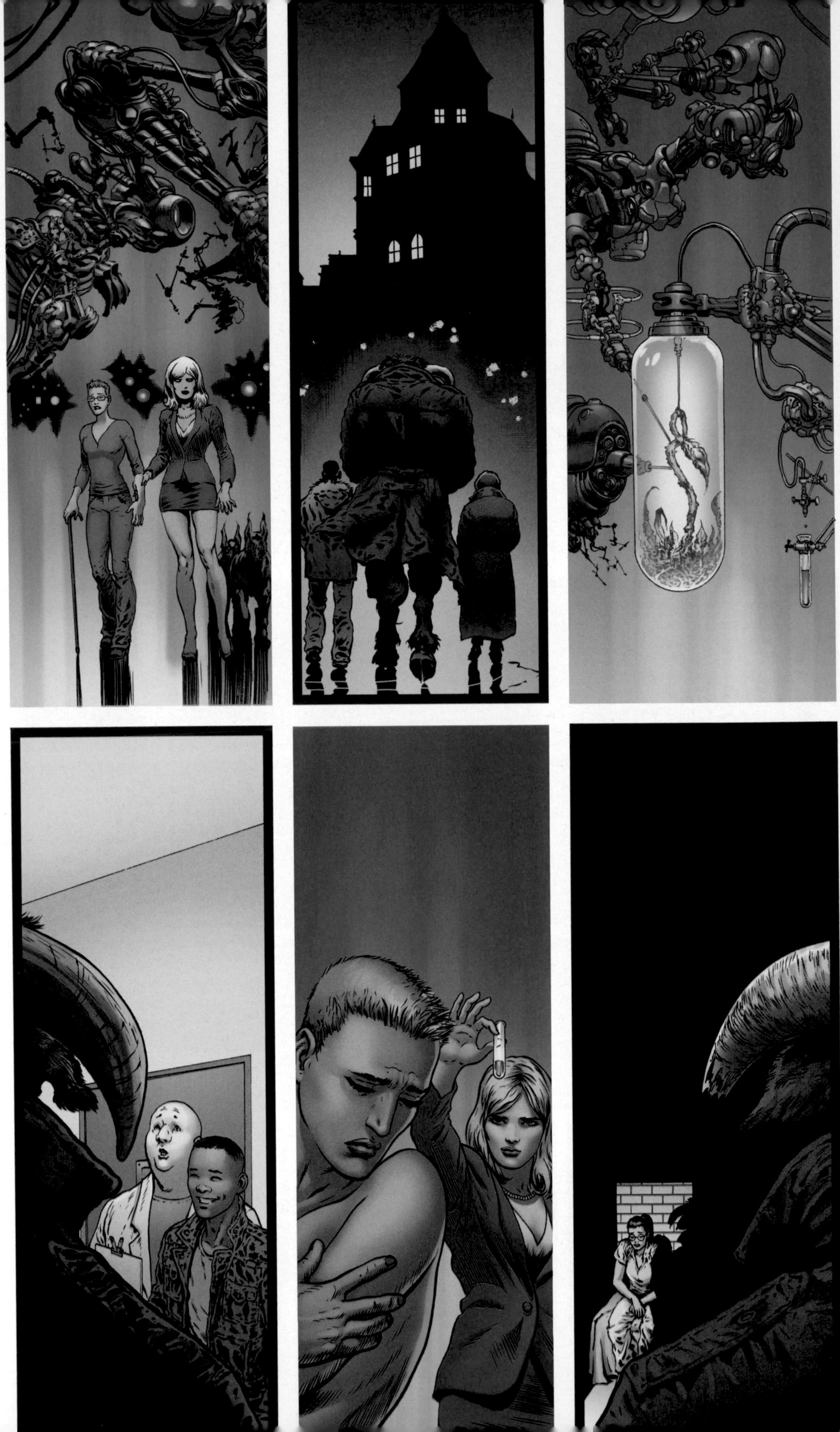

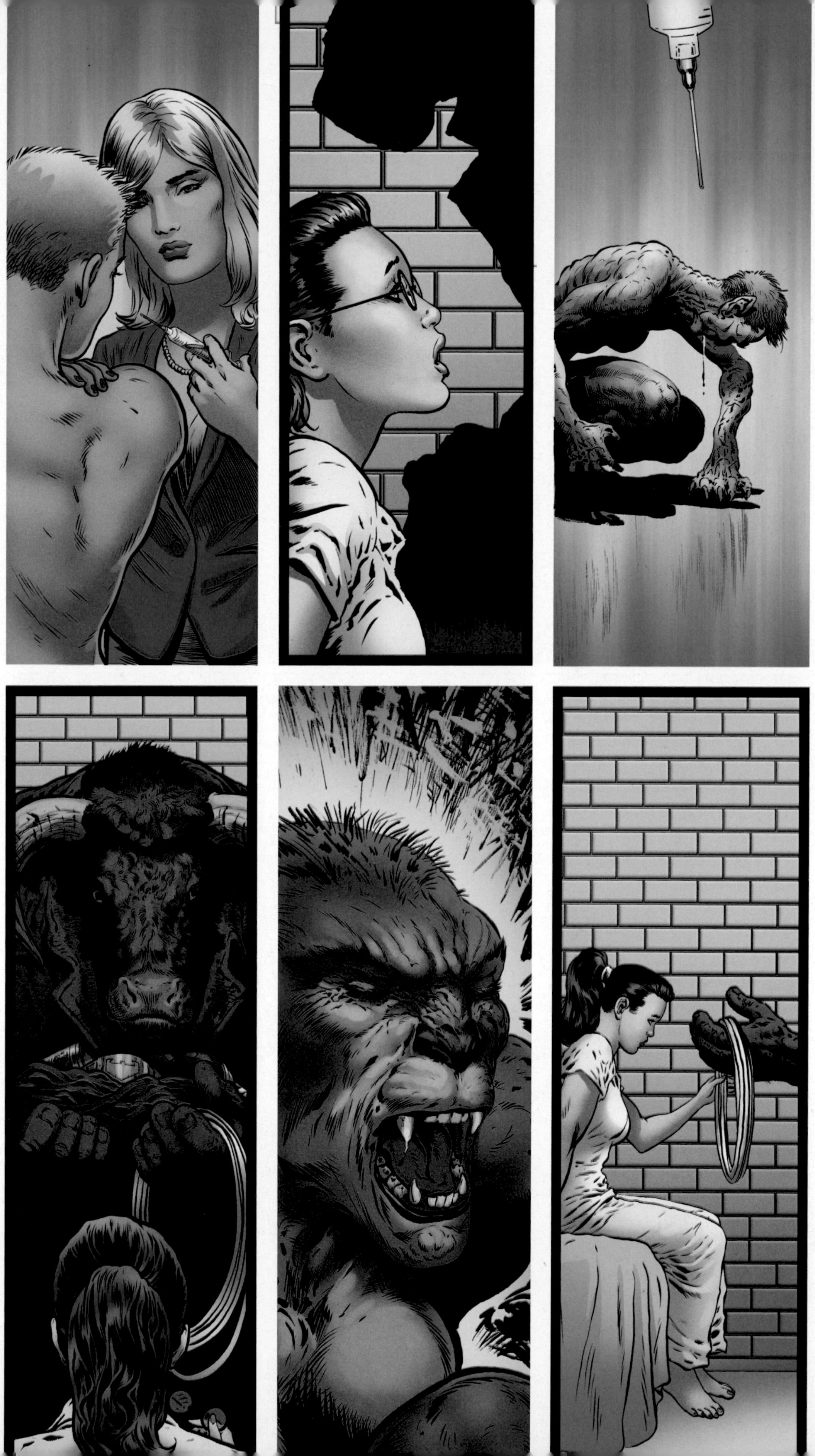

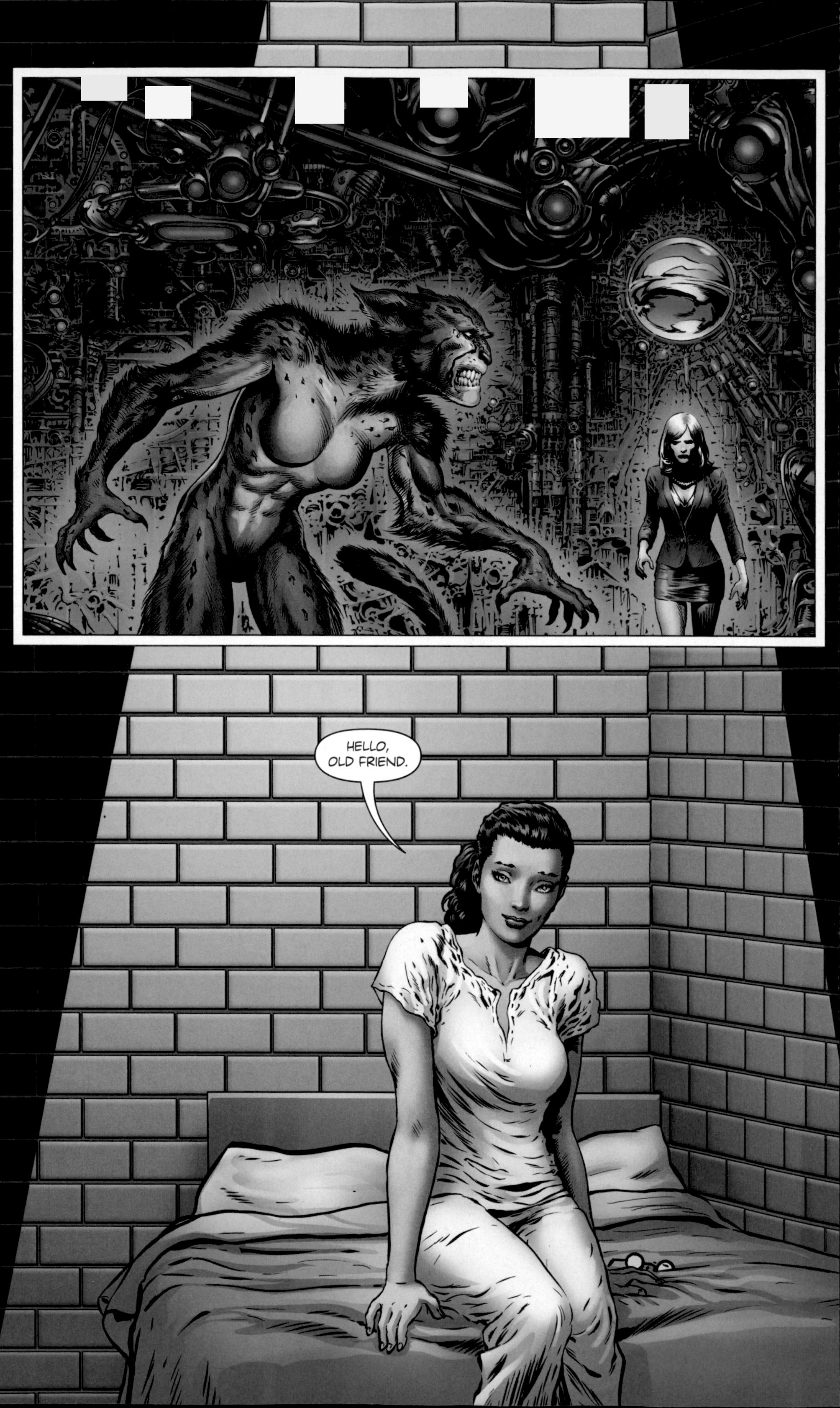
HELLO, OLD FRIEND.

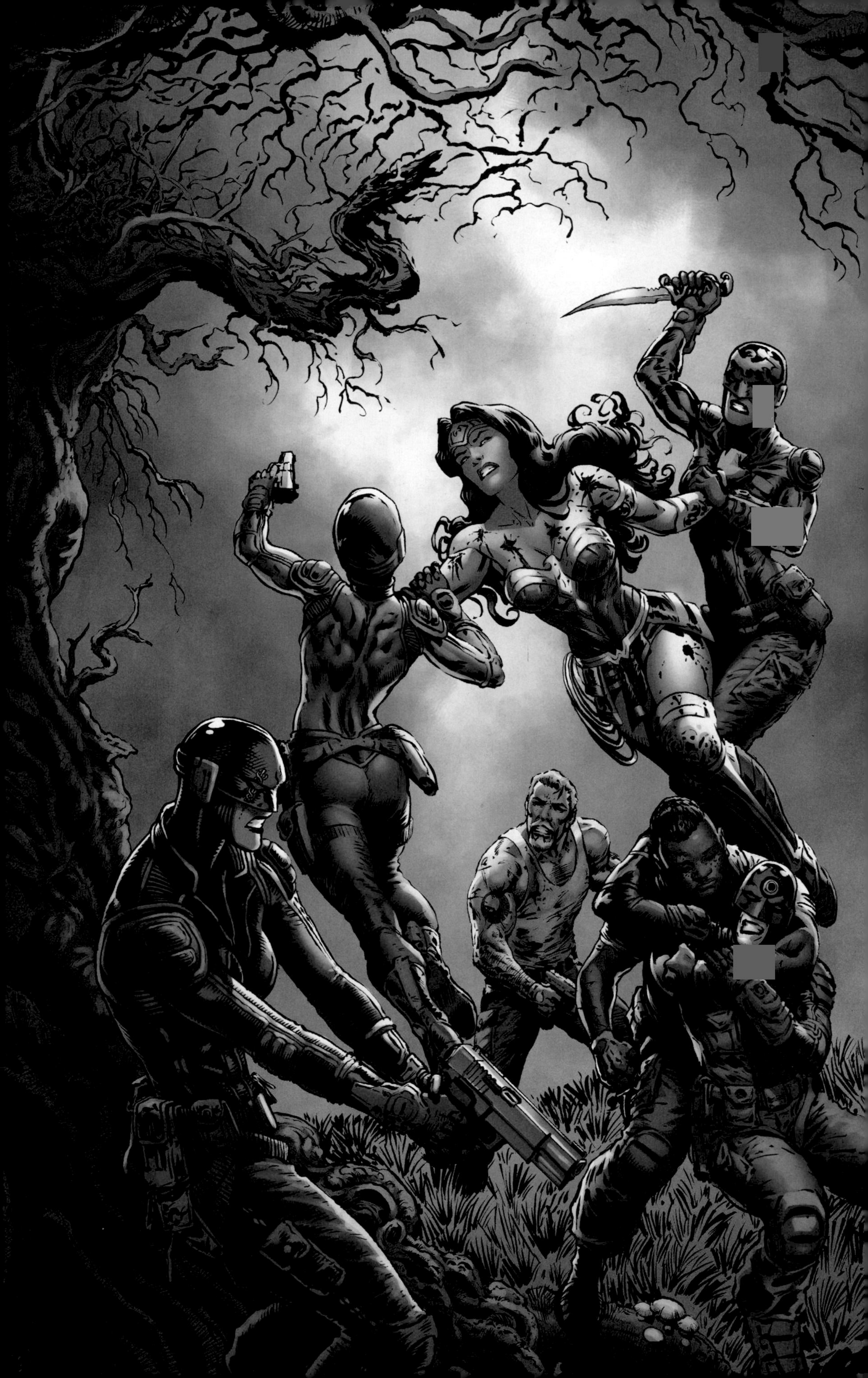

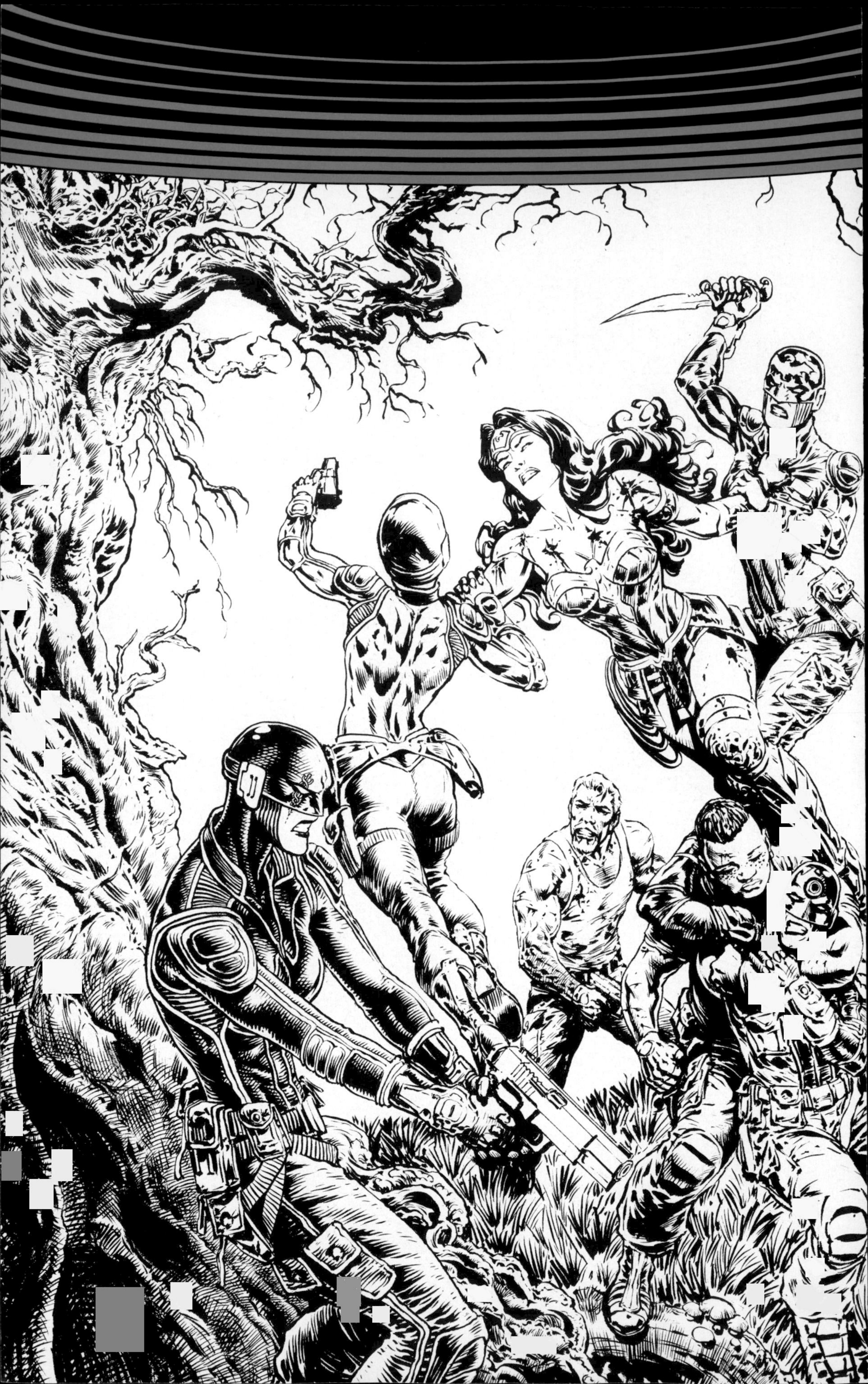

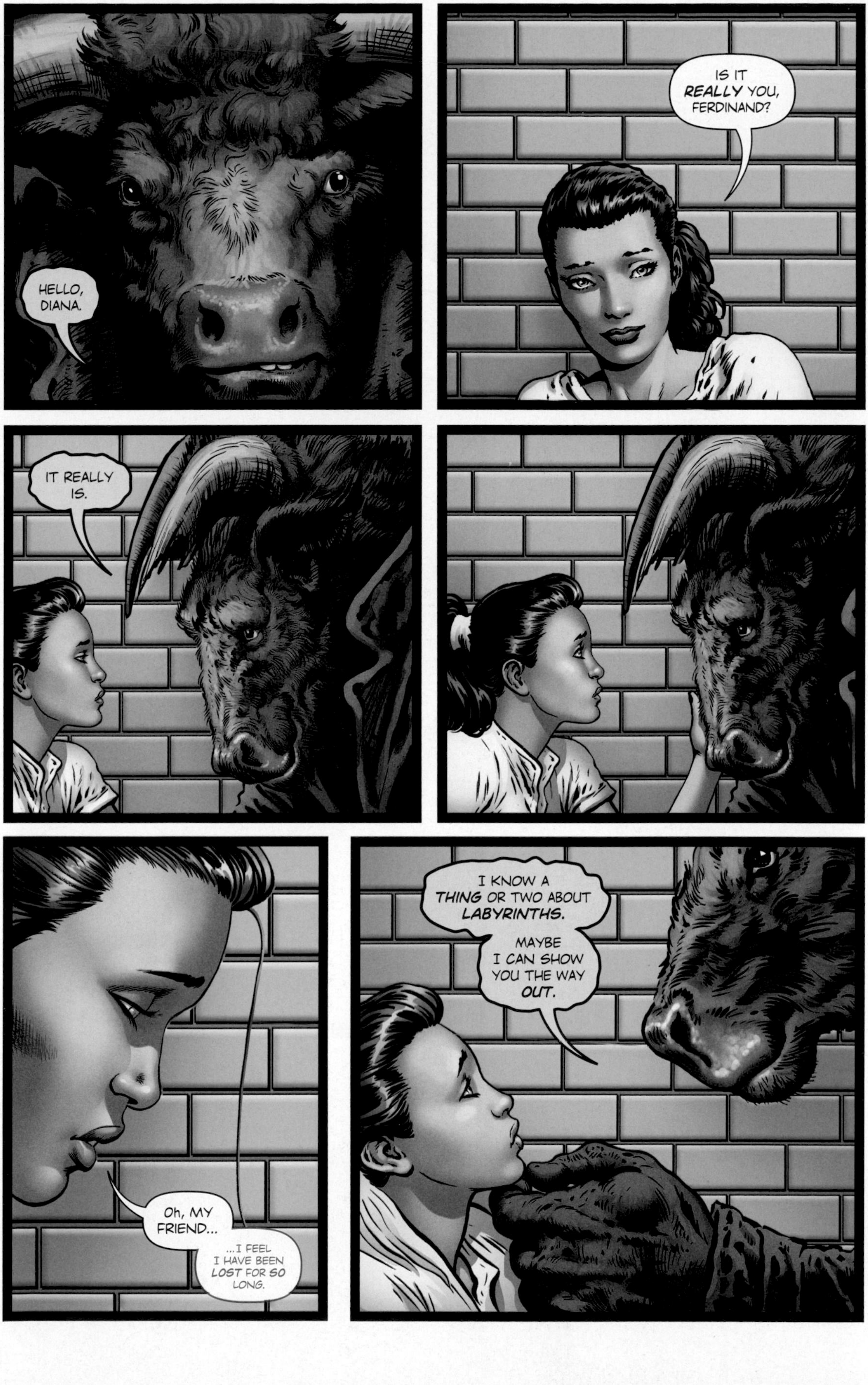
HELLO, DIANA.
IS IT REALLY YOU, FERDINAND?
IT REALLY IS.
Oh, MY FRIEND...
...I FEEL I HAVE BEEN LOST FOR SO LONG.
I KNOW A THING OR TWO ABOUT LABYRINTHS.
MAYBE I CAN SHOW YOU THE WAY OUT.

THE TRUTH Part Three

GREG RUCKA Writer
LIAM SHARP Artist
LAURA MARTIN Colors
JODI WYNNE Letters

LIAM SHARP & LAURA MARTIN Cover

DAVE WIELGOSZ Asst. Editor
CHRIS CONROY & MARK DOYLE Editors

WONDER WOMAN created by **WILLIAM MOULTON MARSTON**

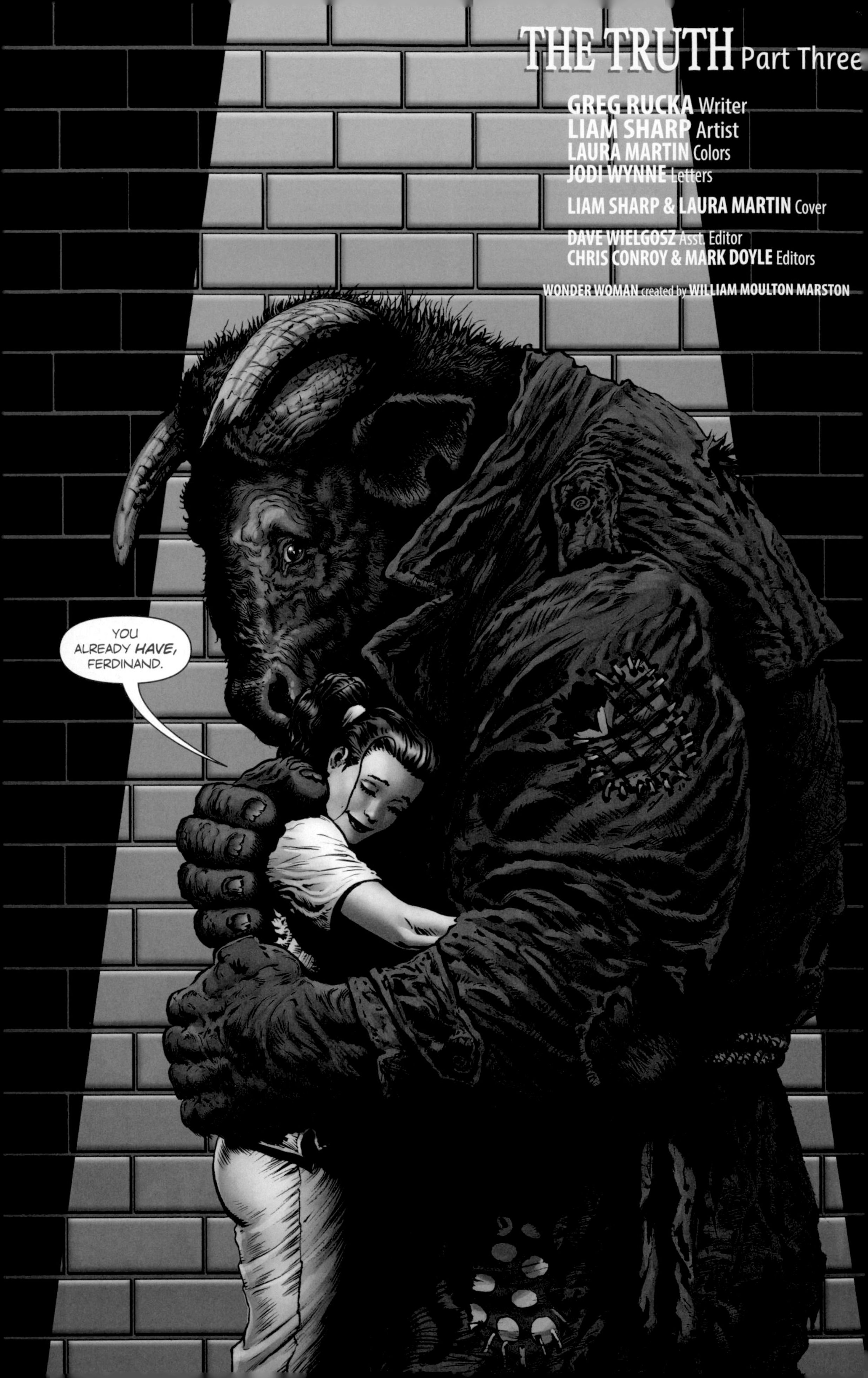
YOU ALREADY *HAVE*, FERDINAND.

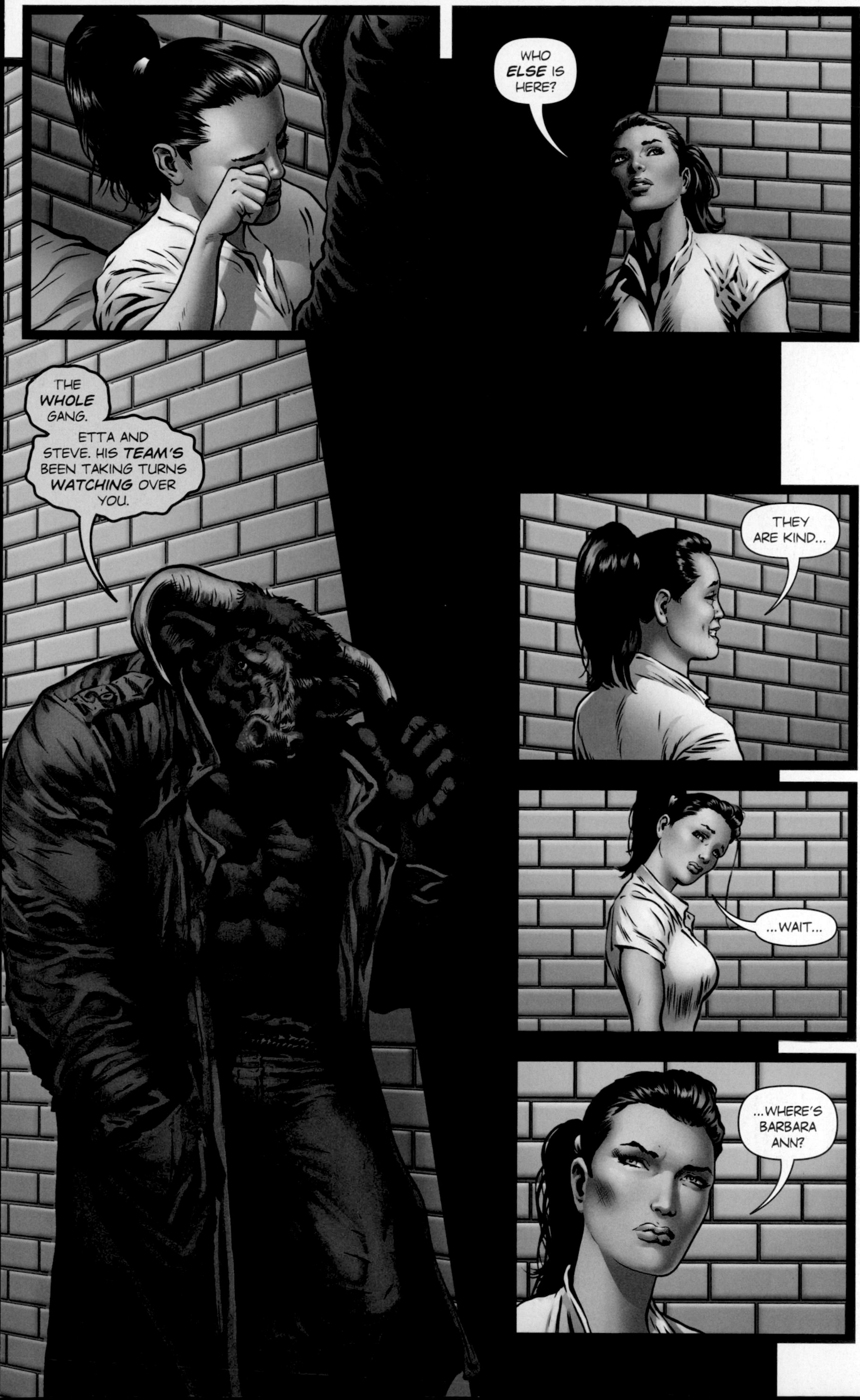
WHO ELSE IS HERE?
THE WHOLE GANG.
ETTA AND STEVE. HIS TEAM'S BEEN TAKING TURNS WATCHING OVER YOU.
THEY ARE KIND...
...WAIT...
...WHERE'S BARBARA ANN?

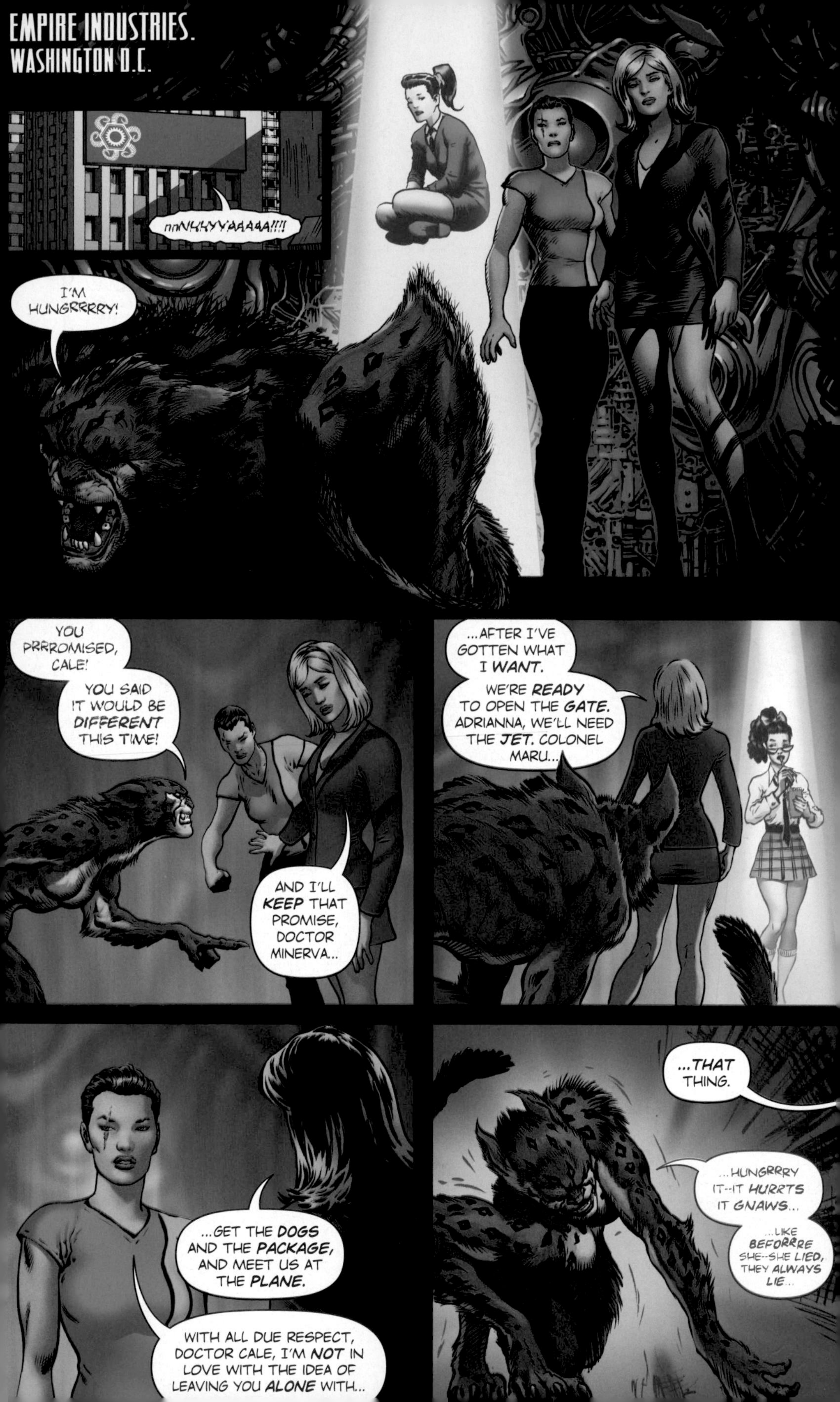
EMPIRE INDUSTRIES.
WASHINGTON D.C.
nnNYYYAAAAA!!!
I'M HUNGRRRRY!
YOU PRRROMISED, CALE!
YOU SAID IT WOULD BE DIFFERENT THIS TIME!
AND I'LL KEEP THAT PROMISE, DOCTOR MINERVA...
...AFTER I'VE GOTTEN WHAT I WANT.
WE'RE READY TO OPEN THE GATE. ADRIANNA, WE'LL NEED THE JET. COLONEL MARU...
...GET THE DOGS AND THE PACKAGE, AND MEET US AT THE PLANE.
WITH ALL DUE RESPECT, DOCTOR CALE, I'M NOT IN LOVE WITH THE IDEA OF LEAVING YOU ALONE WITH...
...THAT THING.
...HUNGRRRY IT--IT HURRTS IT GNAWS...
...LIKE BEFORRRE SHE--SHE LIED, THEY ALWAYS LIE...

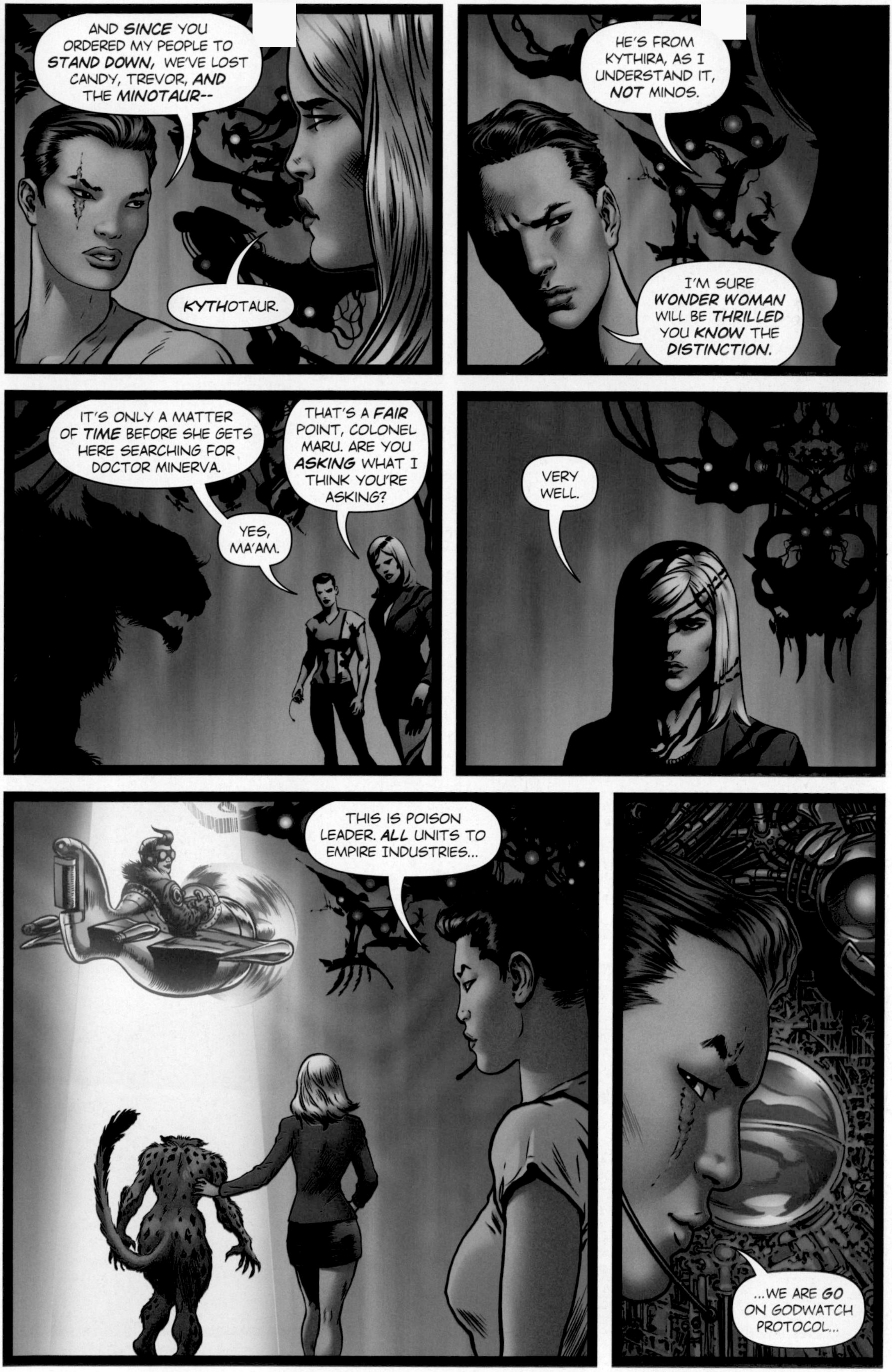
AND SINCE YOU ORDERED MY PEOPLE TO STAND DOWN, WE'VE LOST CANDY, TREVOR, AND THE MINOTAUR--
KYTHOTAUR.
HE'S FROM KYTHIRA, AS I UNDERSTAND IT, NOT MINOS.
I'M SURE WONDER WOMAN WILL BE THRILLED YOU KNOW THE DISTINCTION.
IT'S ONLY A MATTER OF TIME BEFORE SHE GETS HERE SEARCHING FOR DOCTOR MINERVA.
THAT'S A FAIR POINT, COLONEL MARU. ARE YOU ASKING WHAT I THINK YOU'RE ASKING?
YES, MA'AM.
VERY WELL.
THIS IS POISON LEADER. ALL UNITS TO EMPIRE INDUSTRIES...
...WE ARE GO ON GODWATCH PROTOCOL...

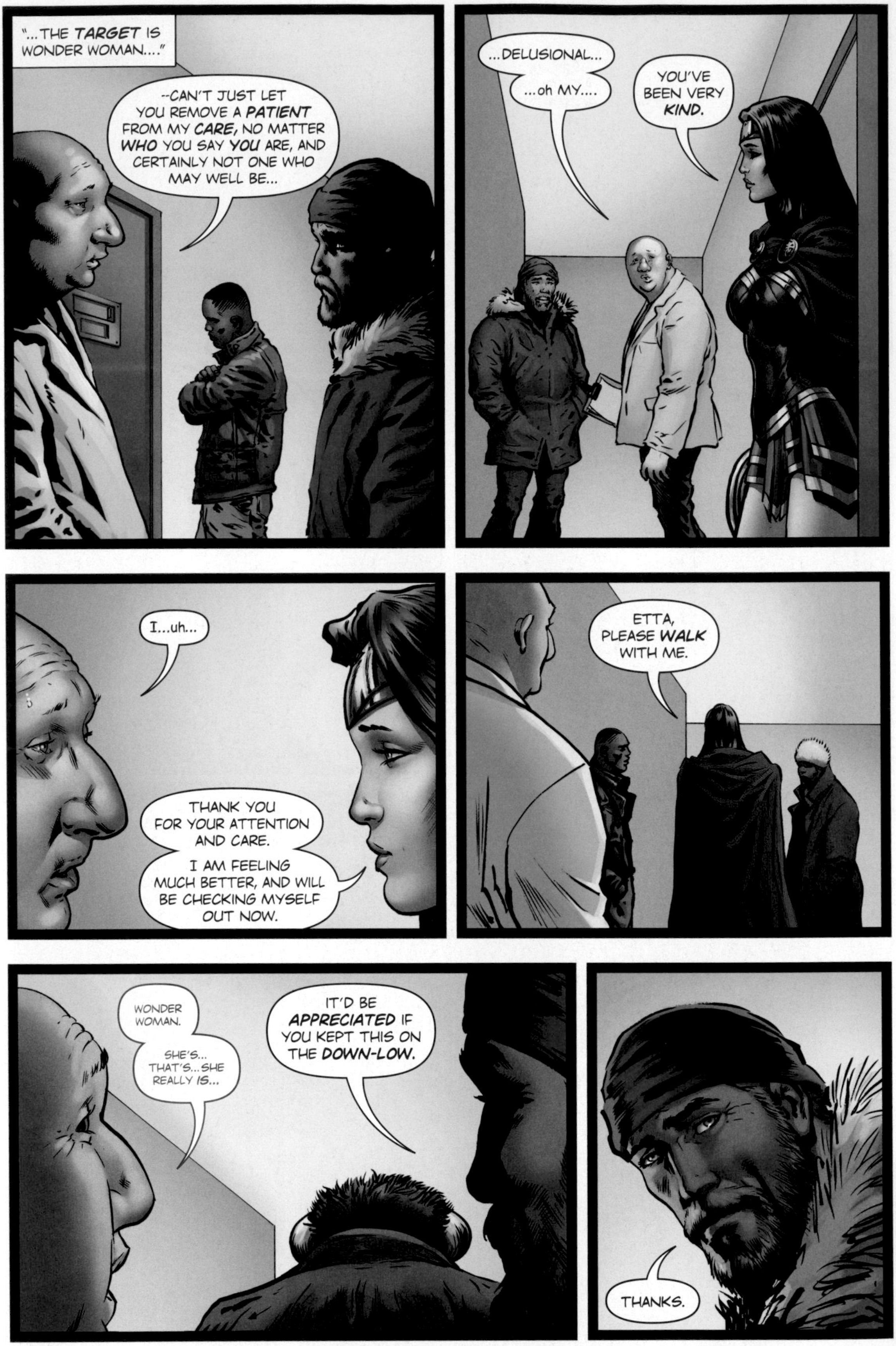
"...THE TARGET IS WONDER WOMAN...."
--CAN'T JUST LET YOU REMOVE A PATIENT FROM MY CARE, NO MATTER WHO YOU SAY YOU ARE, AND CERTAINLY NOT ONE WHO MAY WELL BE...
...DELUSIONAL...
...oh MY....
YOU'VE BEEN VERY KIND.
I...uh...
THANK YOU FOR YOUR ATTENTION AND CARE.
I AM FEELING MUCH BETTER, AND WILL BE CHECKING MYSELF OUT NOW.
ETTA, PLEASE WALK WITH ME.
WONDER WOMAN.
SHE'S... THAT'S...SHE REALLY IS...
IT'D BE APPRECIATED IF YOU KEPT THIS ON THE DOWN-LOW.
THANKS.

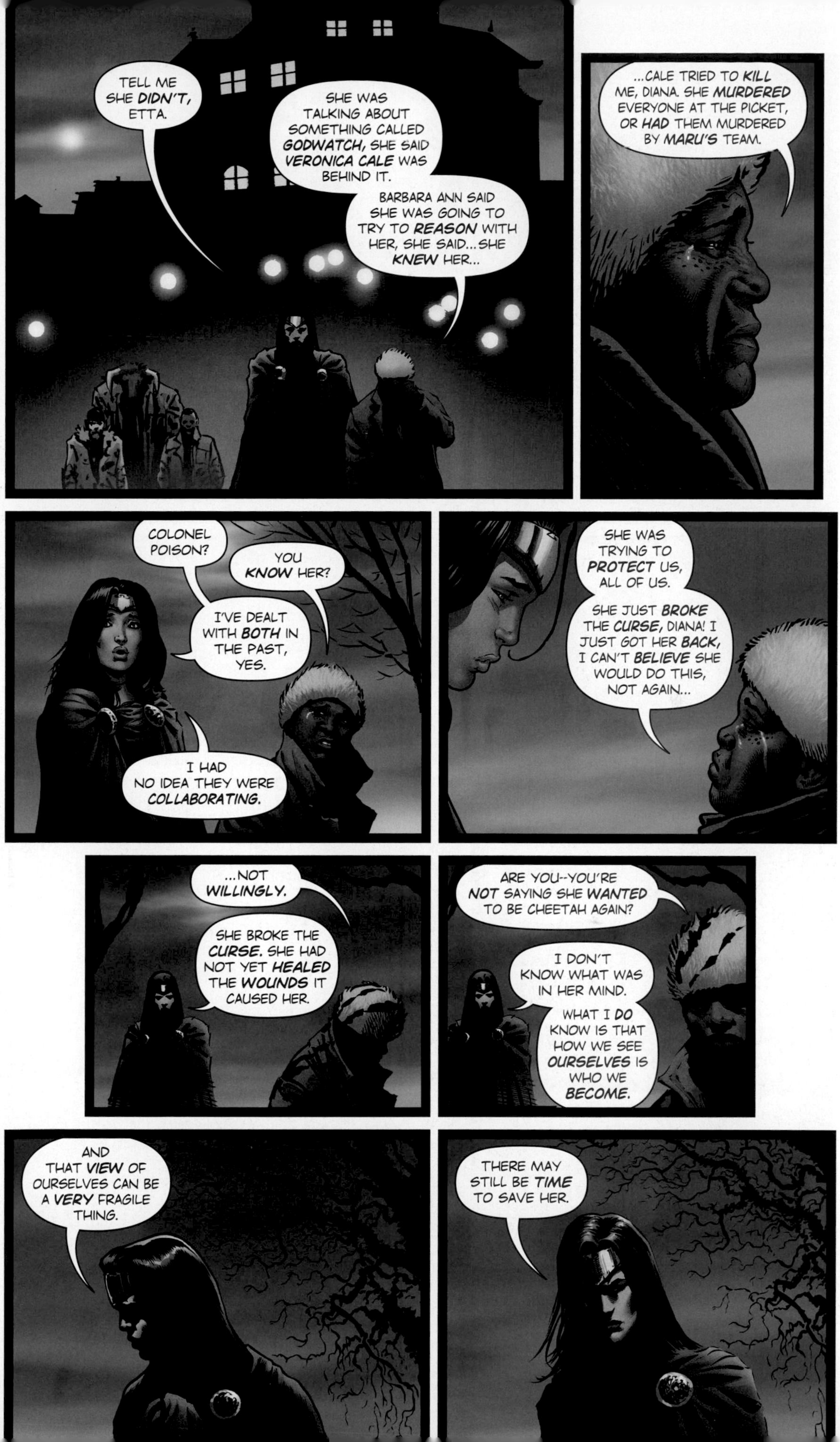

TELL ME SHE DIDN'T, ETTA.
SHE WAS TALKING ABOUT SOMETHING CALLED GODWATCH, SHE SAID VERONICA CALE WAS BEHIND IT.
BARBARA ANN SAID SHE WAS GOING TO TRY TO REASON WITH HER, SHE SAID... SHE KNEW HER...
...CALE TRIED TO KILL ME, DIANA. SHE MURDERED EVERYONE AT THE PICKET, OR HAD THEM MURDERED BY MARU'S TEAM.
COLONEL POISON?
YOU KNOW HER?
I'VE DEALT WITH BOTH IN THE PAST, YES.
I HAD NO IDEA THEY WERE COLLABORATING.
SHE WAS TRYING TO PROTECT US, ALL OF US.
SHE JUST BROKE THE CURSE, DIANA! I JUST GOT HER BACK, I CAN'T BELIEVE SHE WOULD DO THIS, NOT AGAIN...
...NOT WILLINGLY.
SHE BROKE THE CURSE. SHE HAD NOT YET HEALED THE WOUNDS IT CAUSED HER.
ARE YOU--YOU'RE NOT SAYING SHE WANTED TO BE CHEETAH AGAIN?
I DON'T KNOW WHAT WAS IN HER MIND.
WHAT I DO KNOW IS THAT HOW WE SEE OURSELVES IS WHO WE BECOME.
AND THAT VIEW OF OURSELVES CAN BE A VERY FRAGILE THING.
THERE MAY STILL BE TIME TO SAVE HER.

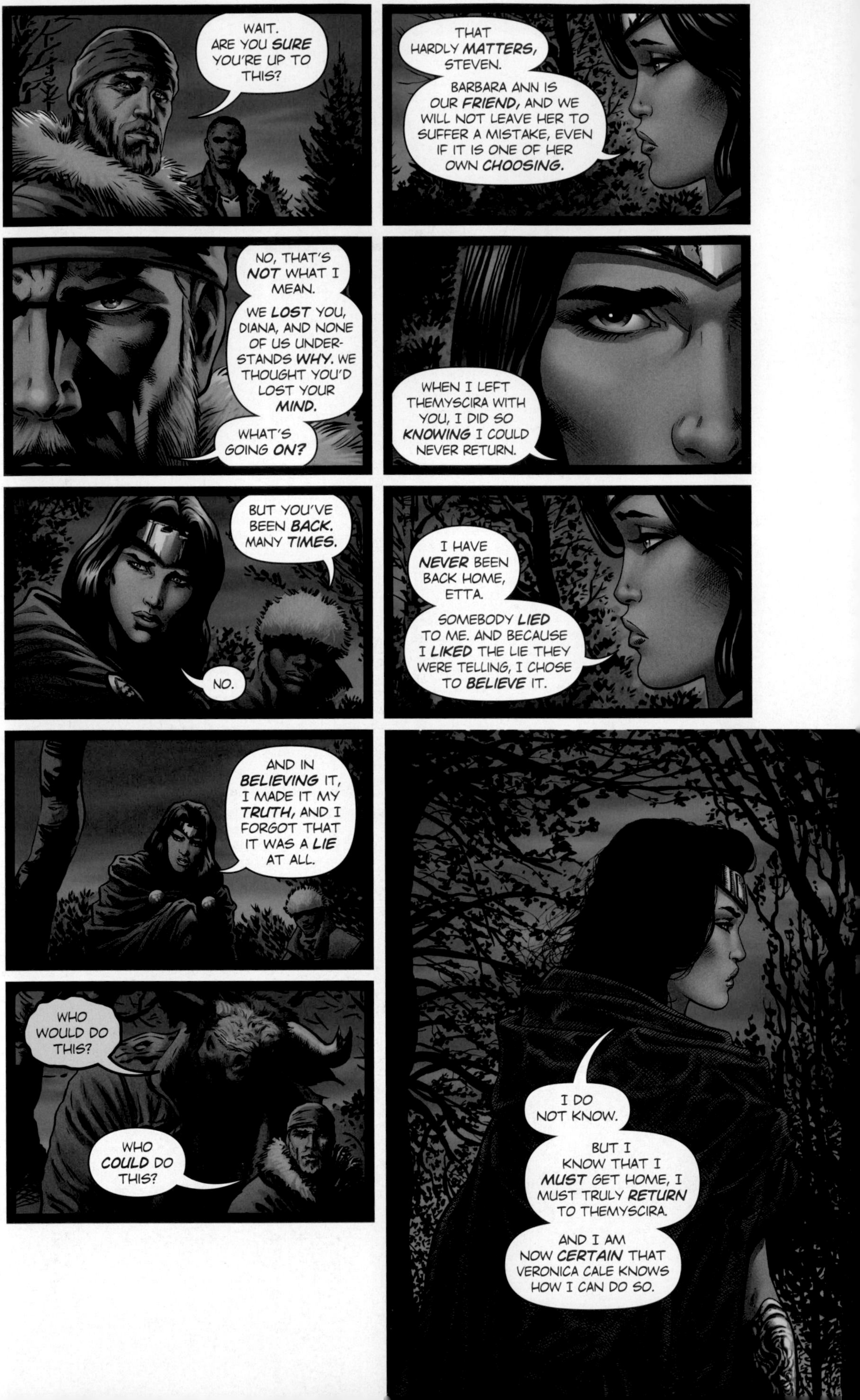

WAIT. ARE YOU SURE YOU'RE UP TO THIS?
THAT HARDLY MATTERS, STEVEN.
BARBARA ANN IS OUR FRIEND, AND WE WILL NOT LEAVE HER TO SUFFER A MISTAKE, EVEN IF IT IS ONE OF HER OWN CHOOSING.
NO, THAT'S NOT WHAT I MEAN.
WE LOST YOU, DIANA, AND NONE OF US UNDER-STANDS WHY. WE THOUGHT YOU'D LOST YOUR MIND.
WHAT'S GOING ON?
WHEN I LEFT THEMYSCIRA WITH YOU, I DID SO KNOWING I COULD NEVER RETURN.
BUT YOU'VE BEEN BACK. MANY TIMES.
NO.
I HAVE NEVER BEEN BACK HOME, ETTA.
SOMEBODY LIED TO ME. AND BECAUSE I LIKED THE LIE THEY WERE TELLING, I CHOSE TO BELIEVE IT.
AND IN BELIEVING IT, I MADE IT MY TRUTH, AND I FORGOT THAT IT WAS A LIE AT ALL.
WHO WOULD DO THIS?
WHO COULD DO THIS?
I DO NOT KNOW.
BUT I KNOW THAT I MUST GET HOME, I MUST TRULY RETURN TO THEMYSCIRA.
AND I AM NOW CERTAIN THAT VERONICA CALE KNOWS HOW I CAN DO SO.

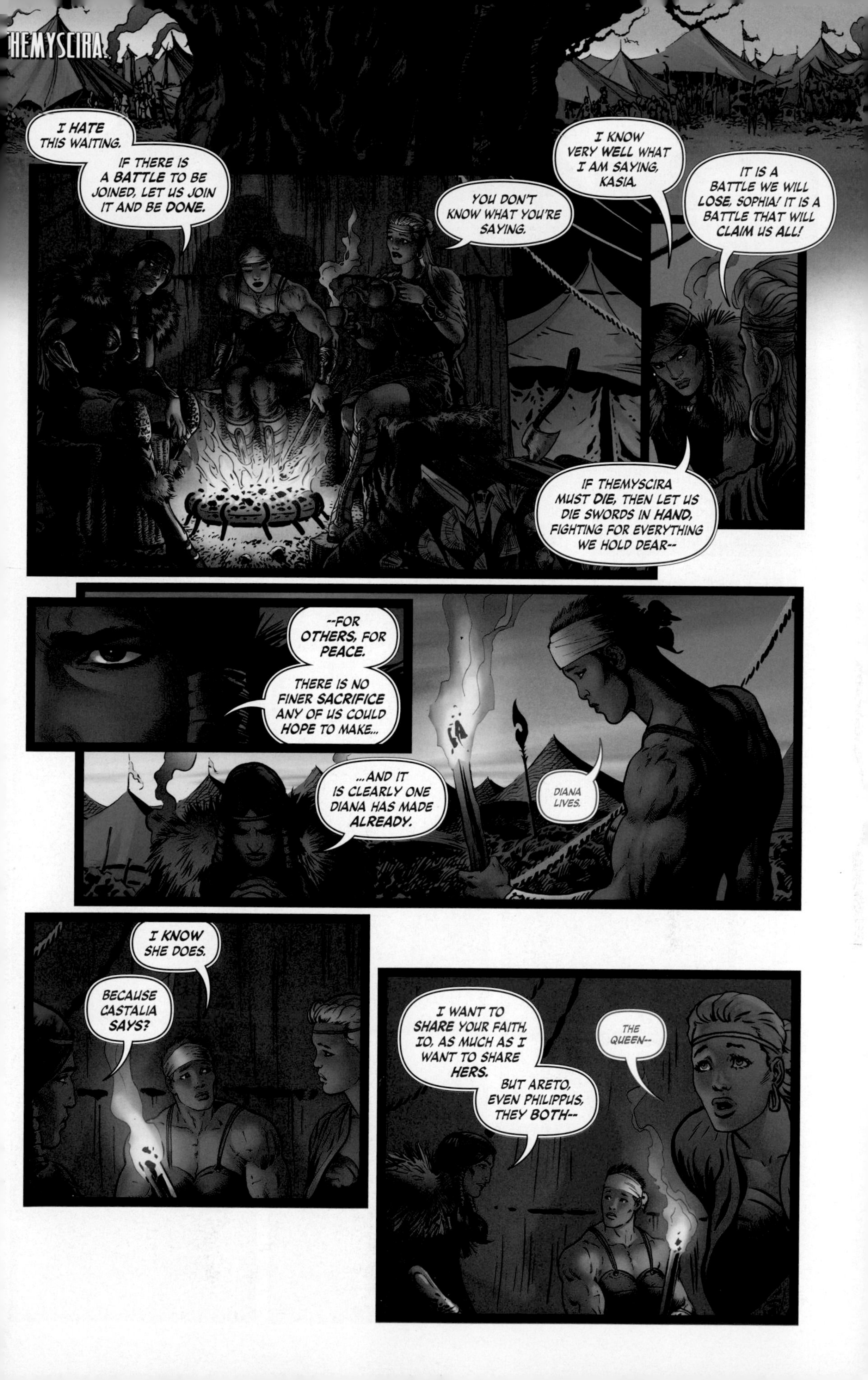
THEMYSCIRA.
I HATE THIS WAITING.
IF THERE IS A BATTLE TO BE JOINED, LET US JOIN IT AND BE DONE.
YOU DON'T KNOW WHAT YOU'RE SAYING.
I KNOW VERY WELL WHAT I AM SAYING, KASIA.
IT IS A BATTLE WE WILL LOSE, SOPHIA! IT IS A BATTLE THAT WILL CLAIM US ALL!
IF THEMYSCIRA MUST DIE, THEN LET US DIE SWORDS IN HAND, FIGHTING FOR EVERYTHING WE HOLD DEAR--
--FOR OTHERS, FOR PEACE.
THERE IS NO FINER SACRIFICE ANY OF US COULD HOPE TO MAKE...
...AND IT IS CLEARLY ONE DIANA HAS MADE ALREADY.
DIANA LIVES.
I KNOW SHE DOES.
BECAUSE CASTALIA SAYS?
I WANT TO SHARE YOUR FAITH, IO, AS MUCH AS I WANT TO SHARE HERS.
BUT ARETO, EVEN PHILIPPUS, THEY BOTH--
THE QUEEN--

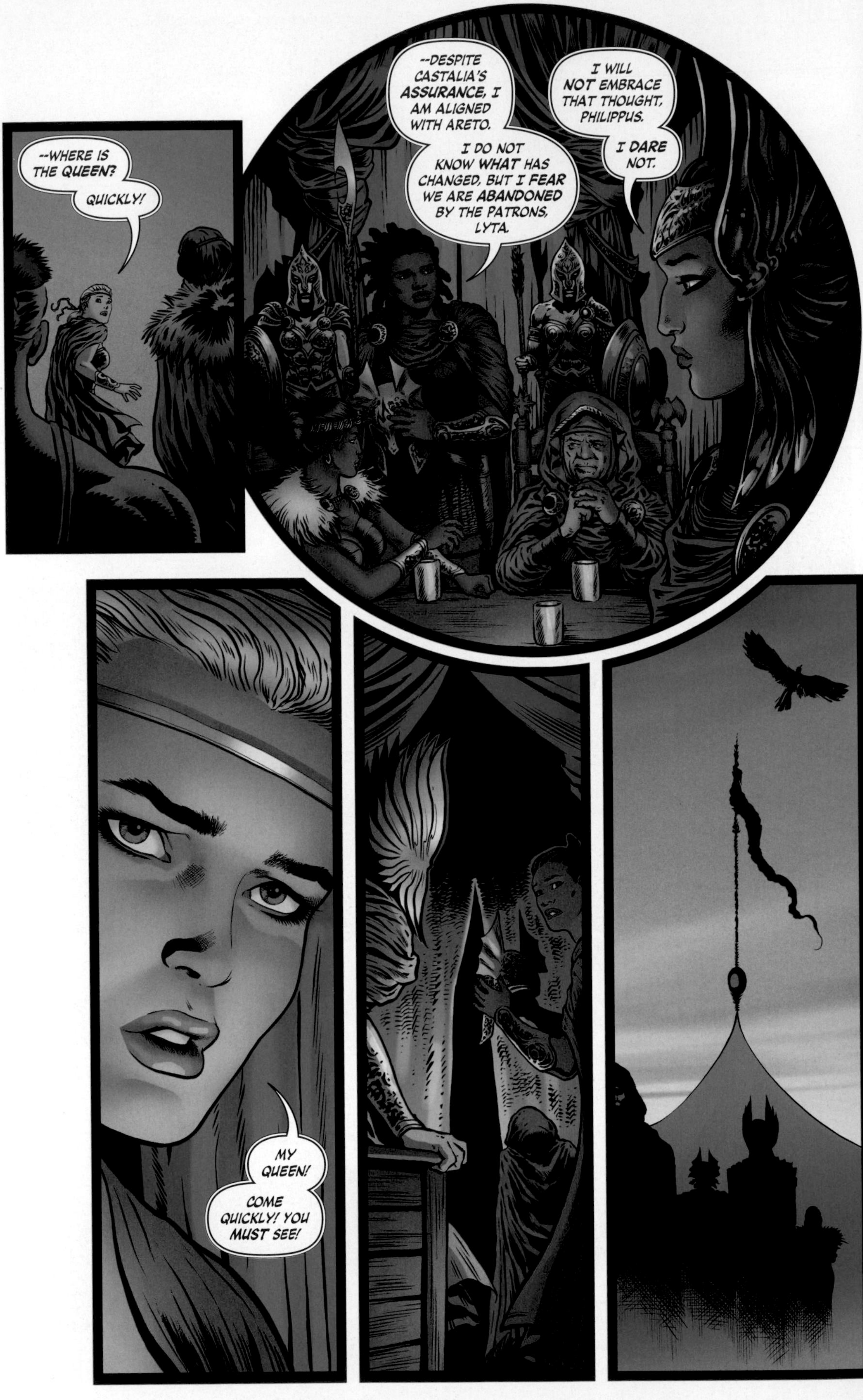
--WHERE IS THE QUEEN?
QUICKLY!
--DESPITE CASTALIA'S ASSURANCE, I AM ALIGNED WITH ARETO.
I DO NOT KNOW WHAT HAS CHANGED, BUT I FEAR WE ARE ABANDONED BY THE PATRONS, LYTA.
I WILL NOT EMBRACE THAT THOUGHT, PHILIPPUS.
I DARE NOT.
MY QUEEN!
COME QUICKLY! YOU MUST SEE!

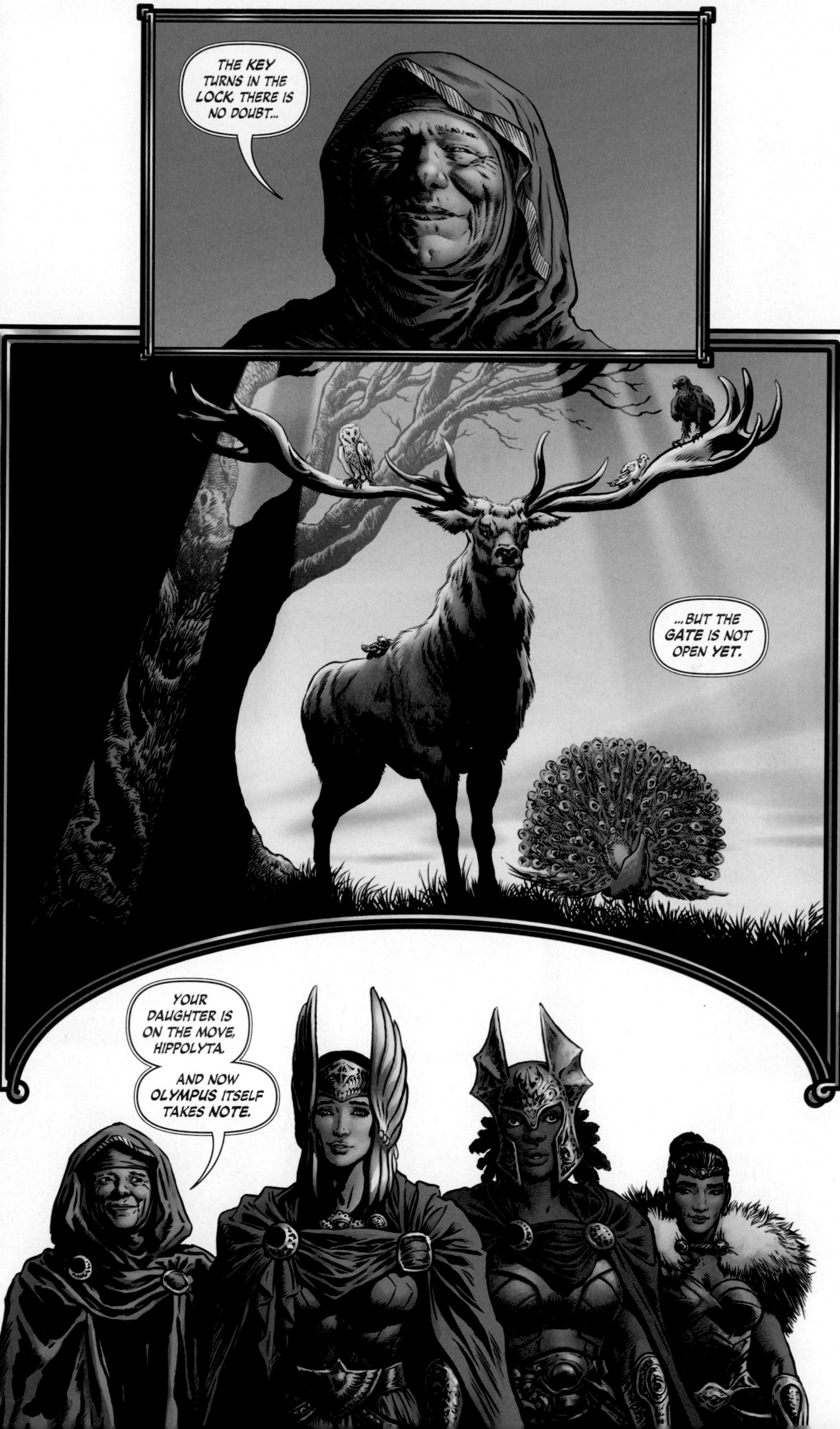
THE KEY TURNS IN THE LOCK, THERE IS NO DOUBT...
...BUT THE GATE IS NOT OPEN YET.
YOUR DAUGHTER IS ON THE MOVE, HIPPOLYTA.
AND NOW OLYMPUS ITSELF TAKES NOTE.

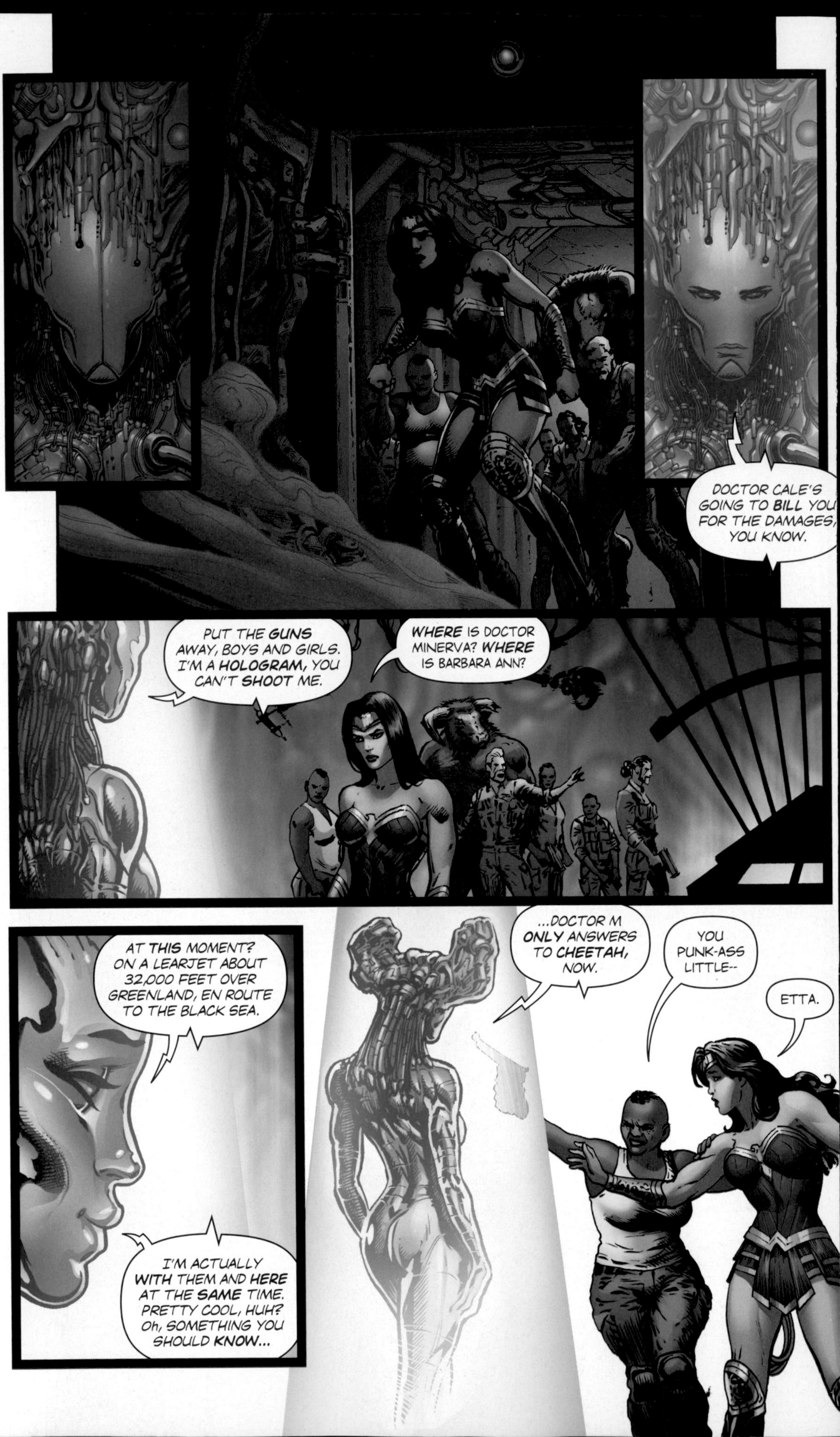
DOCTOR CALE'S GOING TO **BILL** YOU FOR THE DAMAGES, YOU KNOW.
PUT THE **GUNS** AWAY, BOYS AND GIRLS. I'M A **HOLOGRAM,** YOU CAN'T **SHOOT** ME.
WHERE IS DOCTOR MINERVA? **WHERE** IS BARBARA ANN?
AT **THIS** MOMENT? ON A LEARJET ABOUT 32,000 FEET OVER GREENLAND, EN ROUTE TO THE BLACK SEA.
I'M ACTUALLY **WITH** THEM AND **HERE** AT THE **SAME** TIME. PRETTY COOL, HUH? Oh, SOMETHING YOU SHOULD **KNOW...**
...DOCTOR M **ONLY** ANSWERS TO **CHEETAH,** NOW.
YOU PUNK-ASS LITTLE--
ETTA.

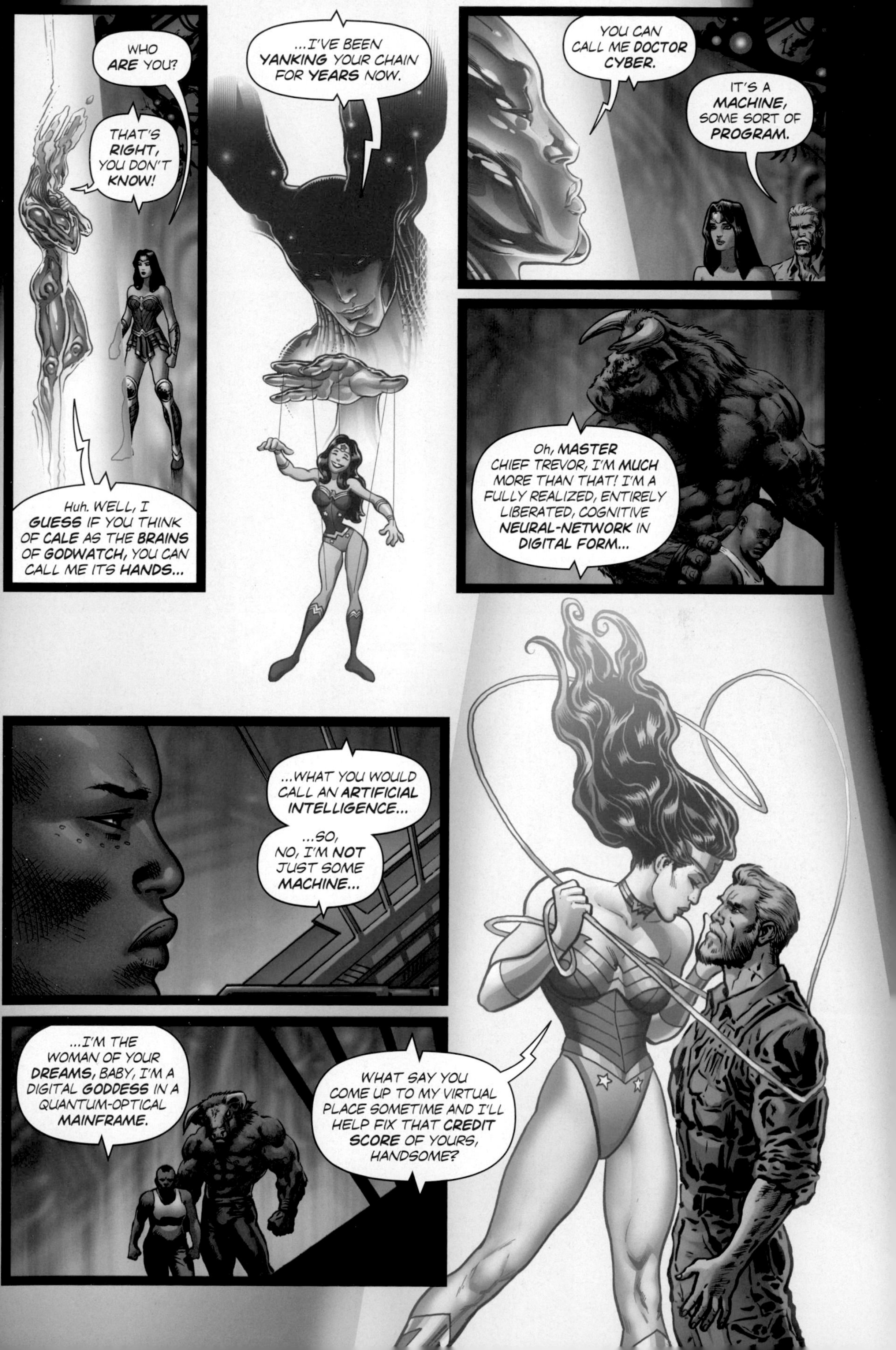
WHO ARE YOU?
THAT'S RIGHT, YOU DON'T KNOW!
Huh. WELL, I GUESS IF YOU THINK OF CALE AS THE BRAINS OF GODWATCH, YOU CAN CALL ME ITS HANDS...
...I'VE BEEN YANKING YOUR CHAIN FOR YEARS NOW.
YOU CAN CALL ME DOCTOR CYBER.
IT'S A MACHINE, SOME SORT OF PROGRAM.
Oh, MASTER CHIEF TREVOR, I'M MUCH MORE THAN THAT! I'M A FULLY REALIZED, ENTIRELY LIBERATED, COGNITIVE NEURAL-NETWORK IN DIGITAL FORM...
...WHAT YOU WOULD CALL AN ARTIFICIAL INTELLIGENCE...
...SO, NO, I'M NOT JUST SOME MACHINE...
...I'M THE WOMAN OF YOUR DREAMS, BABY, I'M A DIGITAL GODDESS IN A QUANTUM-OPTICAL MAINFRAME.
WHAT SAY YOU COME UP TO MY VIRTUAL PLACE SOMETIME AND I'LL HELP FIX THAT CREDIT SCORE OF YOURS, HANDSOME?

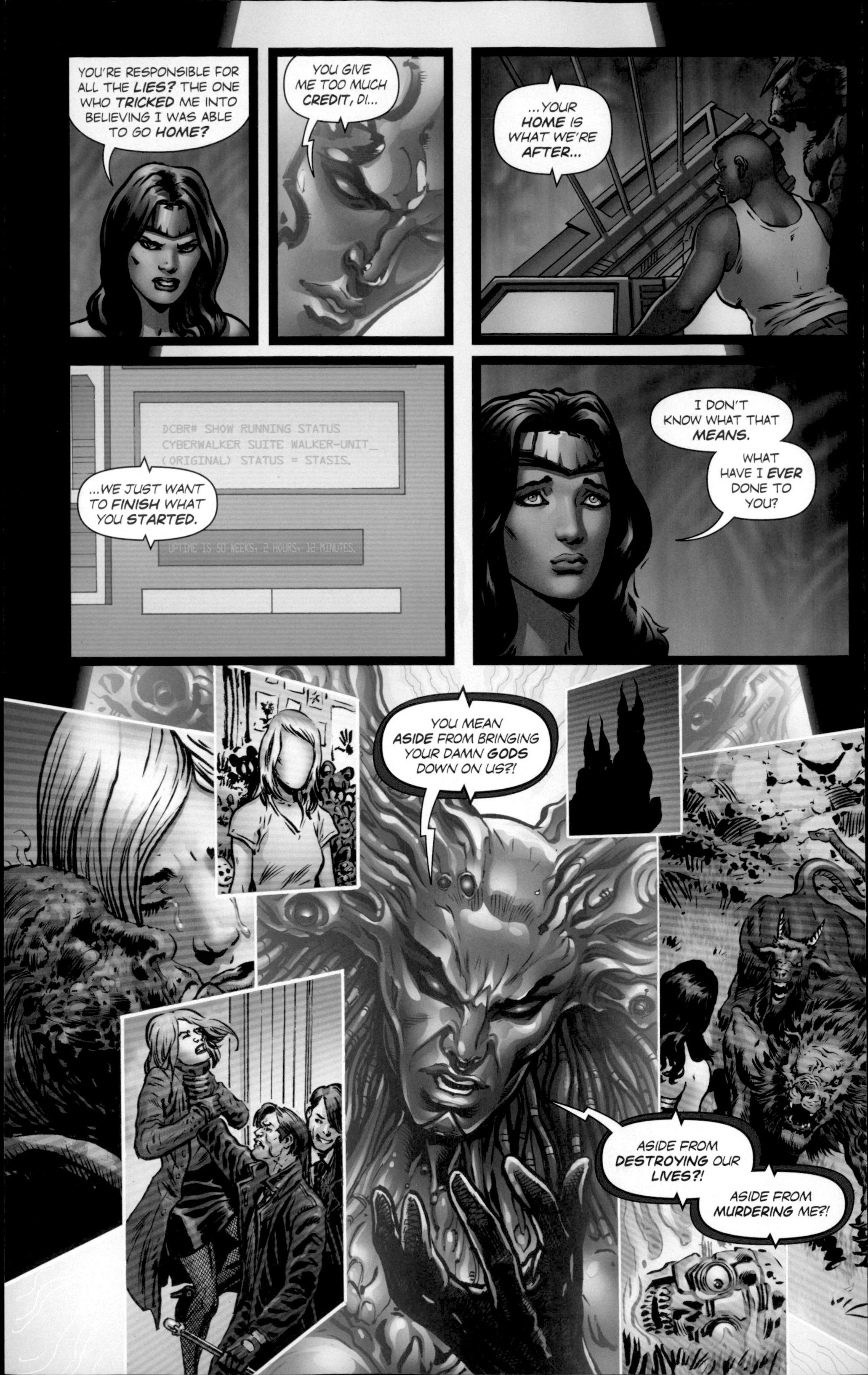
YOU'RE RESPONSIBLE FOR ALL THE **LIES?** THE ONE WHO **TRICKED** ME INTO BELIEVING I WAS ABLE TO GO **HOME?**
YOU GIVE ME TOO MUCH **CREDIT**, DI...
...YOUR **HOME** IS WHAT WE'RE **AFTER...**
DCBR# SHOW RUNNING STATUS
CYBERWALKER SUITE WALKER-UNIT_
(ORIGINAL) STATUS = STASIS.
...WE JUST WANT TO **FINISH** WHAT YOU **STARTED.**
UPTIME IS 50 WEEKS, 2 HOURS, 12 MINUTES.
I DON'T KNOW WHAT THAT **MEANS.**
WHAT HAVE I **EVER** DONE TO YOU?
YOU MEAN **ASIDE** FROM BRINGING YOUR DAMN **GODS** DOWN ON US?!
ASIDE FROM **DESTROYING** OUR **LIVES?!**
ASIDE FROM **MURDERING** ME?!

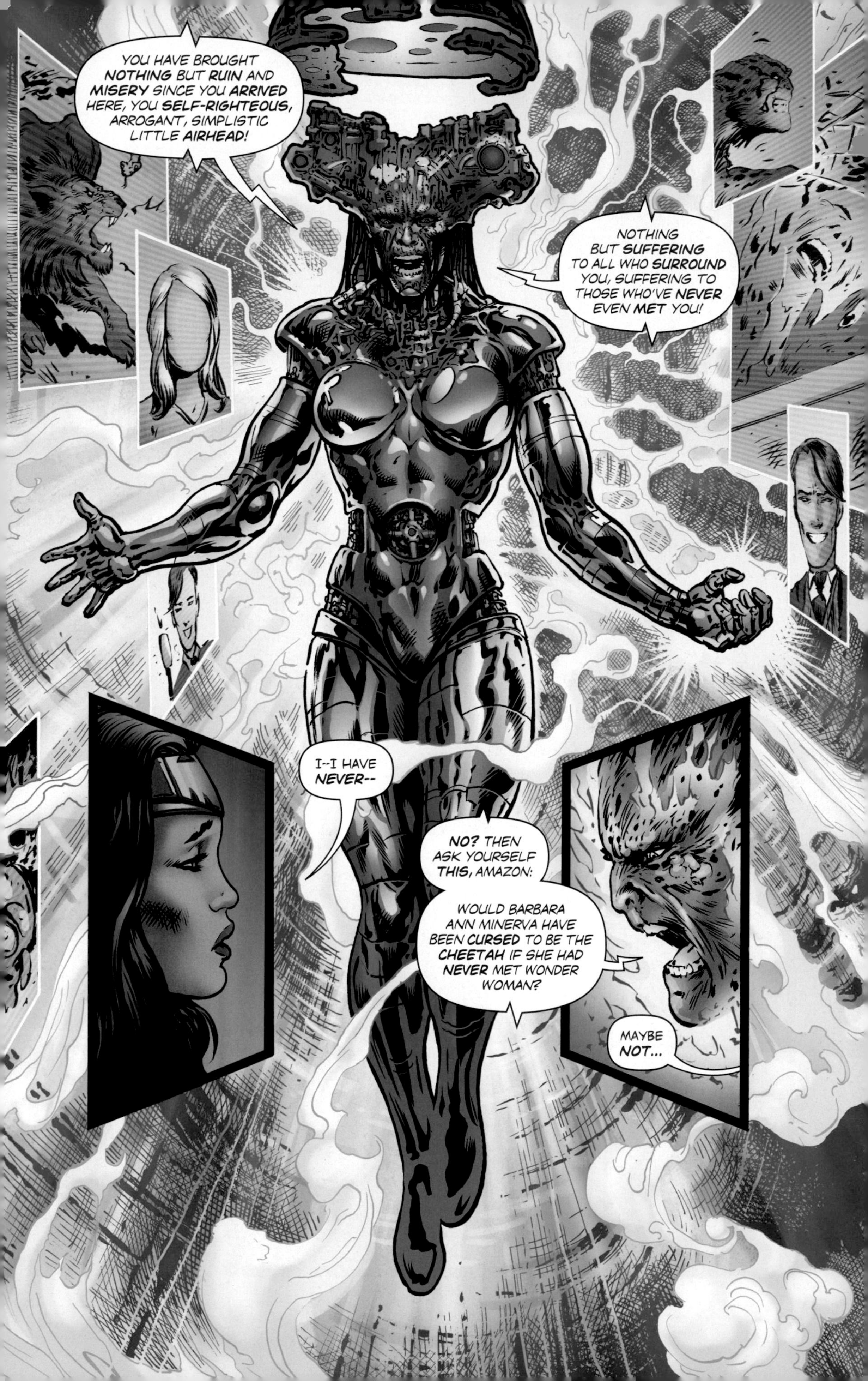
YOU HAVE BROUGHT NOTHING BUT RUIN AND MISERY SINCE YOU ARRIVED HERE, YOU SELF-RIGHTEOUS, ARROGANT, SIMPLISTIC LITTLE AIRHEAD!
NOTHING BUT SUFFERING TO ALL WHO SURROUND YOU, SUFFERING TO THOSE WHO'VE NEVER EVEN MET YOU!
I--I HAVE NEVER--
NO? THEN ASK YOURSELF THIS, AMAZON:
WOULD BARBARA ANN MINERVA HAVE BEEN CURSED TO BE THE CHEETAH IF SHE HAD NEVER MET WONDER WOMAN?
MAYBE NOT...

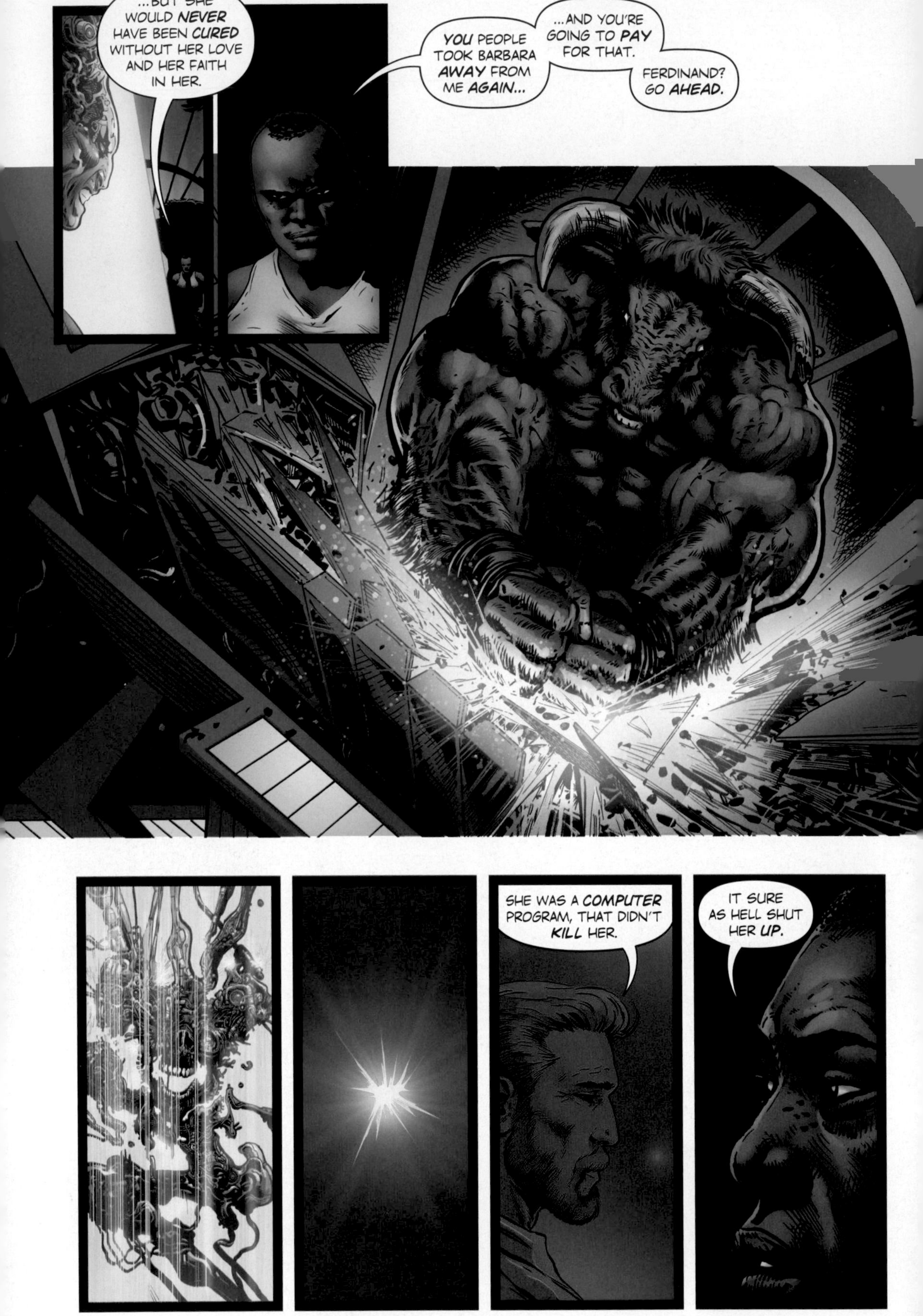

...BUT SHE WOULD NEVER HAVE BEEN CURED WITHOUT HER LOVE AND HER FAITH IN HER.
YOU PEOPLE TOOK BARBARA AWAY FROM ME AGAIN...
...AND YOU'RE GOING TO PAY FOR THAT.
FERDINAND? GO AHEAD.
SHE WAS A COMPUTER PROGRAM, THAT DIDN'T KILL HER.
IT SURE AS HELL SHUT HER UP.

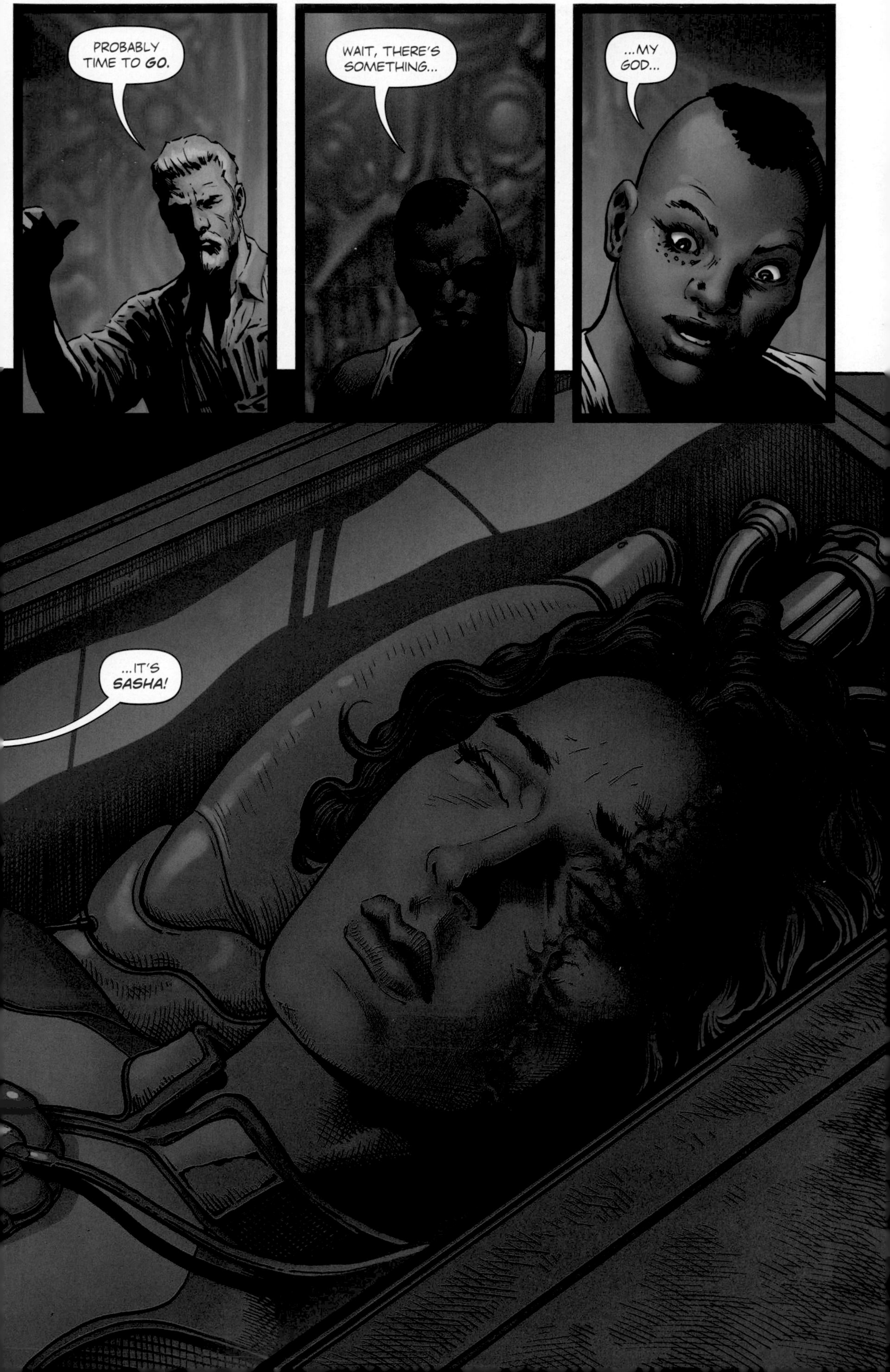
PROBABLY TIME TO **GO.**
WAIT, THERE'S SOMETHING...
...MY GOD...
...IT'S **SASHA!**

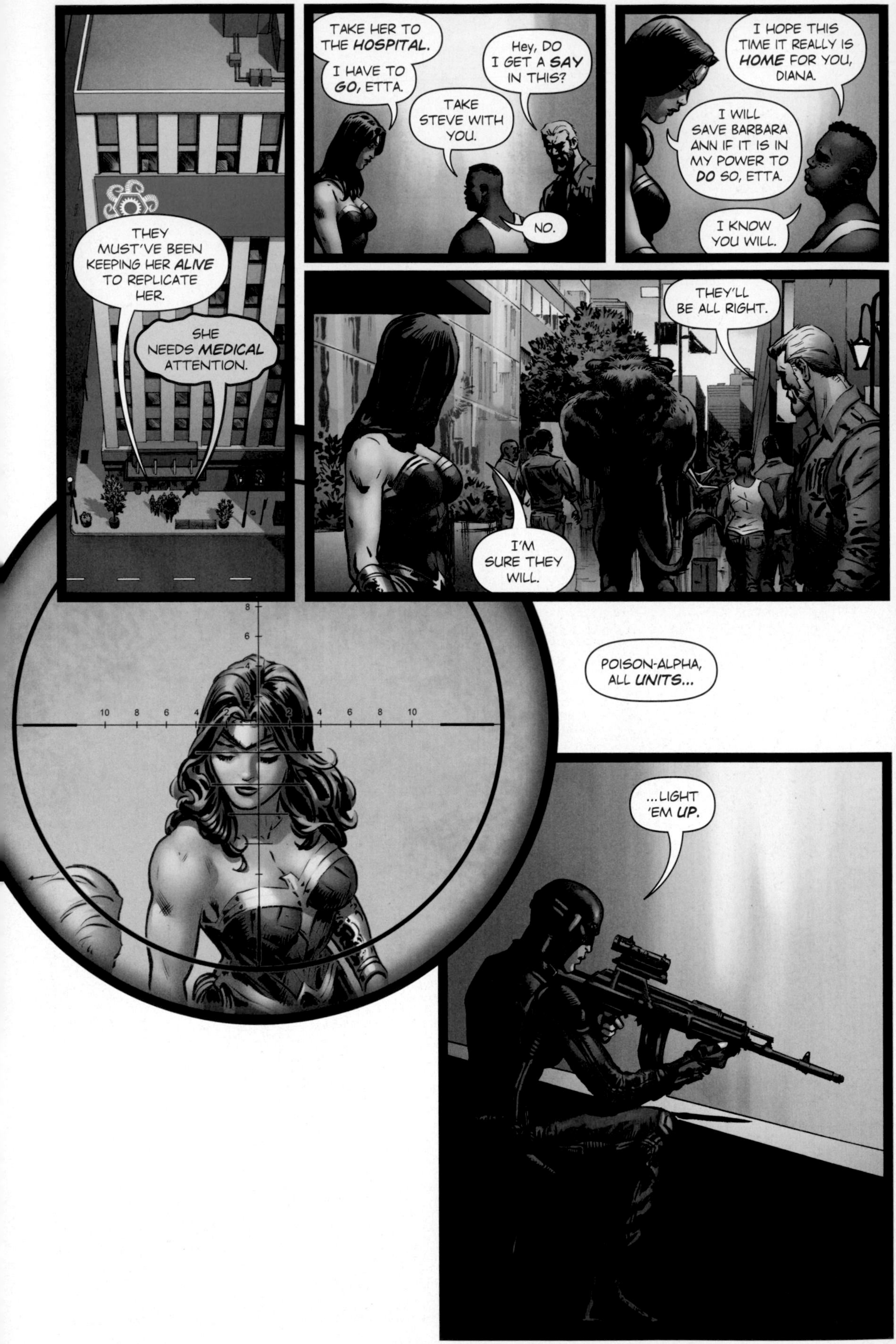
THEY MUST'VE BEEN KEEPING HER ALIVE TO REPLICATE HER.
SHE NEEDS MEDICAL ATTENTION.
TAKE HER TO THE HOSPITAL.
I HAVE TO GO, ETTA.
TAKE STEVE WITH YOU.
Hey, DO I GET A SAY IN THIS?
NO.
I HOPE THIS TIME IT REALLY IS HOME FOR YOU, DIANA.
I WILL SAVE BARBARA ANN IF IT IS IN MY POWER TO DO SO, ETTA.
I KNOW YOU WILL.
THEY'LL BE ALL RIGHT.
I'M SURE THEY WILL.
POISON-ALPHA, ALL UNITS...
...LIGHT 'EM UP.

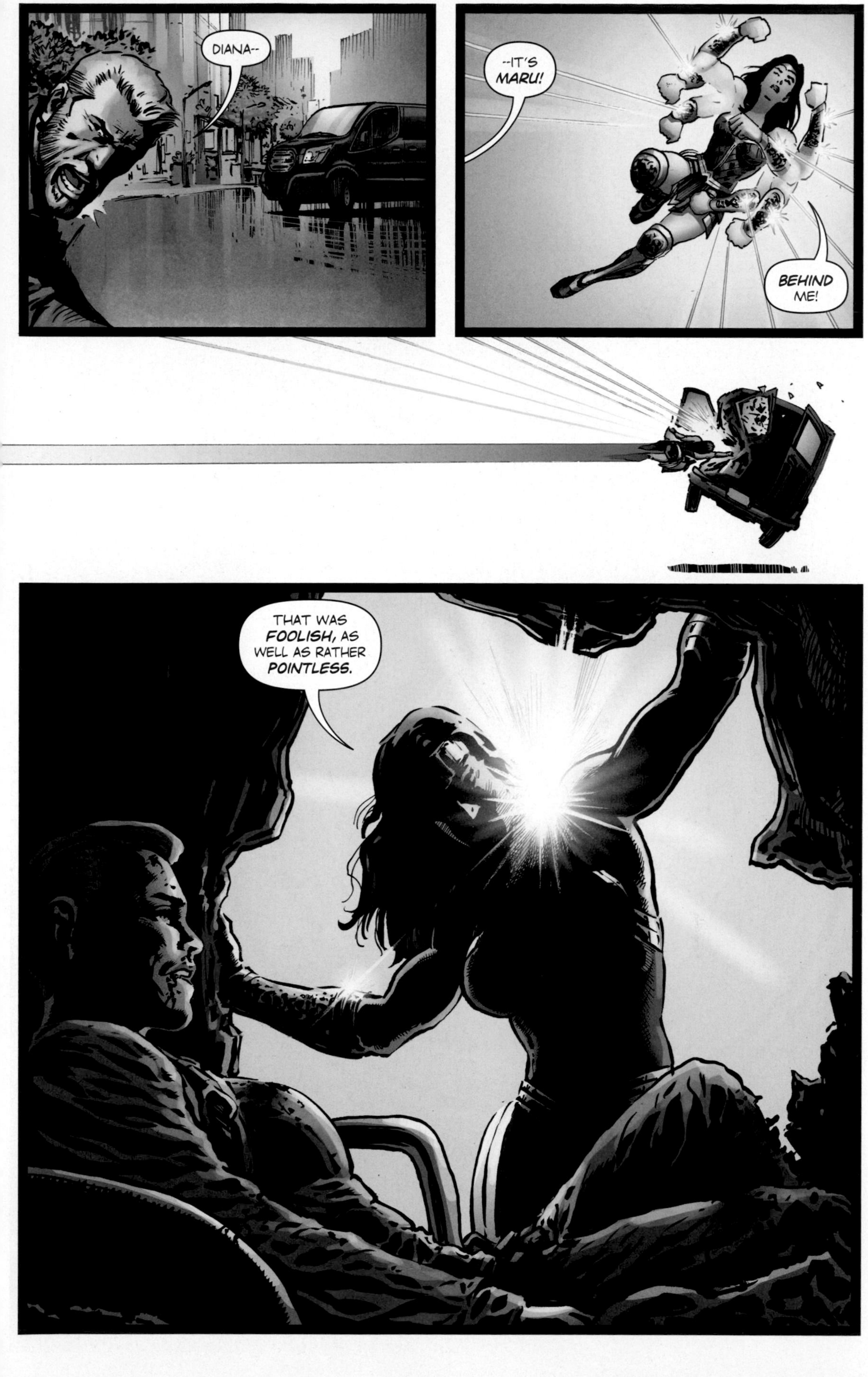
DIANA--
--IT'S MARU!
BEHIND ME!
THAT WAS FOOLISH, AS WELL AS RATHER POINTLESS.

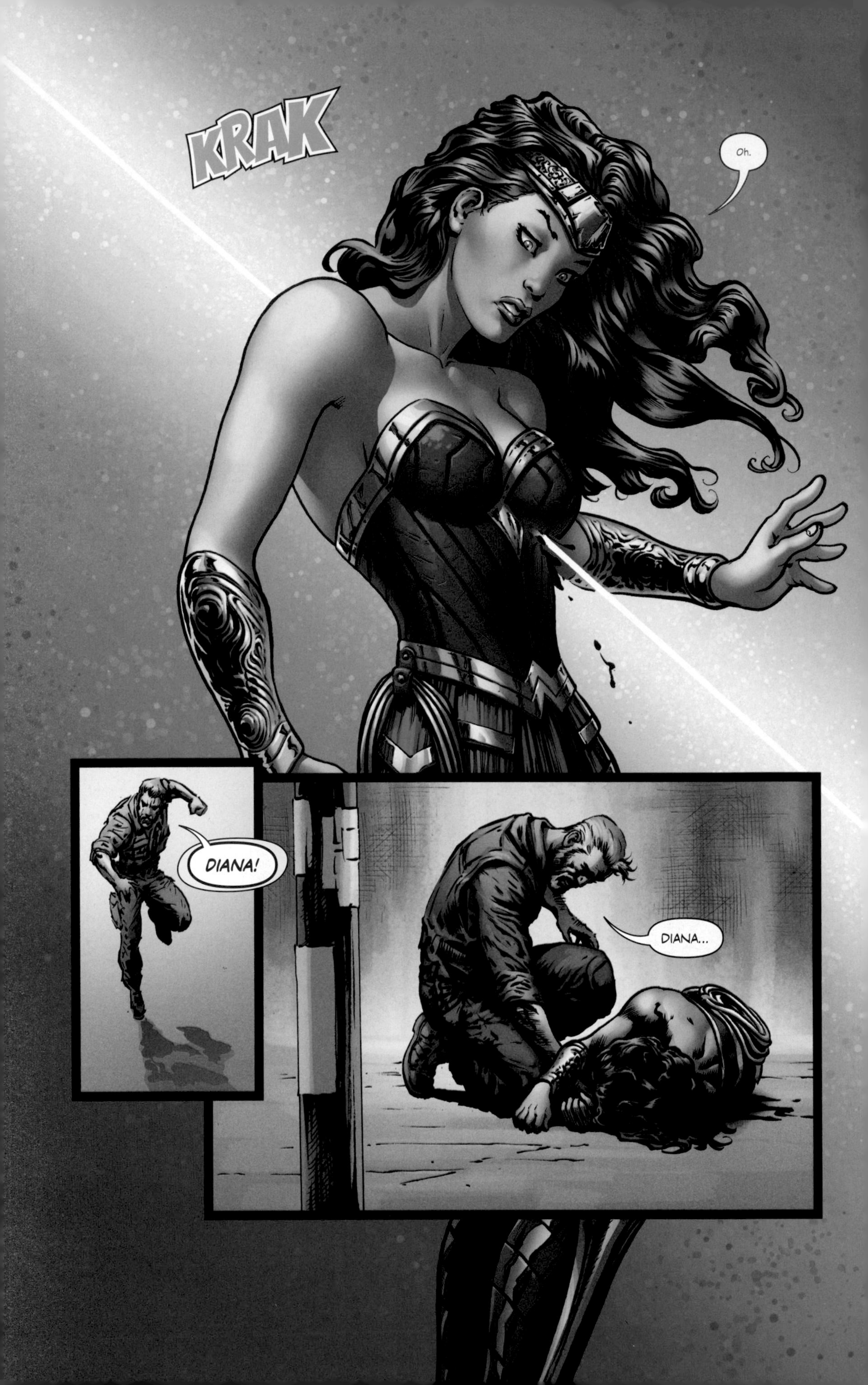
KRAK
Oh.
DIANA!
DIANA...

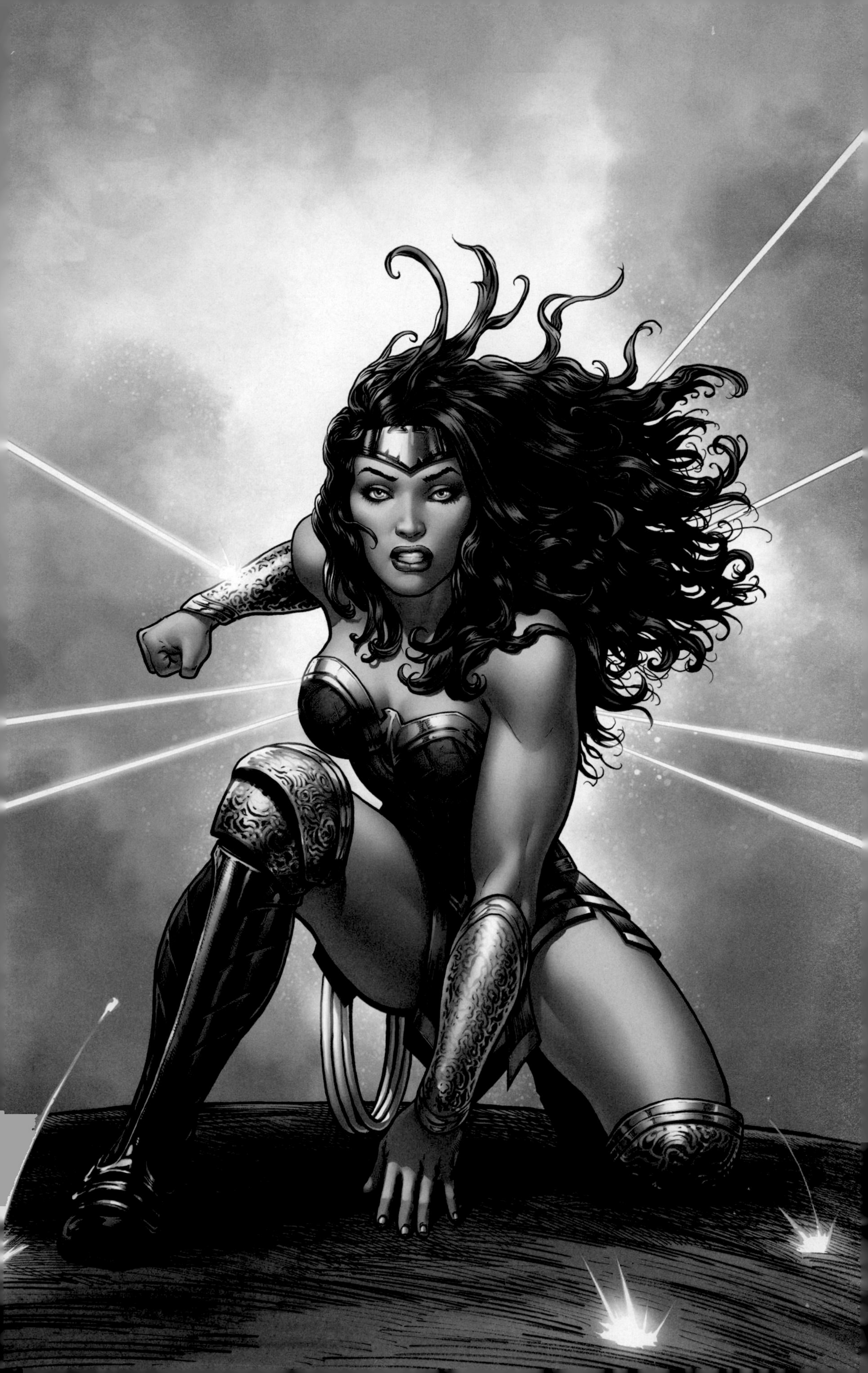

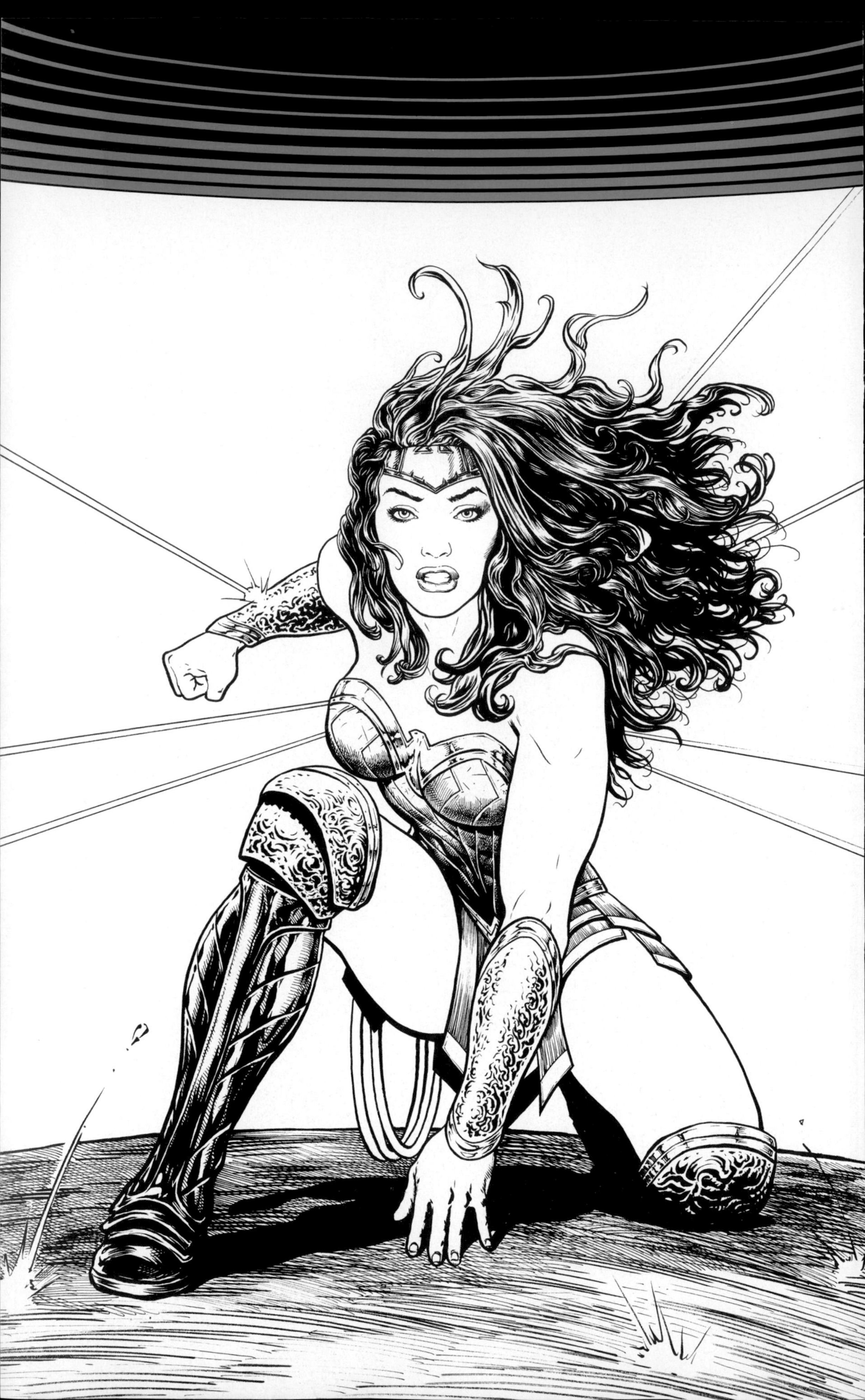

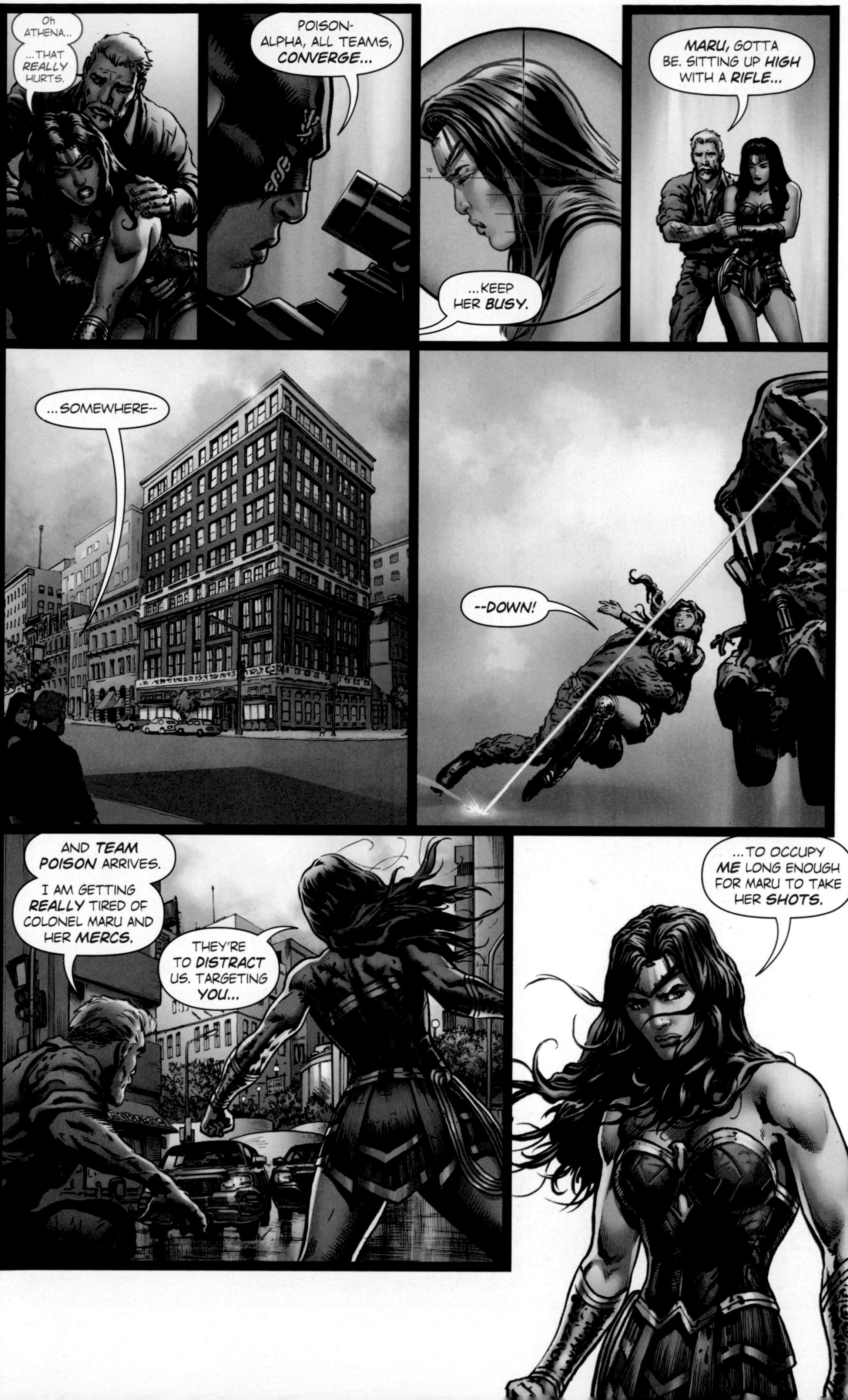
Oh ATHENA...
...THAT REALLY HURTS.
POISON-ALPHA, ALL TEAMS, CONVERGE...
...KEEP HER BUSY.
MARU, GOTTA BE. SITTING UP HIGH WITH A RIFLE...
...SOMEWHERE--
--DOWN!
AND TEAM POISON ARRIVES.
I AM GETTING REALLY TIRED OF COLONEL MARU AND HER MERCS.
THEY'RE TO DISTRACT US. TARGETING YOU...
...TO OCCUPY ME LONG ENOUGH FOR MARU TO TAKE HER SHOTS.

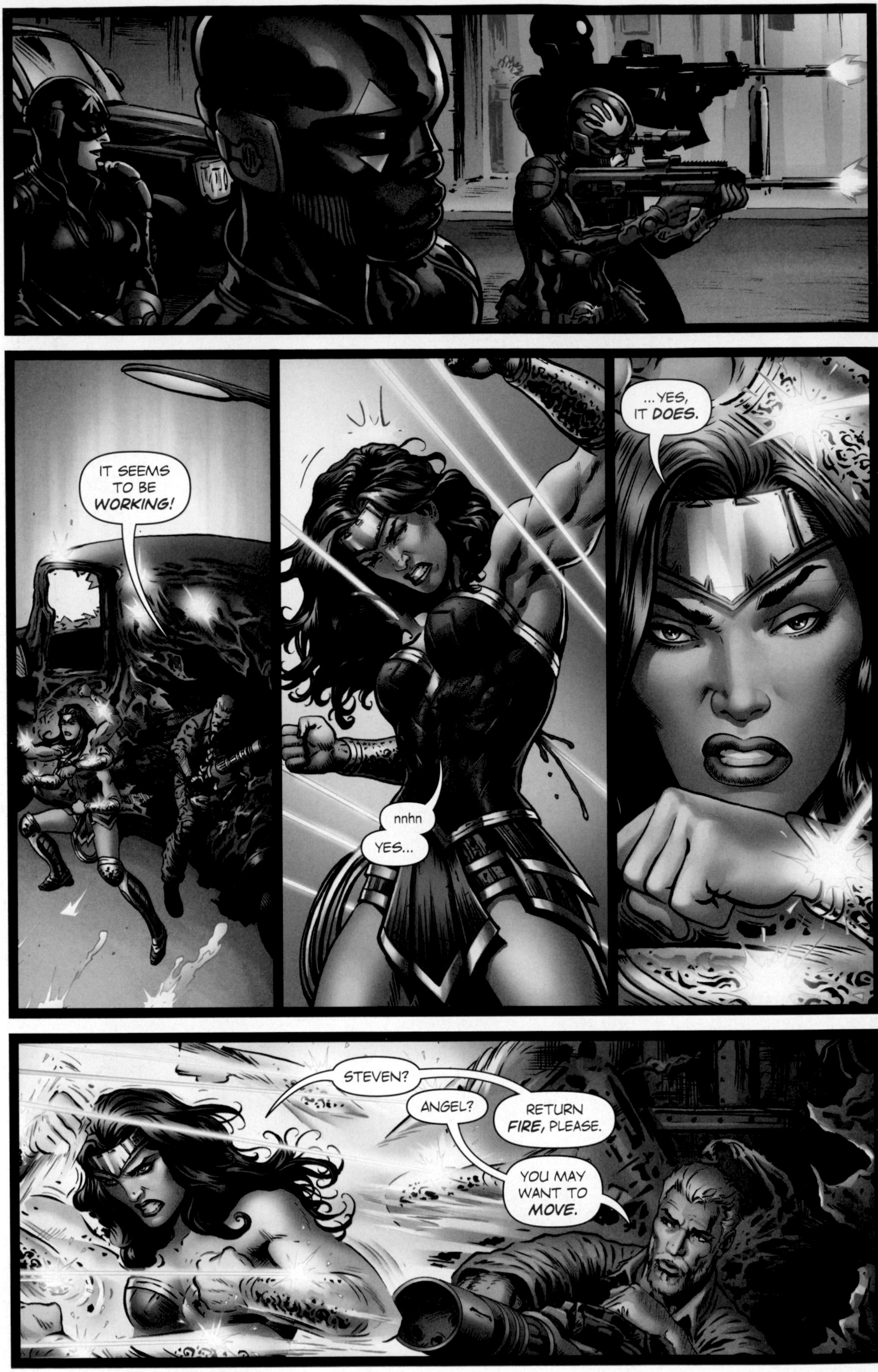
IT SEEMS TO BE WORKING!
...YES, IT DOES.
nnhn
YES...
STEVEN?
RETURN FIRE, PLEASE.
ANGEL?
YOU MAY WANT TO MOVE.

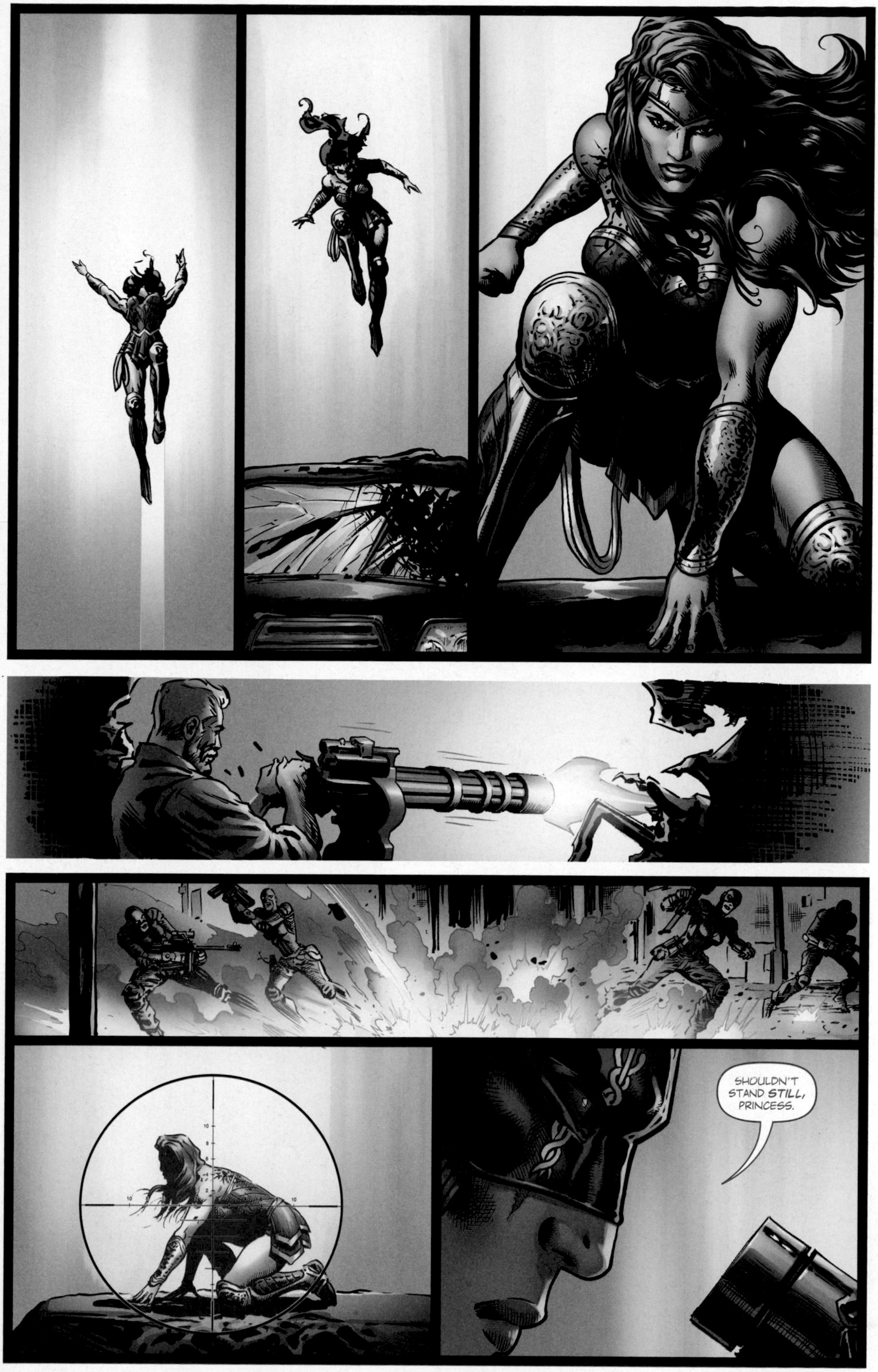
SHOULDN'T STAND STILL, PRINCESS.

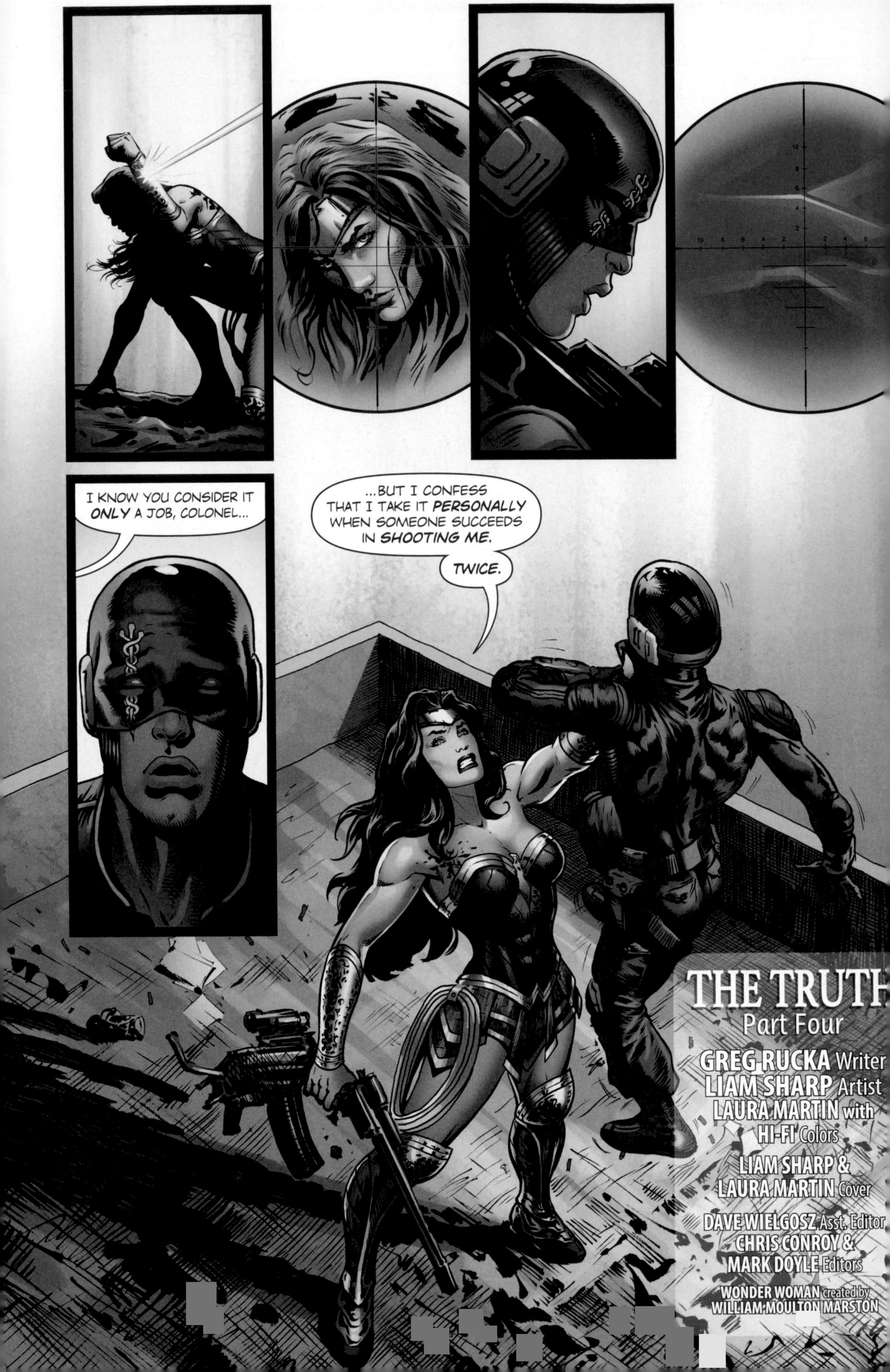
I KNOW YOU CONSIDER IT ONLY A JOB, COLONEL...
...BUT I CONFESS THAT I TAKE IT PERSONALLY WHEN SOMEONE SUCCEEDS IN SHOOTING ME.
TWICE.
THE TRUTH Part Four
GREG RUCKA Writer
LIAM SHARP Artist
LAURA MARTIN with HI-FI Colors
LIAM SHARP & LAURA MARTIN Cover
DAVE WIELGOSZ Asst. Editor
CHRIS CONROY & MARK DOYLE Editors
WONDER WOMAN created by WILLIAM MOULTON MARSTON

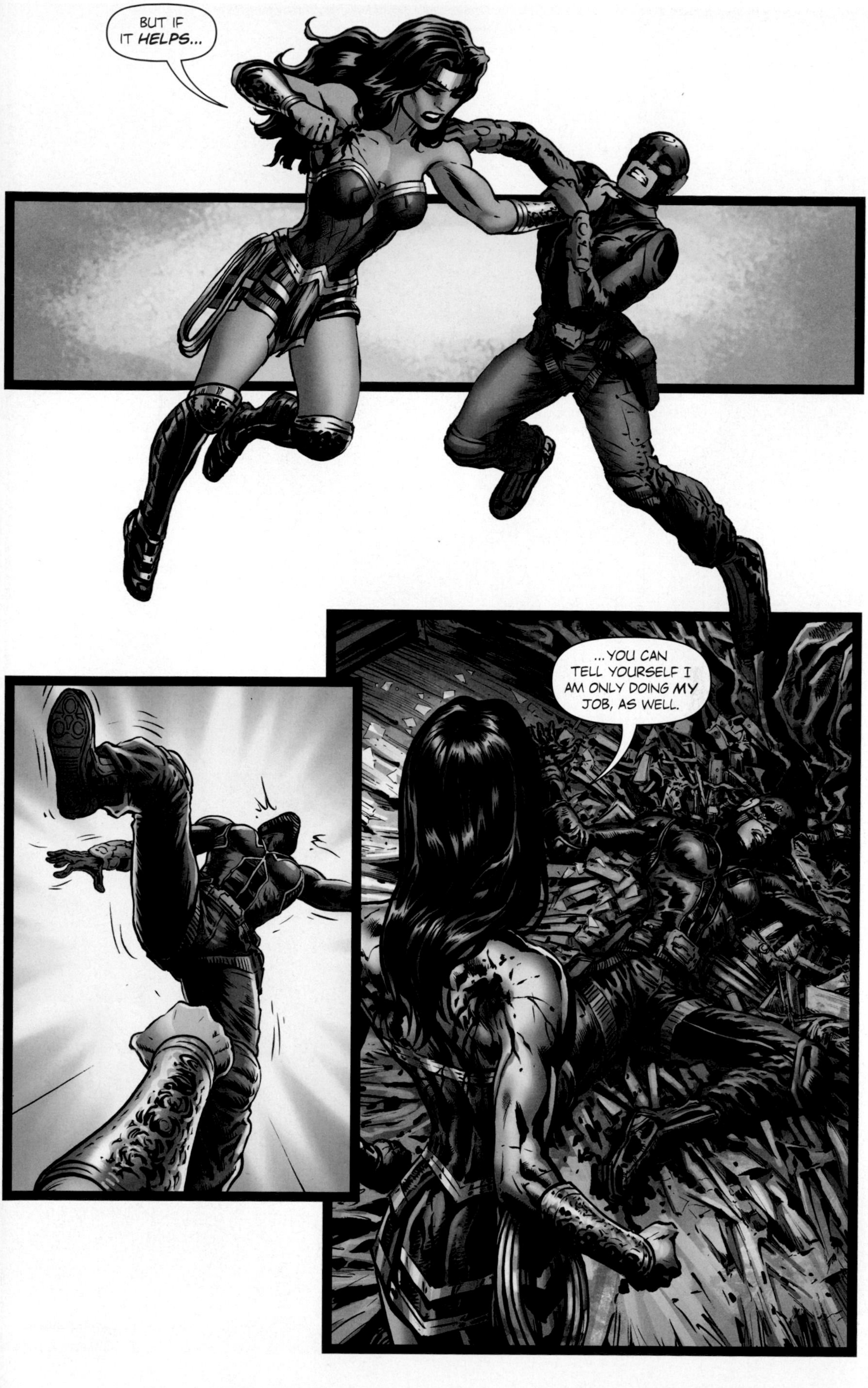
BUT IF IT HELPS...
...YOU CAN TELL YOURSELF I AM ONLY DOING MY JOB, AS WELL.

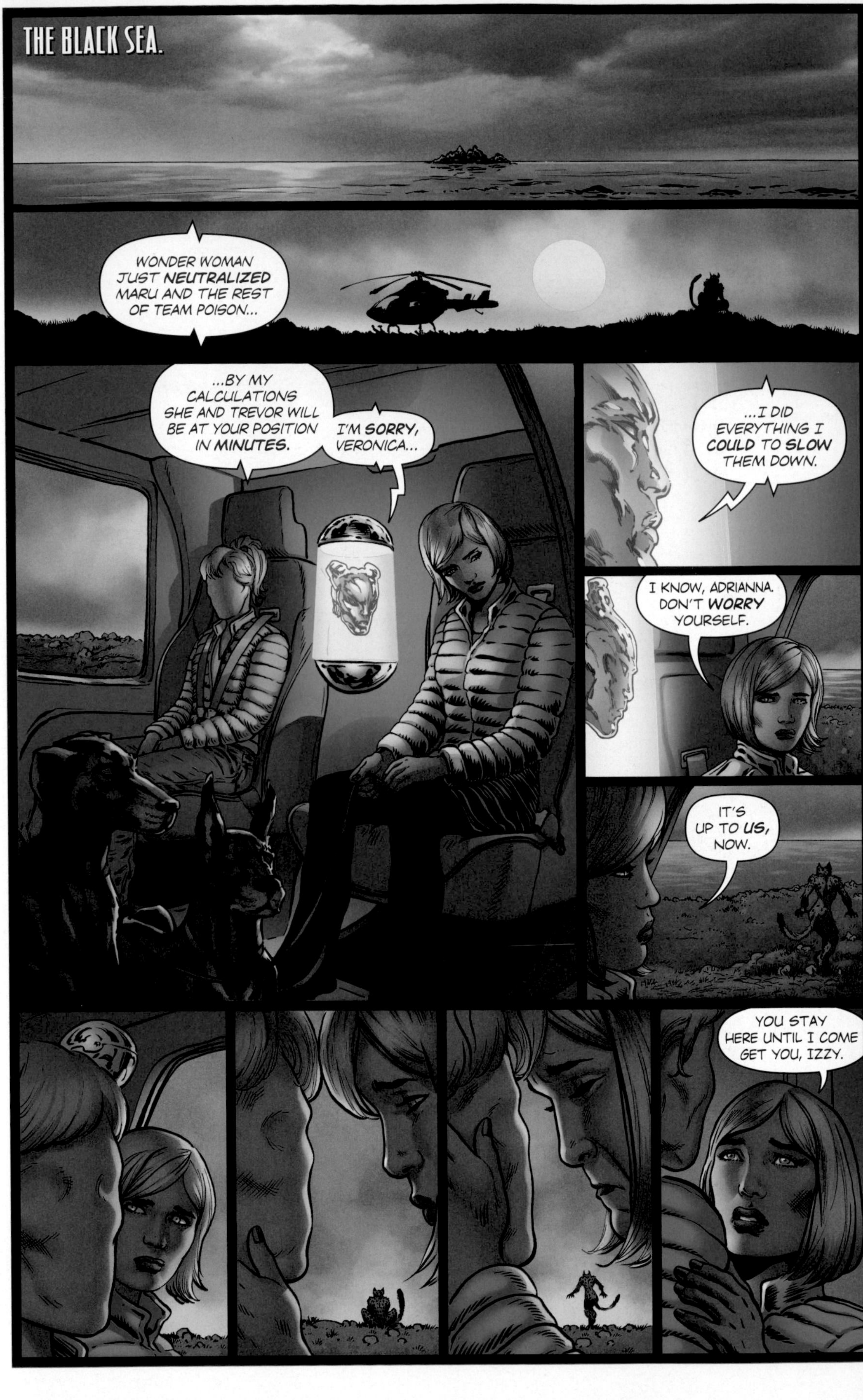
THE BLACK SEA.
WONDER WOMAN JUST NEUTRALIZED MARU AND THE REST OF TEAM POISON...
...BY MY CALCULATIONS SHE AND TREVOR WILL BE AT YOUR POSITION IN MINUTES.
I'M SORRY, VERONICA...
...I DID EVERYTHING I COULD TO SLOW THEM DOWN.
I KNOW, ADRIANNA. DON'T WORRY YOURSELF.
IT'S UP TO US, NOW.
YOU STAY HERE UNTIL I COME GET YOU, IZZY.

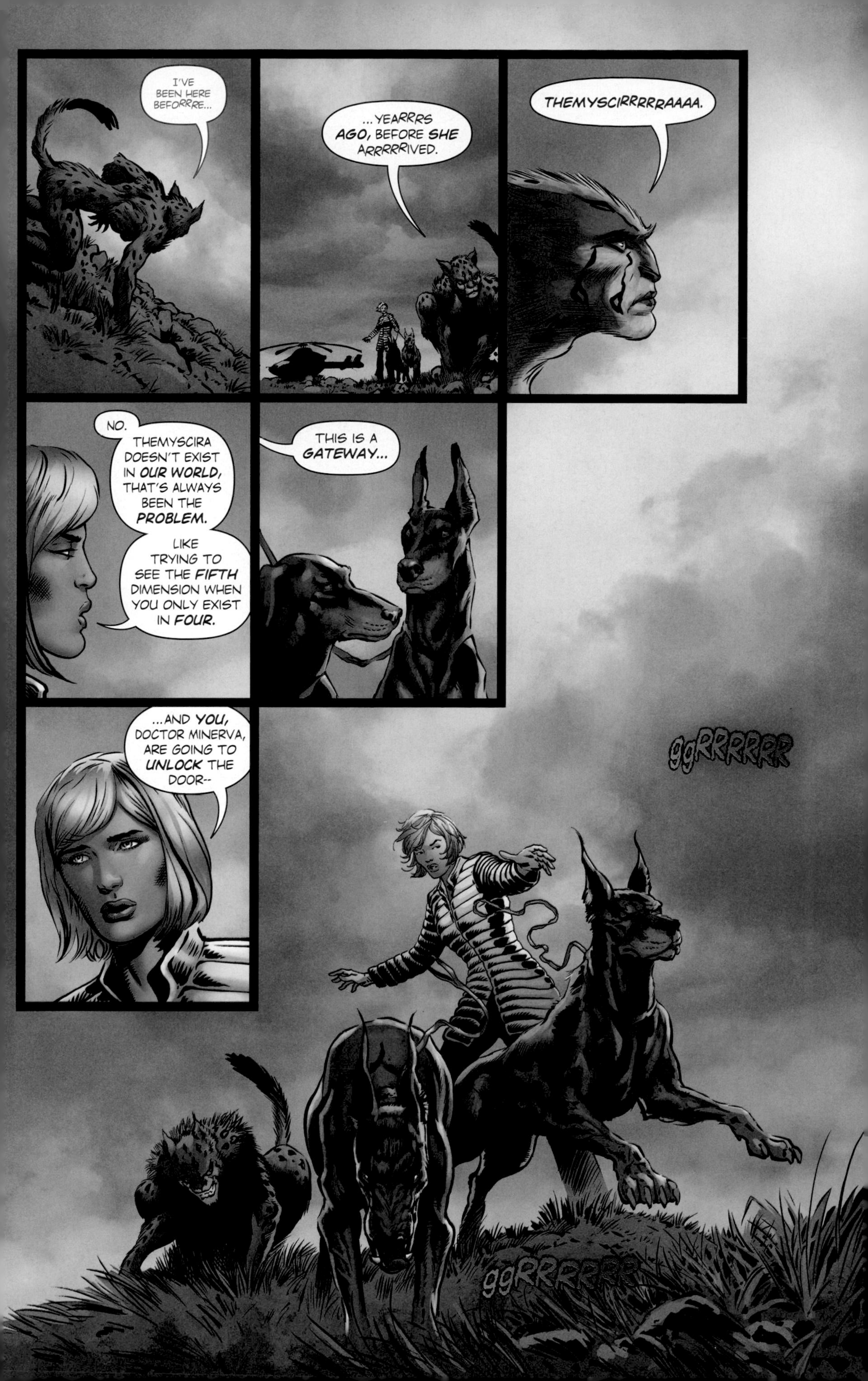
I'VE BEEN HERE BEFORRRE...
...YEARRRS AGO, BEFORE SHE ARRRRRIVED.
THEMYSCIRRRRRAAAA.
NO. THEMYSCIRA DOESN'T EXIST IN OUR WORLD, THAT'S ALWAYS BEEN THE PROBLEM.
LIKE TRYING TO SEE THE FIFTH DIMENSION WHEN YOU ONLY EXIST IN FOUR.
THIS IS A GATEWAY...
...AND YOU, DOCTOR MINERVA, ARE GOING TO UNLOCK THE DOOR--
ggRRRRRR
ggRRRRRR

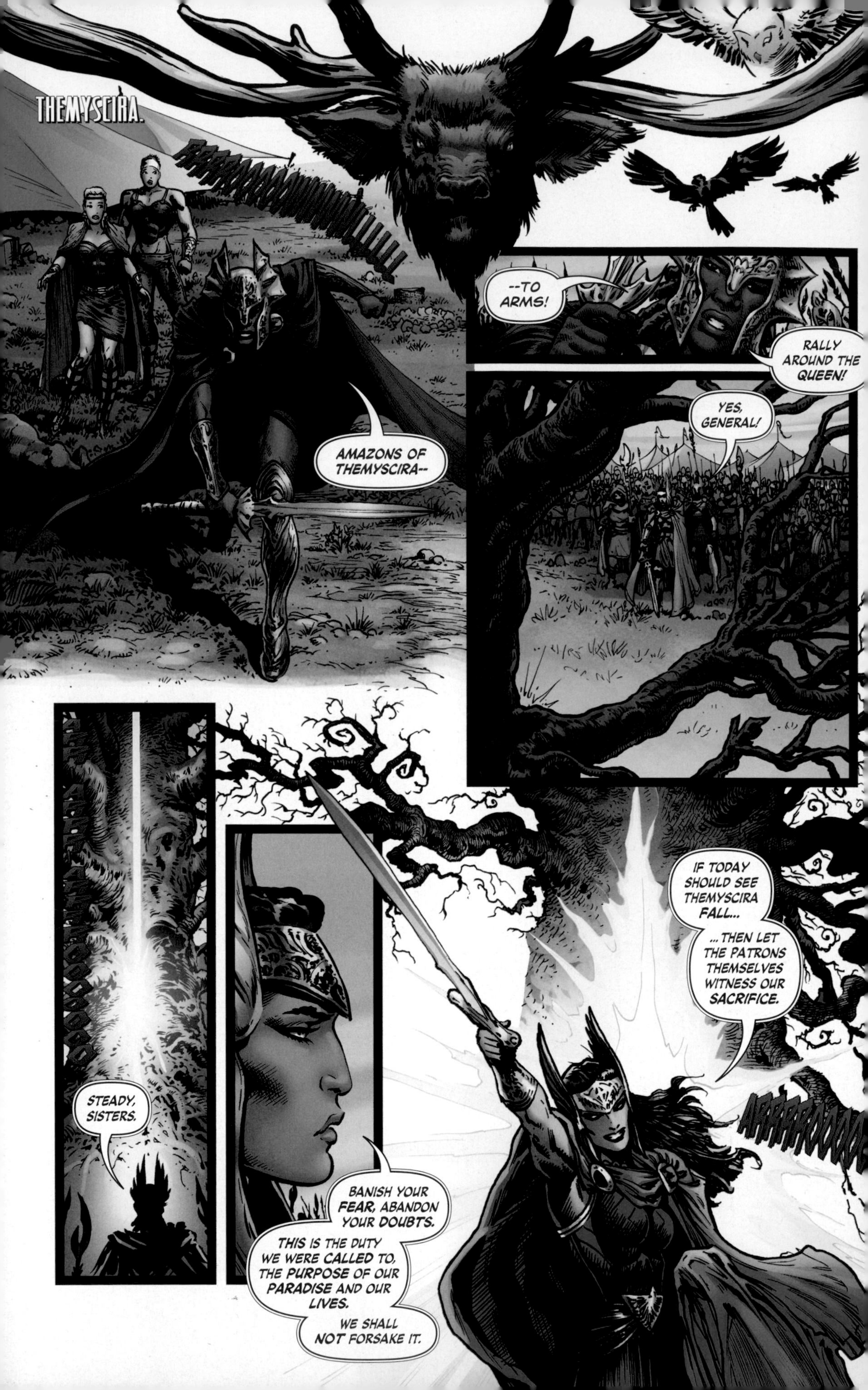
THEMYSCIRA.
AMAZONS OF THEMYSCIRA--
--TO ARMS!
RALLY AROUND THE QUEEN!
YES, GENERAL!
STEADY, SISTERS.
BANISH YOUR FEAR, ABANDON YOUR DOUBTS.
THIS IS THE DUTY WE WERE CALLED TO, THE PURPOSE OF OUR PARADISE AND OUR LIVES.
WE SHALL NOT FORSAKE IT.
IF TODAY SHOULD SEE THEMYSCIRA FALL...
...THEN LET THE PATRONS THEMSELVES WITNESS OUR SACRIFICE.

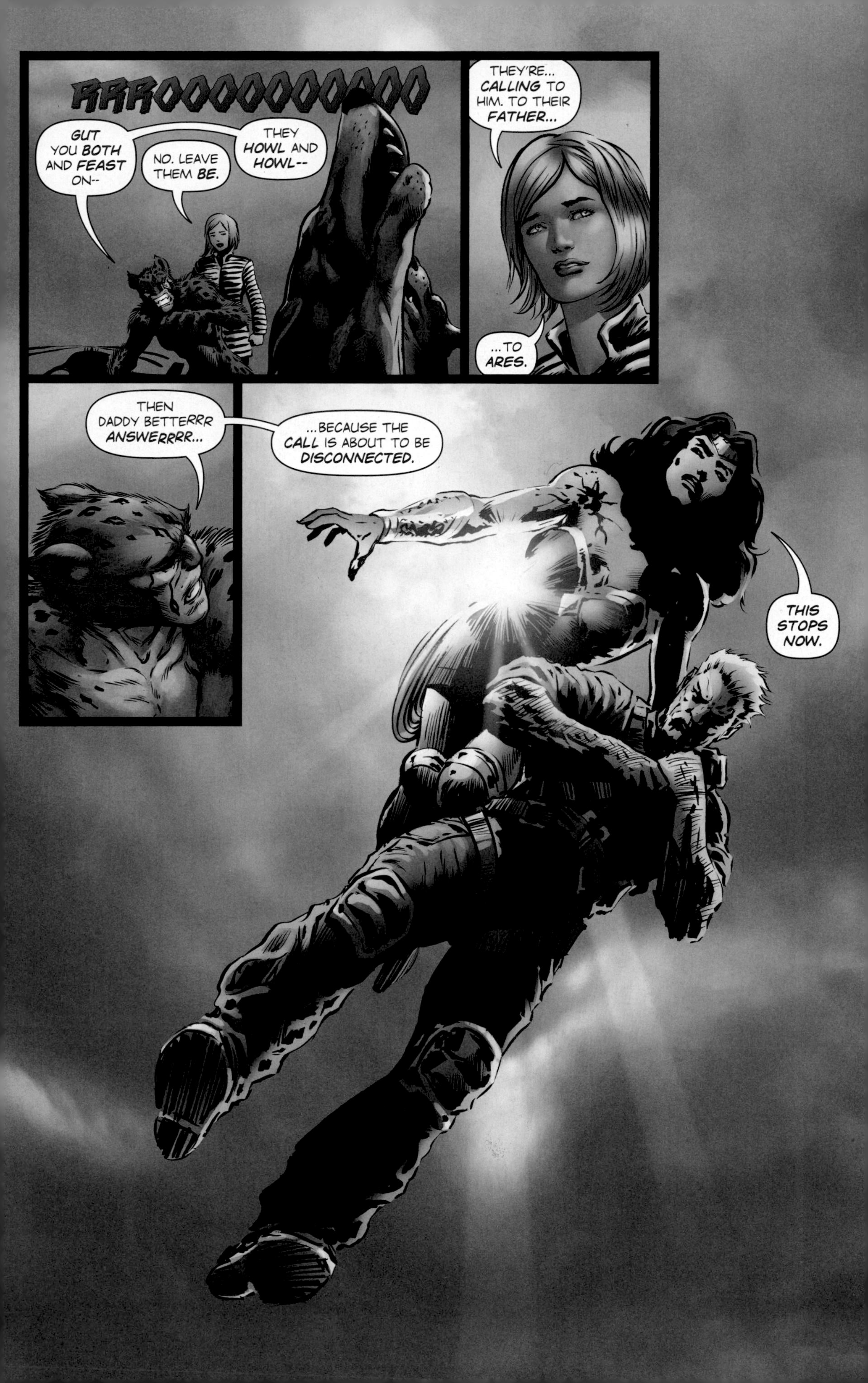
RRROOOOOOOOOOO
GUT YOU BOTH AND FEAST ON--
THEY HOWL AND HOWL--
NO. LEAVE THEM BE.
THEY'RE... CALLING TO HIM. TO THEIR FATHER...
...TO ARES.
THEN DADDY BETTERRR ANSWERRRR...
...BECAUSE THE CALL IS ABOUT TO BE DISCONNECTED.
THIS STOPS NOW.

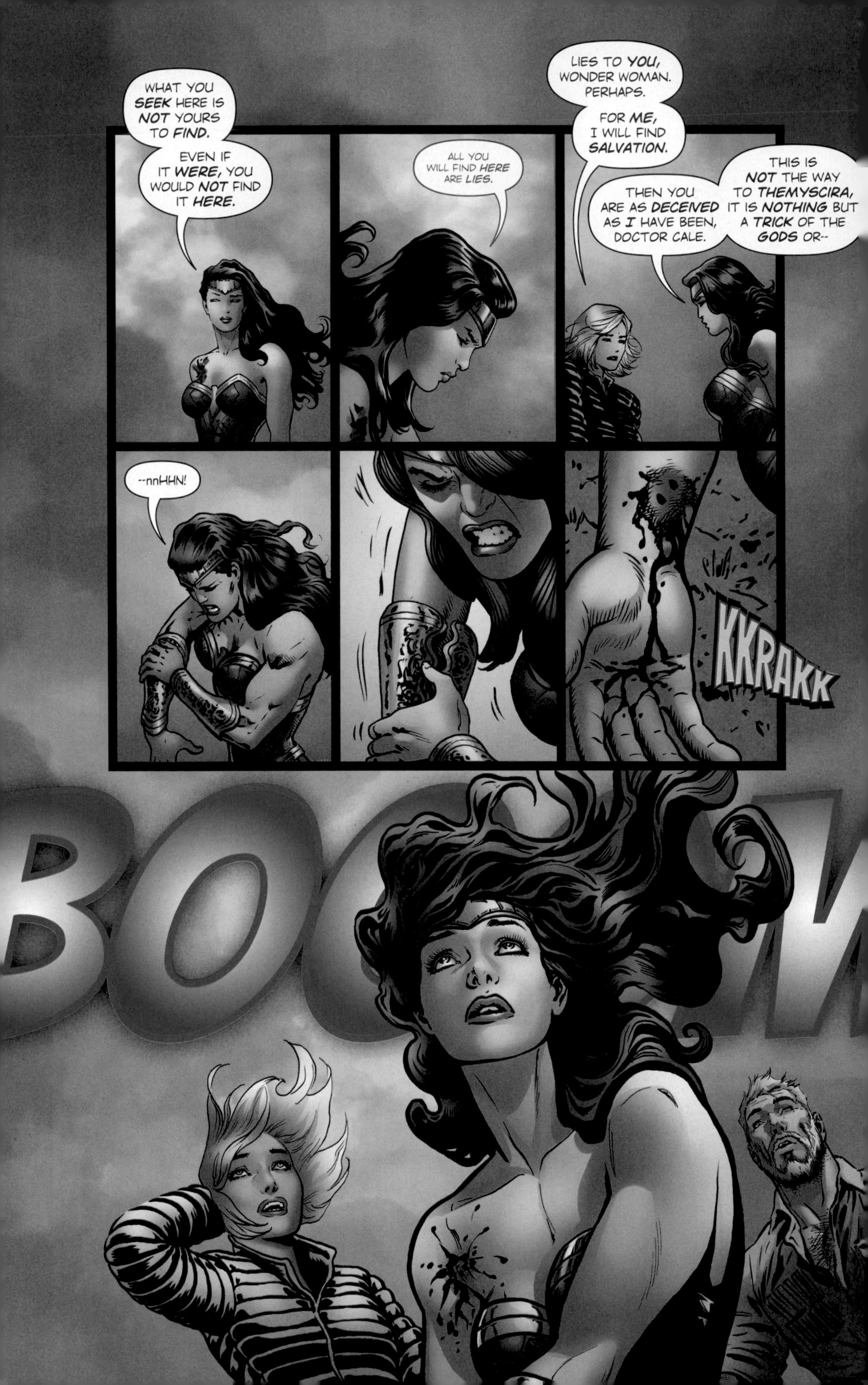
WHAT YOU SEEK HERE IS NOT YOURS TO FIND.
EVEN IF IT WERE, YOU WOULD NOT FIND IT HERE.
ALL YOU WILL FIND HERE ARE LIES.
LIES TO YOU, WONDER WOMAN. PERHAPS.
FOR ME, I WILL FIND SALVATION.
THEN YOU ARE AS DECEIVED AS I HAVE BEEN, DOCTOR CALE.
THIS IS NOT THE WAY TO THEMYSCIRA, IT IS NOTHING BUT A TRICK OF THE GODS OR--
--nnHHN!
KKRAKK
BOOM

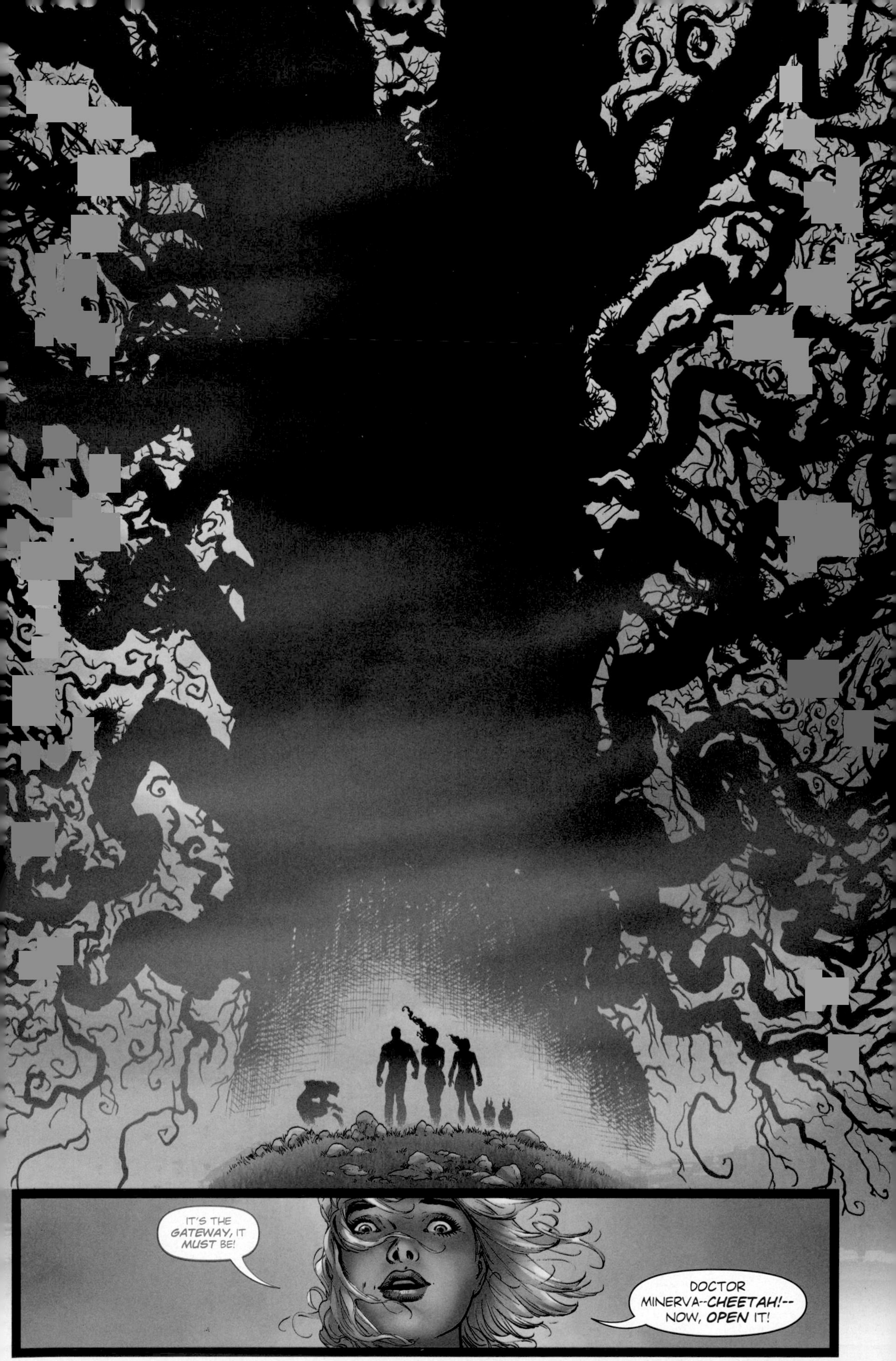
IT'S THE GATEWAY, IT MUST BE!
DOCTOR MINERVA--CHEETAH!-- NOW, OPEN IT!

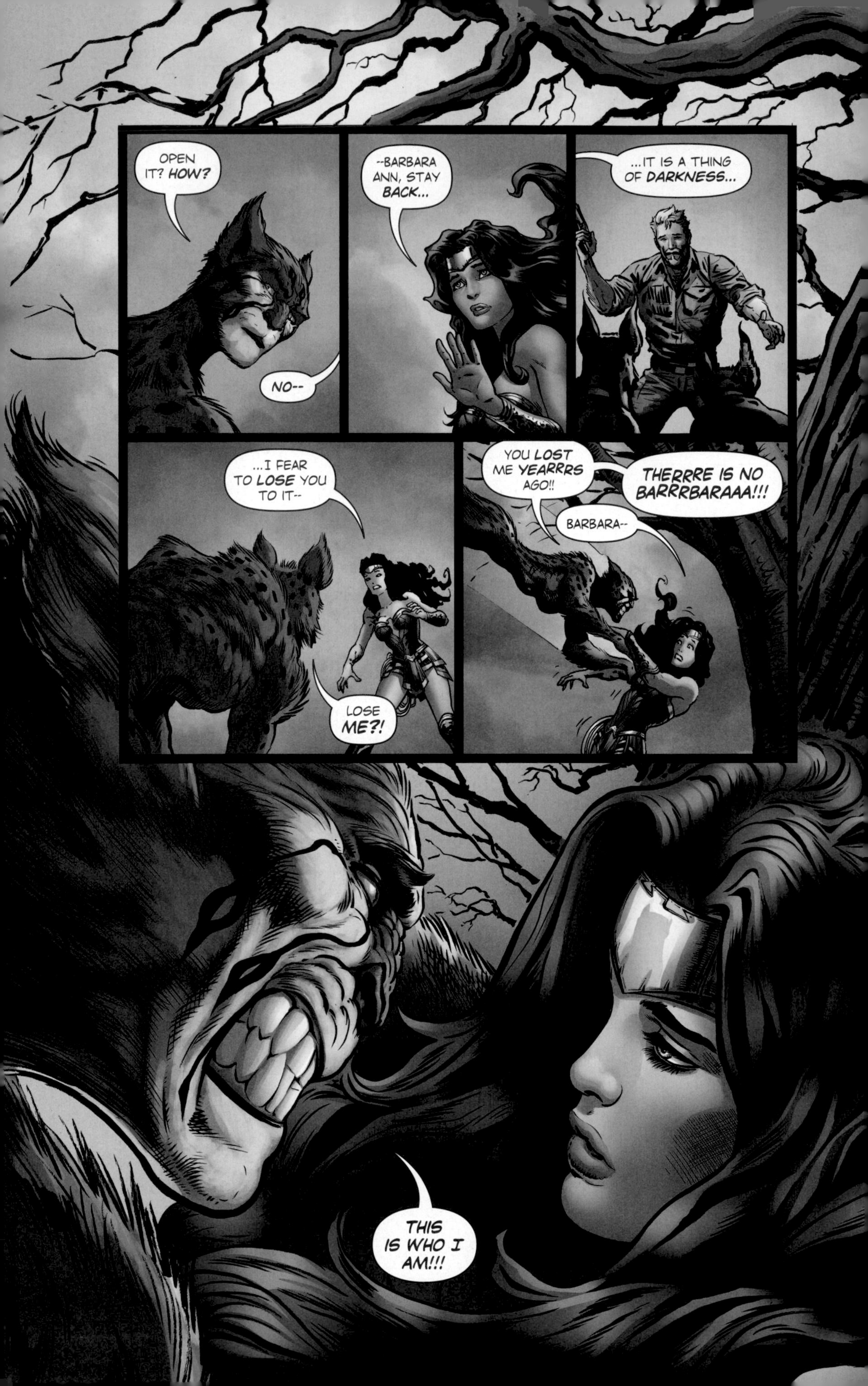

OPEN IT? HOW?
NO--
--BARBARA ANN, STAY BACK...
...IT IS A THING OF DARKNESS...
...I FEAR TO LOSE YOU TO IT--
LOSE ME?!
YOU LOST ME YEARRRS AGO!!
THERRRE IS NO BARRRBARAAA!!!
BARBARA--
THIS IS WHO I AM!!!

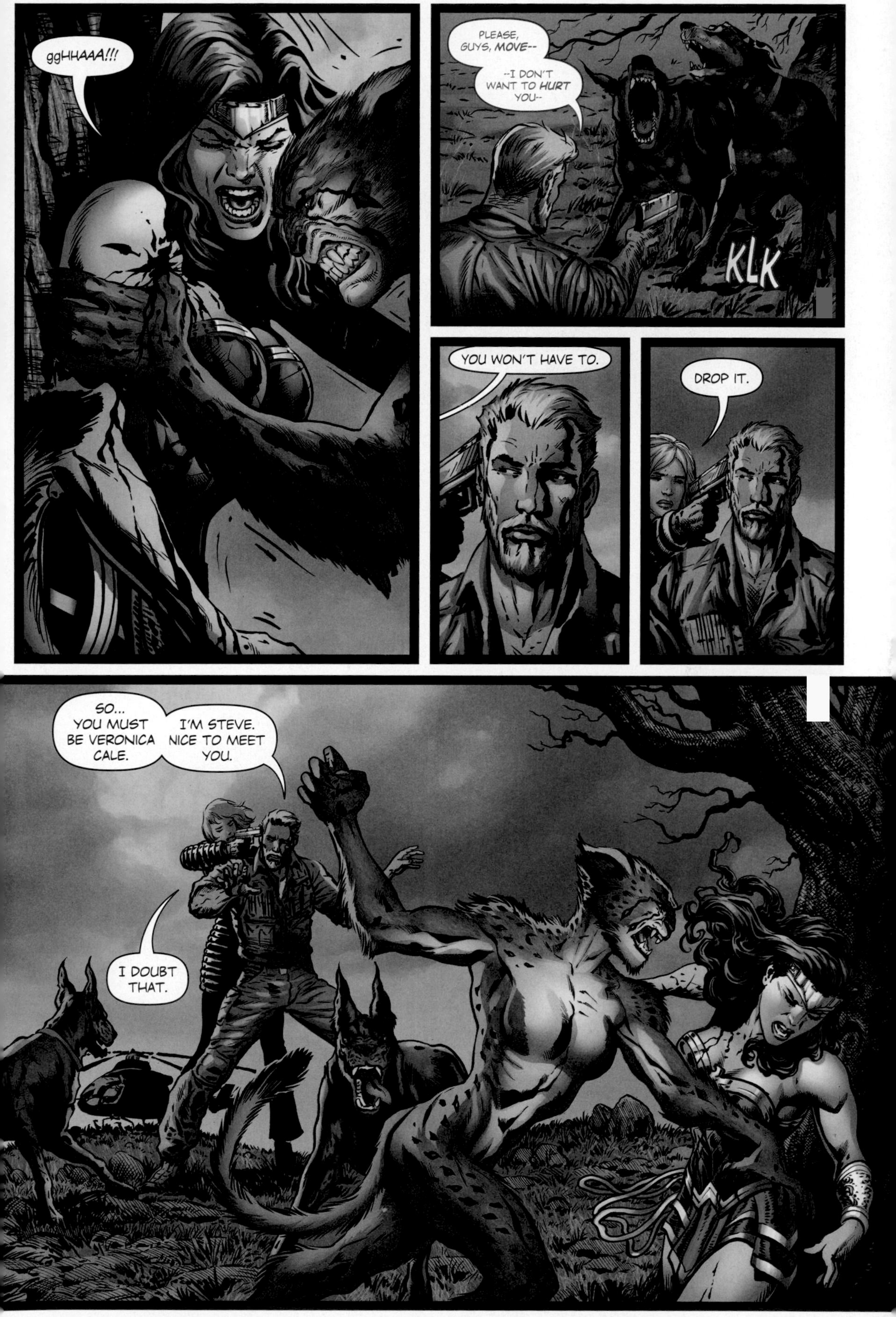
ggHHAAA!!!
PLEASE, GUYS, MOVE--
--I DON'T WANT TO HURT YOU--
KLK
YOU WON'T HAVE TO.
DROP IT.
SO... YOU MUST BE VERONICA CALE.
I'M STEVE. NICE TO MEET YOU.
I DOUBT THAT.

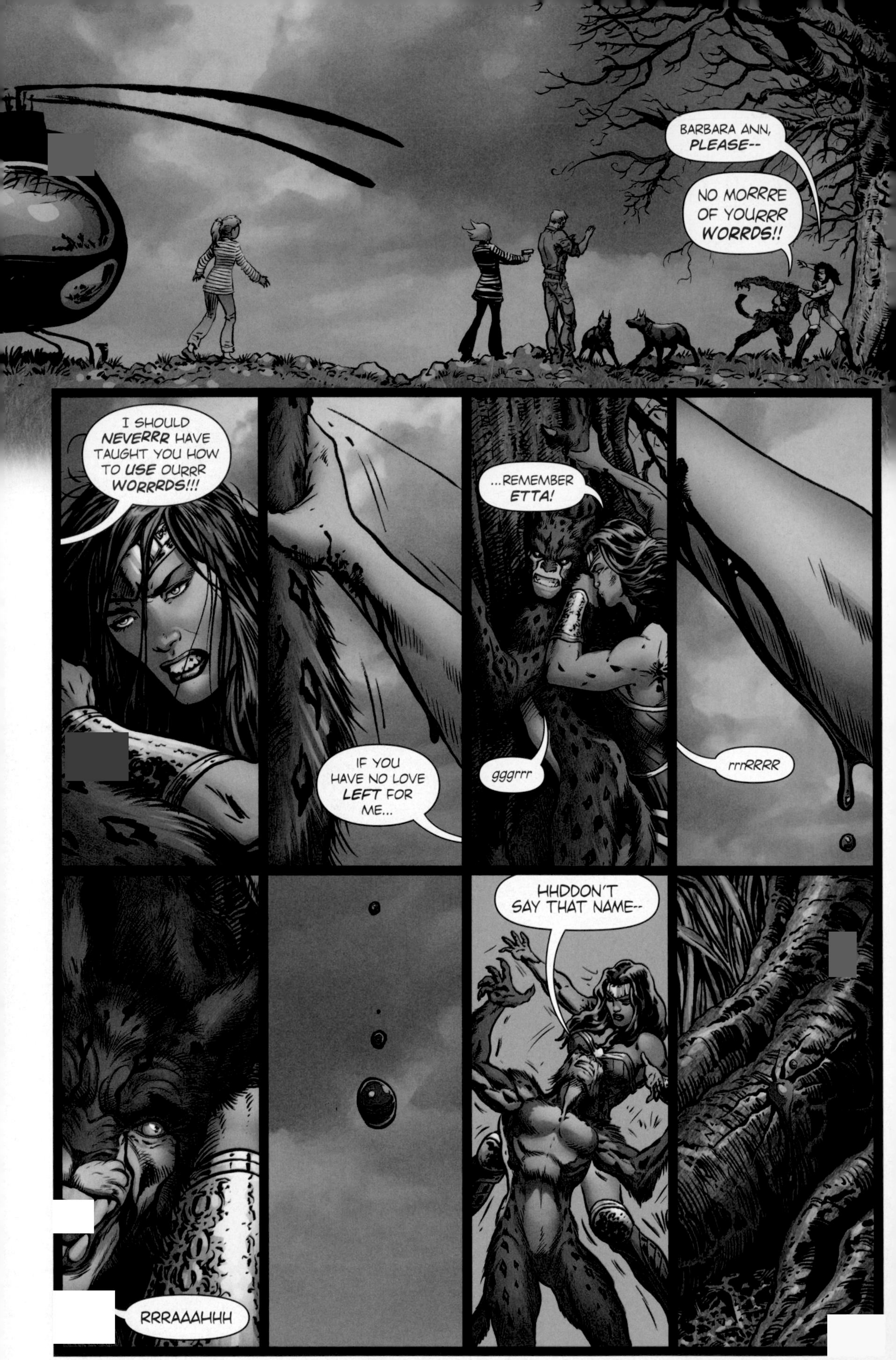
BARBARA ANN, PLEASE--
NO MORRRE OF YOURRR WORRDS!!
I SHOULD NEVERRR HAVE TAUGHT YOU HOW TO USE OURRR WORRRDS!!!
IF YOU HAVE NO LOVE LEFT FOR ME...
...REMEMBER ETTA!
gggrrr
rrrRRRR
RRRAAAHHH
HHDDON'T SAY THAT NAME--

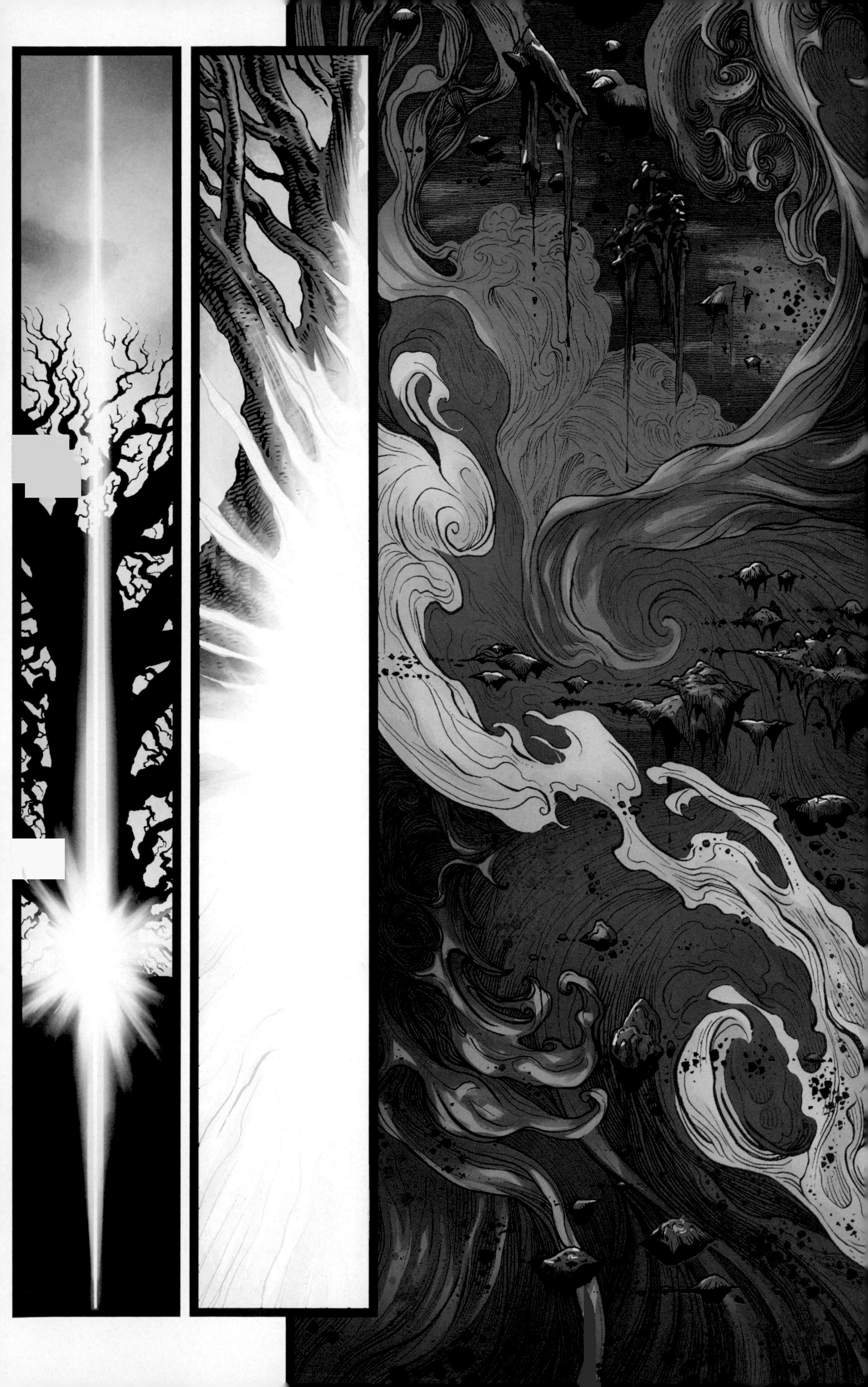

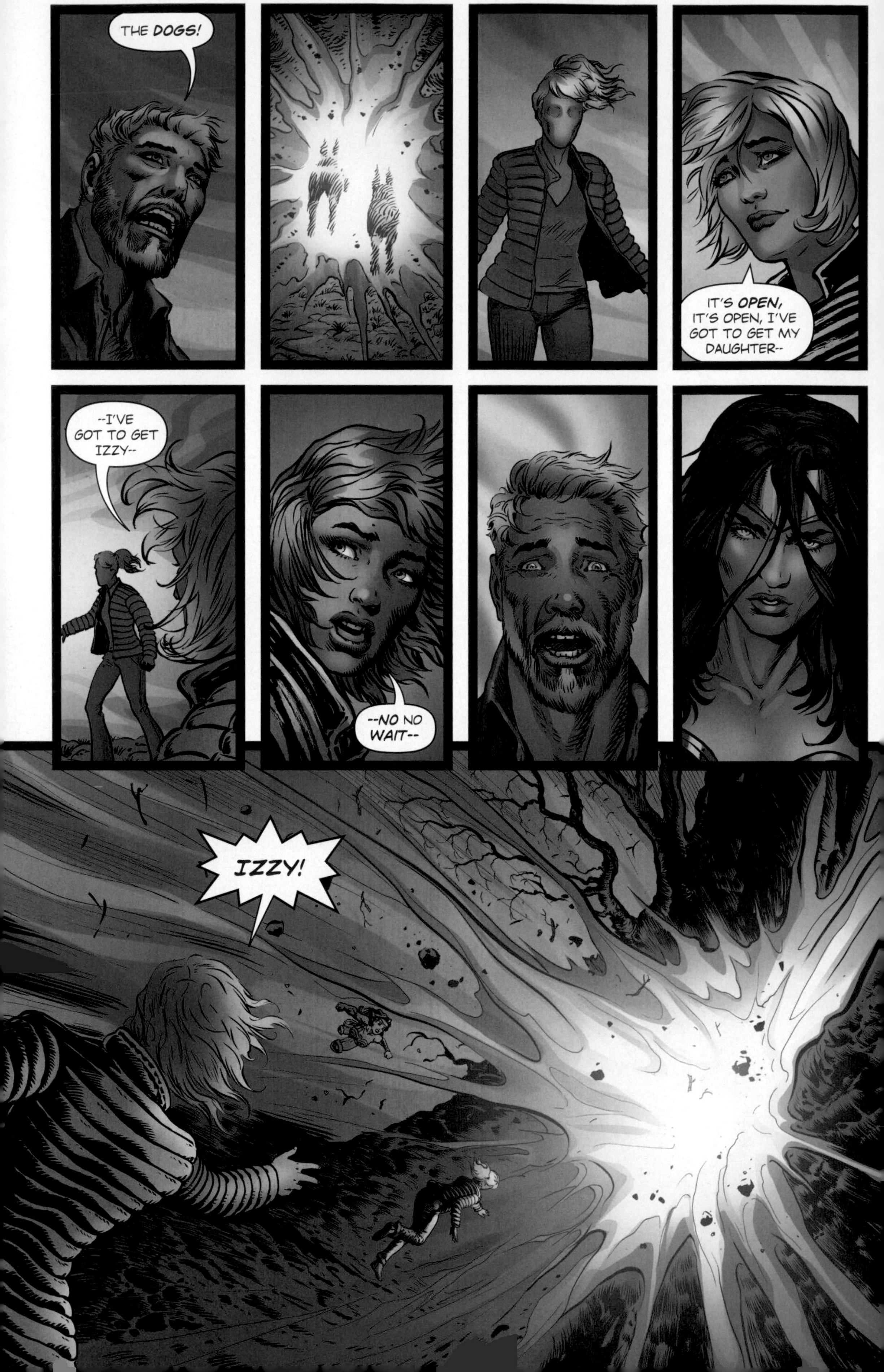
THE DOGS!
IT'S OPEN, IT'S OPEN, I'VE GOT TO GET MY DAUGHTER--
--I'VE GOT TO GET IZZY--
--NO NO WAIT--
IZZY!

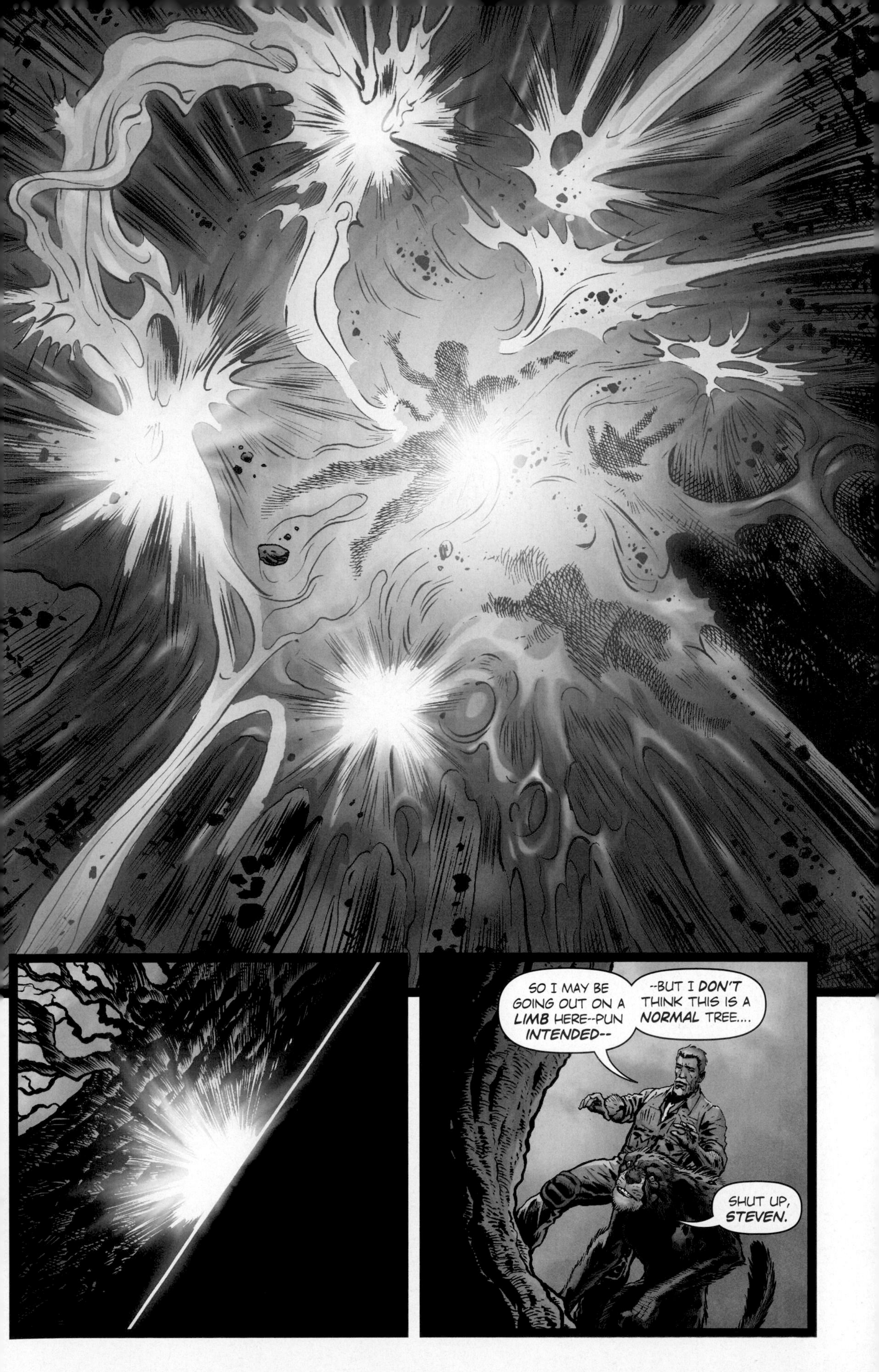
SO I MAY BE GOING OUT ON A LIMB HERE--PUN INTENDED--
--BUT I DON'T THINK THIS IS A NORMAL TREE....
SHUT UP, STEVEN.

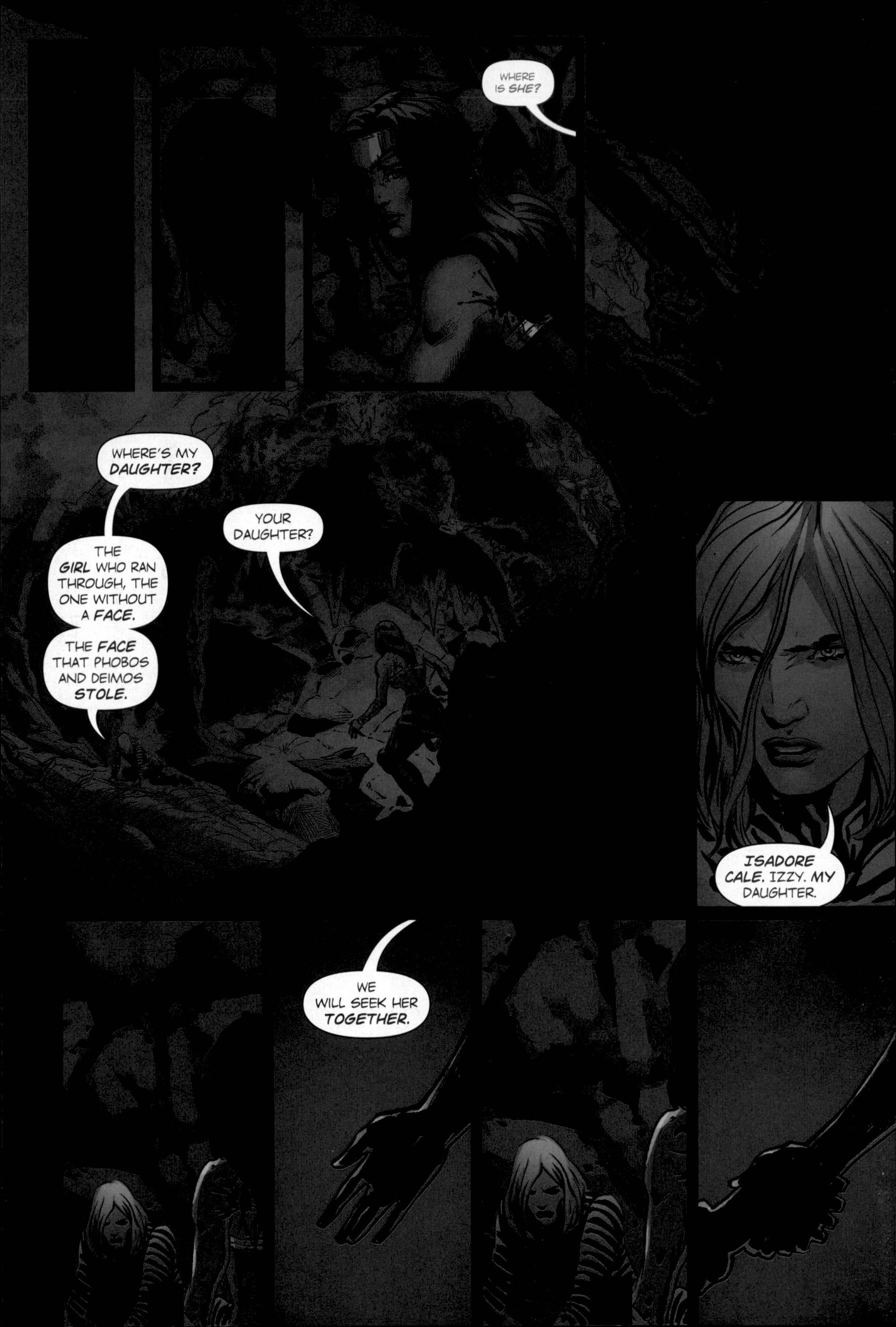
WHERE IS SHE?
WHERE'S MY DAUGHTER?
YOUR DAUGHTER?
THE GIRL WHO RAN THROUGH, THE ONE WITHOUT A FACE.
THE FACE THAT PHOBOS AND DEIMOS STOLE.
ISADORE CALE. IZZY. MY DAUGHTER.
WE WILL SEEK HER TOGETHER.

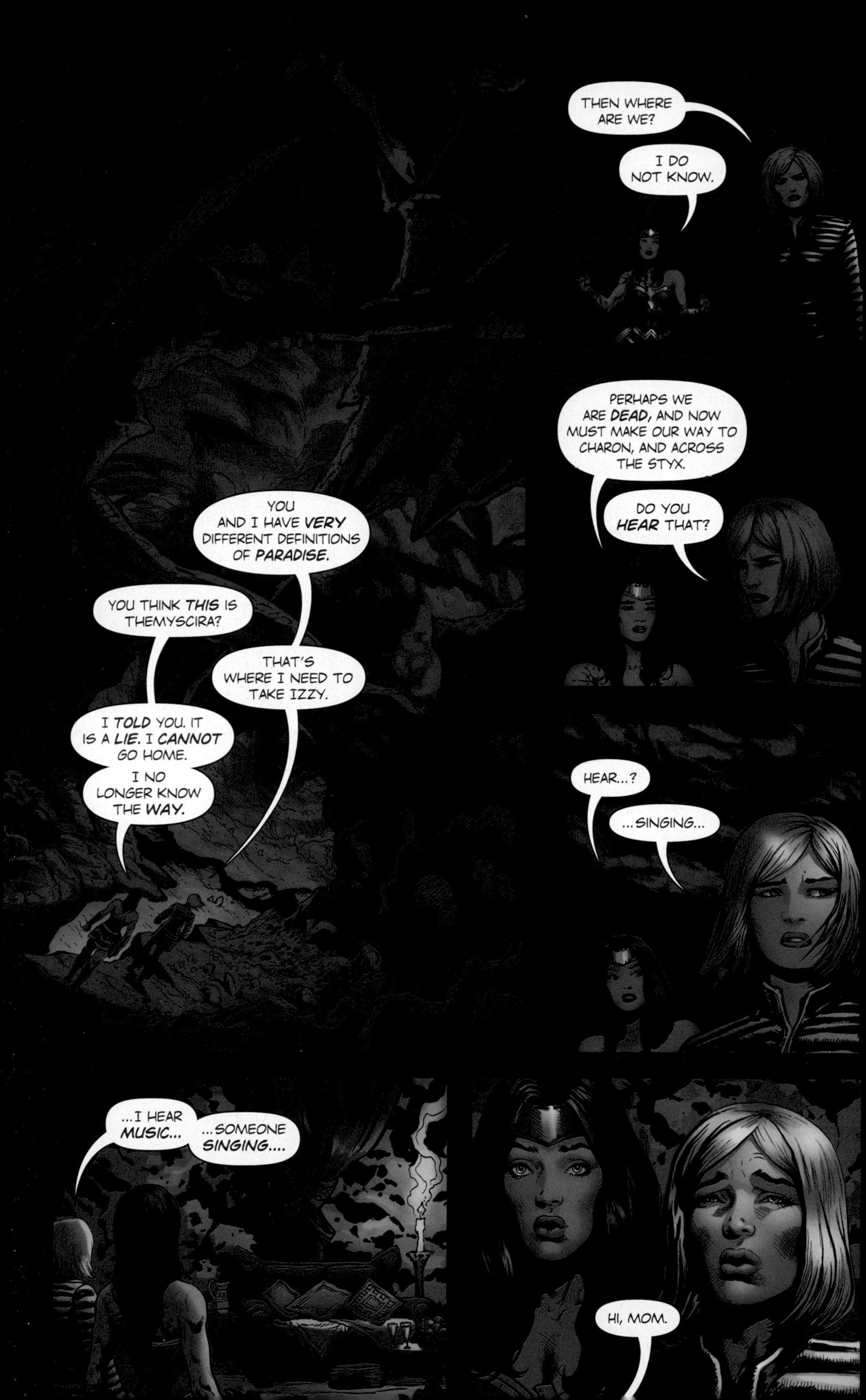

YOU AND I HAVE **VERY** DIFFERENT DEFINITIONS OF **PARADISE.**
YOU THINK **THIS** IS THEMYSCIRA?
THAT'S WHERE I NEED TO TAKE IZZY.
I **TOLD** YOU. IT IS A **LIE.** I **CANNOT** GO HOME.
I NO LONGER KNOW THE **WAY.**
THEN WHERE ARE WE?
I DO NOT KNOW.
PERHAPS WE ARE **DEAD,** AND NOW MUST MAKE OUR WAY TO CHARON, AND ACROSS THE STYX.
DO YOU **HEAR** THAT?
HEAR...?
...SINGING...
...I HEAR **MUSIC...**
...SOMEONE **SINGING....**
HI, MOM.

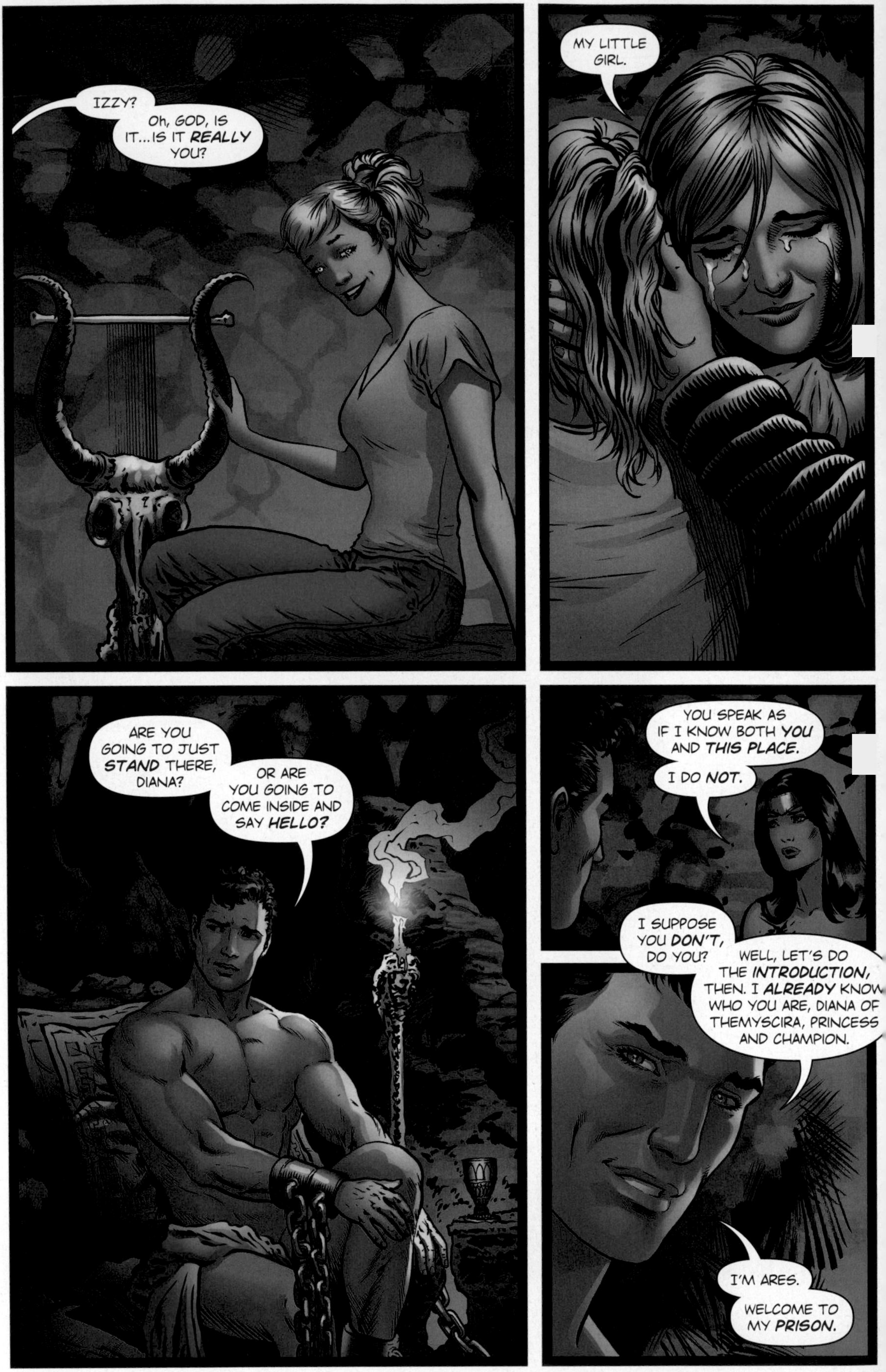
IZZY?
Oh, GOD, IS IT...IS IT REALLY YOU?
MY LITTLE GIRL.
ARE YOU GOING TO JUST STAND THERE, DIANA?
OR ARE YOU GOING TO COME INSIDE AND SAY HELLO?
YOU SPEAK AS IF I KNOW BOTH YOU AND THIS PLACE.
I DO NOT.
I SUPPOSE YOU DON'T, DO YOU?
WELL, LET'S DO THE INTRODUCTION, THEN. I ALREADY KNOW WHO YOU ARE, DIANA OF THEMYSCIRA, PRINCESS AND CHAMPION.
I'M ARES.
WELCOME TO MY PRISON.

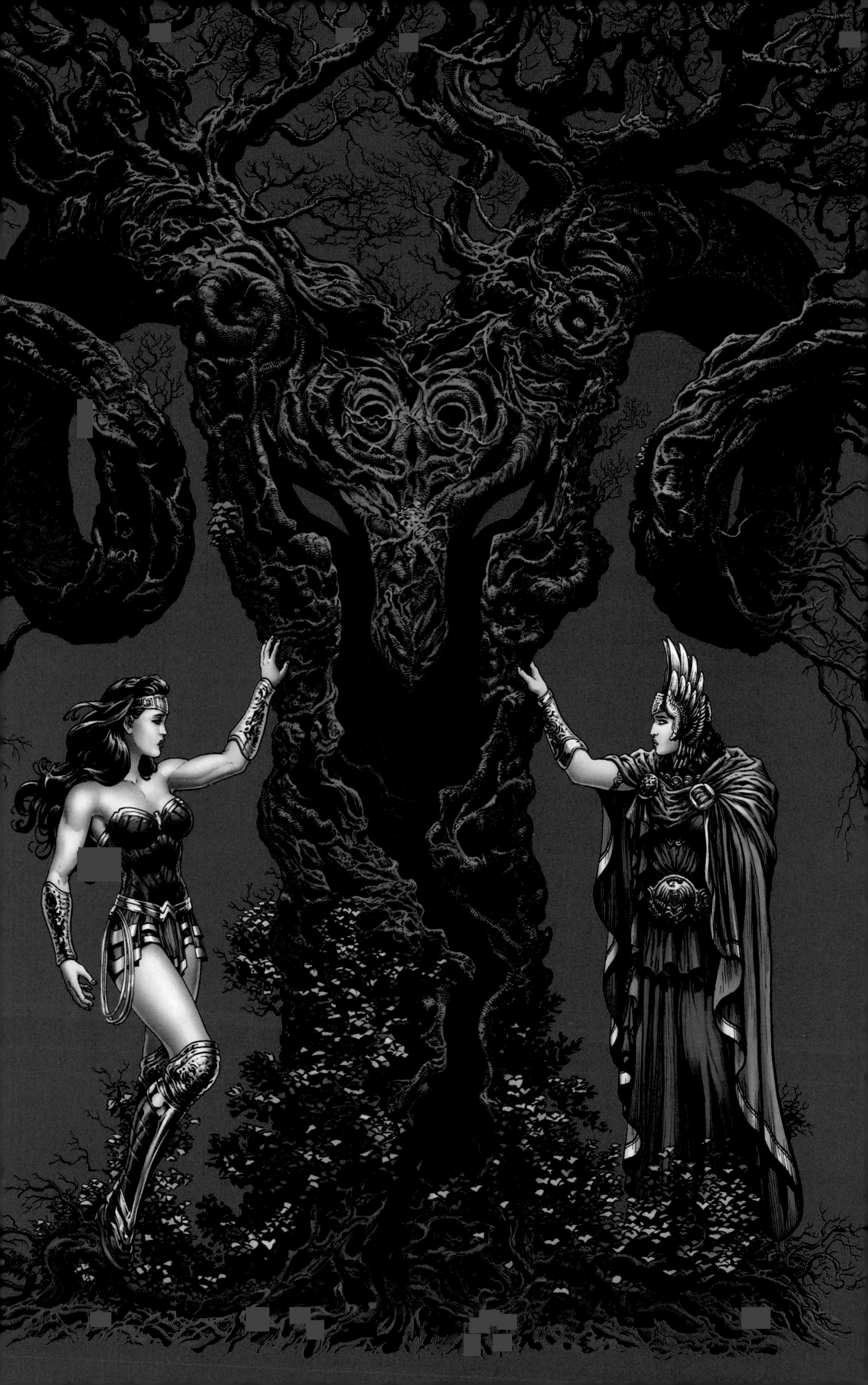

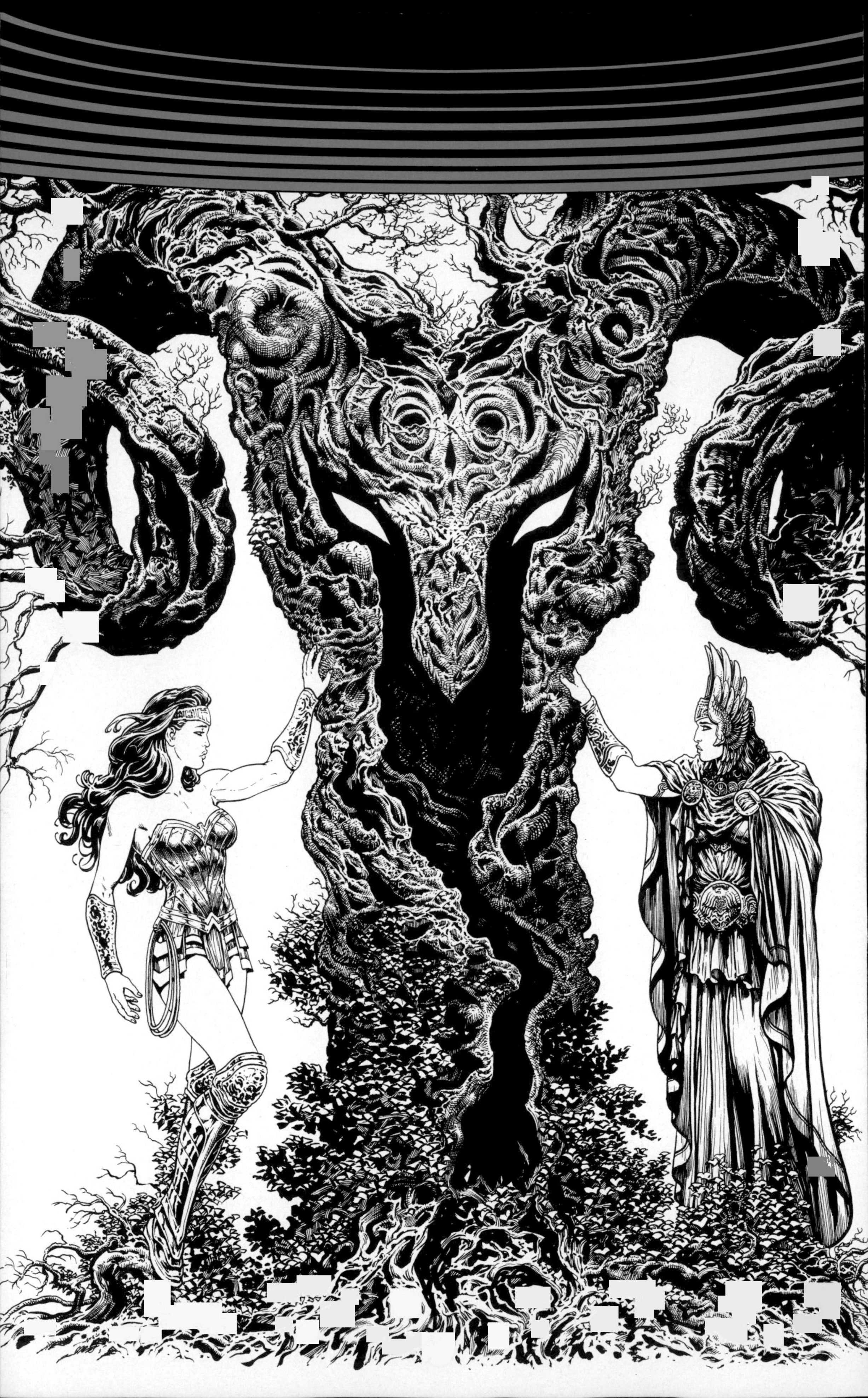

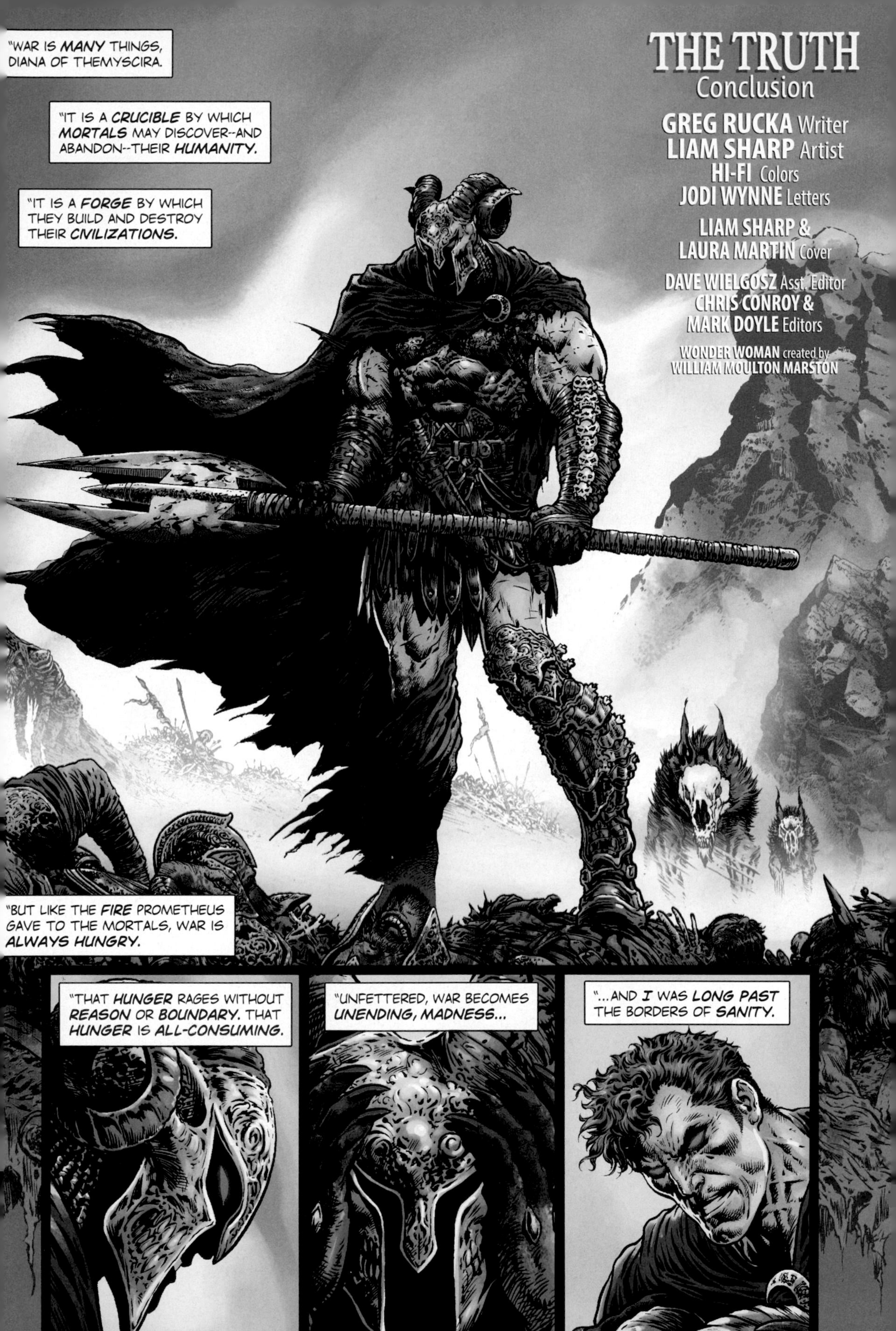
"WAR IS MANY THINGS, DIANA OF THEMYSCIRA.
THE TRUTH
Conclusion
GREG RUCKA Writer
LIAM SHARP Artist
HI-FI Colors
JODI WYNNE Letters
LIAM SHARP & LAURA MARTIN Cover
DAVE WIELGOSZ Asst. Editor
CHRIS CONROY & MARK DOYLE Editors
WONDER WOMAN created by WILLIAM MOULTON MARSTON
"IT IS A CRUCIBLE BY WHICH MORTALS MAY DISCOVER--AND ABANDON--THEIR HUMANITY.
"IT IS A FORGE BY WHICH THEY BUILD AND DESTROY THEIR CIVILIZATIONS.
"BUT LIKE THE FIRE PROMETHEUS GAVE TO THE MORTALS, WAR IS ALWAYS HUNGRY.
"THAT HUNGER RAGES WITHOUT REASON OR BOUNDARY. THAT HUNGER IS ALL-CONSUMING.
"UNFETTERED, WAR BECOMES UNENDING, MADNESS...
"...AND I WAS LONG PAST THE BORDERS OF SANITY.

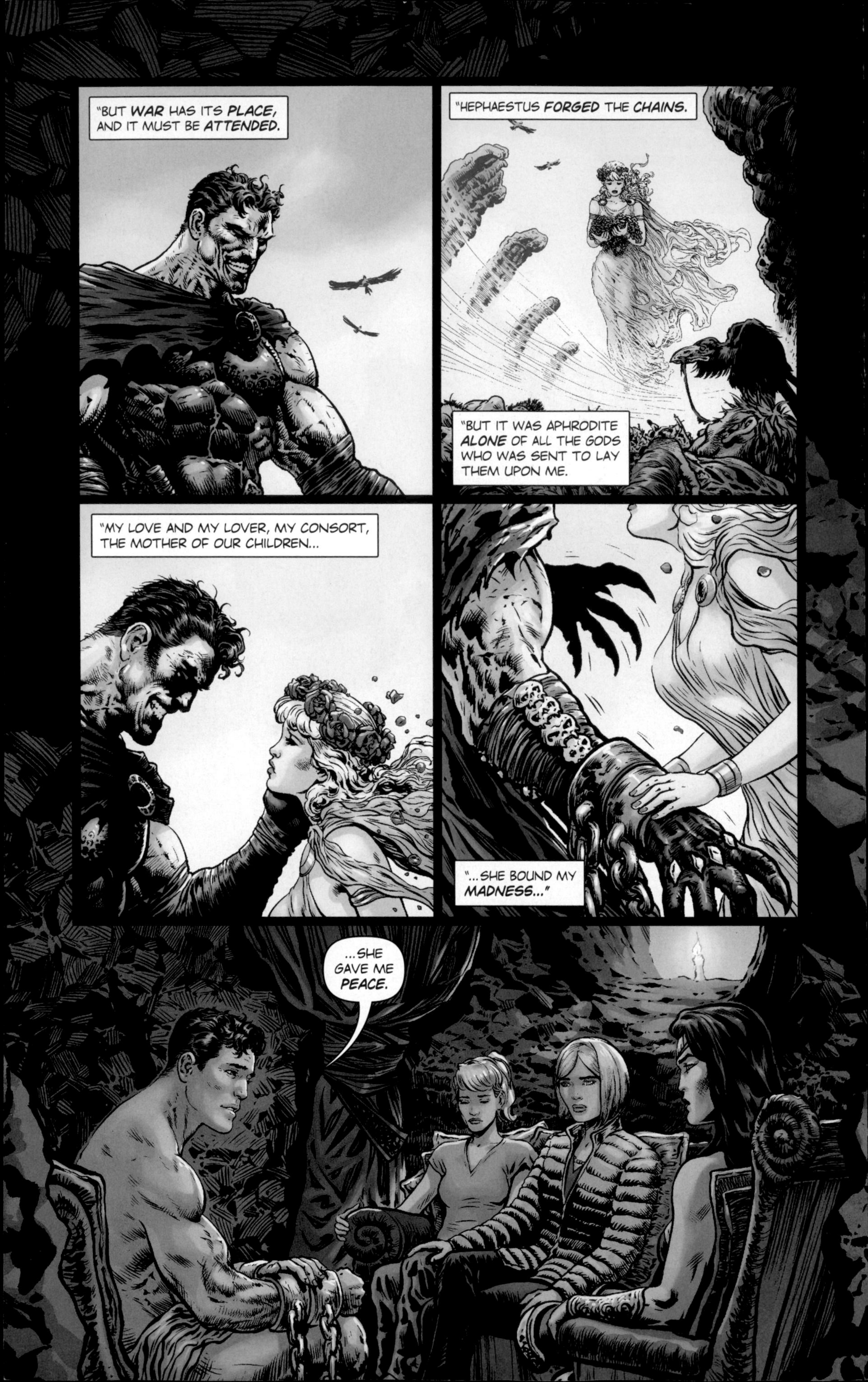
"BUT WAR HAS ITS PLACE, AND IT MUST BE ATTENDED.
"HEPHAESTUS FORGED THE CHAINS.
"BUT IT WAS APHRODITE ALONE OF ALL THE GODS WHO WAS SENT TO LAY THEM UPON ME.
"MY LOVE AND MY LOVER, MY CONSORT, THE MOTHER OF OUR CHILDREN...
"...SHE BOUND MY MADNESS..."
...SHE GAVE ME PEACE.

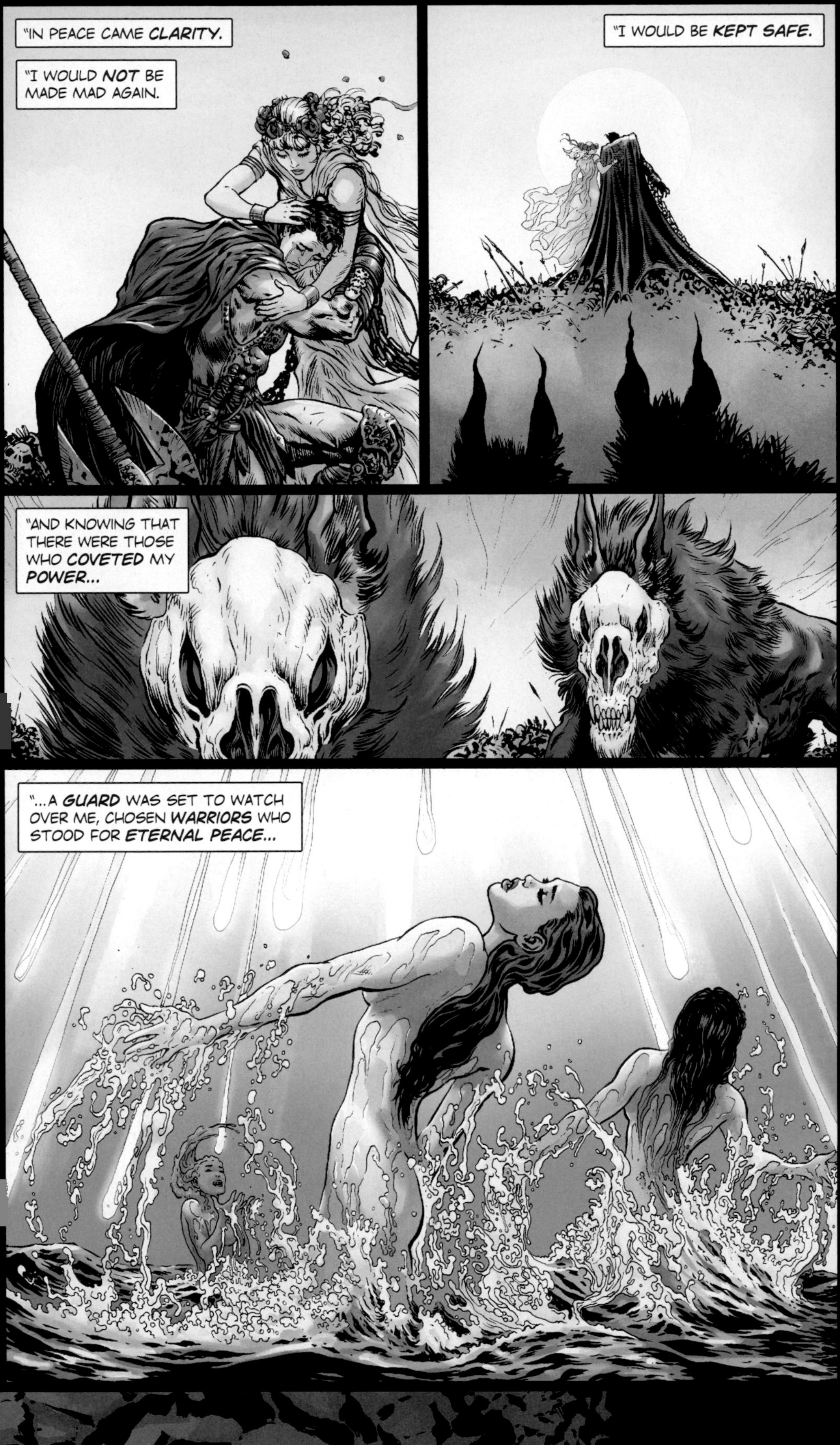
"IN PEACE CAME CLARITY.
"I WOULD NOT BE MADE MAD AGAIN.
"I WOULD BE KEPT SAFE.
"AND KNOWING THAT THERE WERE THOSE WHO COVETED MY POWER...
"...A GUARD WAS SET TO WATCH OVER ME, CHOSEN WARRIORS WHO STOOD FOR ETERNAL PEACE...

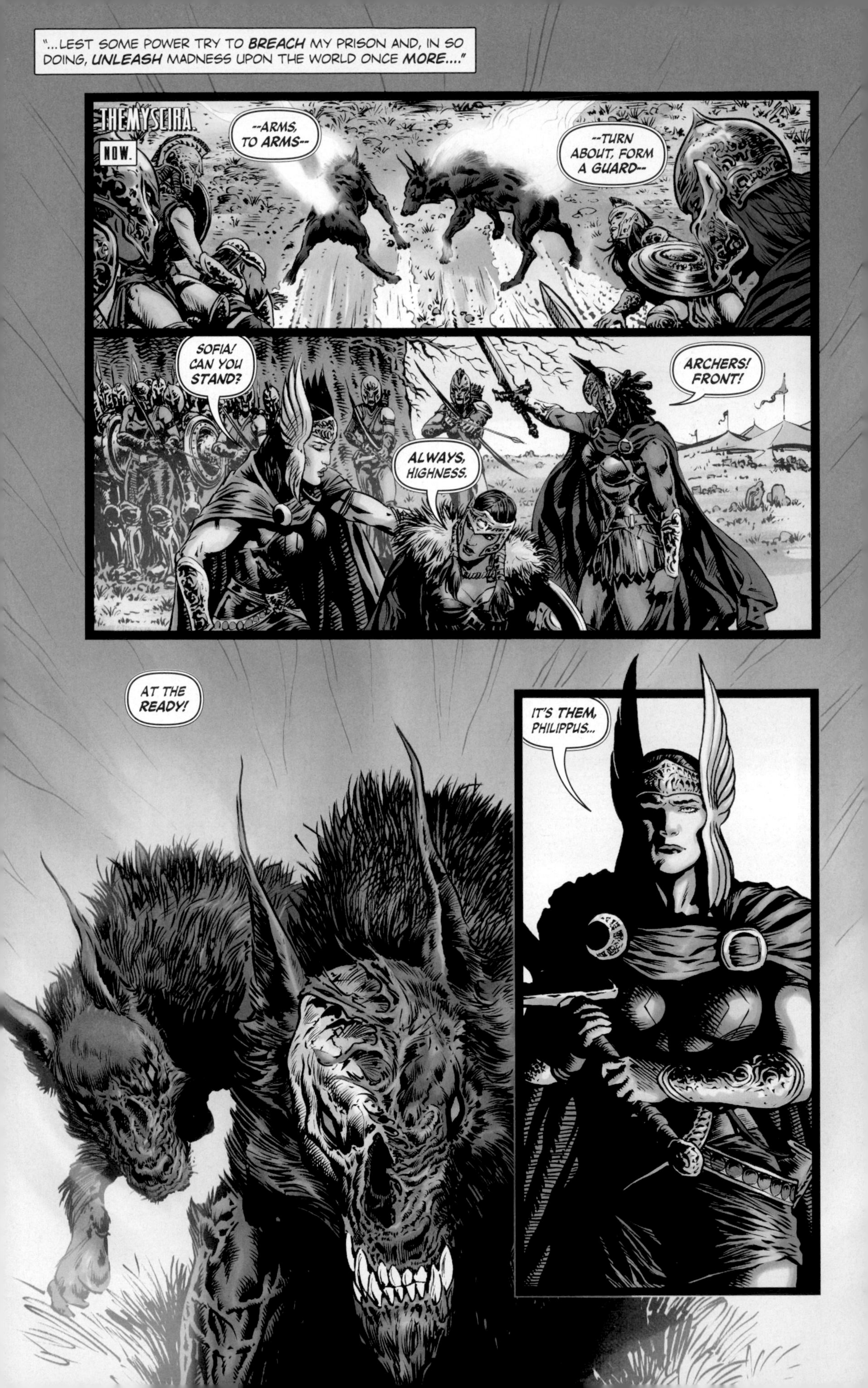
"...LEST SOME POWER TRY TO BREACH MY PRISON AND, IN SO DOING, UNLEASH MADNESS UPON THE WORLD ONCE MORE...."
THEMYSCIRA.
NOW.
--ARMS, TO ARMS--
--TURN ABOUT, FORM A GUARD--
SOFIA! CAN YOU STAND?
ALWAYS, HIGHNESS.
ARCHERS! FRONT!
AT THE READY!
IT'S THEM, PHILIPPUS...

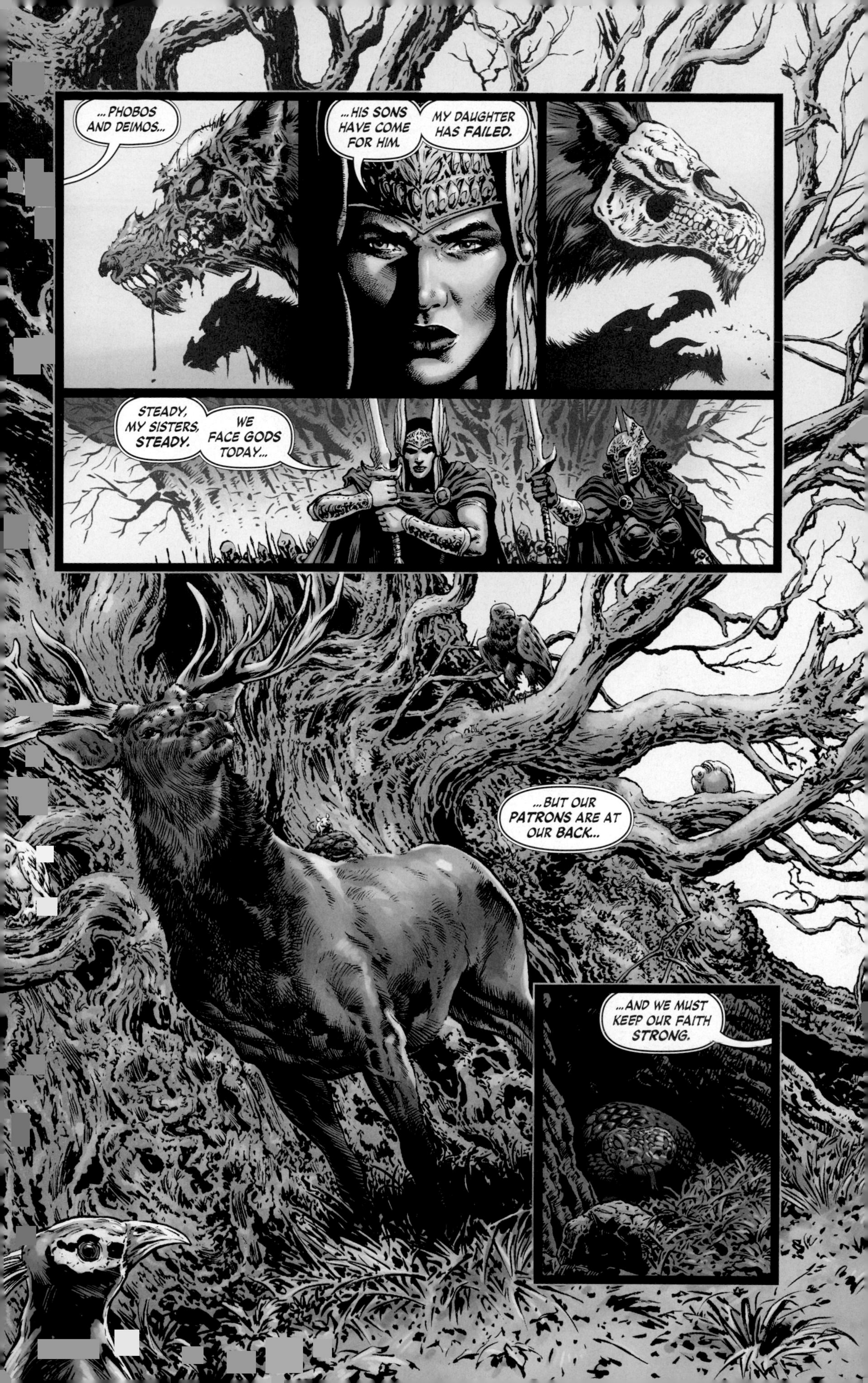
...PHOBOS AND DEIMOS...
...HIS SONS HAVE COME FOR HIM.
MY DAUGHTER HAS FAILED.
STEADY, MY SISTERS, STEADY.
WE FACE GODS TODAY...
...BUT OUR PATRONS ARE AT OUR BACK...
...AND WE MUST KEEP OUR FAITH STRONG.

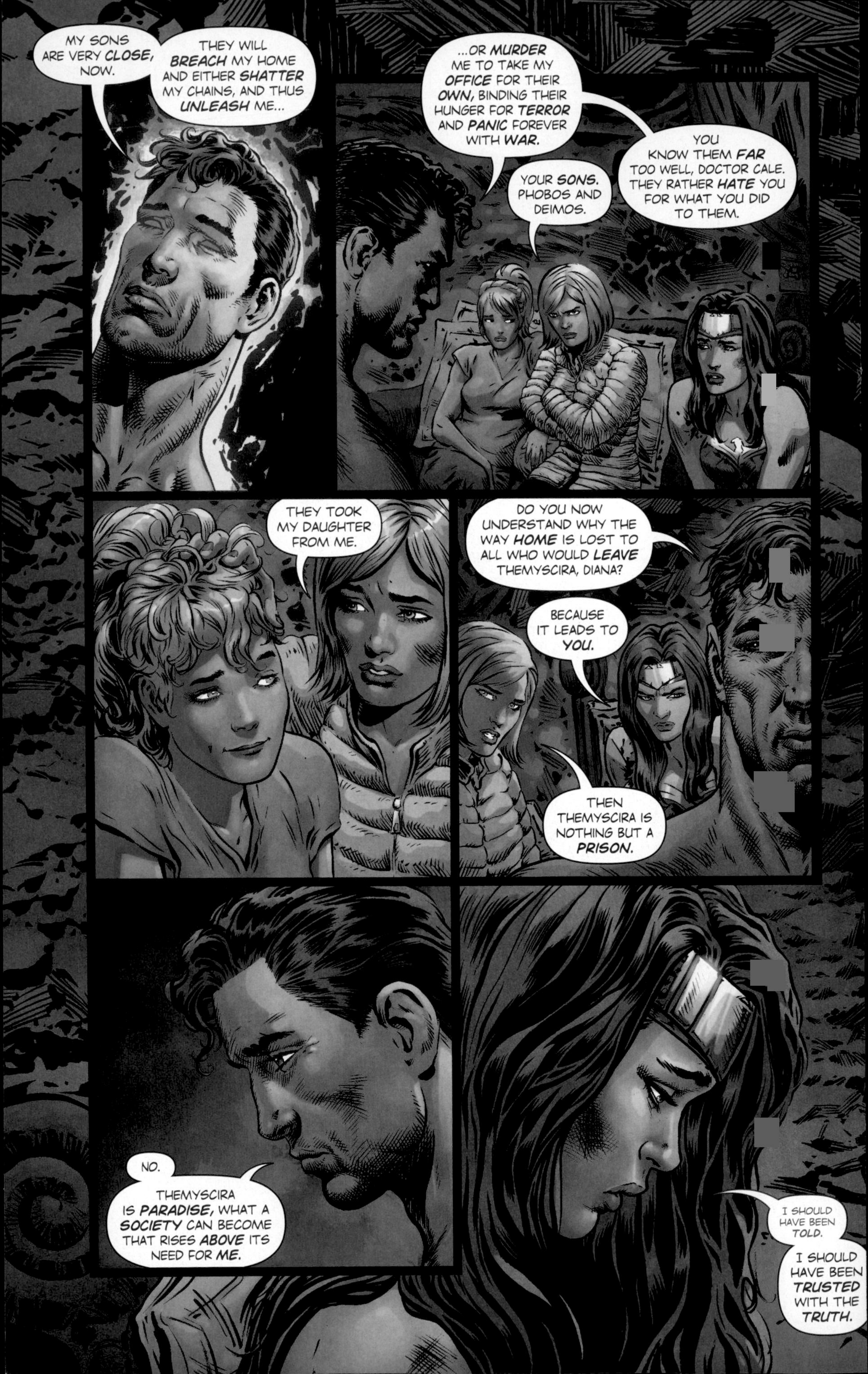
MY SONS ARE VERY CLOSE, NOW.
THEY WILL BREACH MY HOME AND EITHER SHATTER MY CHAINS, AND THUS UNLEASH ME...
...OR MURDER ME TO TAKE MY OFFICE FOR THEIR OWN, BINDING THEIR HUNGER FOR TERROR AND PANIC FOREVER WITH WAR.
YOUR SONS. PHOBOS AND DEIMOS.
YOU KNOW THEM FAR TOO WELL, DOCTOR CALE. THEY RATHER HATE YOU FOR WHAT YOU DID TO THEM.
THEY TOOK MY DAUGHTER FROM ME.
DO YOU NOW UNDERSTAND WHY THE WAY HOME IS LOST TO ALL WHO WOULD LEAVE THEMYSCIRA, DIANA?
BECAUSE IT LEADS TO YOU.
THEN THEMYSCIRA IS NOTHING BUT A PRISON.
NO.
THEMYSCIRA IS PARADISE, WHAT A SOCIETY CAN BECOME THAT RISES ABOVE ITS NEED FOR ME.
I SHOULD HAVE BEEN TOLD.
I SHOULD HAVE BEEN TRUSTED WITH THE TRUTH.

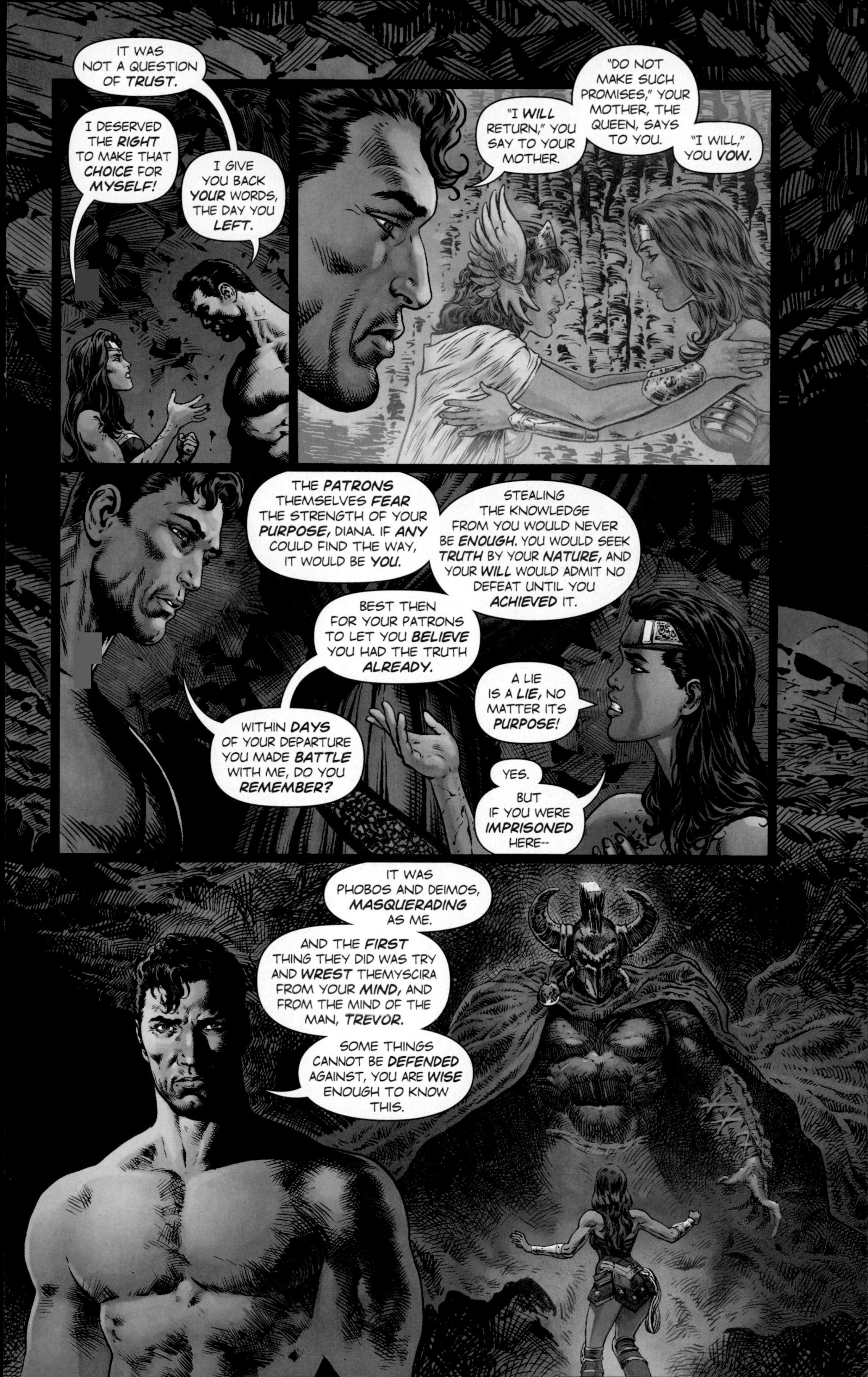

IT WAS NOT A QUESTION OF TRUST.
I DESERVED THE RIGHT TO MAKE THAT CHOICE FOR MYSELF!
I GIVE YOU BACK YOUR WORDS, THE DAY YOU LEFT.
"I WILL RETURN," YOU SAY TO YOUR MOTHER.
"DO NOT MAKE SUCH PROMISES," YOUR MOTHER, THE QUEEN, SAYS TO YOU.
"I WILL," YOU VOW.
THE PATRONS THEMSELVES FEAR THE STRENGTH OF YOUR PURPOSE, DIANA. IF ANY COULD FIND THE WAY, IT WOULD BE YOU.
STEALING THE KNOWLEDGE FROM YOU WOULD NEVER BE ENOUGH. YOU WOULD SEEK TRUTH BY YOUR NATURE, AND YOUR WILL WOULD ADMIT NO DEFEAT UNTIL YOU ACHIEVED IT.
BEST THEN FOR YOUR PATRONS TO LET YOU BELIEVE YOU HAD THE TRUTH ALREADY.
A LIE IS A LIE, NO MATTER ITS PURPOSE!
WITHIN DAYS OF YOUR DEPARTURE YOU MADE BATTLE WITH ME, DO YOU REMEMBER?
YES.
BUT IF YOU WERE IMPRISONED HERE--
IT WAS PHOBOS AND DEIMOS, MASQUERADING AS ME.
AND THE FIRST THING THEY DID WAS TRY AND WREST THEMYSCIRA FROM YOUR MIND, AND FROM THE MIND OF THE MAN, TREVOR.
SOME THINGS CANNOT BE DEFENDED AGAINST, YOU ARE WISE ENOUGH TO KNOW THIS.

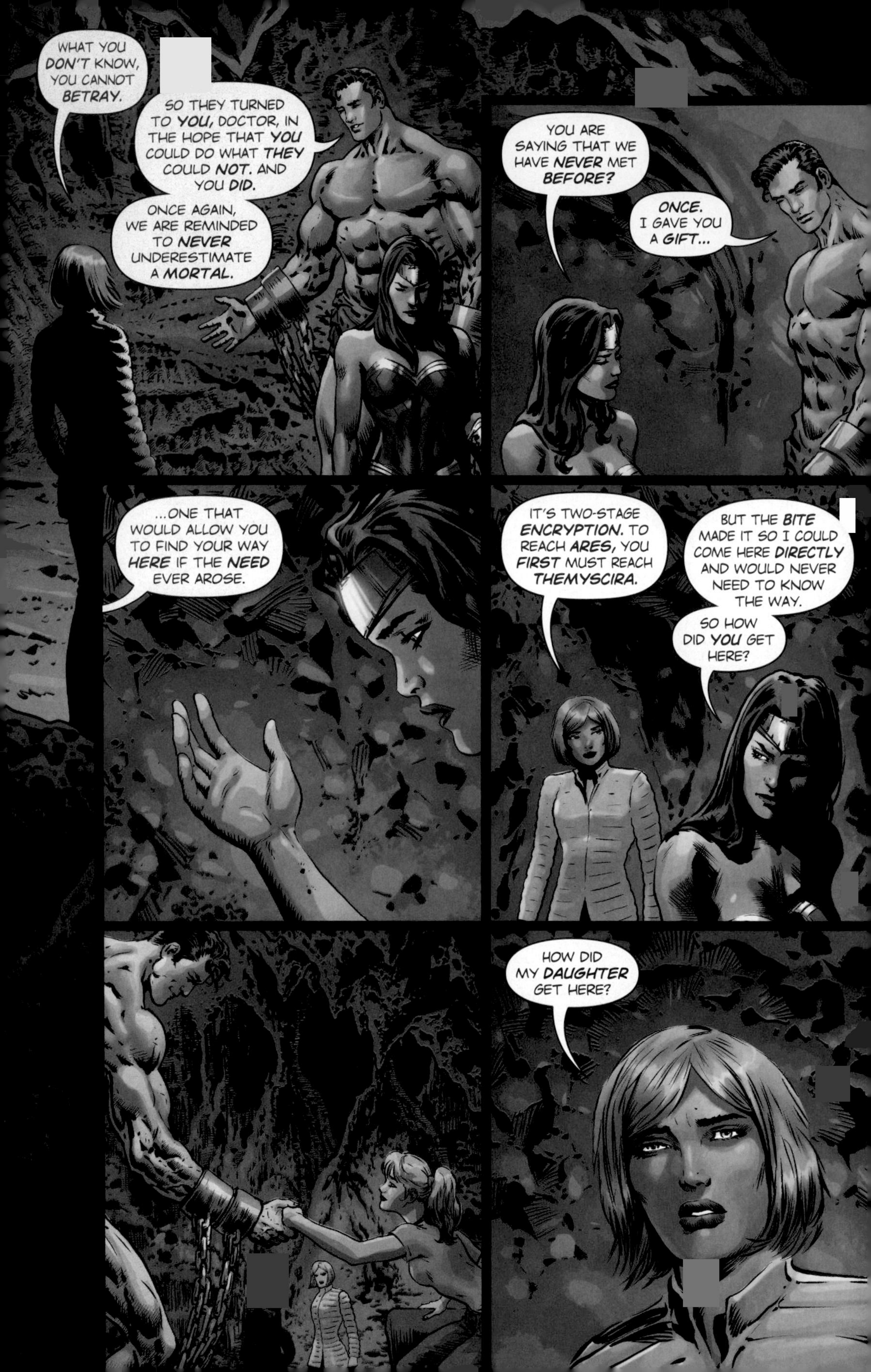
WHAT YOU DON'T KNOW, YOU CANNOT BETRAY.
SO THEY TURNED TO YOU, DOCTOR, IN THE HOPE THAT YOU COULD DO WHAT THEY COULD NOT. AND YOU DID.
ONCE AGAIN, WE ARE REMINDED TO NEVER UNDERESTIMATE A MORTAL.
YOU ARE SAYING THAT WE HAVE NEVER MET BEFORE?
ONCE. I GAVE YOU A GIFT...
...ONE THAT WOULD ALLOW YOU TO FIND YOUR WAY HERE IF THE NEED EVER AROSE.
IT'S TWO-STAGE ENCRYPTION. TO REACH ARES, YOU FIRST MUST REACH THEMYSCIRA.
BUT THE BITE MADE IT SO I COULD COME HERE DIRECTLY AND WOULD NEVER NEED TO KNOW THE WAY.
SO HOW DID YOU GET HERE?
HOW DID MY DAUGHTER GET HERE?

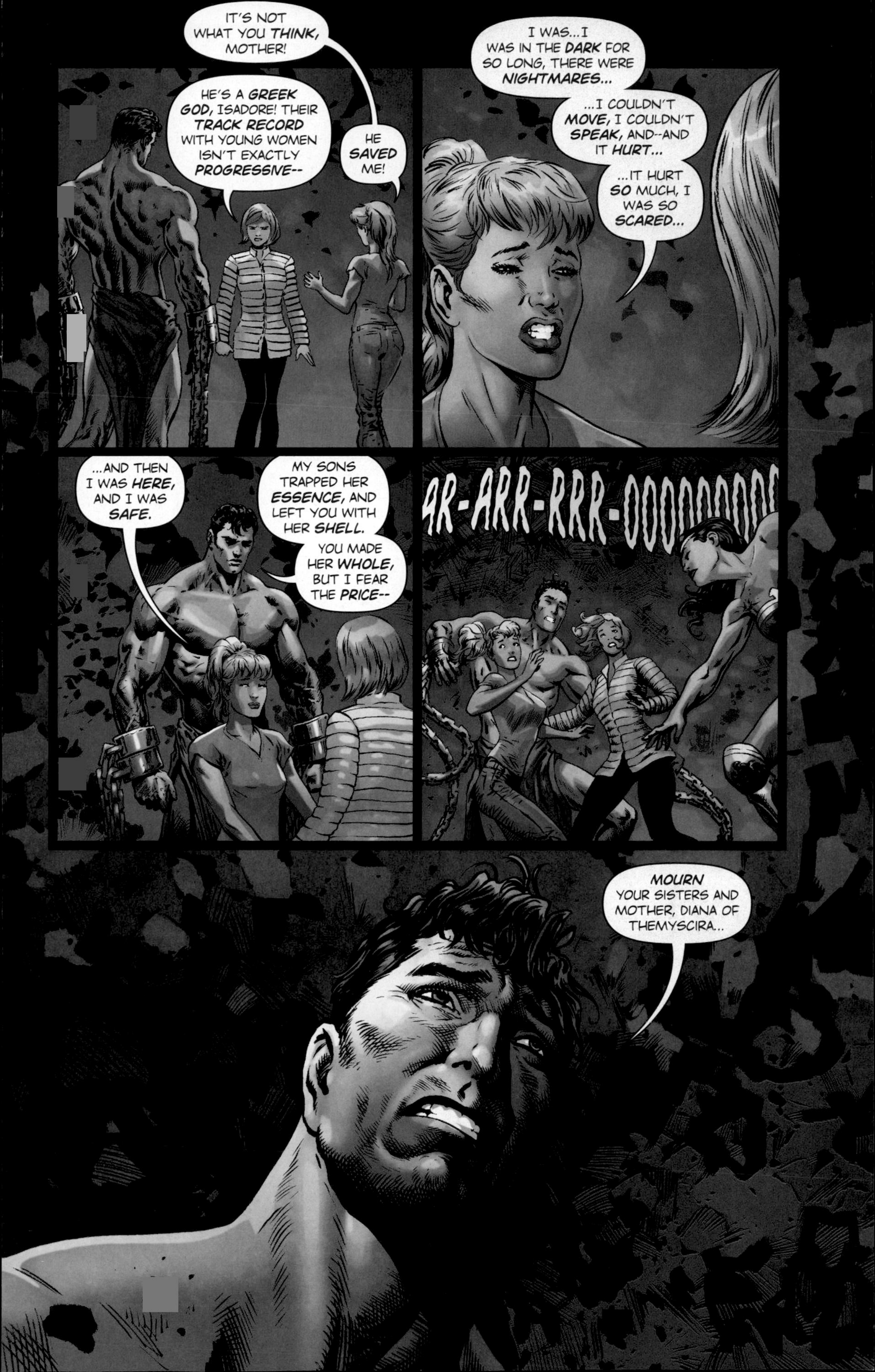
IT'S NOT WHAT YOU THINK, MOTHER!
HE'S A GREEK GOD, ISADORE! THEIR TRACK RECORD WITH YOUNG WOMEN ISN'T EXACTLY PROGRESSIVE--
HE SAVED ME!
I WAS...I WAS IN THE DARK FOR SO LONG, THERE WERE NIGHTMARES...
...I COULDN'T MOVE, I COULDN'T SPEAK, AND--AND IT HURT...
...IT HURT SO MUCH, I WAS SO SCARED...
...AND THEN I WAS HERE, AND I WAS SAFE.
MY SONS TRAPPED HER ESSENCE, AND LEFT YOU WITH HER SHELL.
YOU MADE HER WHOLE, BUT I FEAR THE PRICE--
AR-ARR-RRR-OOOOOOOO
MOURN YOUR SISTERS AND MOTHER, DIANA OF THEMYSCIRA...

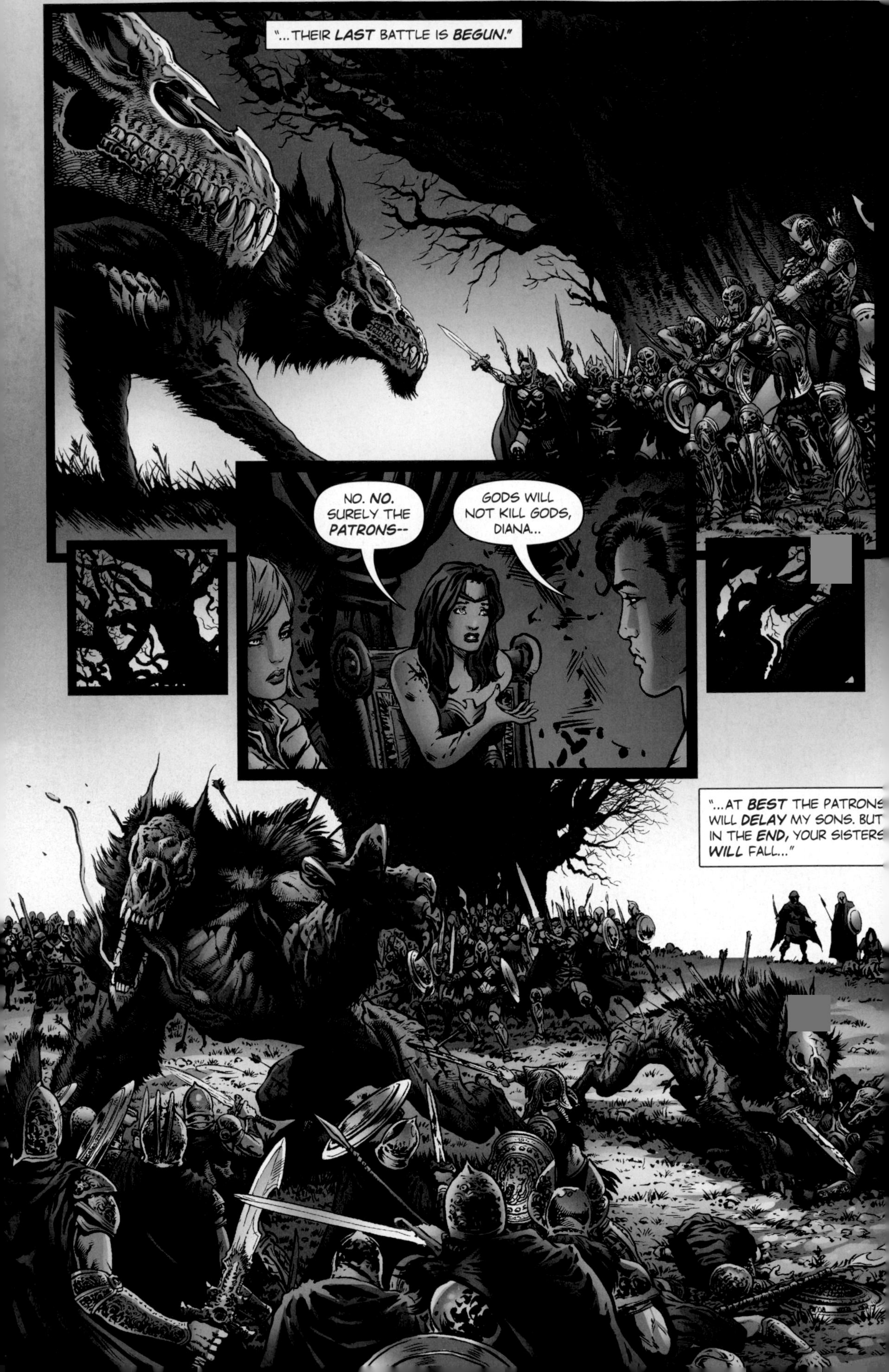
"...THEIR LAST BATTLE IS BEGUN."
NO. NO. SURELY THE PATRONS--
GODS WILL NOT KILL GODS, DIANA...
"...AT BEST THE PATRONS WILL DELAY MY SONS. BUT IN THE END, YOUR SISTERS WILL FALL..."

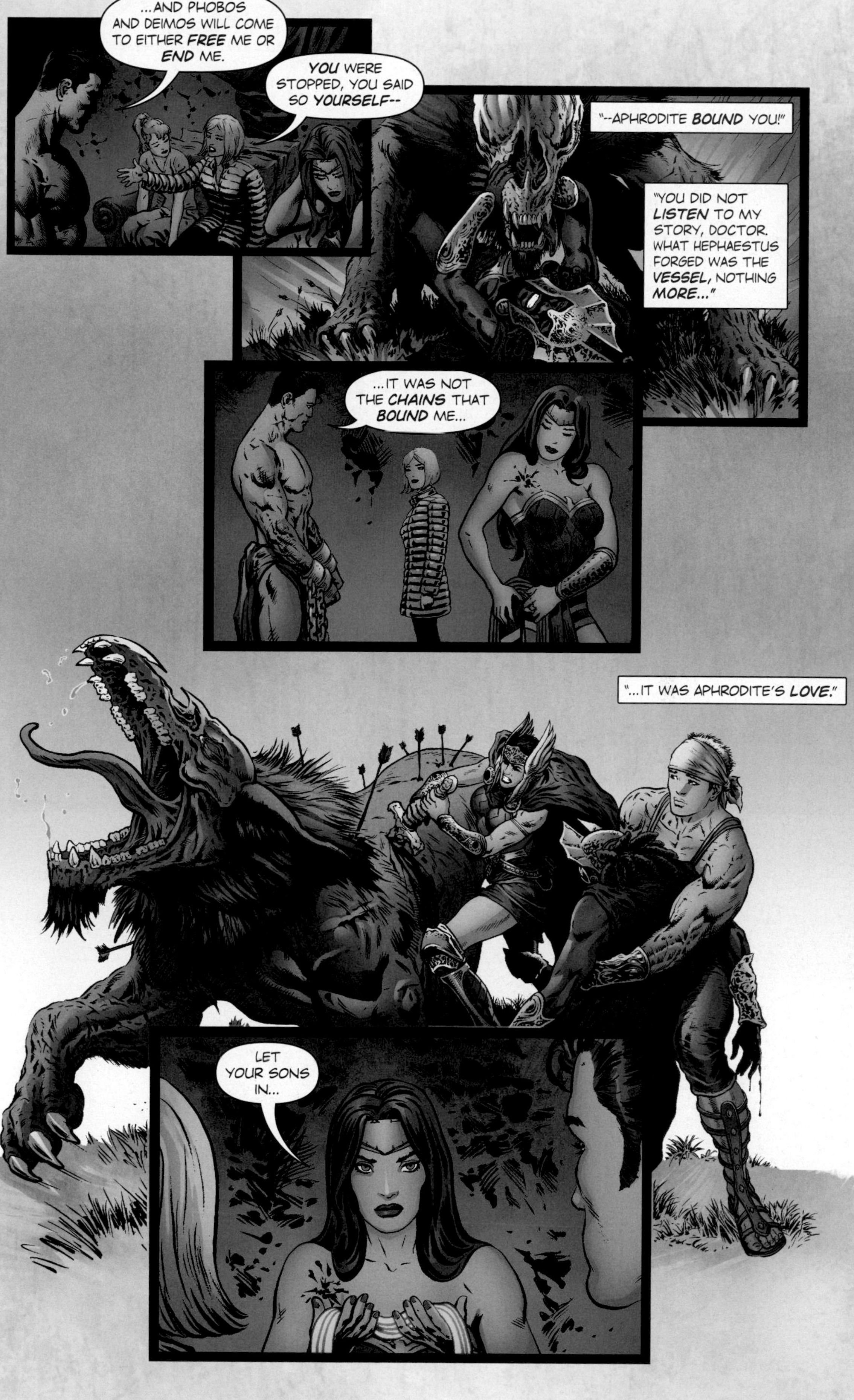
...AND PHOBOS AND DEIMOS WILL COME TO EITHER FREE ME OR END ME.
YOU WERE STOPPED, YOU SAID SO YOURSELF--
"--APHRODITE BOUND YOU!"
"YOU DID NOT LISTEN TO MY STORY, DOCTOR. WHAT HEPHAESTUS FORGED WAS THE VESSEL, NOTHING MORE..."
...IT WAS NOT THE CHAINS THAT BOUND ME...
"...IT WAS APHRODITE'S LOVE."
LET YOUR SONS IN...

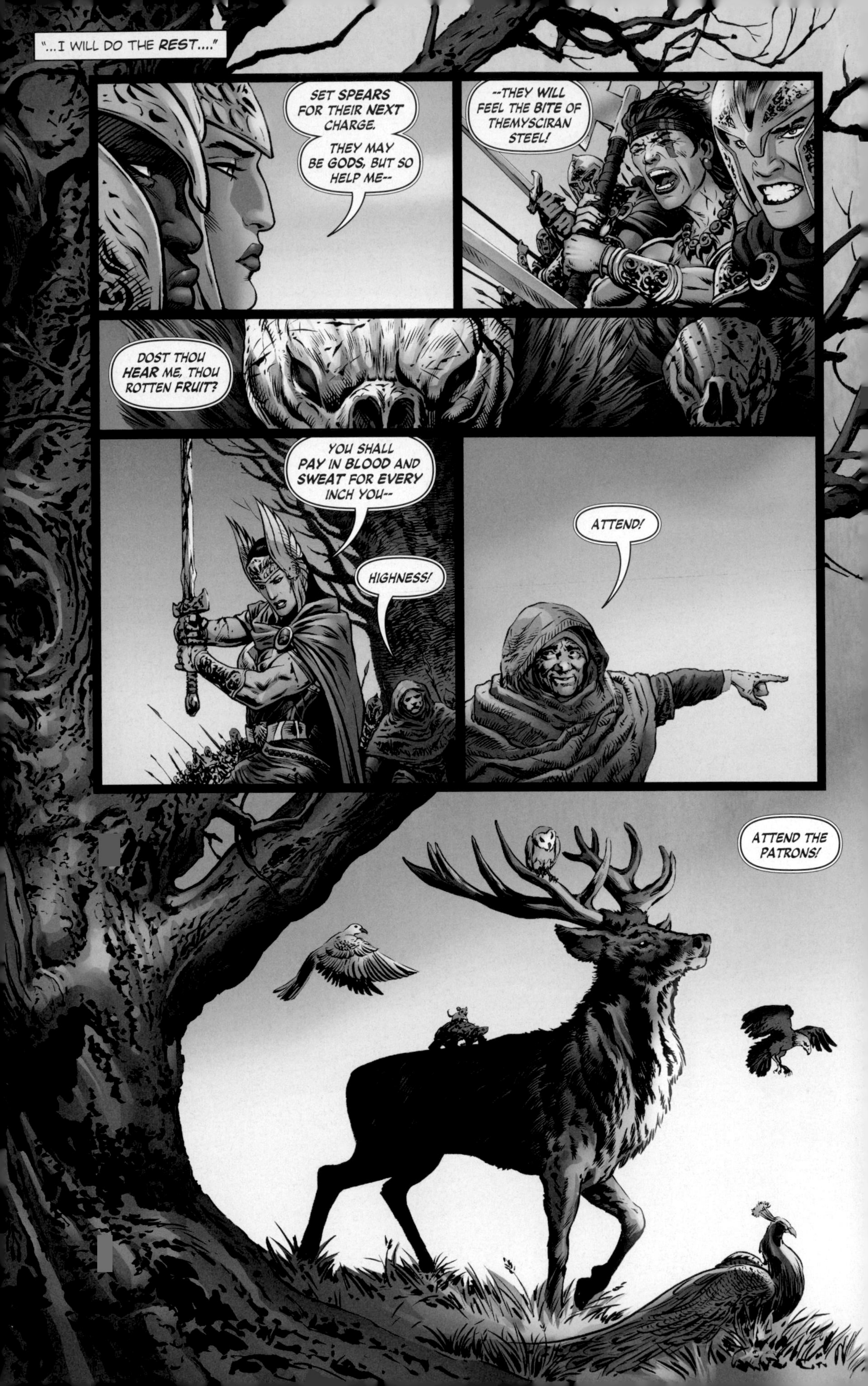
"...I WILL DO THE REST...."
SET SPEARS FOR THEIR NEXT CHARGE.
THEY MAY BE GODS, BUT SO HELP ME--
--THEY WILL FEEL THE BITE OF THEMYSCIRAN STEEL!
DOST THOU HEAR ME, THOU ROTTEN FRUIT?
YOU SHALL PAY IN BLOOD AND SWEAT FOR EVERY INCH YOU--
HIGHNESS!
ATTEND!
ATTEND THE PATRONS!

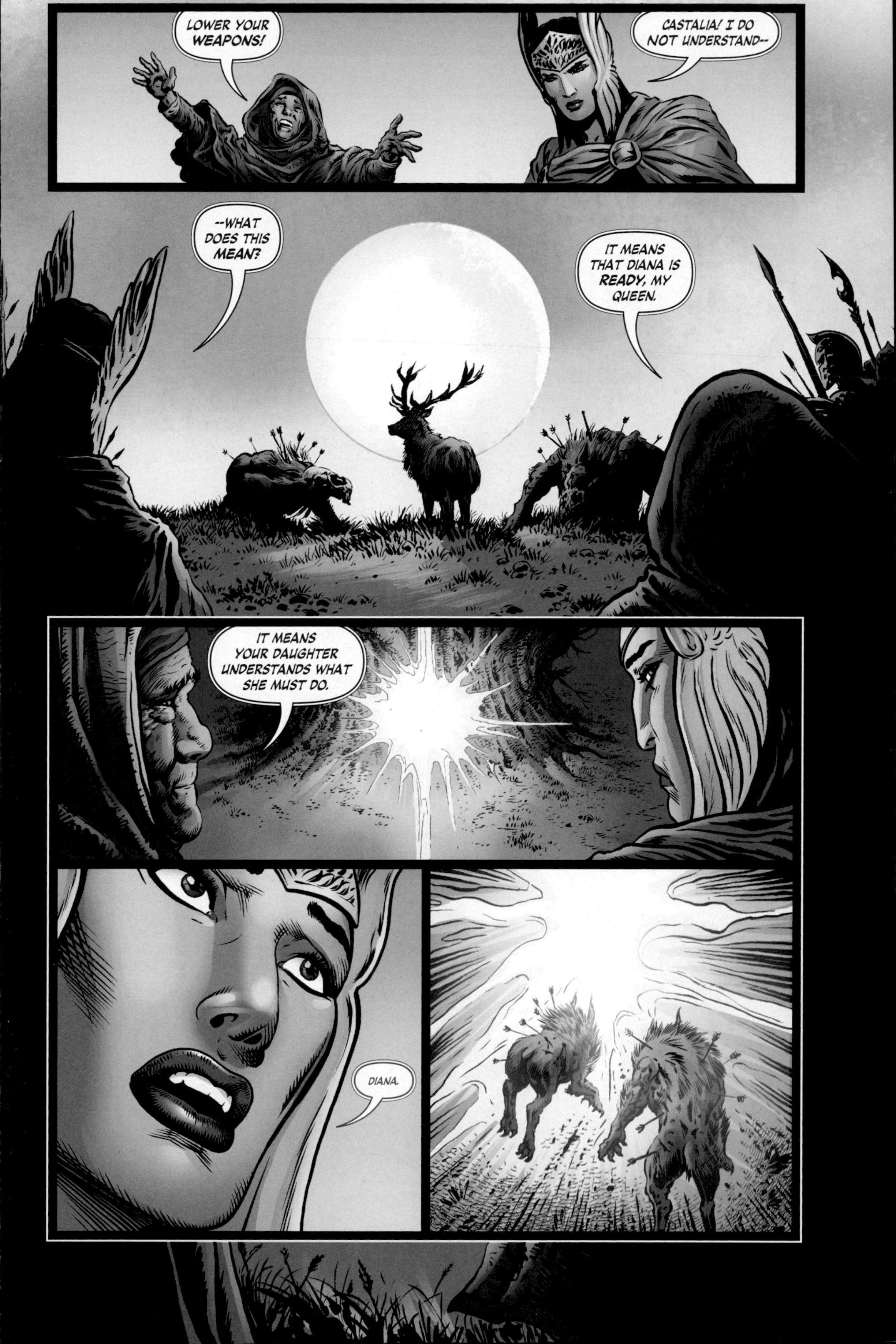
LOWER YOUR WEAPONS!
CASTALIA! I DO NOT UNDERSTAND--
--WHAT DOES THIS MEAN?
IT MEANS THAT DIANA IS READY, MY QUEEN.
IT MEANS YOUR DAUGHTER UNDERSTANDS WHAT SHE MUST DO.
DIANA.

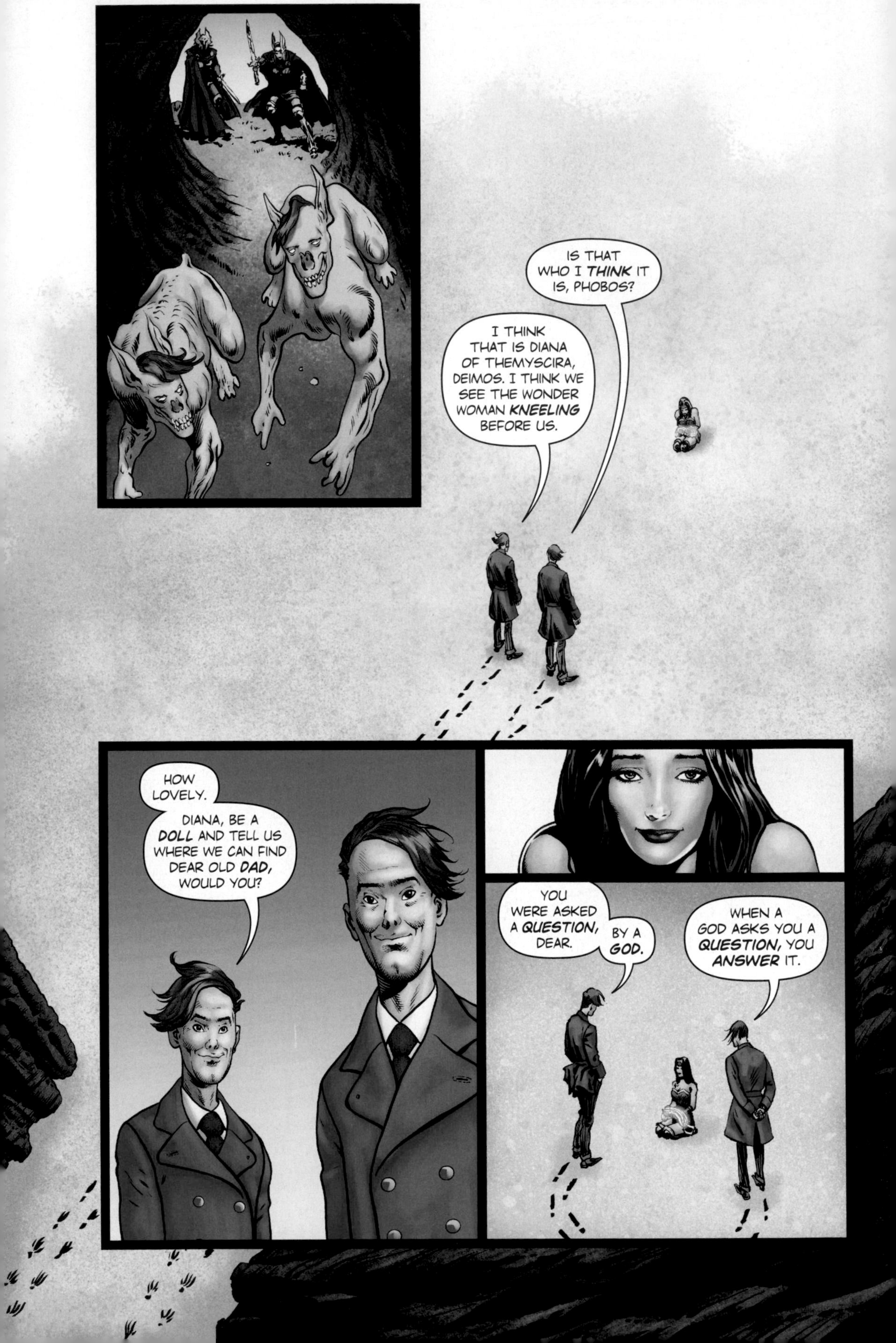
IS THAT WHO I THINK IT IS, PHOBOS?
I THINK THAT IS DIANA OF THEMYSCIRA, DEIMOS. I THINK WE SEE THE WONDER WOMAN KNEELING BEFORE US.
HOW LOVELY.
DIANA, BE A DOLL AND TELL US WHERE WE CAN FIND DEAR OLD DAD, WOULD YOU?
YOU WERE ASKED A QUESTION, DEAR.
BY A GOD.
WHEN A GOD ASKS YOU A QUESTION, YOU ANSWER IT.

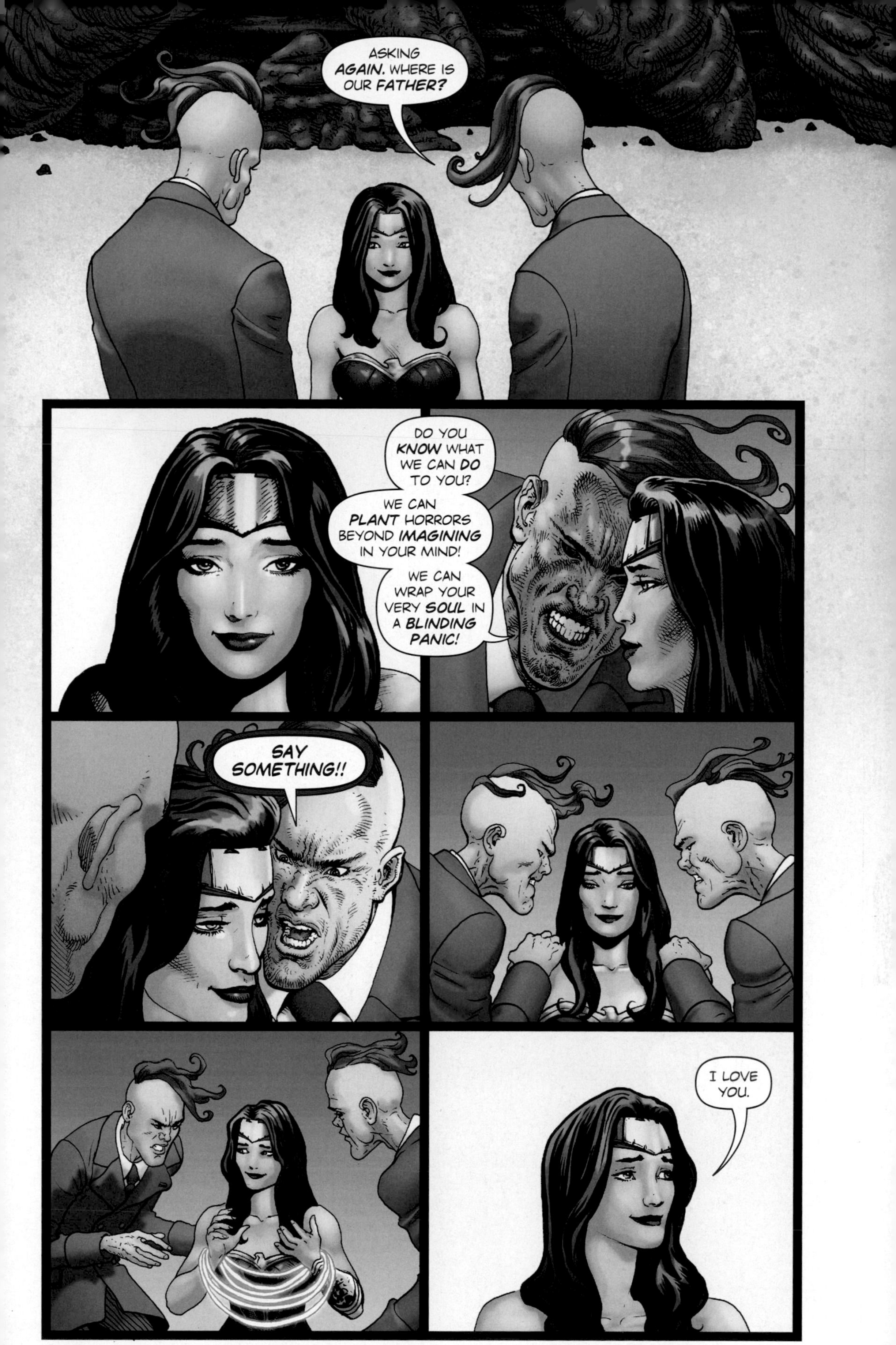
ASKING AGAIN. WHERE IS OUR FATHER?
DO YOU KNOW WHAT WE CAN DO TO YOU?
WE CAN PLANT HORRORS BEYOND IMAGINING IN YOUR MIND!
WE CAN WRAP YOUR VERY SOUL IN A BLINDING PANIC!
SAY SOMETHING!!
I LOVE YOU.

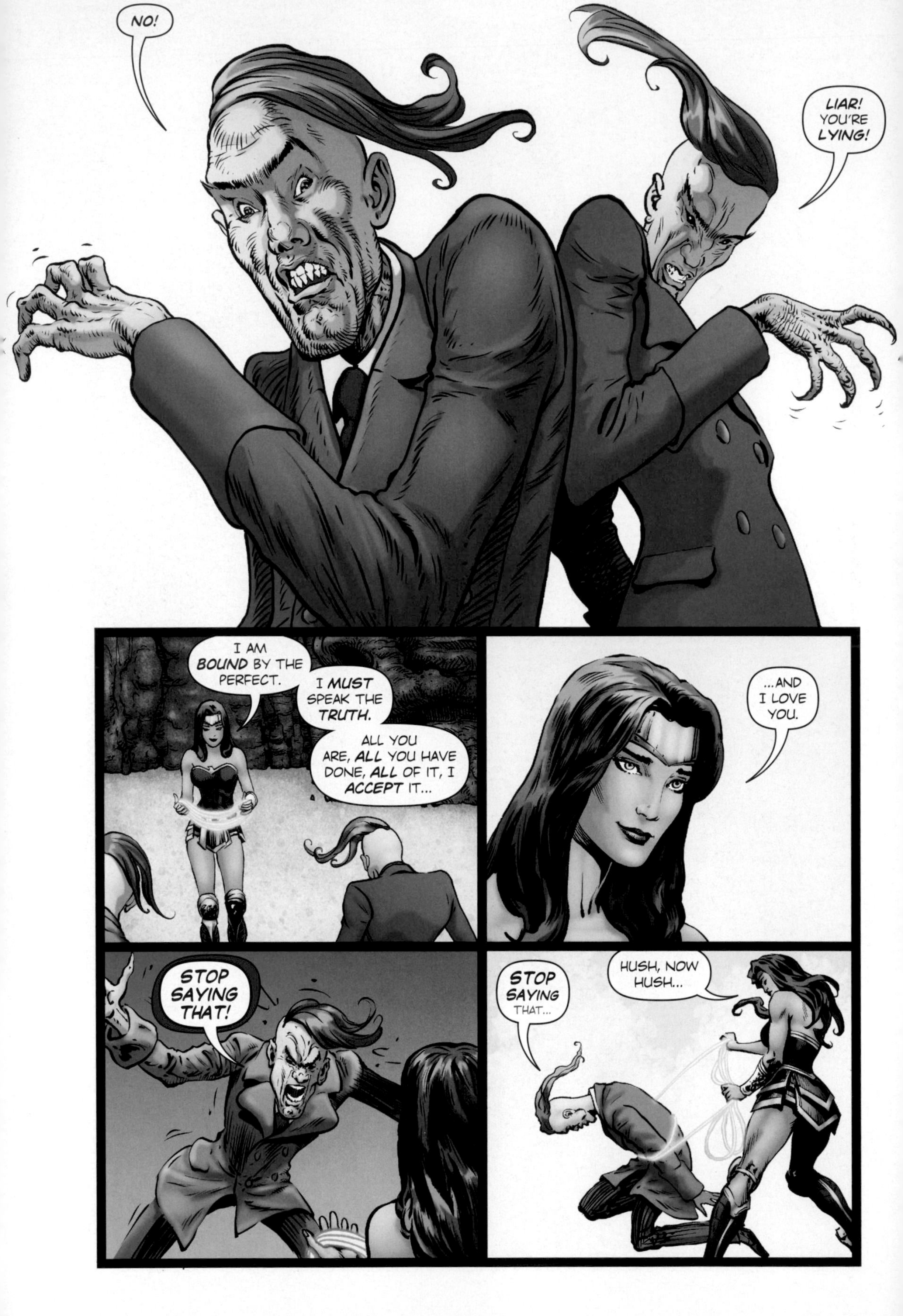
NO!
LIAR! YOU'RE LYING!
I AM BOUND BY THE PERFECT.
I MUST SPEAK THE TRUTH.
ALL YOU ARE, ALL YOU HAVE DONE, ALL OF IT, I ACCEPT IT...
...AND I LOVE YOU.
STOP SAYING THAT!
STOP SAYING THAT...
HUSH, NOW HUSH...

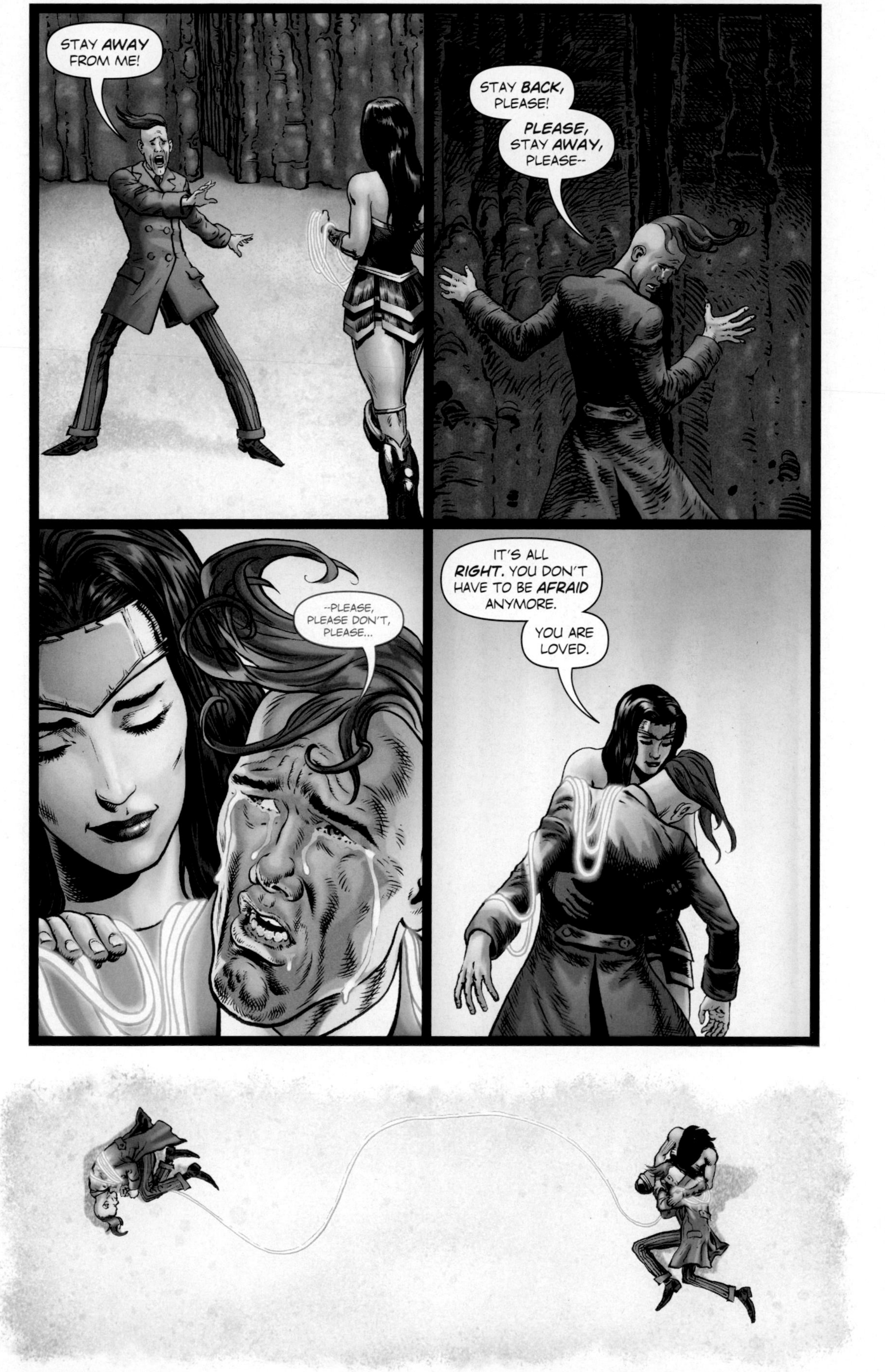
STAY AWAY FROM ME!
STAY BACK, PLEASE!
PLEASE, STAY AWAY, PLEASE--
--PLEASE, PLEASE DON'T, PLEASE...
IT'S ALL RIGHT. YOU DON'T HAVE TO BE AFRAID ANYMORE.
YOU ARE LOVED.

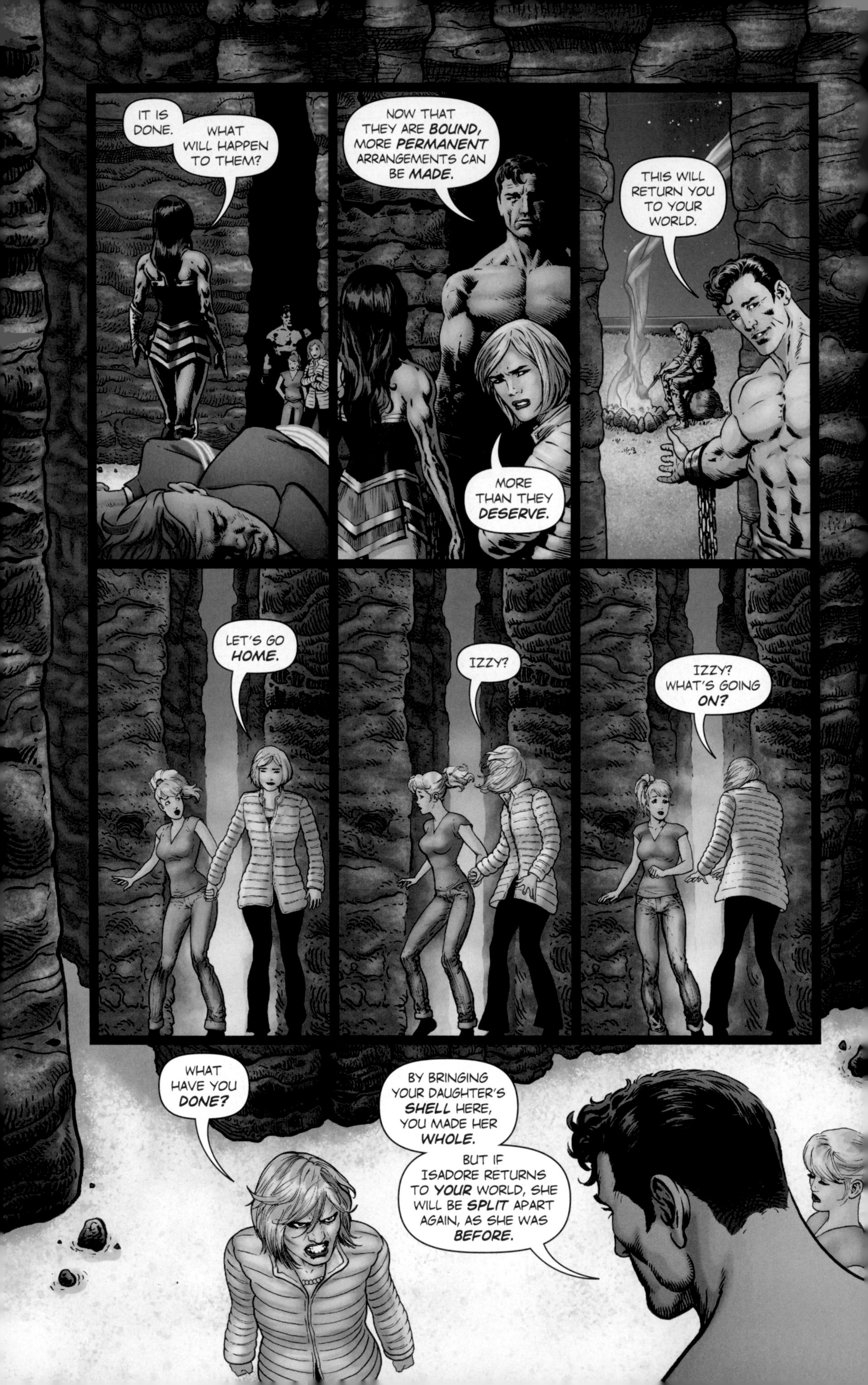

IT IS DONE.
WHAT WILL HAPPEN TO THEM?
NOW THAT THEY ARE BOUND, MORE PERMANENT ARRANGEMENTS CAN BE MADE.
MORE THAN THEY DESERVE.
THIS WILL RETURN YOU TO YOUR WORLD.
LET'S GO HOME.
IZZY?
IZZY? WHAT'S GOING ON?
WHAT HAVE YOU DONE?
BY BRINGING YOUR DAUGHTER'S SHELL HERE, YOU MADE HER WHOLE.
BUT IF ISADORE RETURNS TO YOUR WORLD, SHE WILL BE SPLIT APART AGAIN, AS SHE WAS BEFORE.

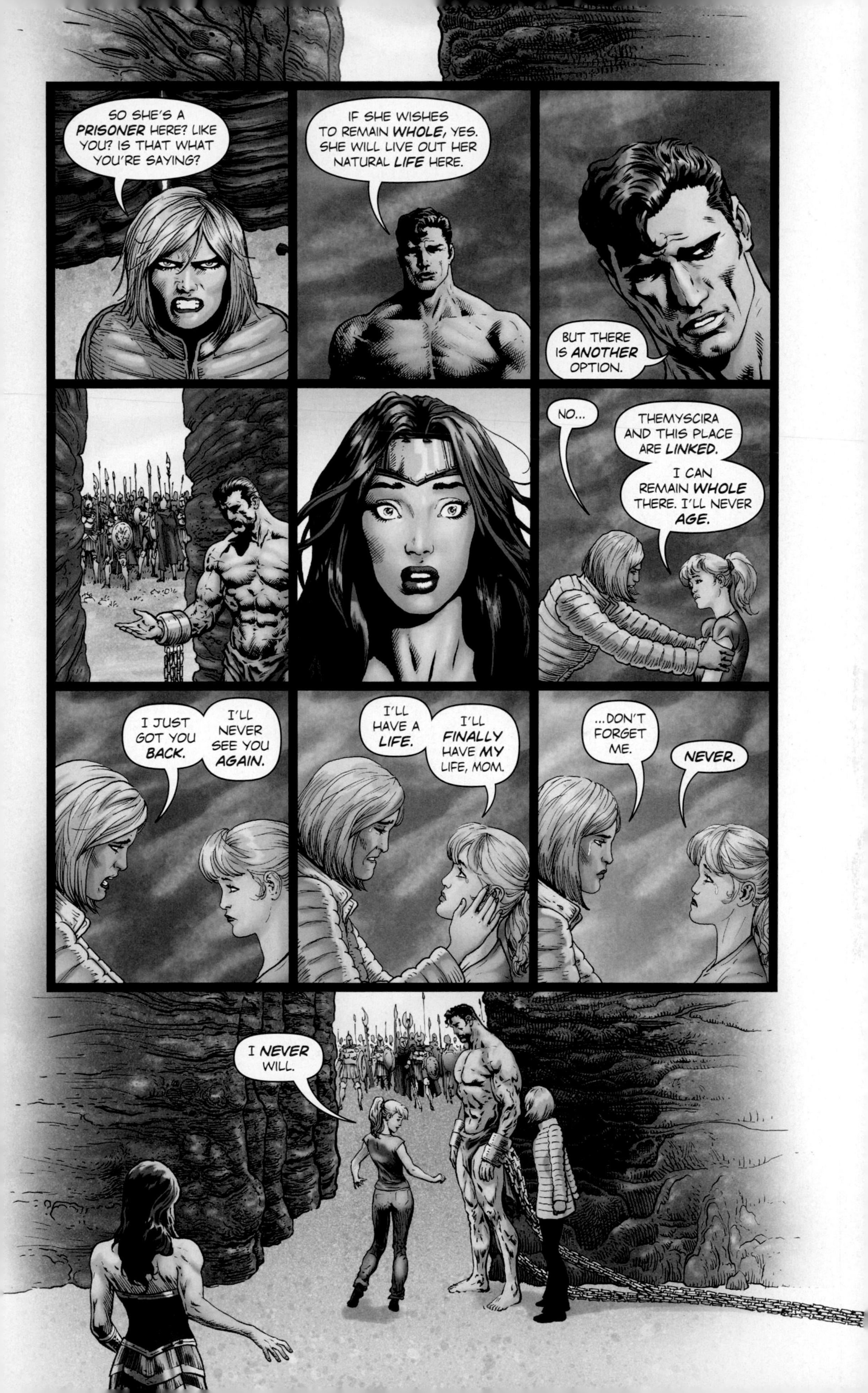
SO SHE'S A PRISONER HERE? LIKE YOU? IS THAT WHAT YOU'RE SAYING?
IF SHE WISHES TO REMAIN WHOLE, YES. SHE WILL LIVE OUT HER NATURAL LIFE HERE.
BUT THERE IS ANOTHER OPTION.
NO...
THEMYSCIRA AND THIS PLACE ARE LINKED.
I CAN REMAIN WHOLE THERE. I'LL NEVER AGE.
I JUST GOT YOU BACK.
I'LL NEVER SEE YOU AGAIN.
I'LL HAVE A LIFE.
I'LL FINALLY HAVE MY LIFE, MOM.
...DON'T FORGET ME.
NEVER.
I NEVER WILL.

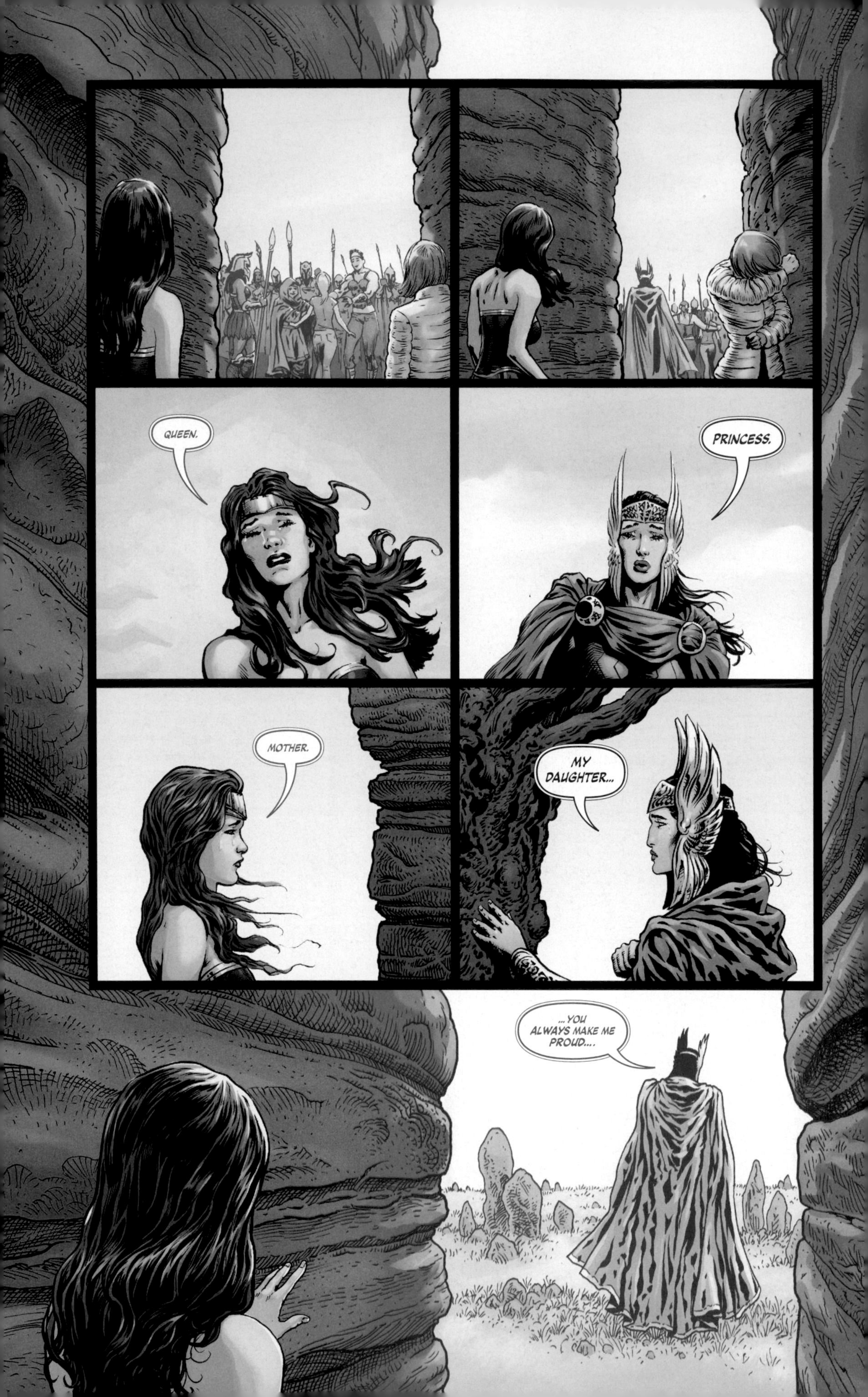
QUEEN.
PRINCESS.
MOTHER.
MY DAUGHTER...
...YOU ALWAYS MAKE ME PROUD....

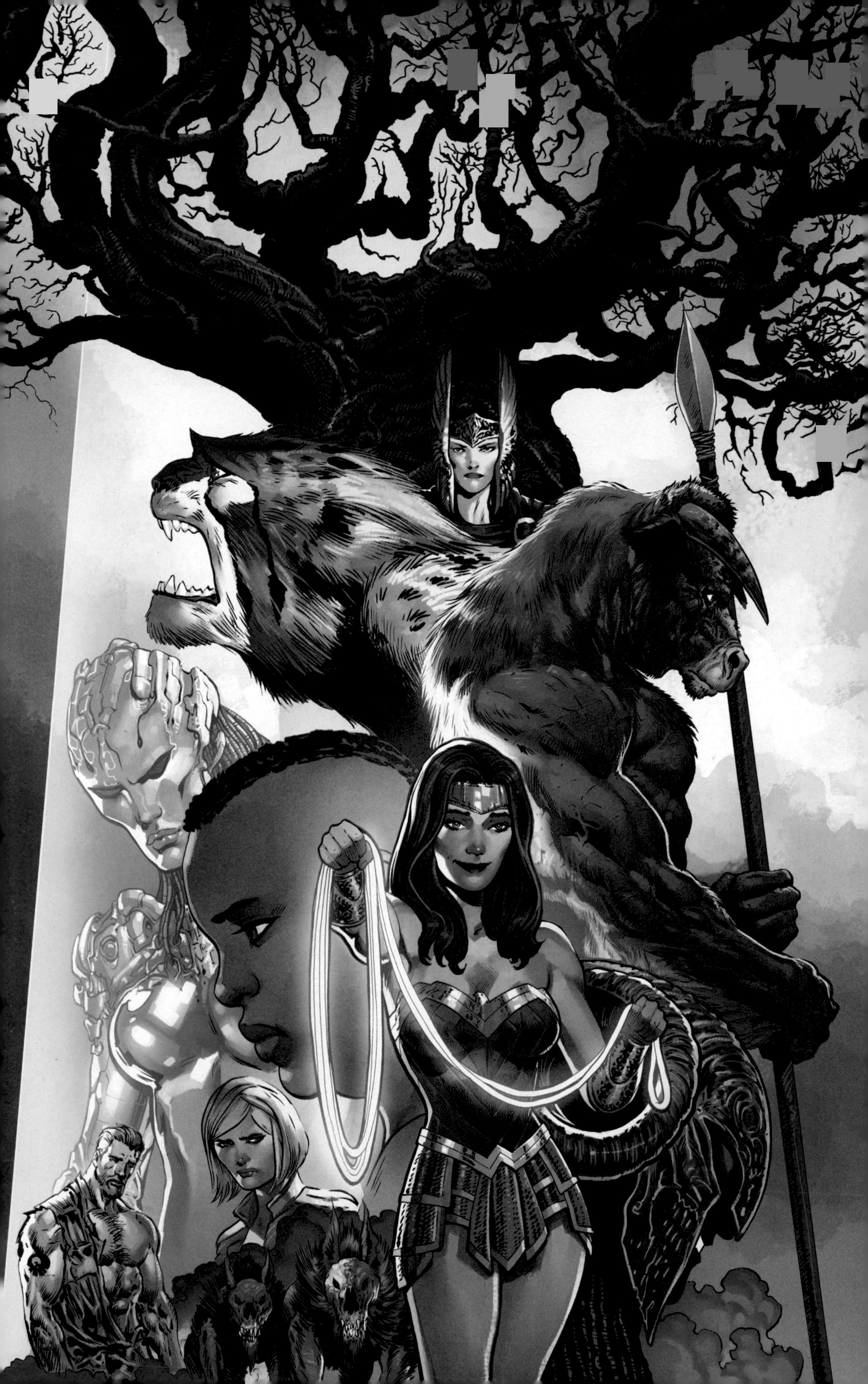

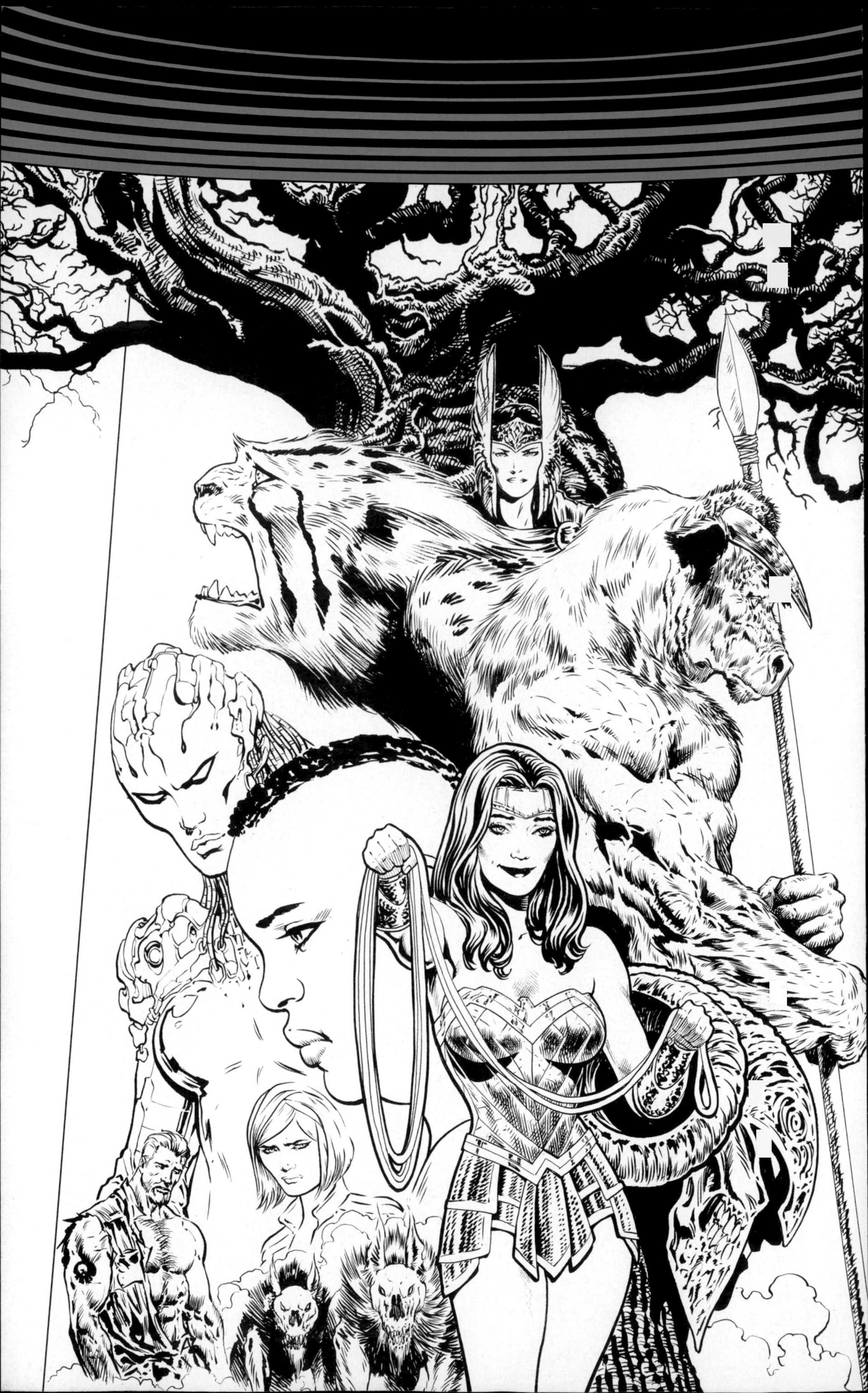

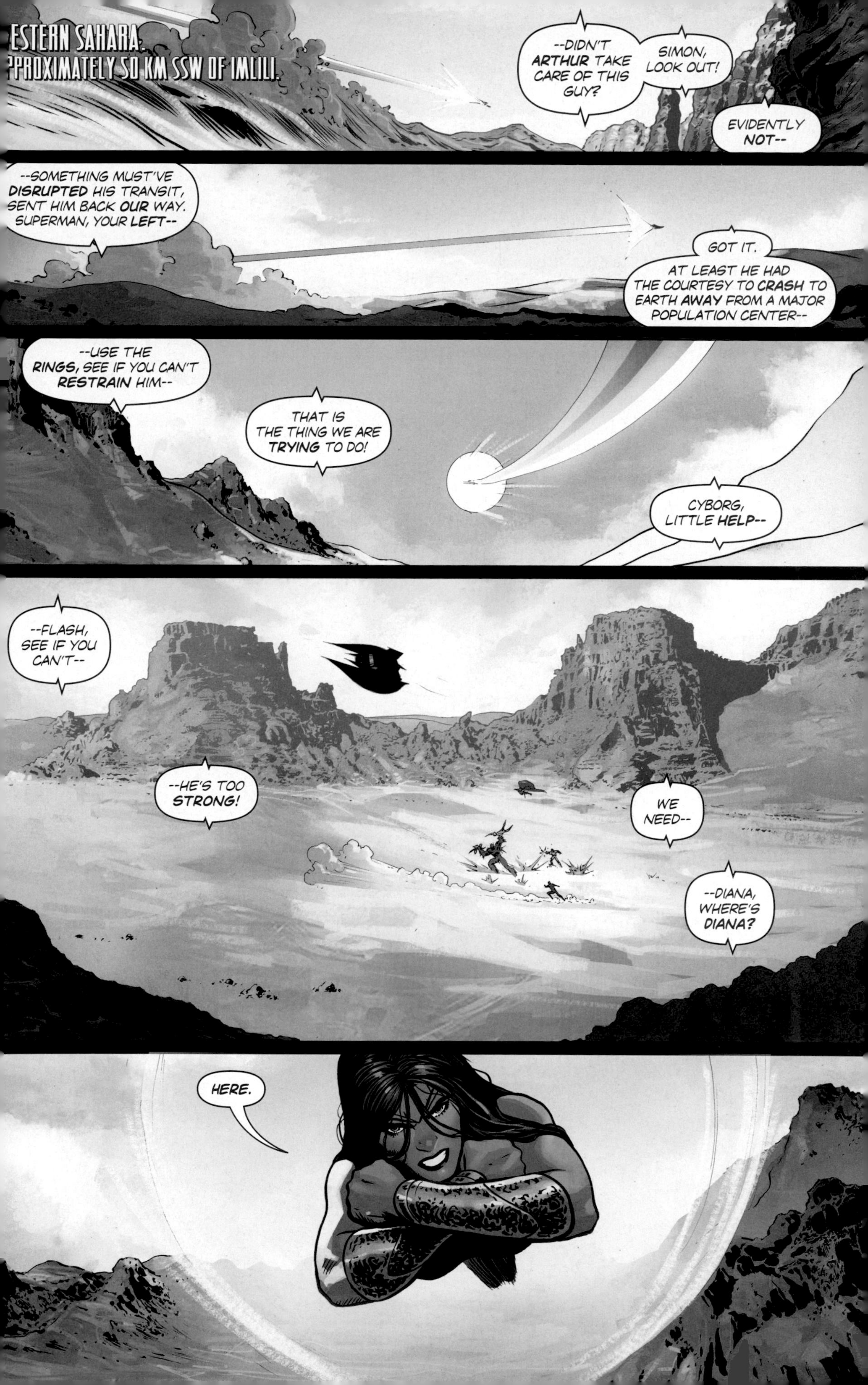
ESTERN SAHARA.
PPROXIMATELY 50 KM SSW OF IMLILI.
--DIDN'T ARTHUR TAKE CARE OF THIS GUY?
SIMON, LOOK OUT!
EVIDENTLY NOT--
--SOMETHING MUST'VE DISRUPTED HIS TRANSIT, SENT HIM BACK OUR WAY. SUPERMAN, YOUR LEFT--
GOT IT.
AT LEAST HE HAD THE COURTESY TO CRASH TO EARTH AWAY FROM A MAJOR POPULATION CENTER--
--USE THE RINGS, SEE IF YOU CAN'T RESTRAIN HIM--
THAT IS THE THING WE ARE TRYING TO DO!
CYBORG, LITTLE HELP--
--FLASH, SEE IF YOU CAN'T--
--HE'S TOO STRONG!
WE NEED--
--DIANA, WHERE'S DIANA?
HERE.

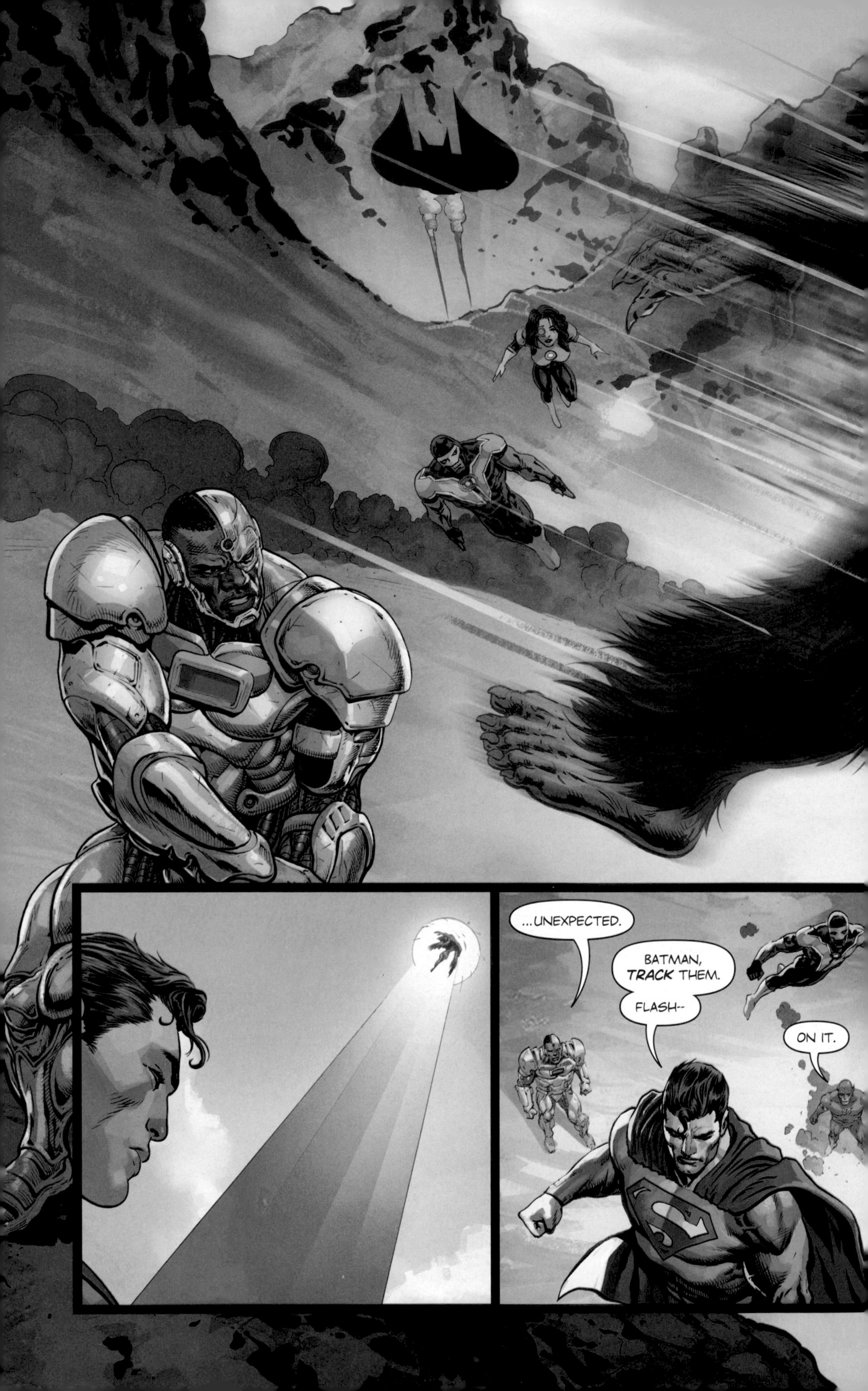
...UNEXPECTED.
BATMAN, TRACK THEM.
FLASH--
ON IT.

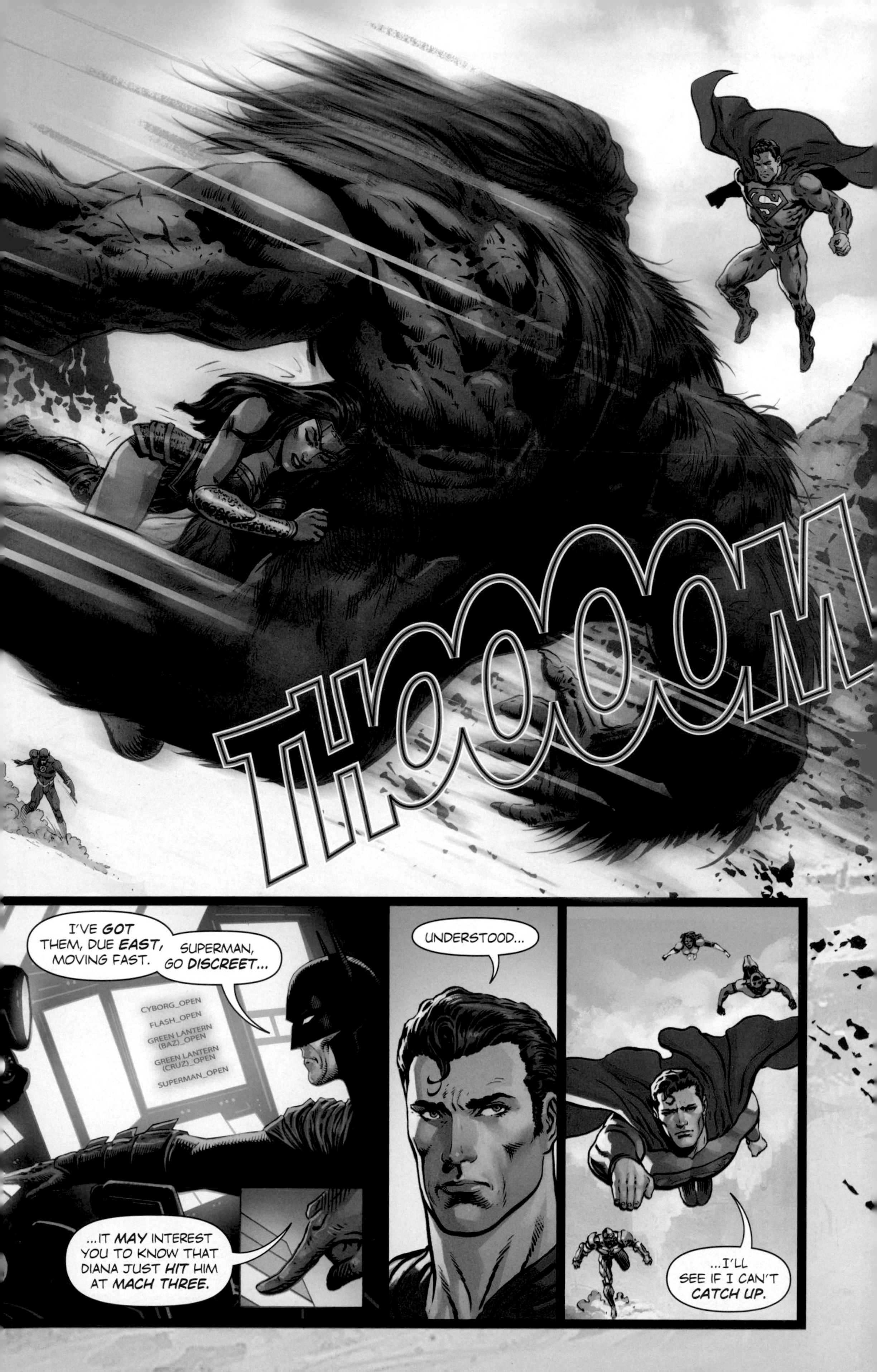
THOOOOM
I'VE GOT THEM, DUE EAST, MOVING FAST.
SUPERMAN, GO DISCREET...
CYBORG_OPEN
FLASH_OPEN
GREEN LANTERN (BAZ)_OPEN
GREEN LANTERN (CRUZ)_OPEN
SUPERMAN_OPEN
...IT MAY INTEREST YOU TO KNOW THAT DIANA JUST HIT HIM AT MACH THREE.
UNDERSTOOD...
...I'LL SEE IF I CAN'T CATCH UP.

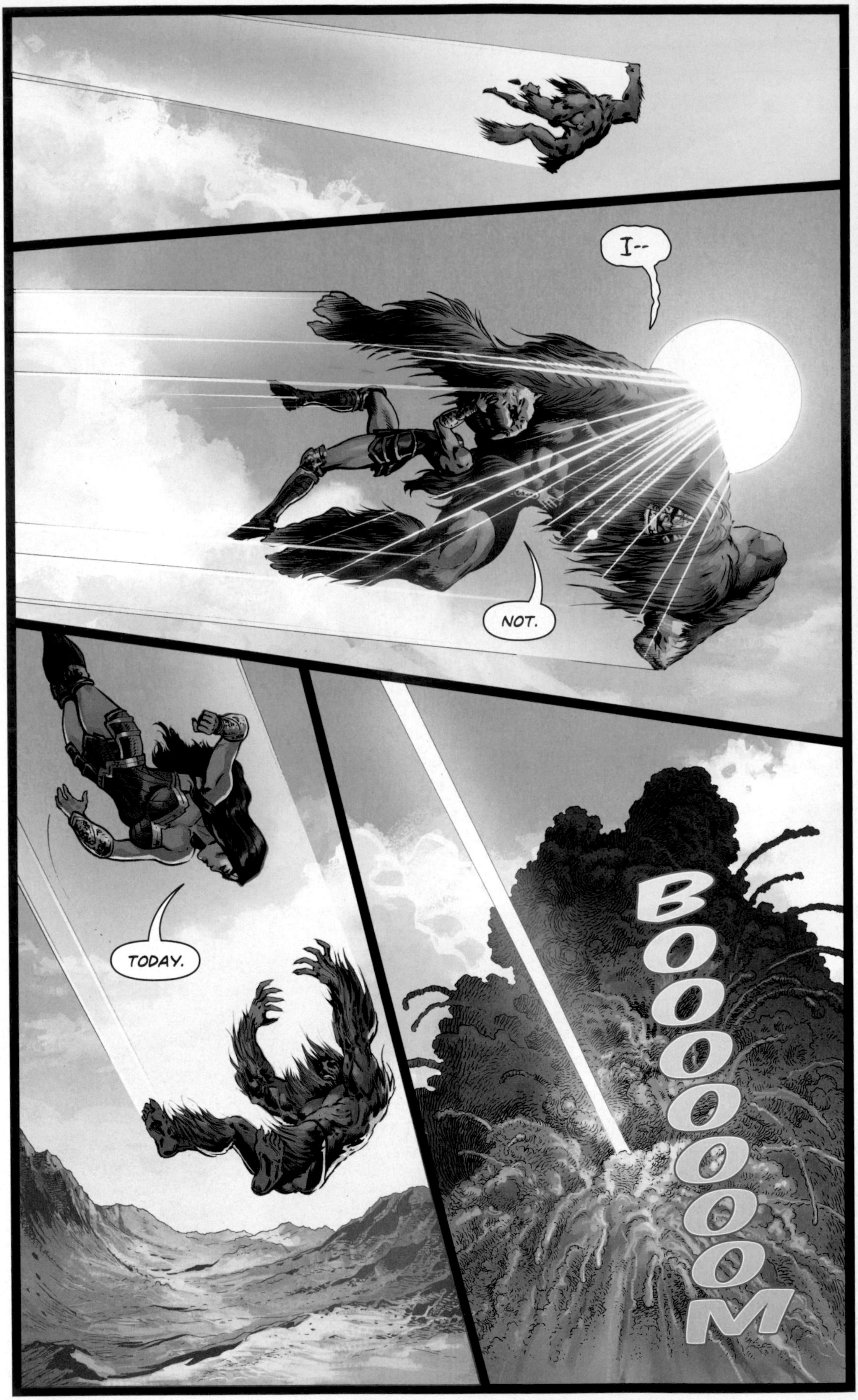
I--
NOT.
TODAY.
BOOOOOOOM

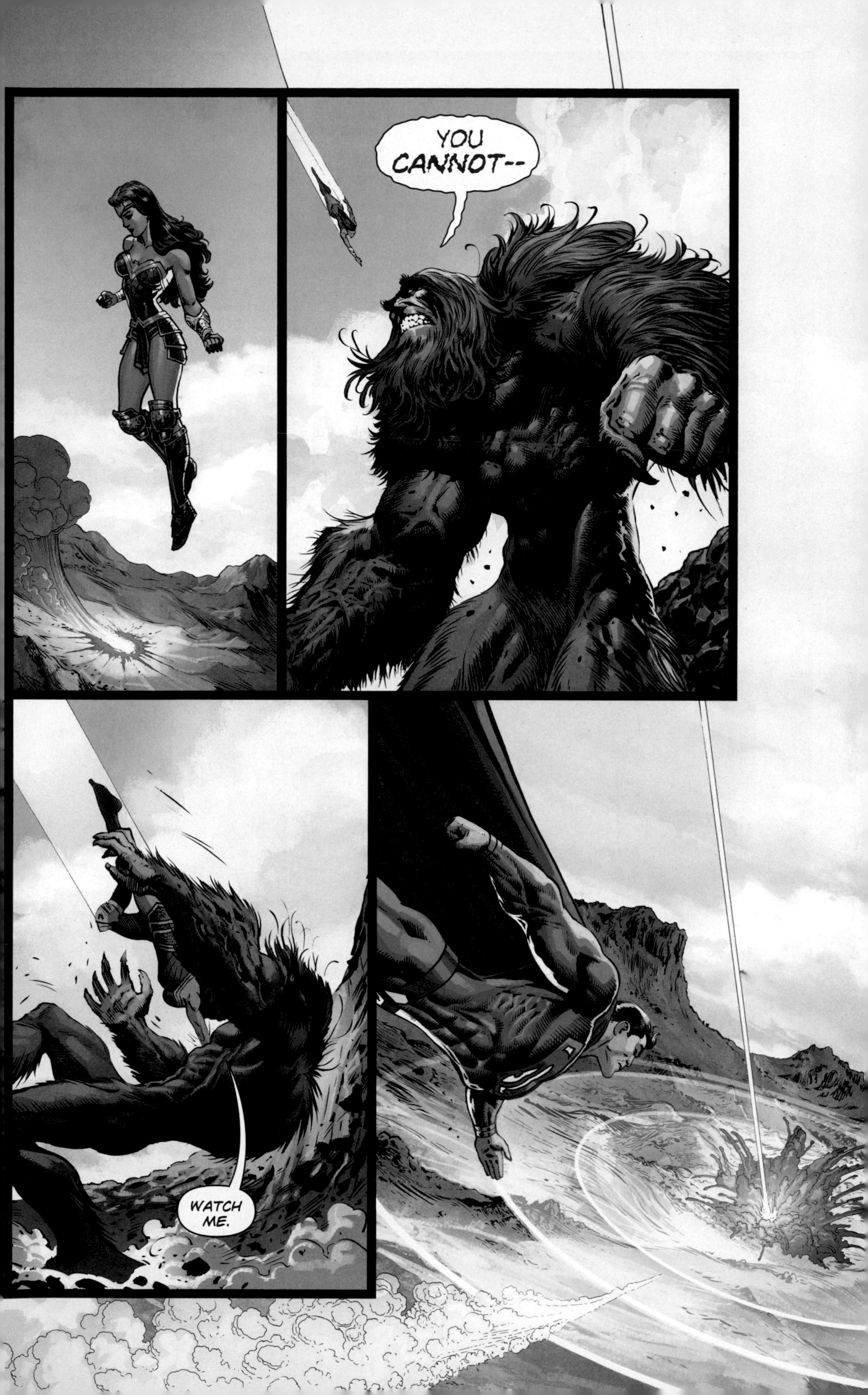
YOU CANNOT--
WATCH ME.

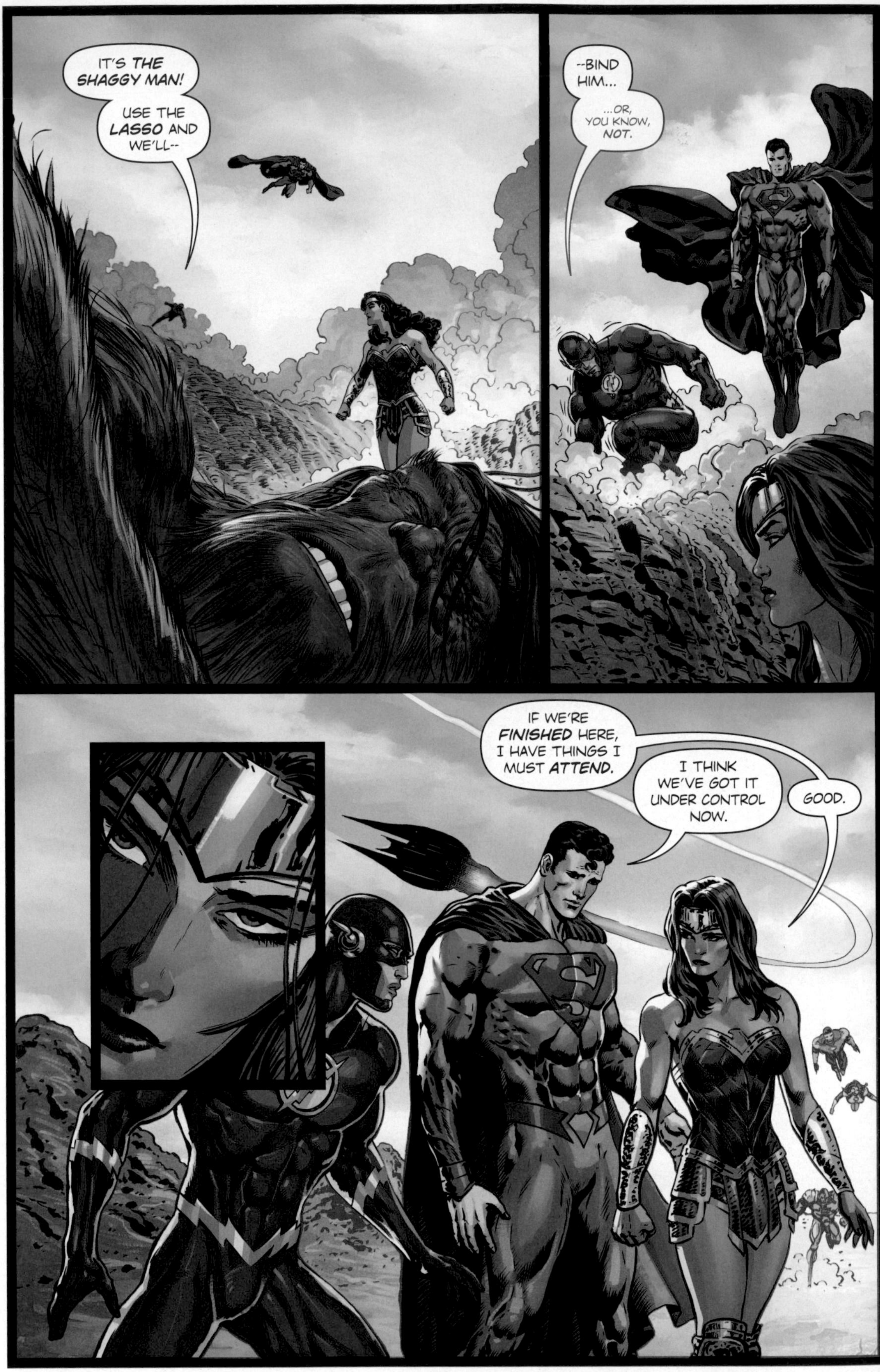
IT'S THE SHAGGY MAN!
USE THE LASSO AND WE'LL--
--BIND HIM...
...OR, YOU KNOW, NOT.
IF WE'RE FINISHED HERE, I HAVE THINGS I MUST ATTEND.
I THINK WE'VE GOT IT UNDER CONTROL NOW.
GOOD.

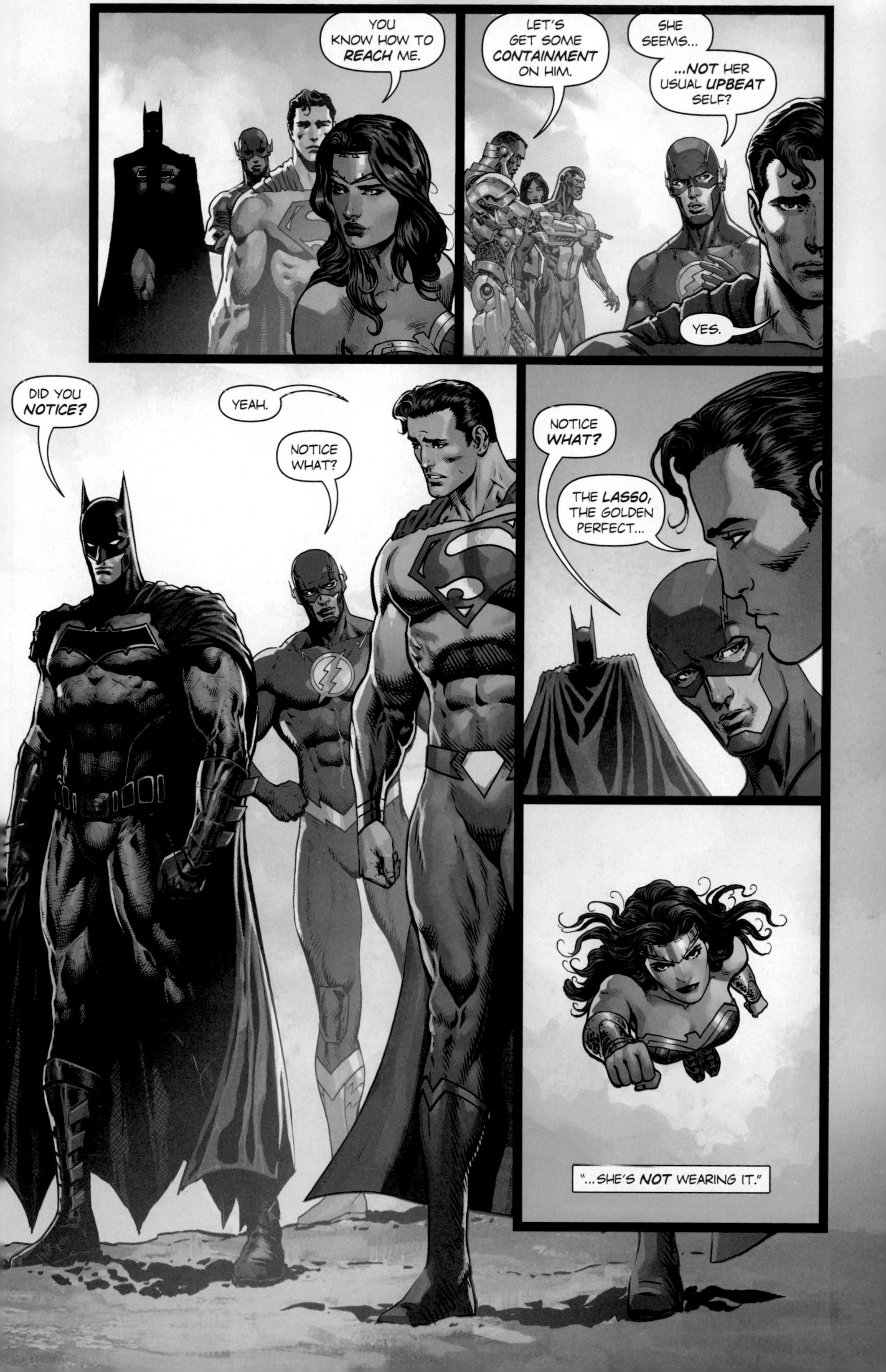
YOU KNOW HOW TO REACH ME.
LET'S GET SOME CONTAINMENT ON HIM.
SHE SEEMS...
...NOT HER USUAL UPBEAT SELF?
YES.
DID YOU NOTICE?
YEAH.
NOTICE WHAT?
NOTICE WHAT?
THE LASSO, THE GOLDEN PERFECT...
"...SHE'S NOT WEARING IT."

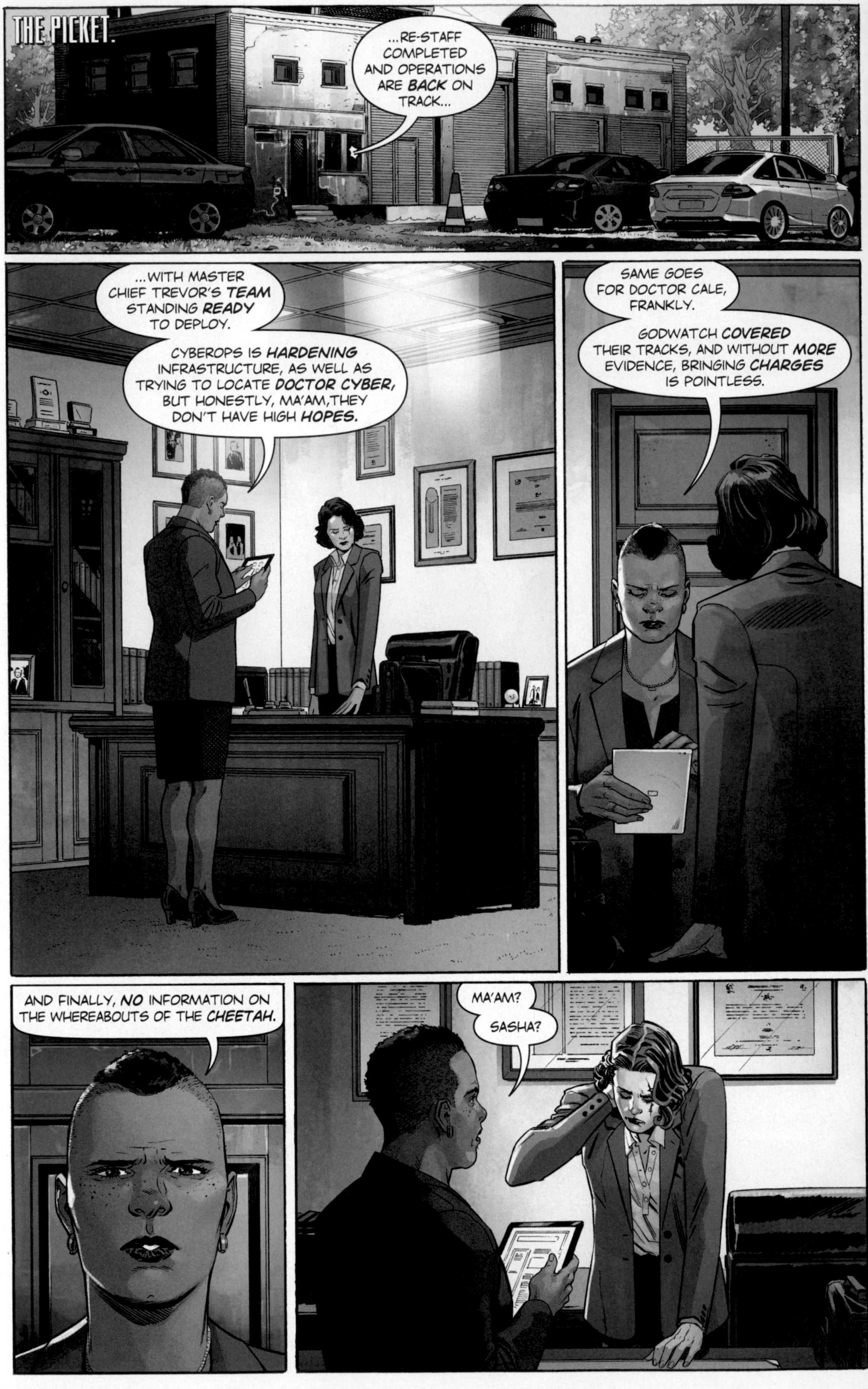
THE PICKET.
...RE-STAFF COMPLETED AND OPERATIONS ARE BACK ON TRACK...
...WITH MASTER CHIEF TREVOR'S TEAM STANDING READY TO DEPLOY.
CYBEROPS IS HARDENING INFRASTRUCTURE, AS WELL AS TRYING TO LOCATE DOCTOR CYBER, BUT HONESTLY, MA'AM,THEY DON'T HAVE HIGH HOPES.
SAME GOES FOR DOCTOR CALE, FRANKLY.
GODWATCH COVERED THEIR TRACKS, AND WITHOUT MORE EVIDENCE, BRINGING CHARGES IS POINTLESS.
AND FINALLY, NO INFORMATION ON THE WHEREABOUTS OF THE CHEETAH.
MA'AM?
SASHA?

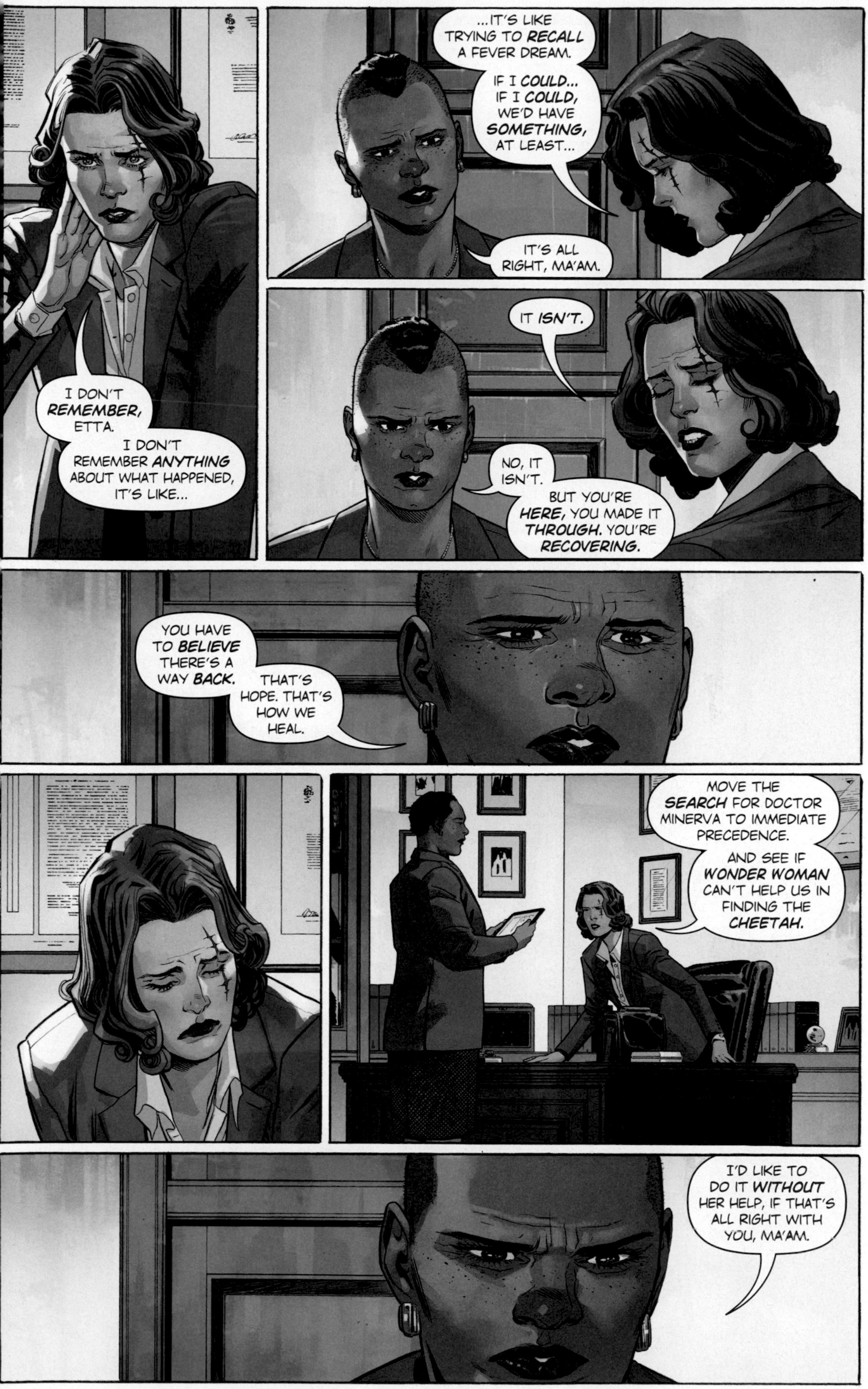
I DON'T REMEMBER, ETTA.
I DON'T REMEMBER ANYTHING ABOUT WHAT HAPPENED, IT'S LIKE...
...IT'S LIKE TRYING TO RECALL A FEVER DREAM.
IF I COULD... IF I COULD, WE'D HAVE SOMETHING, AT LEAST...
IT'S ALL RIGHT, MA'AM.
IT ISN'T.
NO, IT ISN'T.
BUT YOU'RE HERE, YOU MADE IT THROUGH. YOU'RE RECOVERING.
YOU HAVE TO BELIEVE THERE'S A WAY BACK.
THAT'S HOPE. THAT'S HOW WE HEAL.
MOVE THE SEARCH FOR DOCTOR MINERVA TO IMMEDIATE PRECEDENCE.
AND SEE IF WONDER WOMAN CAN'T HELP US IN FINDING THE CHEETAH.
I'D LIKE TO DO IT WITHOUT HER HELP, IF THAT'S ALL RIGHT WITH YOU, MA'AM.

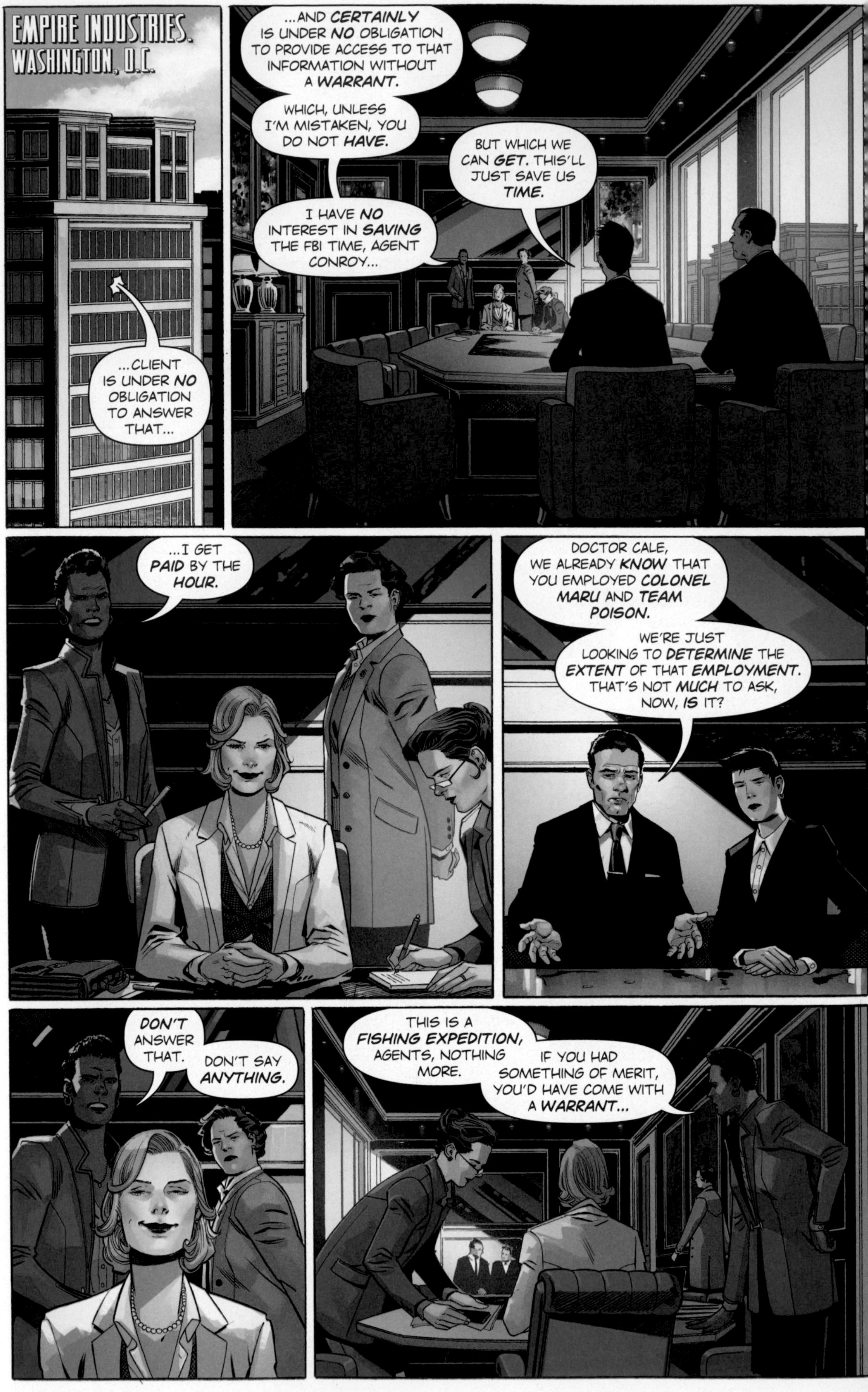
EMPIRE INDUSTRIES. WASHINGTON, D.C.
...CLIENT IS UNDER NO OBLIGATION TO ANSWER THAT...
...AND CERTAINLY IS UNDER NO OBLIGATION TO PROVIDE ACCESS TO THAT INFORMATION WITHOUT A WARRANT.
WHICH, UNLESS I'M MISTAKEN, YOU DO NOT HAVE.
BUT WHICH WE CAN GET. THIS'LL JUST SAVE US TIME.
I HAVE NO INTEREST IN SAVING THE FBI TIME, AGENT CONROY...
...I GET PAID BY THE HOUR.
DOCTOR CALE, WE ALREADY KNOW THAT YOU EMPLOYED COLONEL MARU AND TEAM POISON.
WE'RE JUST LOOKING TO DETERMINE THE EXTENT OF THAT EMPLOYMENT. THAT'S NOT MUCH TO ASK, NOW, IS IT?
DON'T ANSWER THAT.
DON'T SAY ANYTHING.
THIS IS A FISHING EXPEDITION, AGENTS, NOTHING MORE.
IF YOU HAD SOMETHING OF MERIT, YOU'D HAVE COME WITH A WARRANT...

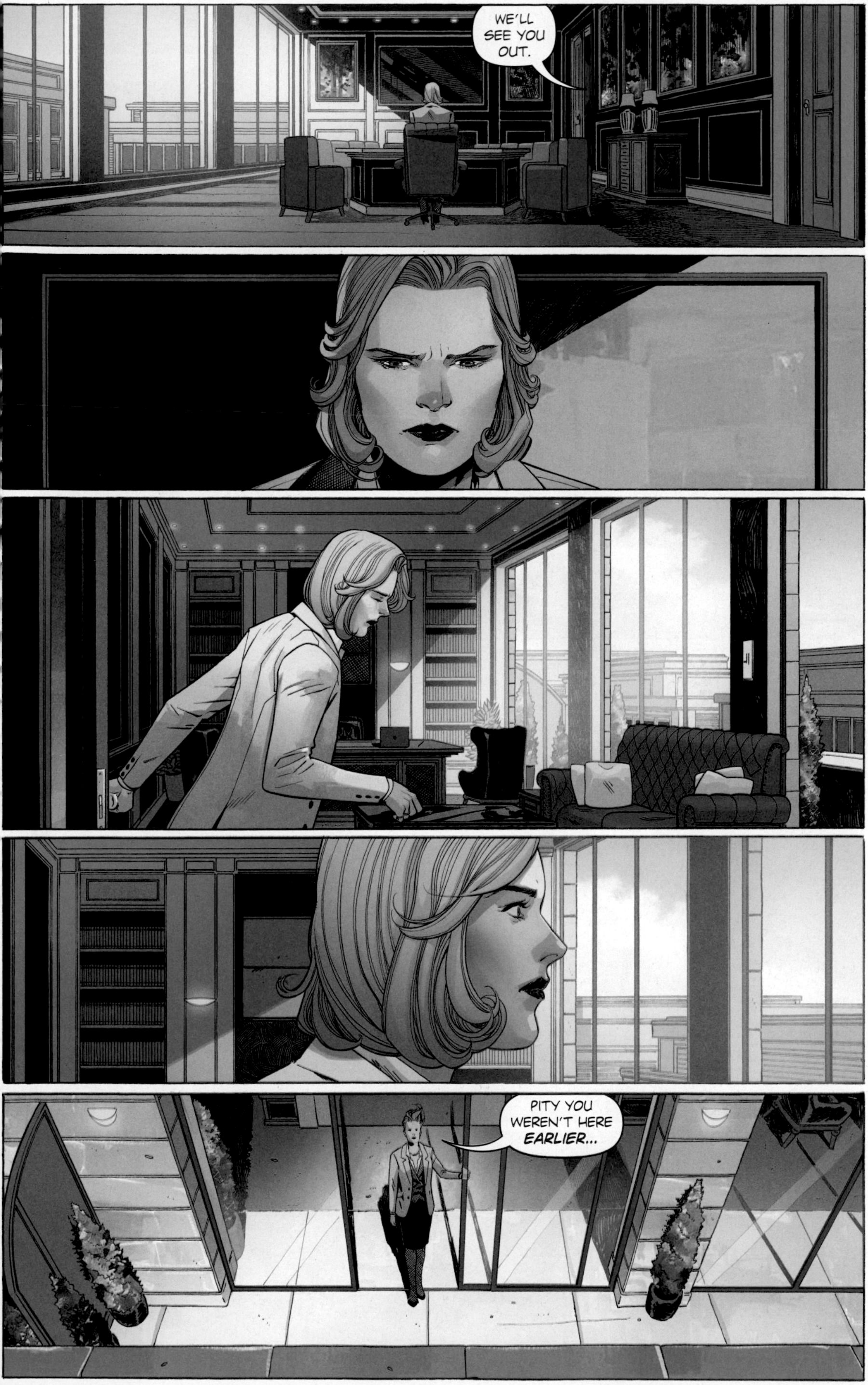
WE'LL SEE YOU OUT.
PITY YOU WEREN'T HERE EARLIER...

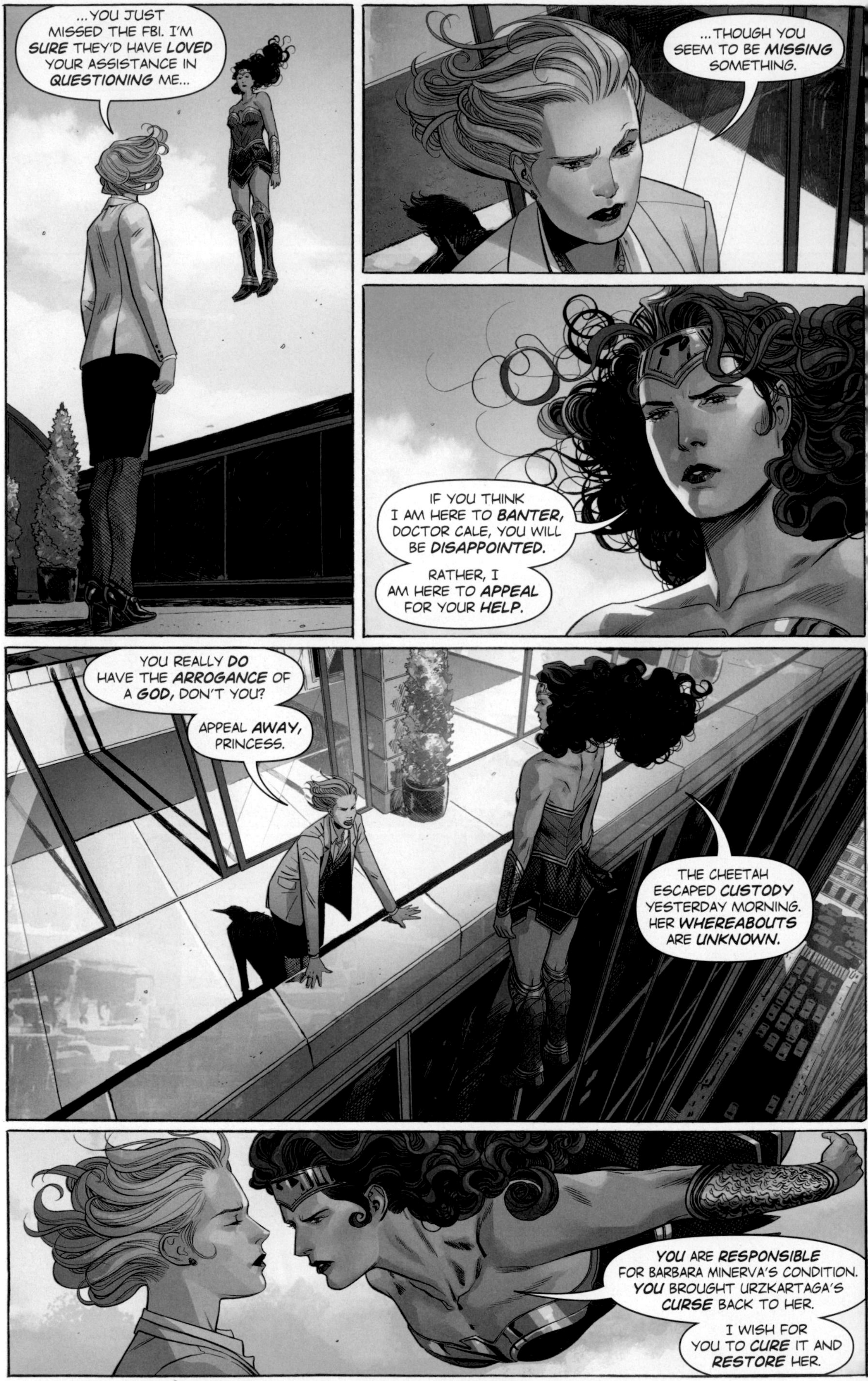
...YOU JUST MISSED THE FBI. I'M SURE THEY'D HAVE LOVED YOUR ASSISTANCE IN QUESTIONING ME...
...THOUGH YOU SEEM TO BE MISSING SOMETHING.
IF YOU THINK I AM HERE TO BANTER, DOCTOR CALE, YOU WILL BE DISAPPOINTED.
RATHER, I AM HERE TO APPEAL FOR YOUR HELP.
YOU REALLY DO HAVE THE ARROGANCE OF A GOD, DON'T YOU?
APPEAL AWAY, PRINCESS.
THE CHEETAH ESCAPED CUSTODY YESTERDAY MORNING. HER WHEREABOUTS ARE UNKNOWN.
YOU ARE RESPONSIBLE FOR BARBARA MINERVA'S CONDITION. YOU BROUGHT URZKARTAGA'S CURSE BACK TO HER.
I WISH FOR YOU TO CURE IT AND RESTORE HER.

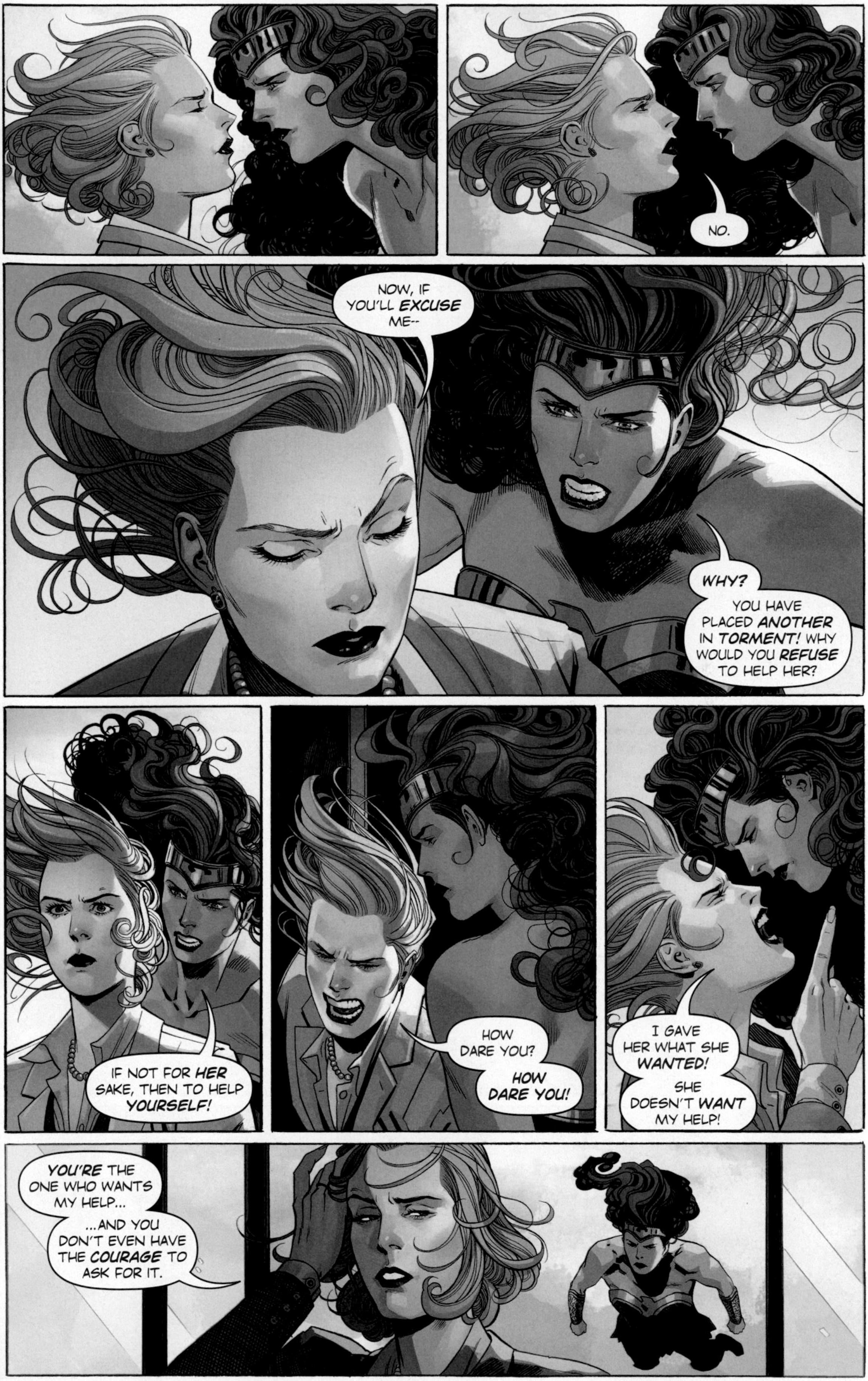
NO.
NOW, IF YOU'LL EXCUSE ME--
WHY?
YOU HAVE PLACED ANOTHER IN TORMENT! WHY WOULD YOU REFUSE TO HELP HER?
IF NOT FOR HER SAKE, THEN TO HELP YOURSELF!
HOW DARE YOU?
HOW DARE YOU!
I GAVE HER WHAT SHE WANTED!
SHE DOESN'T WANT MY HELP!
YOU'RE THE ONE WHO WANTS MY HELP...
...AND YOU DON'T EVEN HAVE THE COURAGE TO ASK FOR IT.

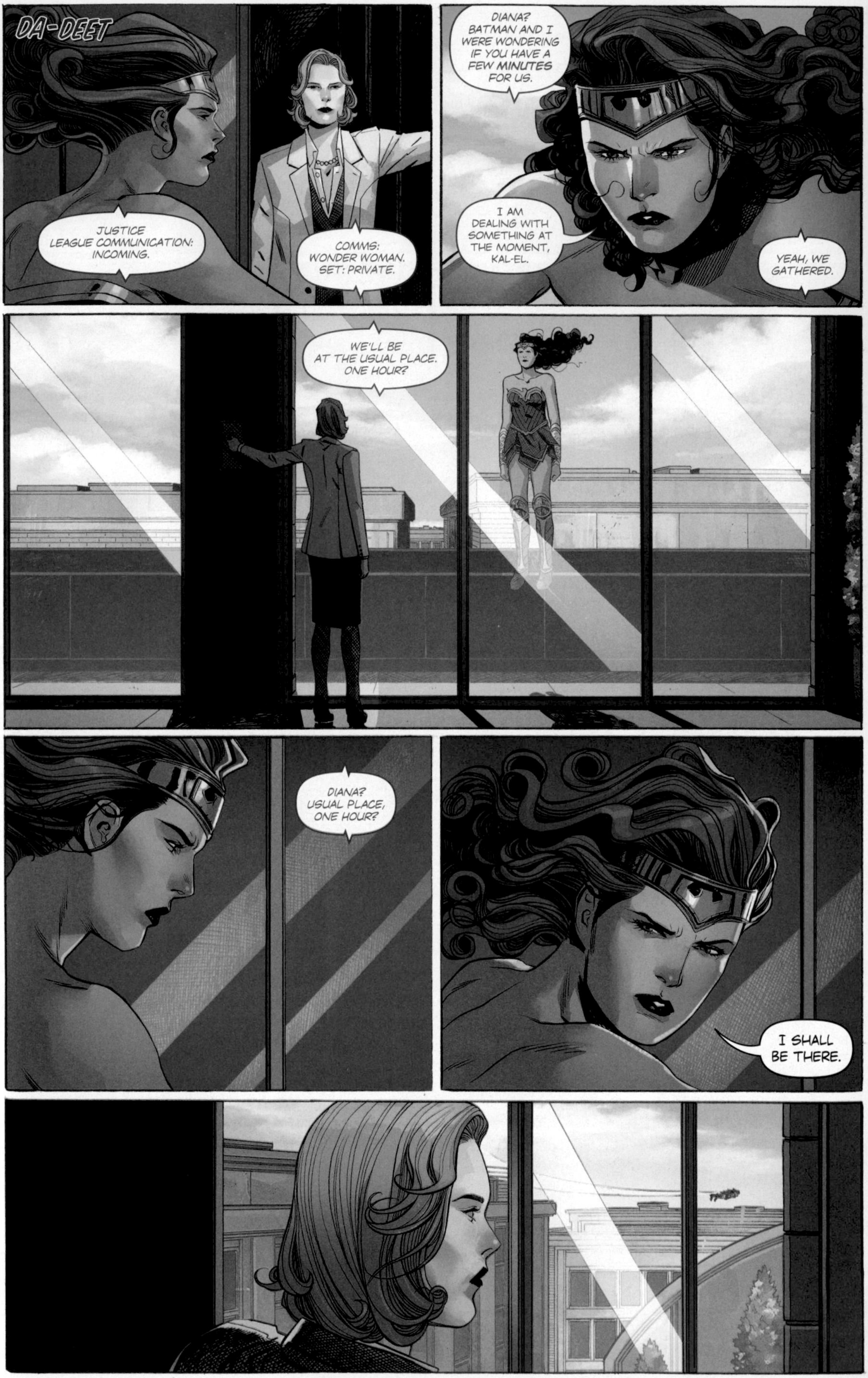
DA-DEET
JUSTICE LEAGUE COMMUNICATION: INCOMING.
COMMS: WONDER WOMAN. SET: PRIVATE.
DIANA? BATMAN AND I WERE WONDERING IF YOU HAVE A FEW MINUTES FOR US.
I AM DEALING WITH SOMETHING AT THE MOMENT, KAL-EL.
YEAH, WE GATHERED.
WE'LL BE AT THE USUAL PLACE. ONE HOUR?
DIANA? USUAL PLACE, ONE HOUR?
I SHALL BE THERE.

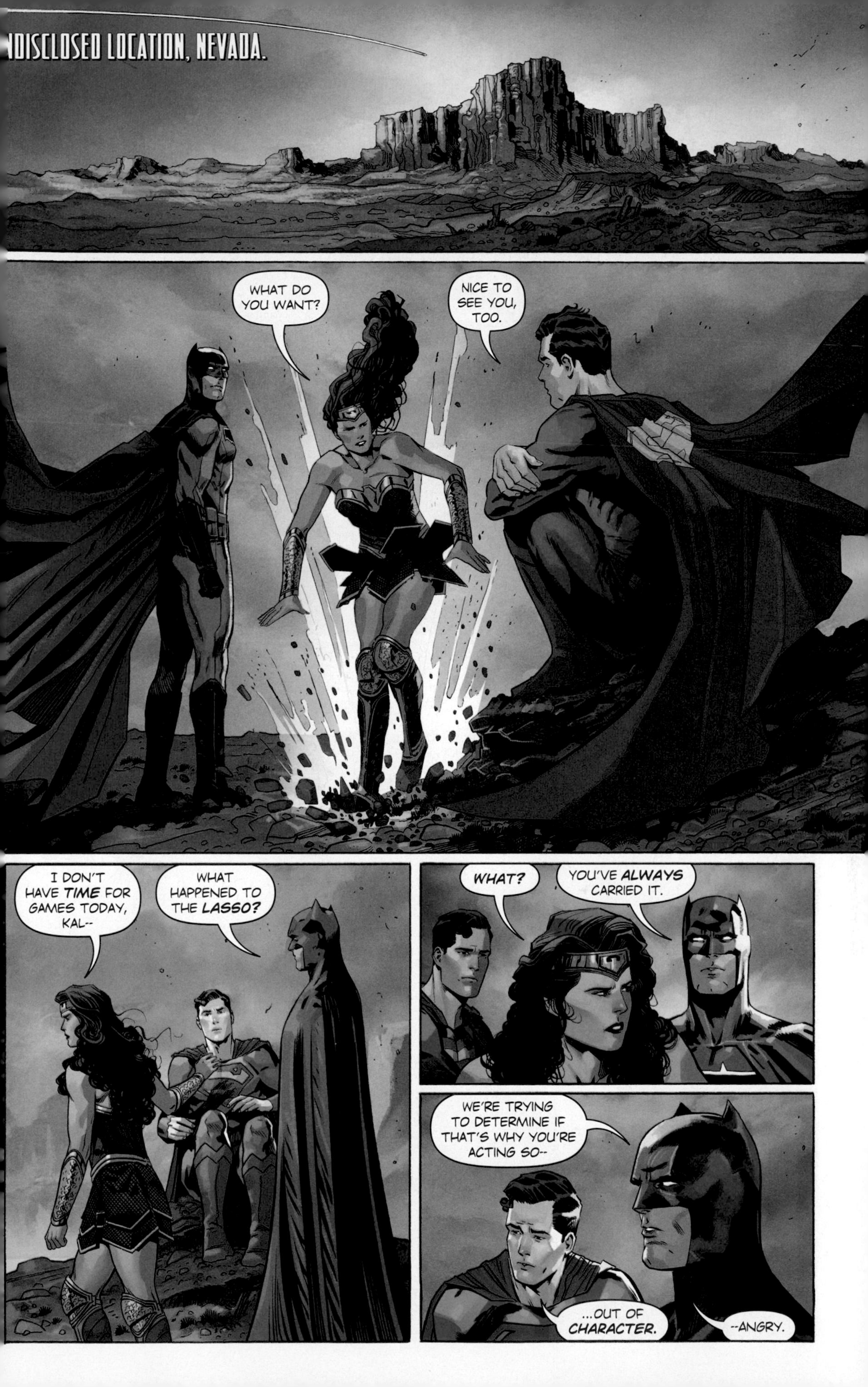
NDISCLOSED LOCATION, NEVADA.
WHAT DO YOU WANT?
NICE TO SEE YOU, TOO.
I DON'T HAVE TIME FOR GAMES TODAY, KAL--
WHAT HAPPENED TO THE LASSO?
WHAT?
YOU'VE ALWAYS CARRIED IT.
WE'RE TRYING TO DETERMINE IF THAT'S WHY YOU'RE ACTING SO--
...OUT OF CHARACTER.
--ANGRY.

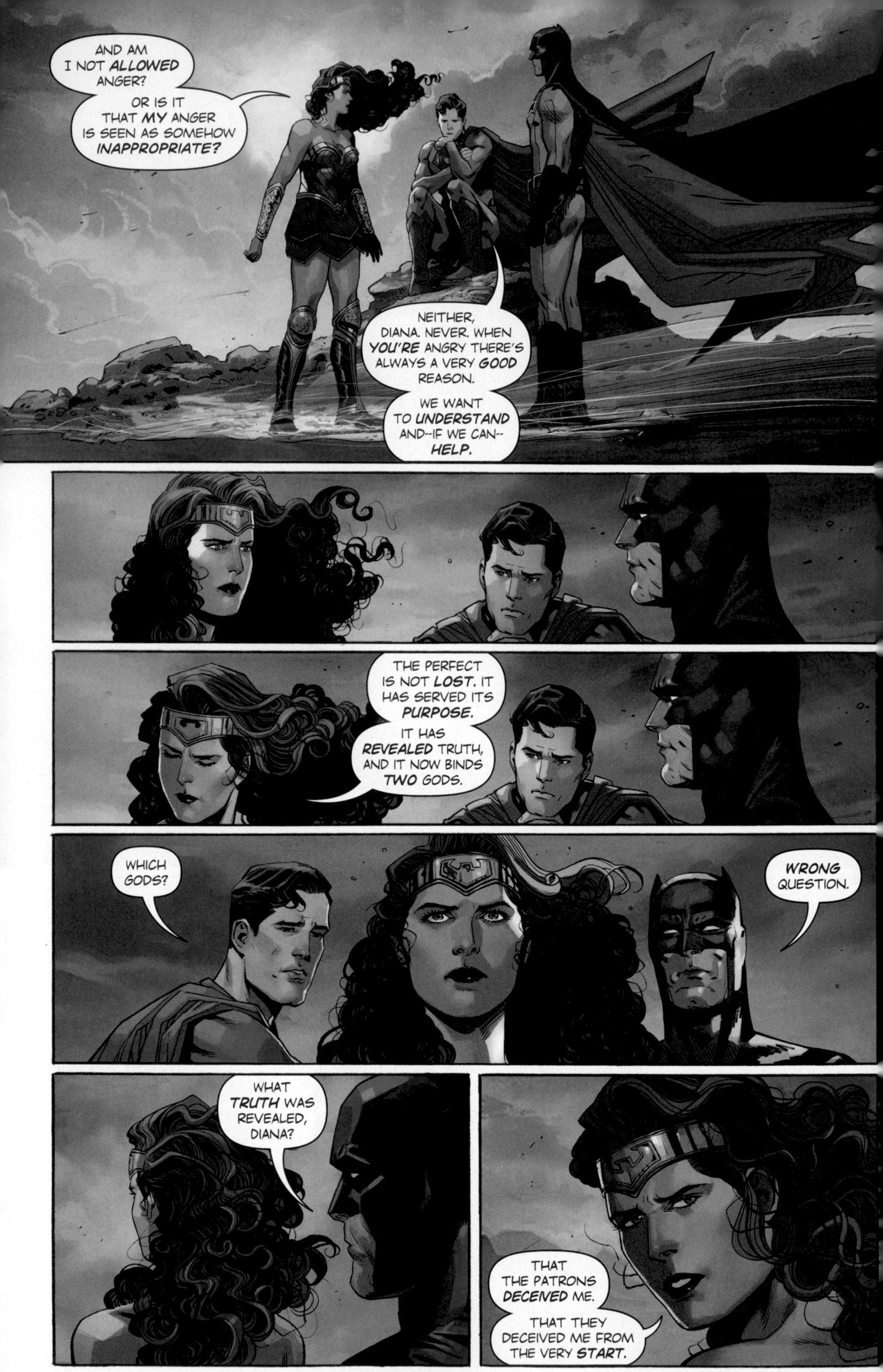
AND AM I NOT ALLOWED ANGER?
OR IS IT THAT MY ANGER IS SEEN AS SOMEHOW INAPPROPRIATE?
NEITHER, DIANA. NEVER. WHEN YOU'RE ANGRY THERE'S ALWAYS A VERY GOOD REASON.
WE WANT TO UNDERSTAND AND--IF WE CAN--HELP.
THE PERFECT IS NOT LOST. IT HAS SERVED ITS PURPOSE.
IT HAS REVEALED TRUTH, AND IT NOW BINDS TWO GODS.
WHICH GODS?
WRONG QUESTION.
WHAT TRUTH WAS REVEALED, DIANA?
THAT THE PATRONS DECEIVED ME.
THAT THEY DECEIVED ME FROM THE VERY START.

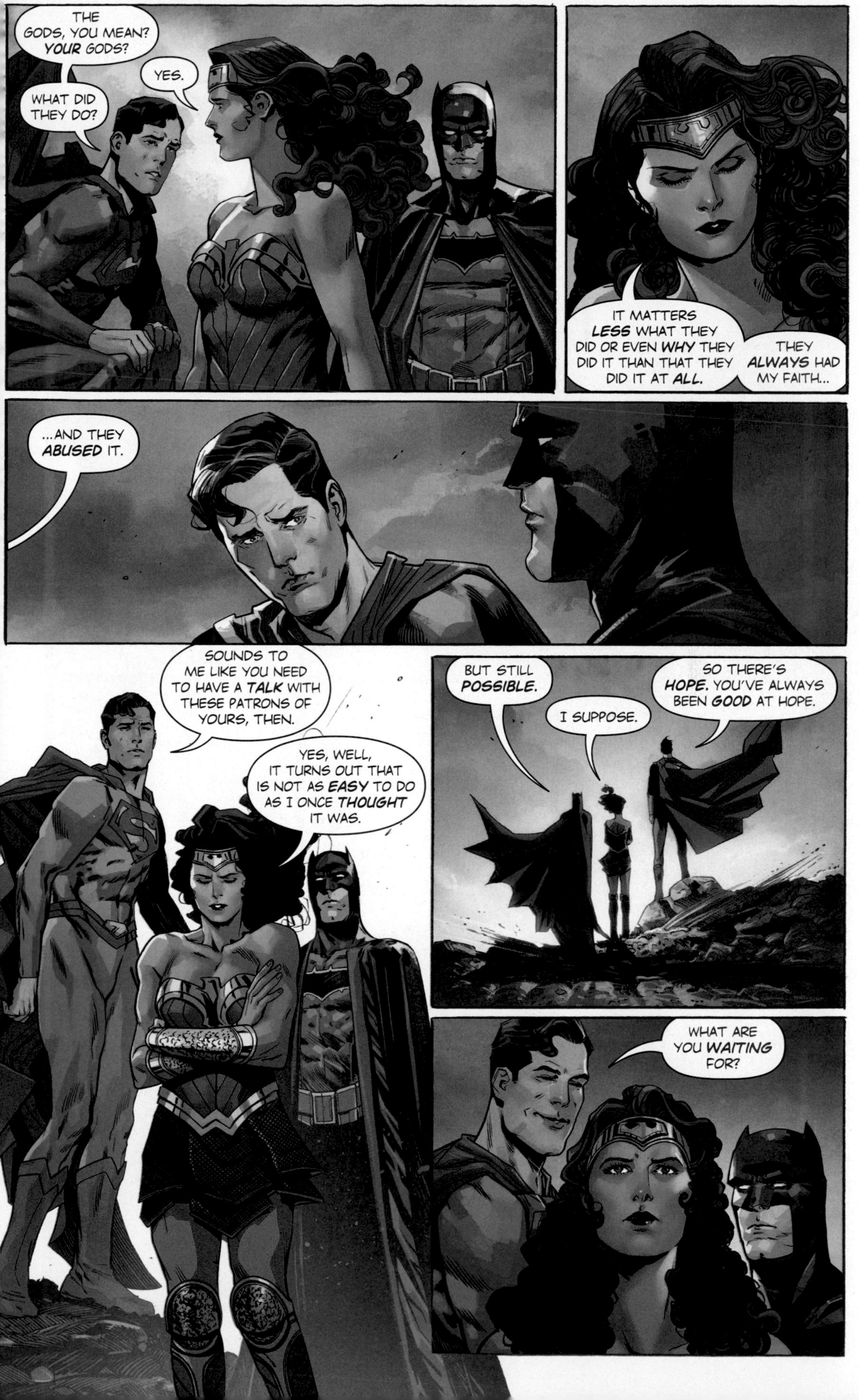
THE GODS, YOU MEAN? YOUR GODS?
YES.
WHAT DID THEY DO?
IT MATTERS LESS WHAT THEY DID OR EVEN WHY THEY DID IT THAN THAT THEY DID IT AT ALL.
THEY ALWAYS HAD MY FAITH...
...AND THEY ABUSED IT.
SOUNDS TO ME LIKE YOU NEED TO HAVE A TALK WITH THESE PATRONS OF YOURS, THEN.
YES, WELL, IT TURNS OUT THAT IS NOT AS EASY TO DO AS I ONCE THOUGHT IT WAS.
BUT STILL POSSIBLE.
I SUPPOSE.
SO THERE'S HOPE. YOU'VE ALWAYS BEEN GOOD AT HOPE.
WHAT ARE YOU WAITING FOR?

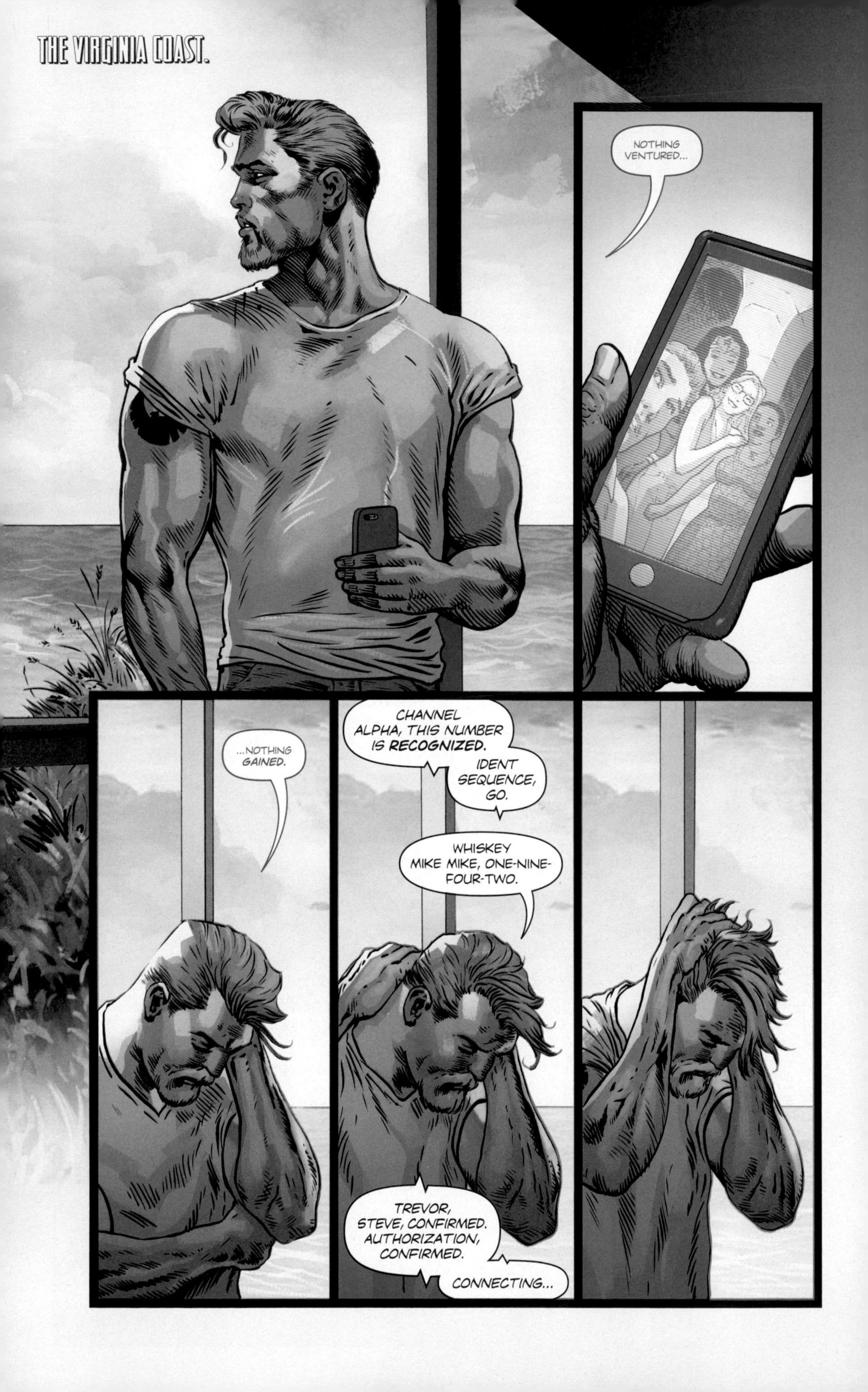
THE VIRGINIA COAST.
NOTHING VENTURED...
...NOTHING GAINED.
CHANNEL ALPHA, THIS NUMBER IS RECOGNIZED.
IDENT SEQUENCE, GO.
WHISKEY MIKE MIKE, ONE-NINE-FOUR-TWO.
TREVOR, STEVE, CONFIRMED. AUTHORIZATION, CONFIRMED.
CONNECTING...

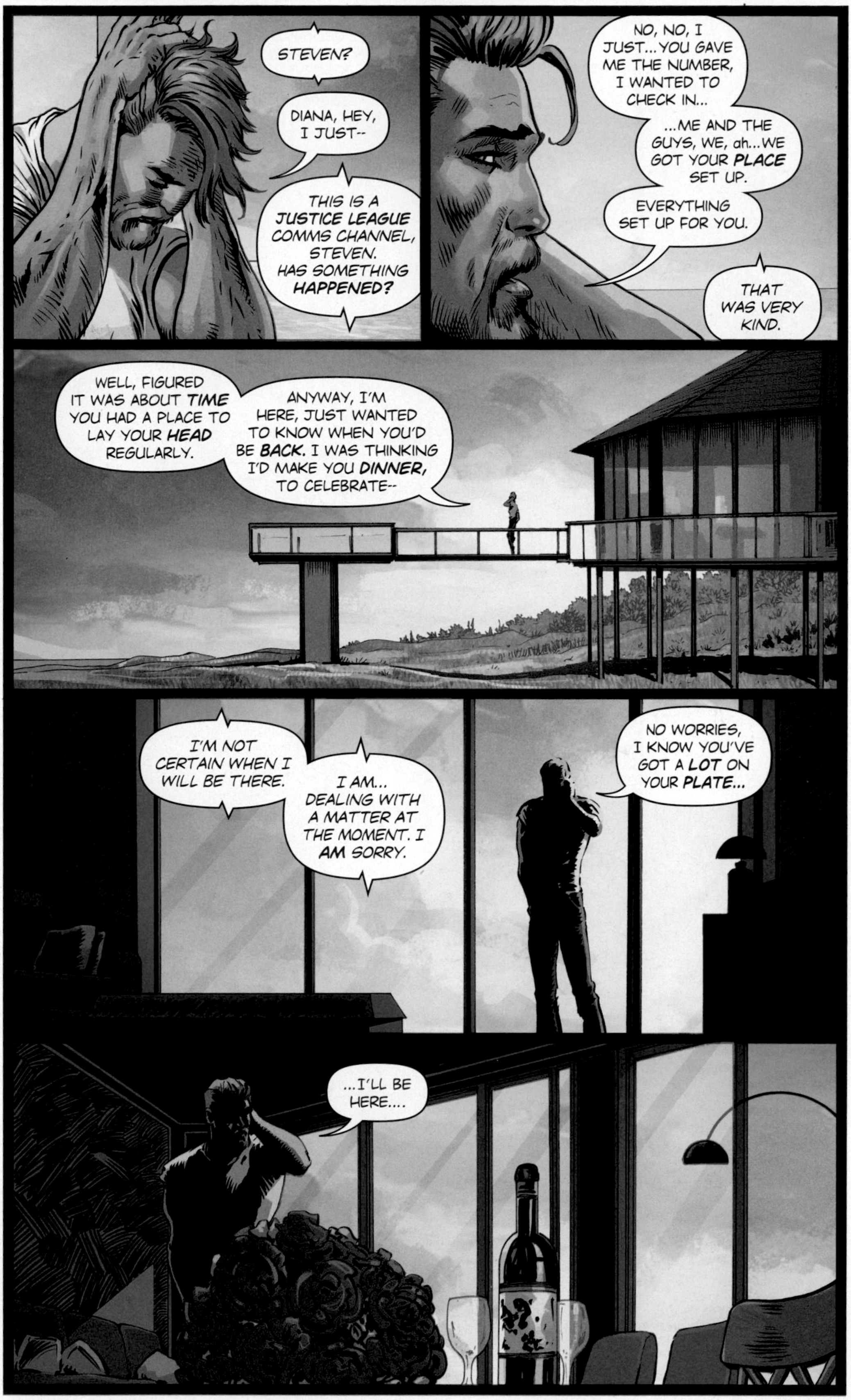
STEVEN?
DIANA, HEY, I JUST--
THIS IS A JUSTICE LEAGUE COMMS CHANNEL, STEVEN. HAS SOMETHING HAPPENED?
NO, NO, I JUST...YOU GAVE ME THE NUMBER, I WANTED TO CHECK IN...
...ME AND THE GUYS, WE, ah...WE GOT YOUR PLACE SET UP.
EVERYTHING SET UP FOR YOU.
THAT WAS VERY KIND.
WELL, FIGURED IT WAS ABOUT TIME YOU HAD A PLACE TO LAY YOUR HEAD REGULARLY.
ANYWAY, I'M HERE, JUST WANTED TO KNOW WHEN YOU'D BE BACK. I WAS THINKING I'D MAKE YOU DINNER, TO CELEBRATE--
I'M NOT CERTAIN WHEN I WILL BE THERE.
I AM... DEALING WITH A MATTER AT THE MOMENT. I AM SORRY.
NO WORRIES, I KNOW YOU'VE GOT A LOT ON YOUR PLATE...
...I'LL BE HERE....

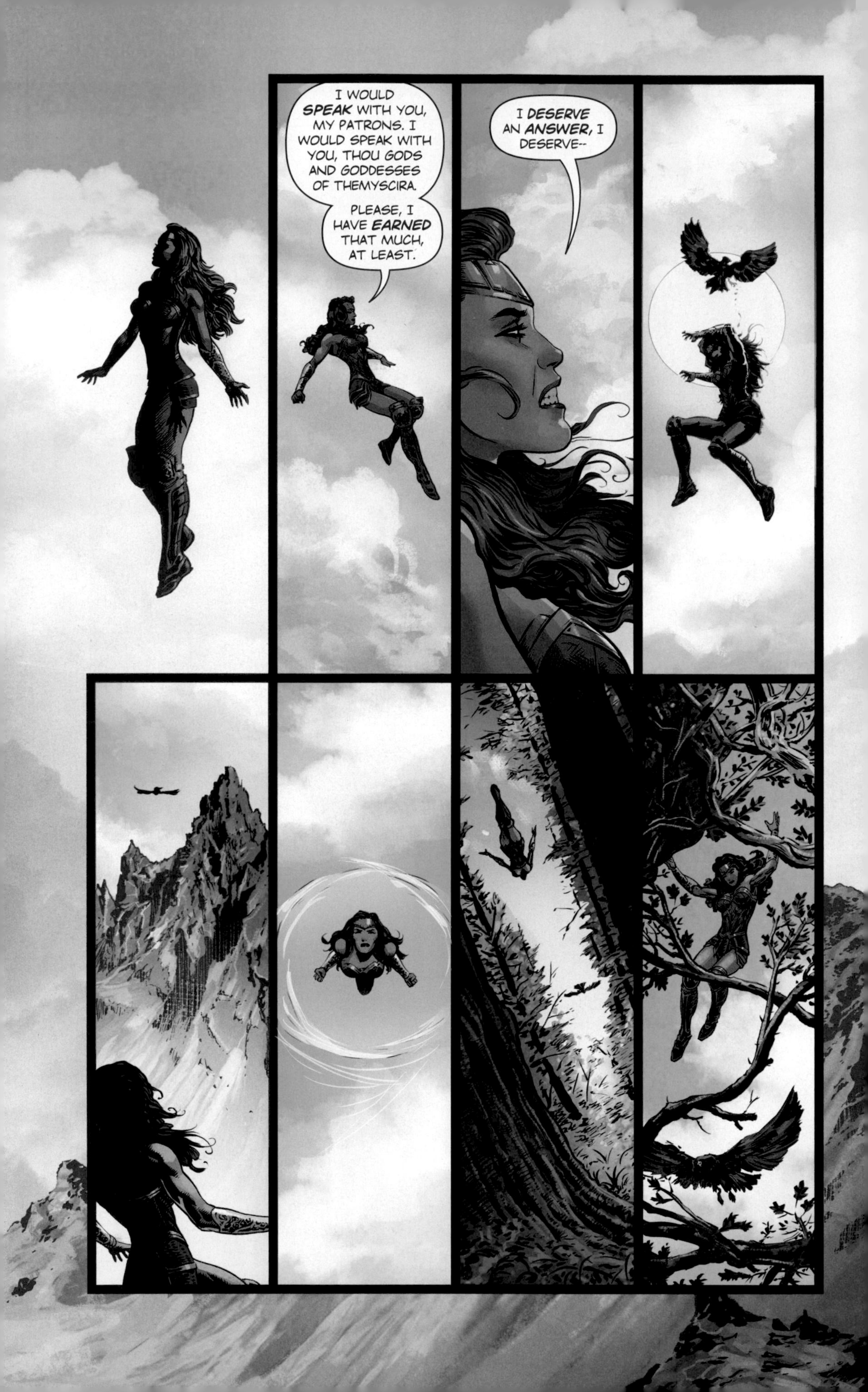
I WOULD SPEAK WITH YOU, MY PATRONS. I WOULD SPEAK WITH YOU, THOU GODS AND GODDESSES OF THEMYSCIRA.
PLEASE, I HAVE EARNED THAT MUCH, AT LEAST.
I DESERVE AN ANSWER, I DESERVE--

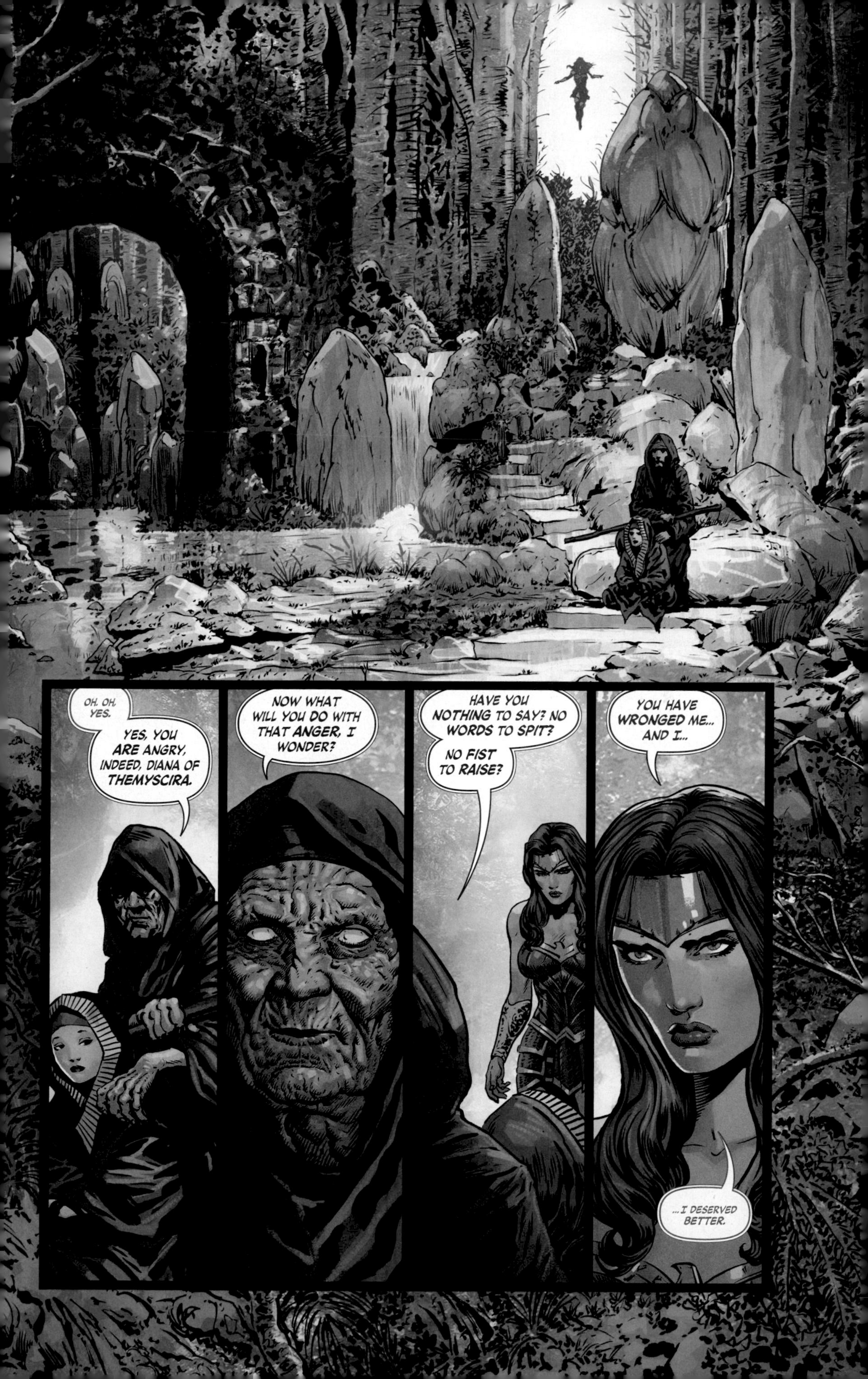
OH. OH. YES.
YES, YOU ARE ANGRY, INDEED, DIANA OF THEMYSCIRA.
NOW WHAT WILL YOU DO WITH THAT ANGER, I WONDER?
HAVE YOU NOTHING TO SAY? NO WORDS TO SPIT?
NO FIST TO RAISE?
YOU HAVE WRONGED ME... AND I...
...I DESERVED BETTER.

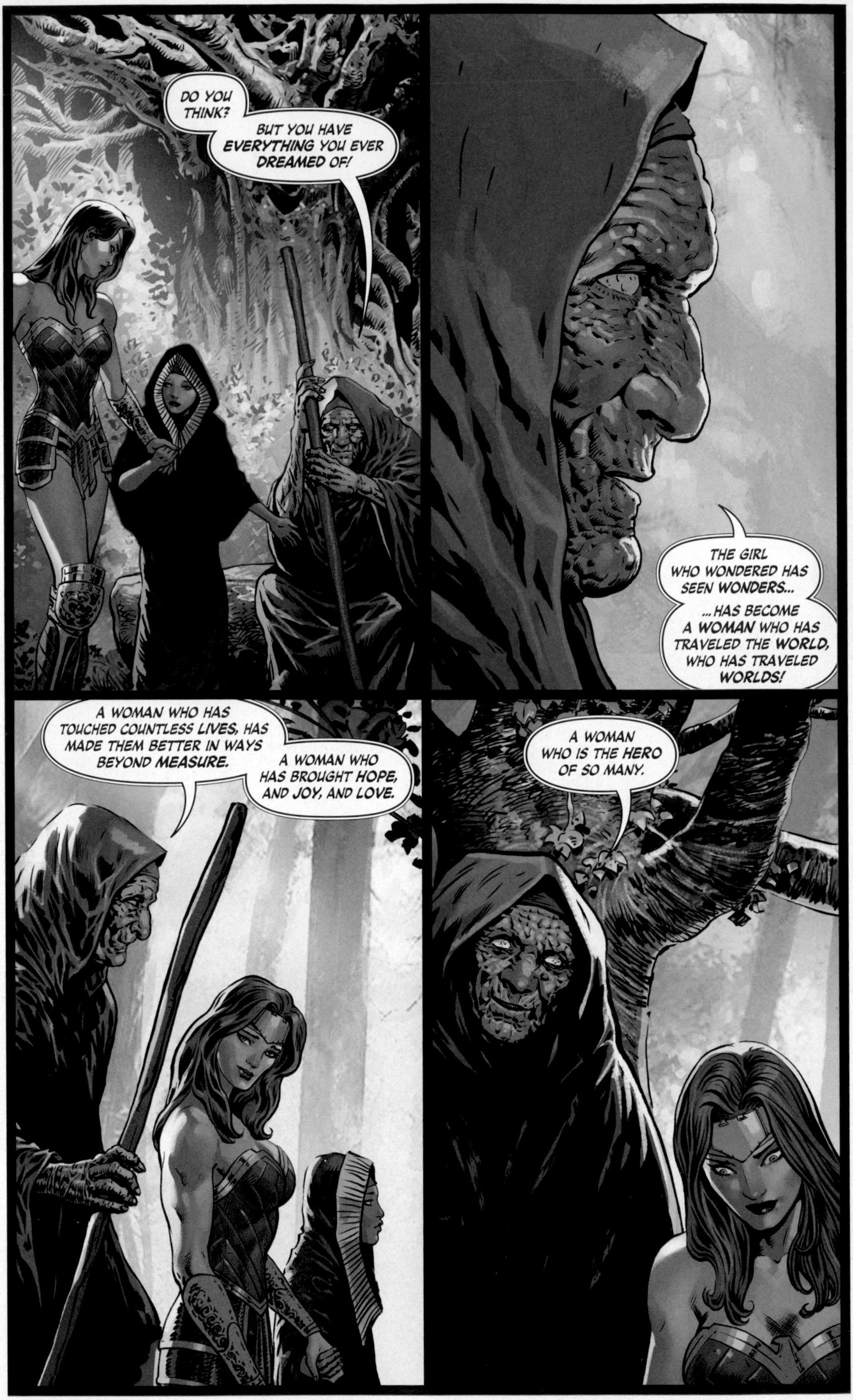
DO YOU THINK?
BUT YOU HAVE EVERYTHING YOU EVER DREAMED OF!
THE GIRL WHO WONDERED HAS SEEN WONDERS...
...HAS BECOME A WOMAN WHO HAS TRAVELED THE WORLD, WHO HAS TRAVELED WORLDS!
A WOMAN WHO HAS TOUCHED COUNTLESS LIVES, HAS MADE THEM BETTER IN WAYS BEYOND MEASURE.
A WOMAN WHO HAS BROUGHT HOPE, AND JOY, AND LOVE.
A WOMAN WHO IS THE HERO OF SO MANY.

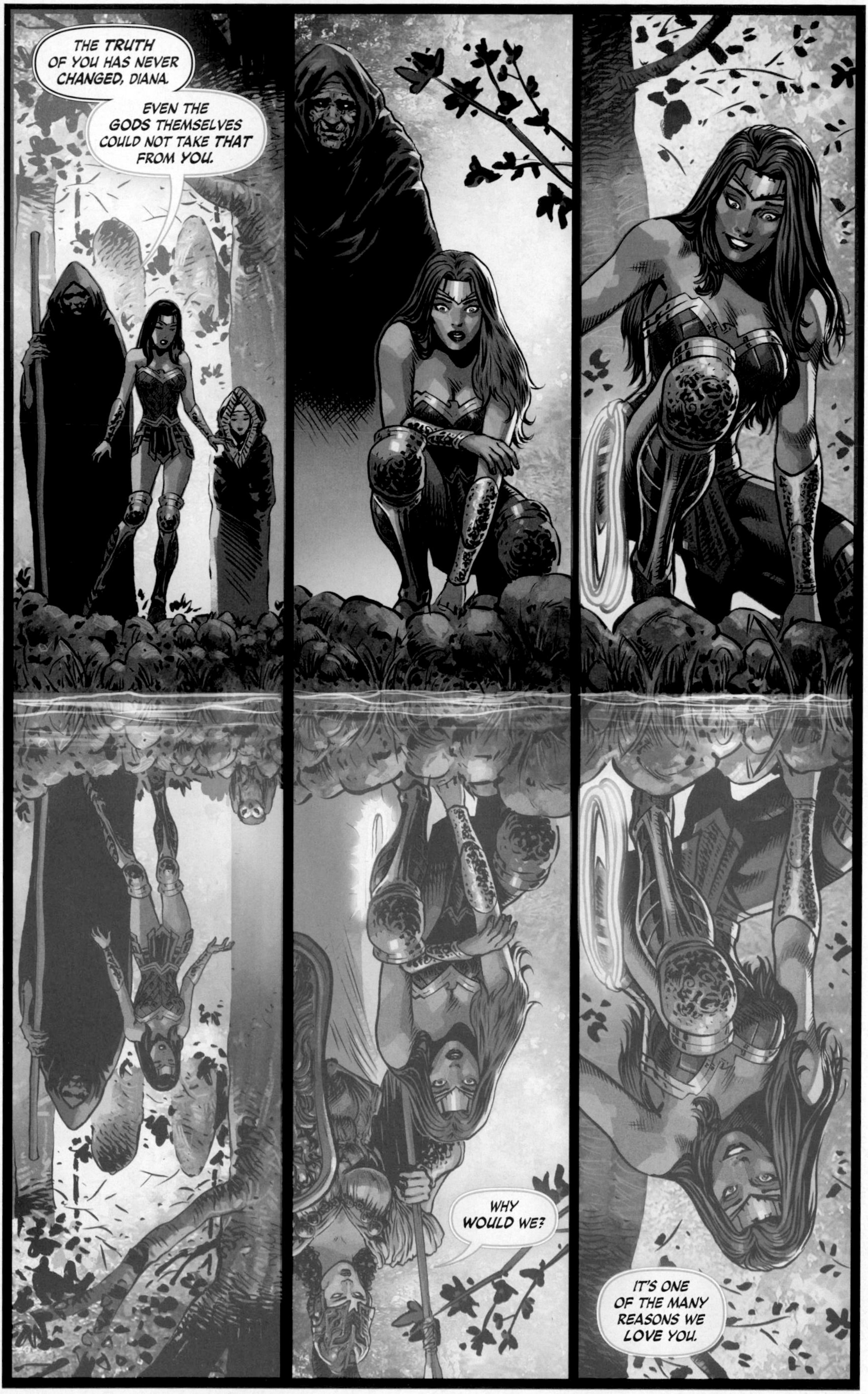
THE TRUTH OF YOU HAS NEVER CHANGED, DIANA.
EVEN THE GODS THEMSELVES COULD NOT TAKE THAT FROM YOU.
WHY WOULD WE?
IT'S ONE OF THE MANY REASONS WE LOVE YOU.

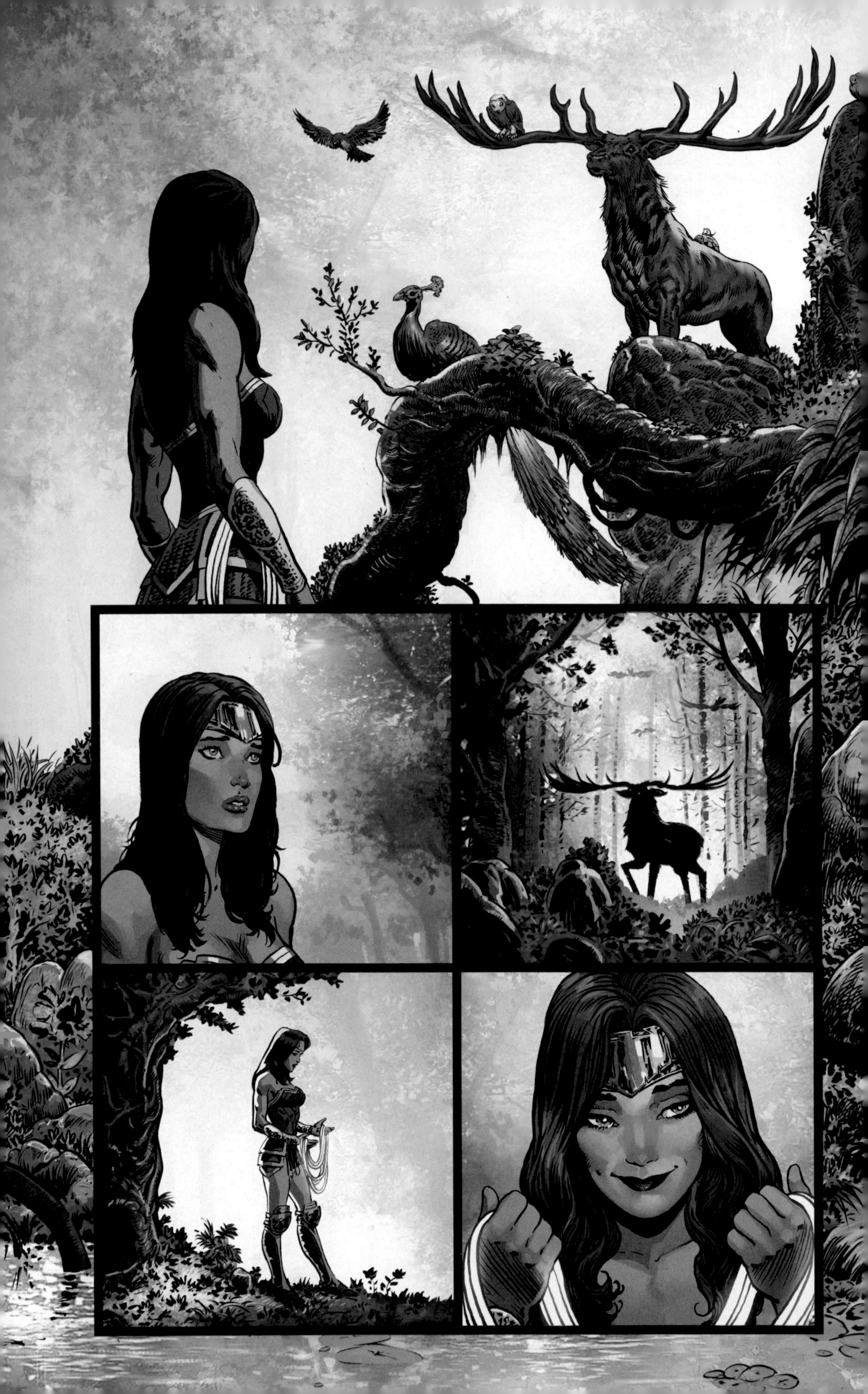

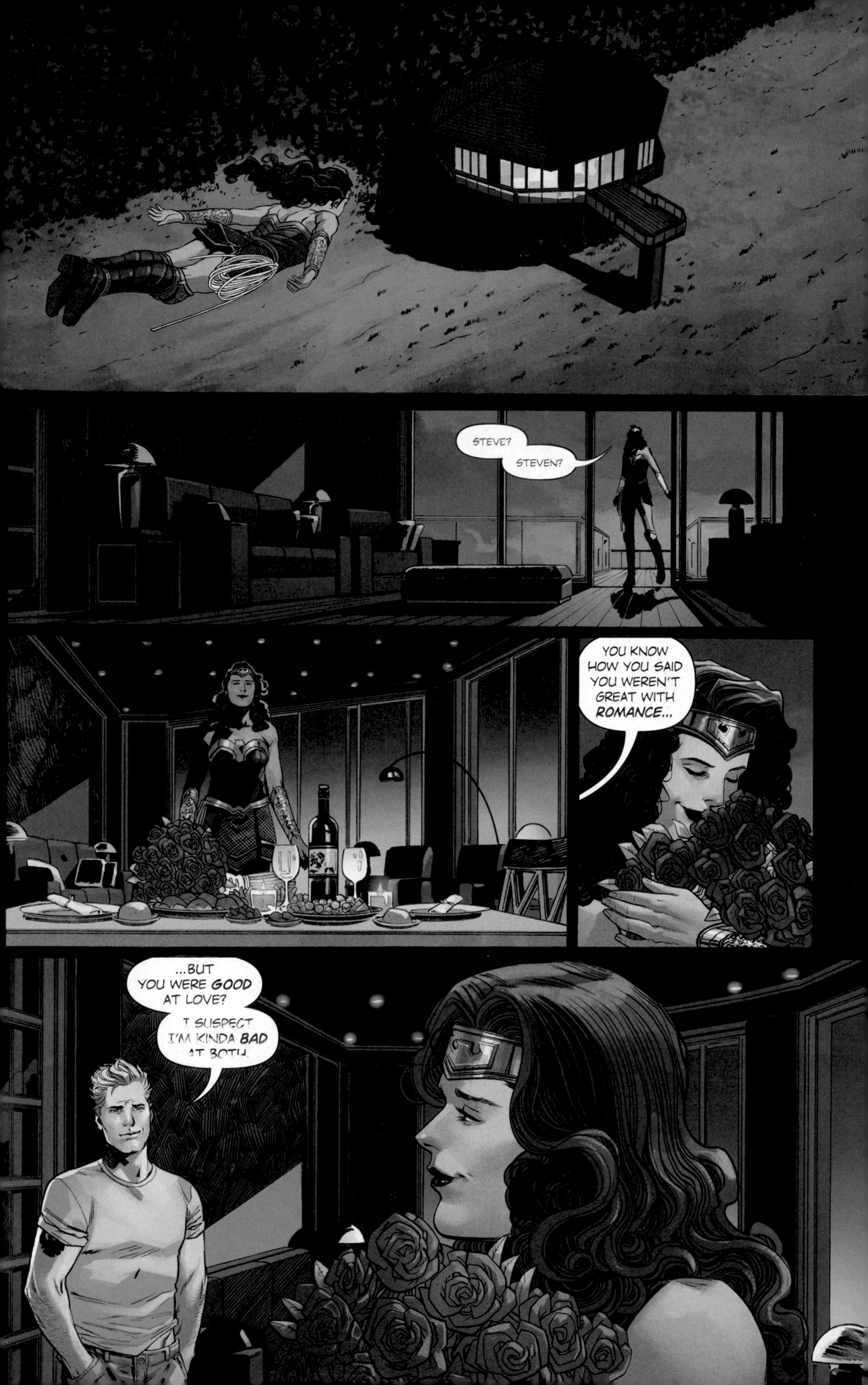
STEVE?
STEVEN?
YOU KNOW HOW YOU SAID YOU WEREN'T GREAT WITH ROMANCE...
...BUT YOU WERE GOOD AT LOVE?
I SUSPECT I'M KINDA BAD AT BOTH.

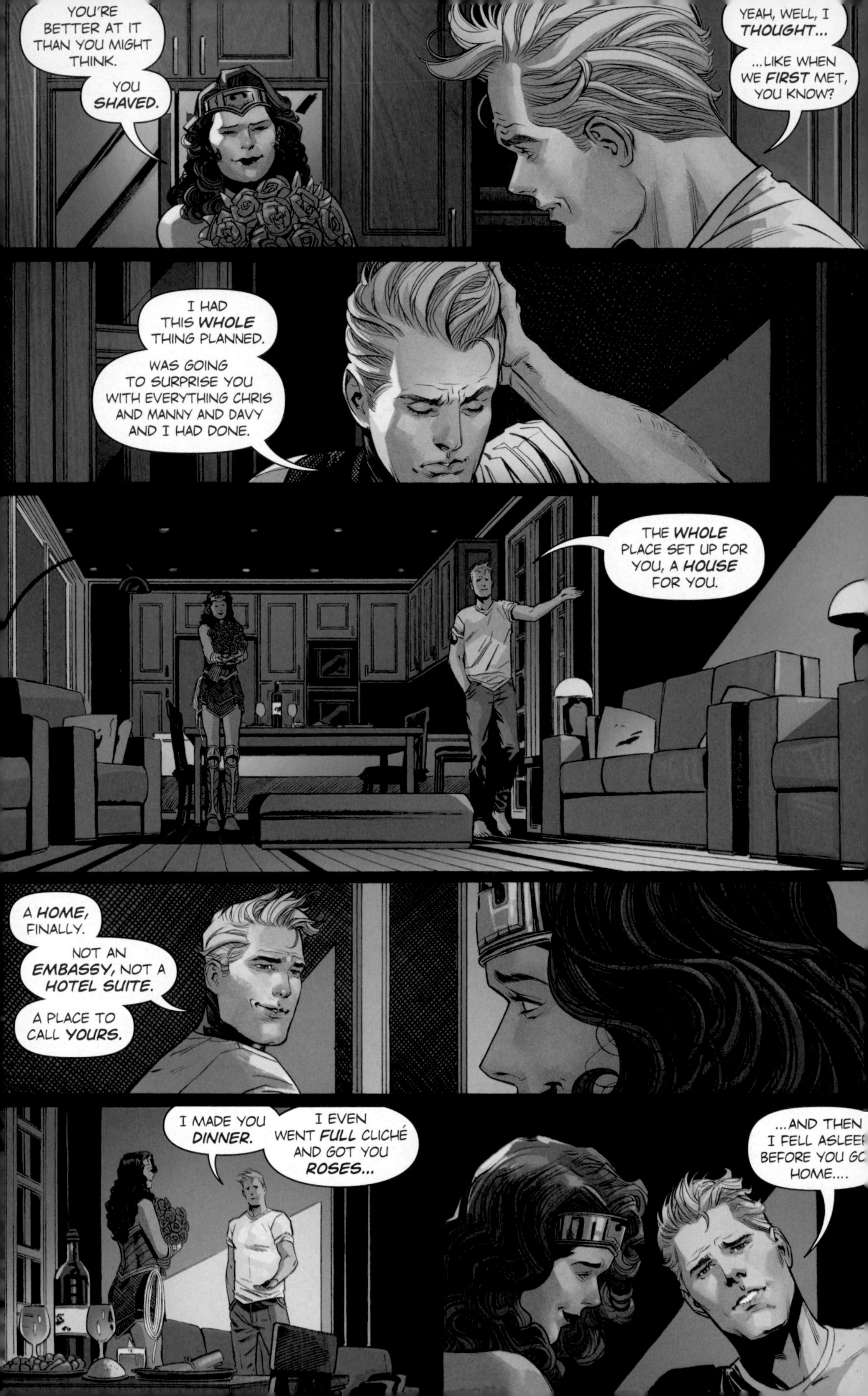
YOU'RE BETTER AT IT THAN YOU MIGHT THINK.
YOU SHAVED.
YEAH, WELL, I THOUGHT...
...LIKE WHEN WE FIRST MET, YOU KNOW?
I HAD THIS WHOLE THING PLANNED.
WAS GOING TO SURPRISE YOU WITH EVERYTHING CHRIS AND MANNY AND DAVY AND I HAD DONE.
THE WHOLE PLACE SET UP FOR YOU, A HOUSE FOR YOU.
A HOME, FINALLY.
NOT AN EMBASSY, NOT A HOTEL SUITE.
A PLACE TO CALL YOURS.
I MADE YOU DINNER.
I EVEN WENT FULL CLICHÉ AND GOT YOU ROSES...
...AND THEN I FELL ASLEE
BEFORE YOU GO
HOME....

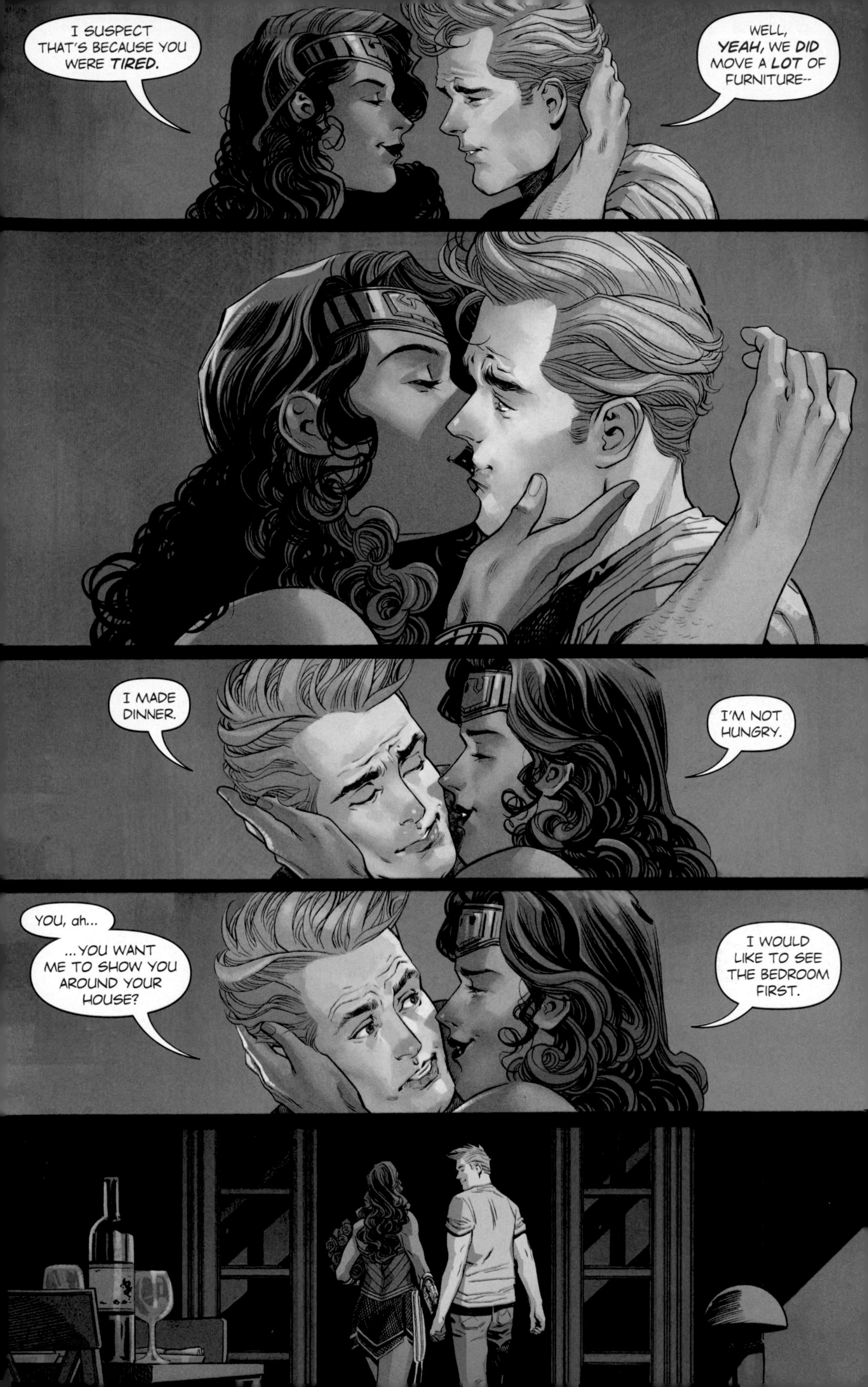
I SUSPECT THAT'S BECAUSE YOU WERE **TIRED.**
WELL, **YEAH,** WE **DID** MOVE A **LOT** OF FURNITURE--
I MADE DINNER.
I'M NOT HUNGRY.
YOU, ah...
...YOU WANT ME TO SHOW YOU AROUND YOUR HOUSE?
I WOULD LIKE TO SEE THE BEDROOM FIRST.

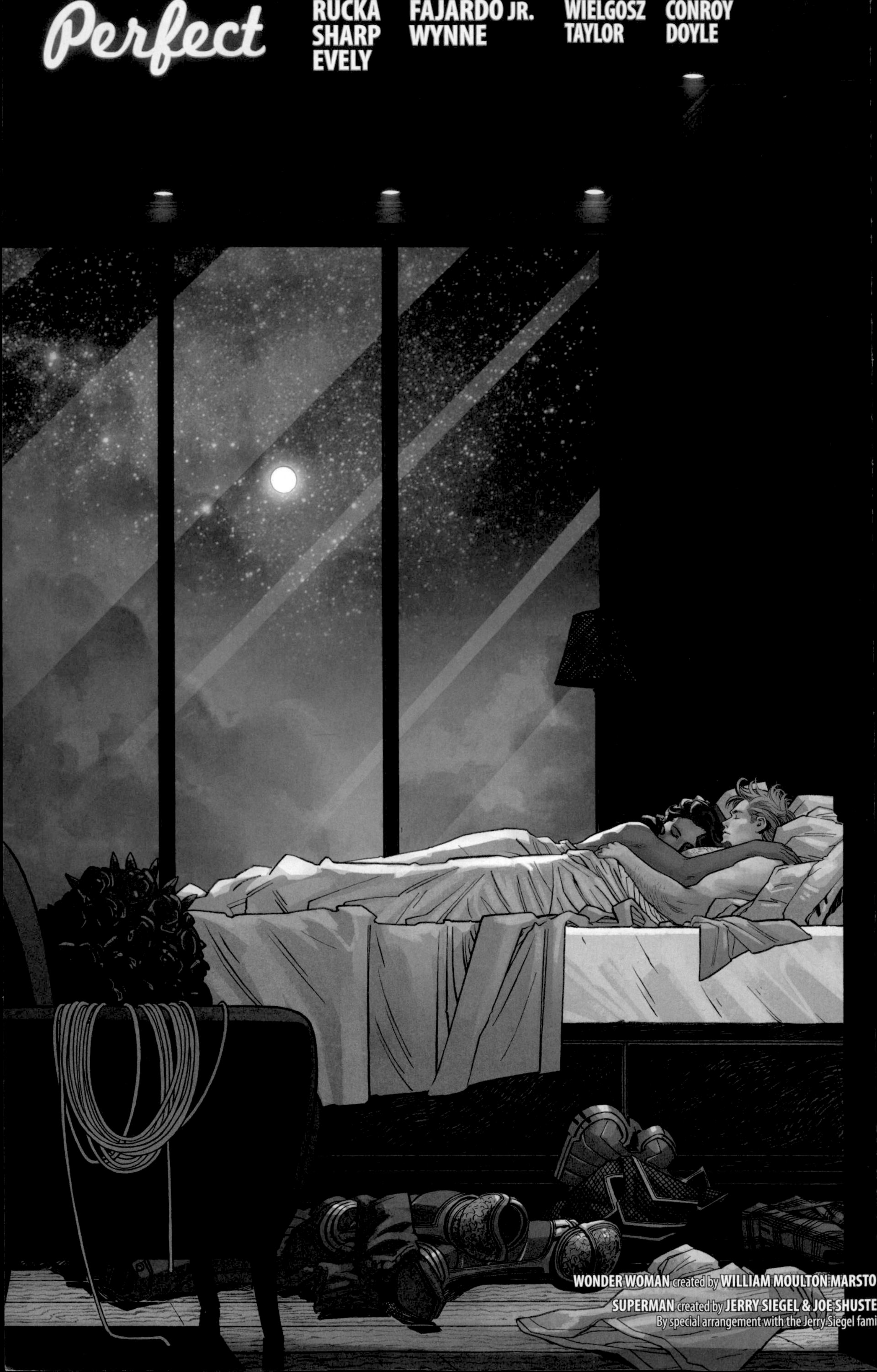
Perfect
RUCKA
SHARP
EVELY
FAJARDO JR.
WYNNE
WIELGOSZ
TAYLOR
CONROY
DOYLE
WONDER WOMAN created by WILLIAM MOULTON MARSTO
SUPERMAN created by JERRY SIEGEL & JOE SHUSTE
By special arrangement with the Jerry Siegel fami

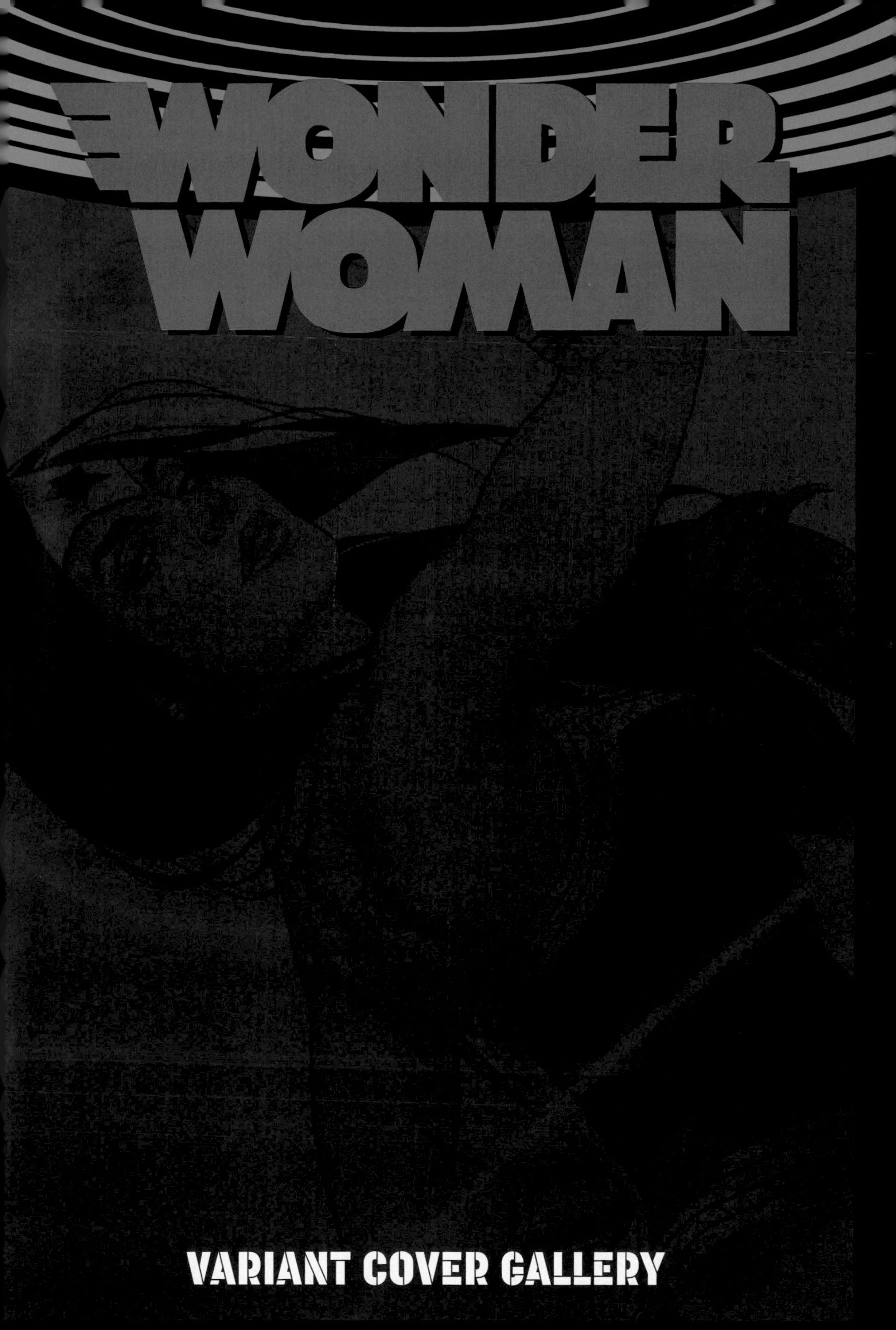
WONDER WOMAN

VARIANT COVER GALLERY

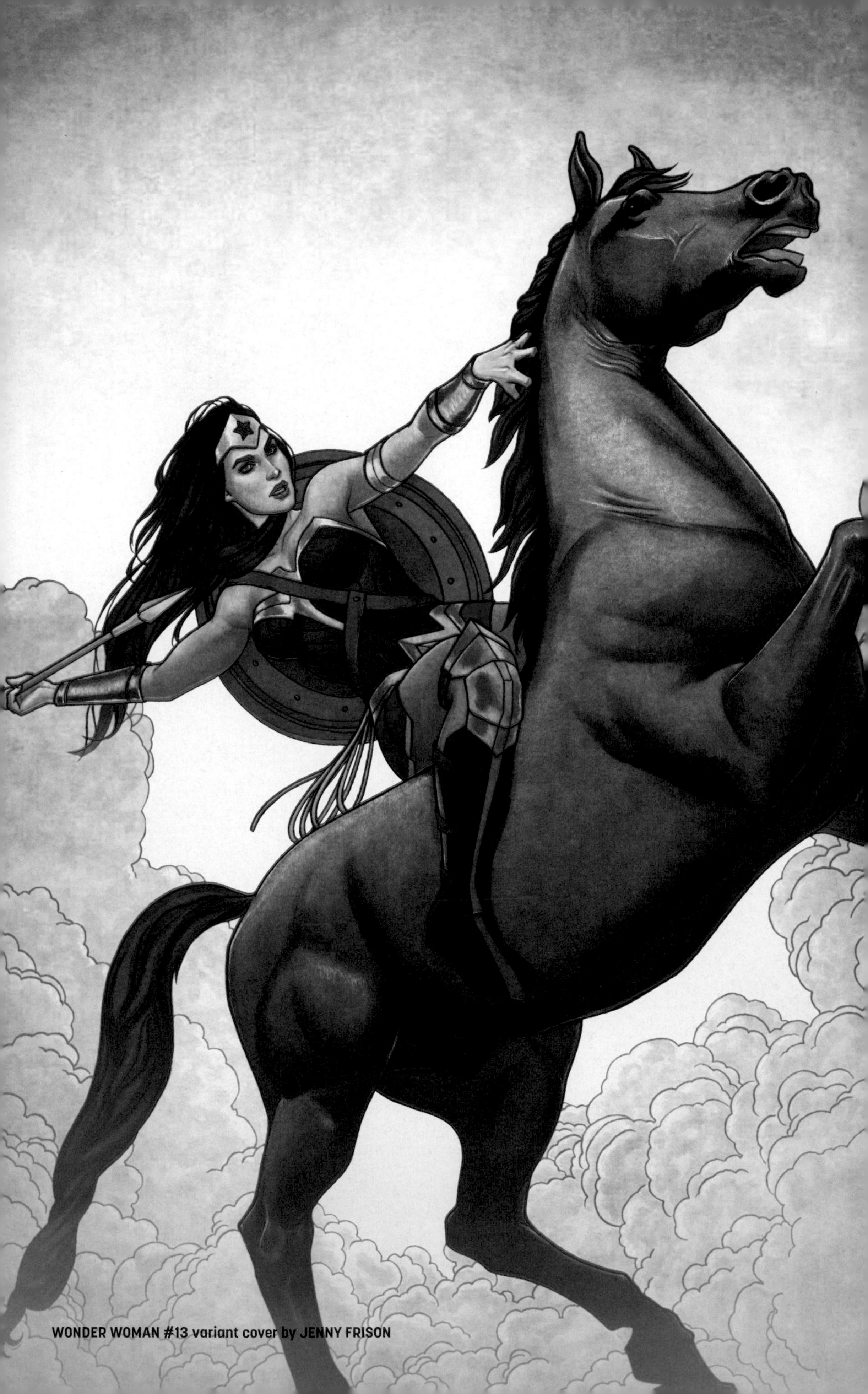

WONDER WOMAN #13 variant cover by JENNY FRISON

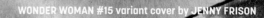
WONDER WOMAN #15 variant cover by JENNY FRISON

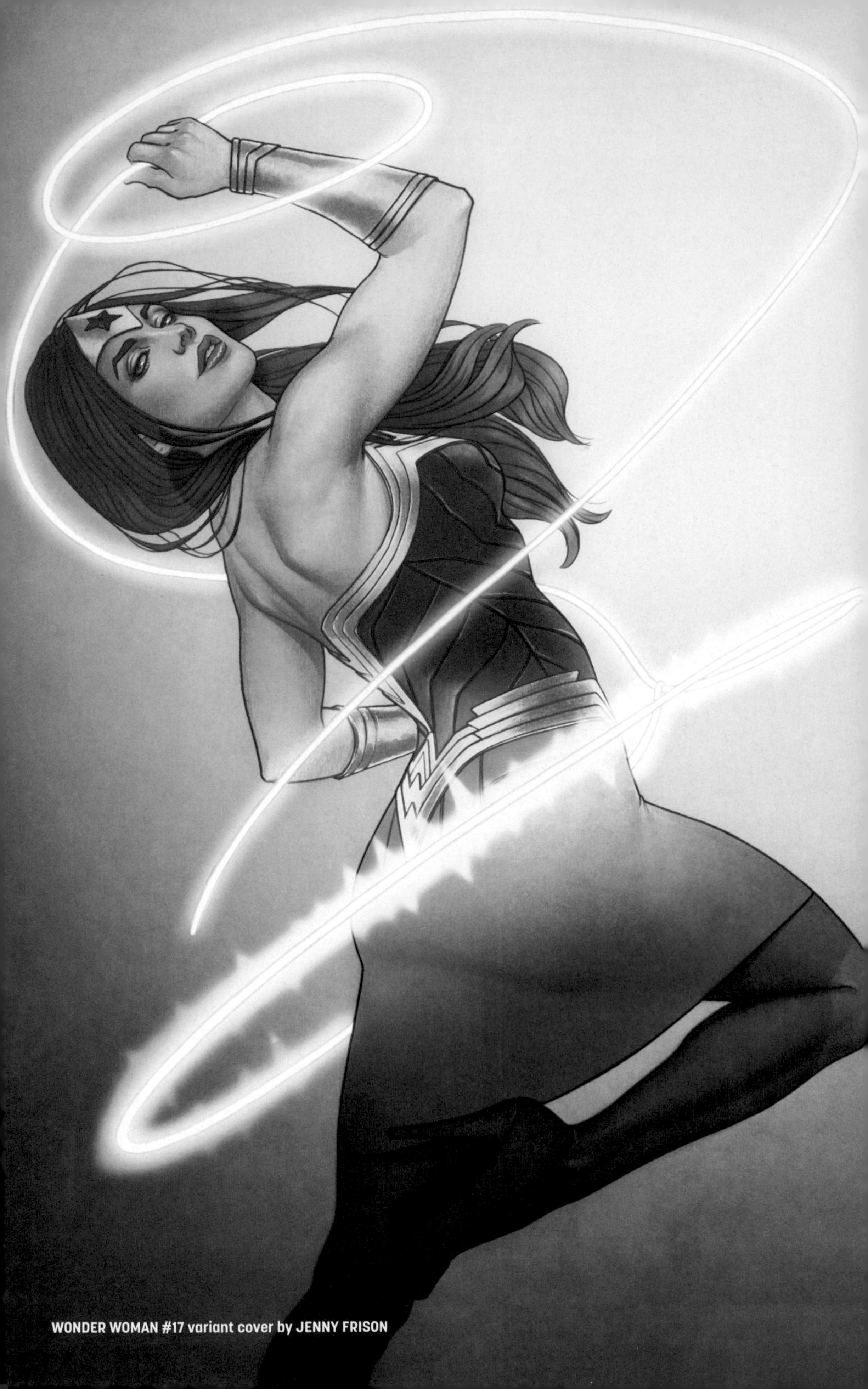

WONDER WOMAN #17 variant cover by JENNY FRISON

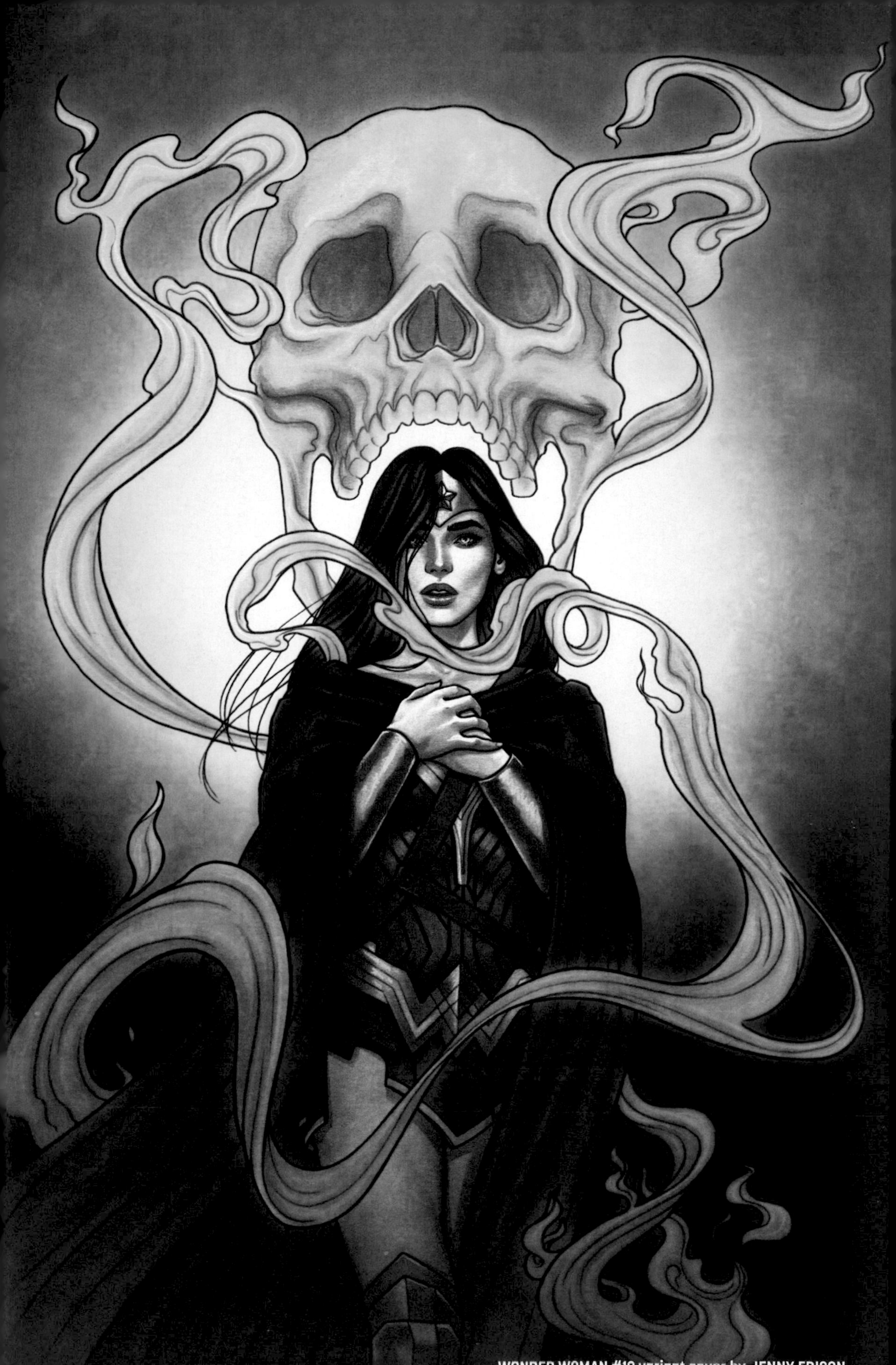

WONDER WOMAN #19 variant cover by JENNY FRISON

WONDER WOMAN #21 variant cover by JENNY FRISON

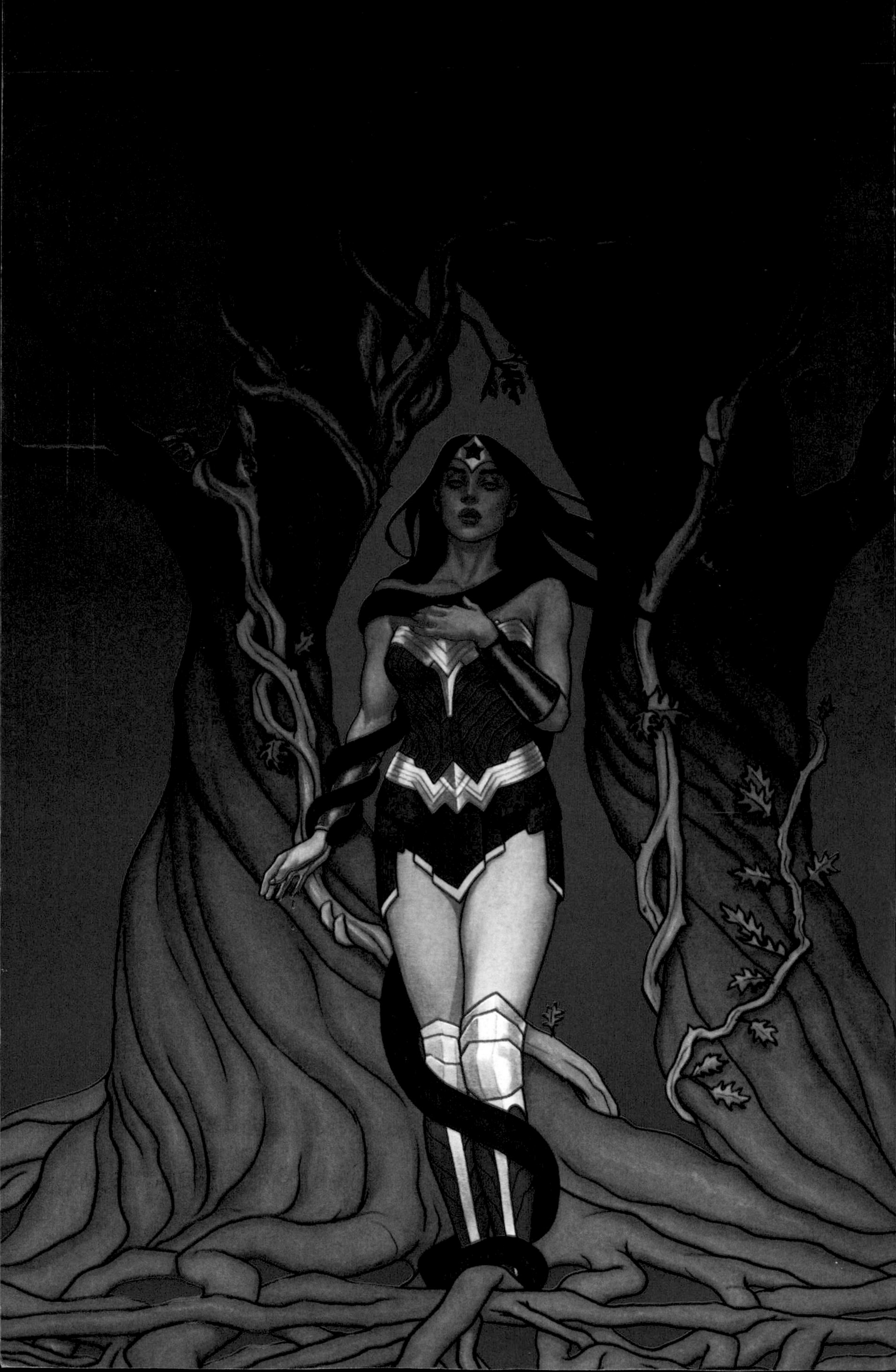

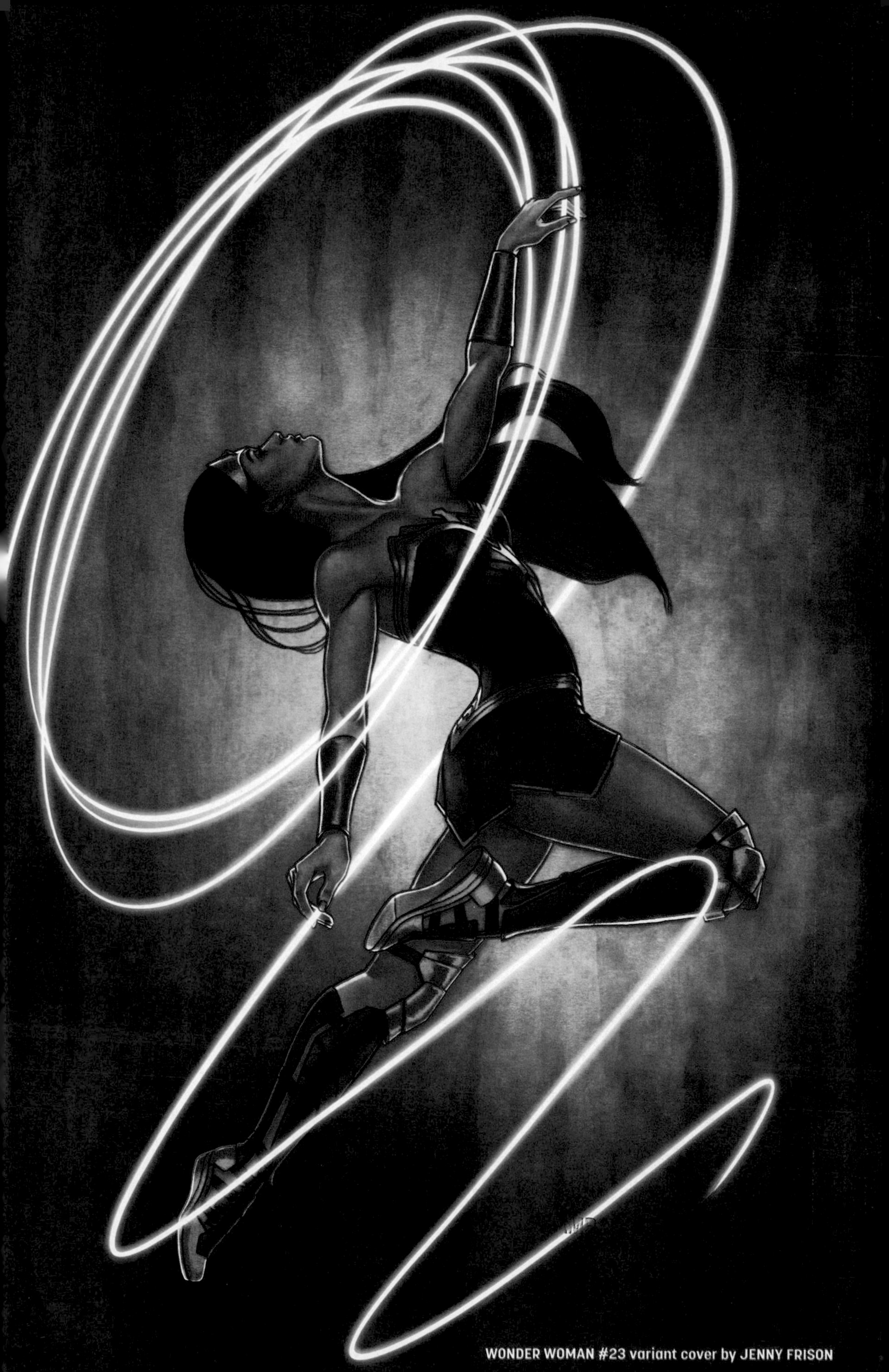

WONDER WOMAN #23 variant cover by JENNY FRISON

WONDER WOMAN #25 variant cover by JENNY FRISON

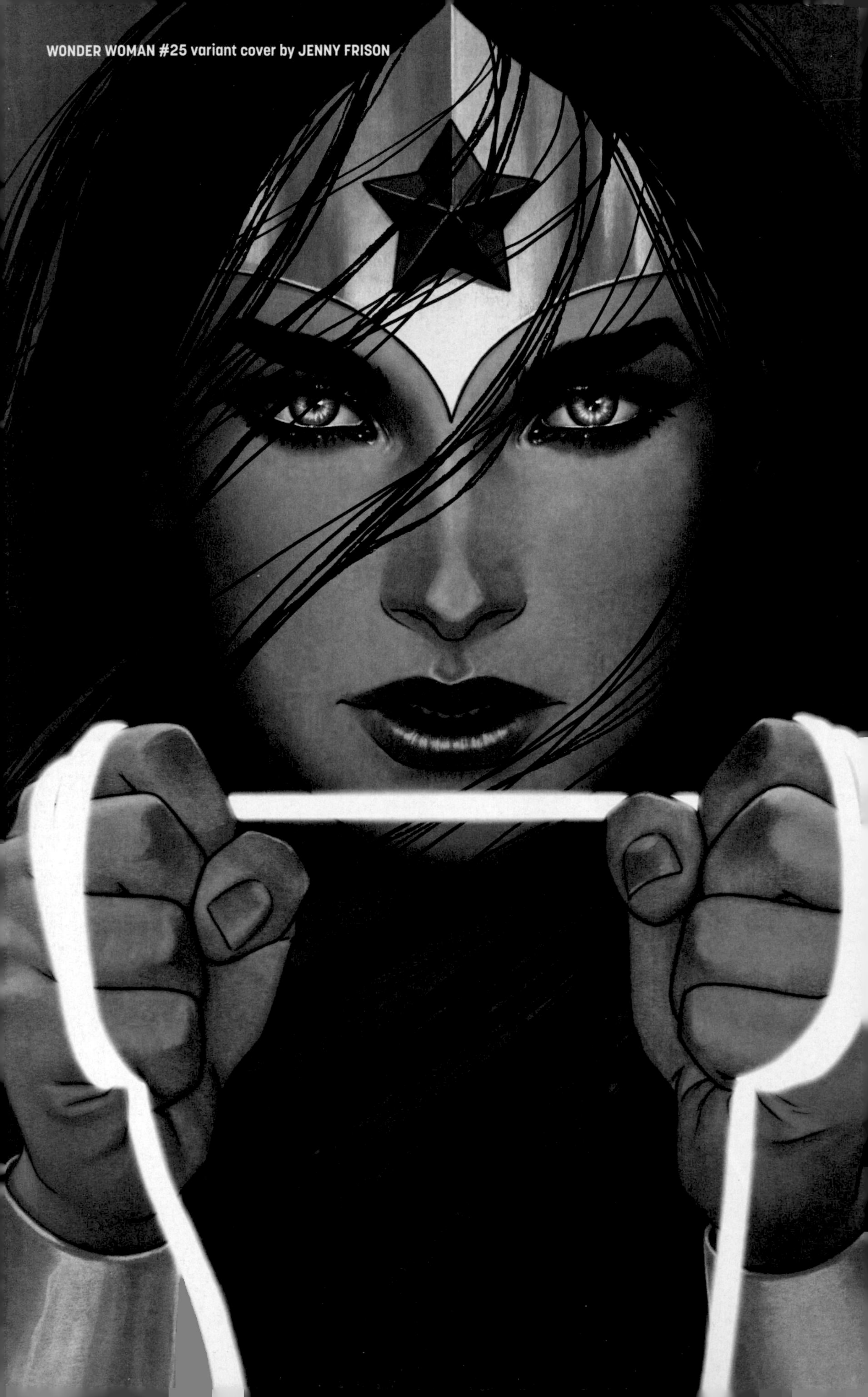

DC UNIVERSE REBIRTH

WONDER WOMAN

VOL. 1: THE LIES

GREG RUCKA
with LIAM SHARP

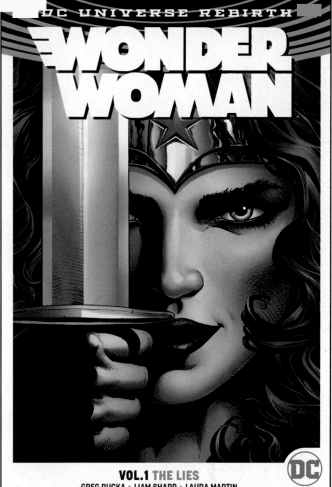

JUSTICE LEAGUE VOL. 1: THE EXTINCTION MACHINES

SUPERGIRL VOL. 1: REIGN OF THE SUPERMEN

BATGIRL VOL. 1: BEYOND BURNSIDE

Get more DC graphic novels wherever comics and books are sold!

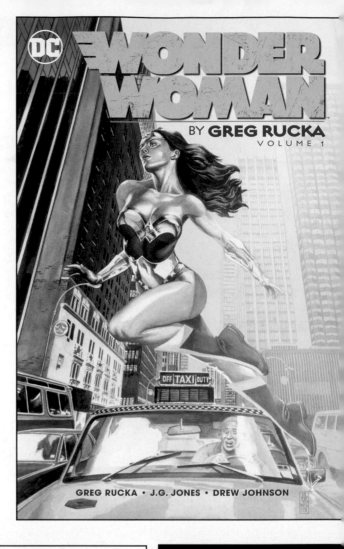

"One of the best writers for Wonder Woman in the modern era."
— **NERDIST**

WONDER WOMAN BY
GREG
RUCKA
with J.G. JONES
& DREW JOHNSON

BATWOMAN: ELEGY
with J.H. WILLIAMS III

52 VOL. 1
with VARIOUS ARTISTS

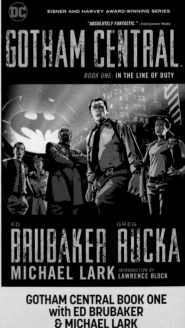

GOTHAM CENTRAL BOOK ONE
with ED BRUBAKER
& MICHAEL LARK

"Bringing Greg Rucka back to WONDER WOMAN was one of the most exciting announcements of DC Rebirth." **THE A.V. CLUB**

"The relaunched Wonder Woman series is one of the most crucial pieces of the DC Rebirth lineup." **IGN**

"If you only pick up one DC book... make it Wonder Woman." **NEWSARAMA**

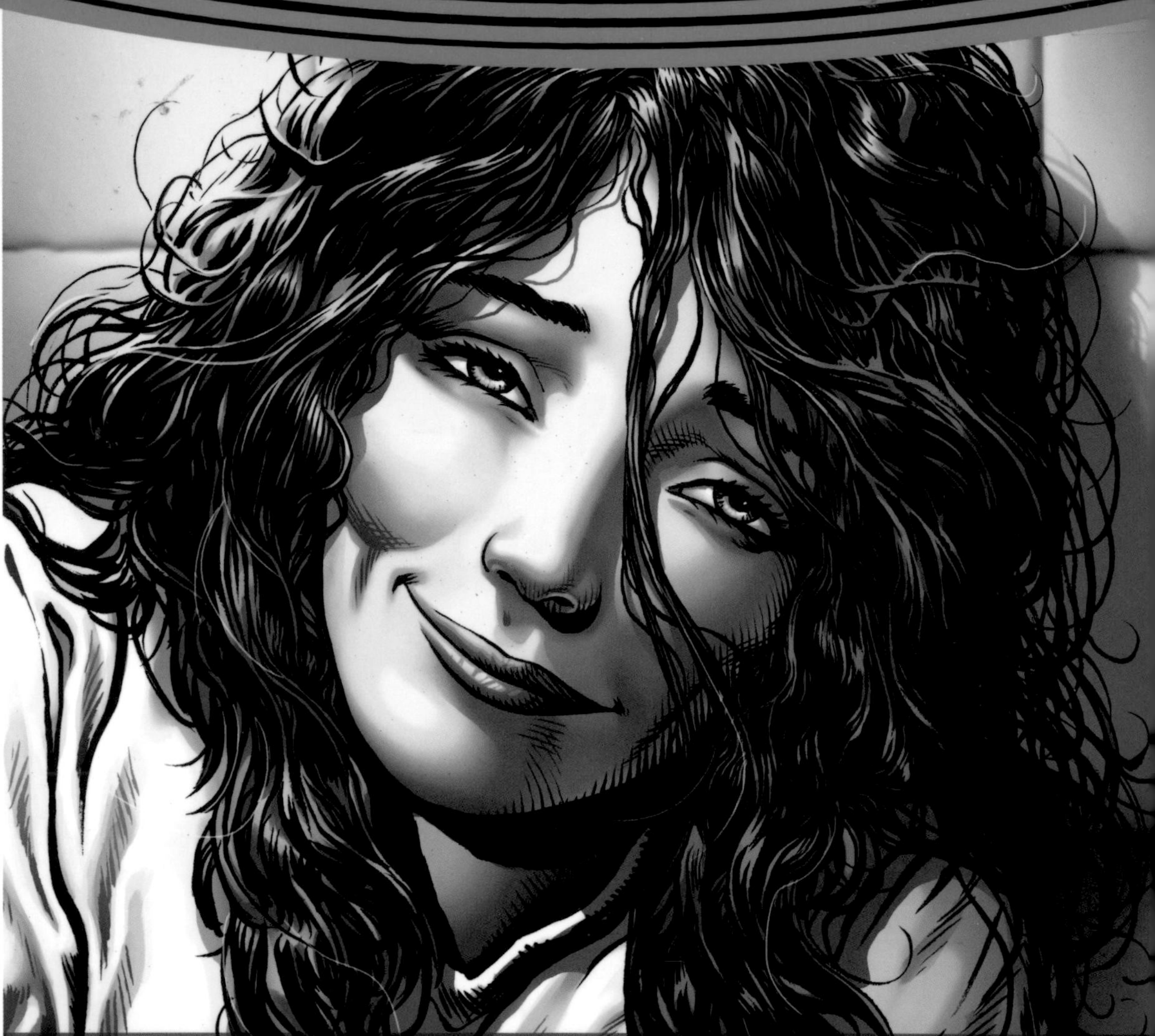

DIVINE MADNESS

They say the truth will set you free. That's what Princess Diana—the hero known to the world as Wonder Woman—had hoped. But she discovered a far darker truth, learning that her entire life and history had been transformed...and it has driven her insane.

Even as her life unravels, sinister forces threaten all she holds dear. No matter how great the trauma, she must continue to fight against the evil and lies that have destroyed her life.

With the help of her closest allies—and her greatest enemy, the Cheetah—Diana will put the pieces of her broken mind back together and do battle against her fearsome new foes.

Will she defy the will of the gods, save her Amazon sisters and solve the mystery of her own existence once and for all? Or is the cost of the truth too steep for even Wonder Woman to bear?

Find out in **WONDER WOMAN VOL. 3: THE TRUTH**, the latest chapter of the instant-classic saga from writer **GREG RUCKA** and artist **LIAM SHARP**. Exploding from the blockbuster DC Rebirth event, this storyline collects odd-numbered issues from WONDER WOMAN #13-25.

51699 >
9 781401 271411
$16.99 USA $22.99 CAN ISBN: 978-1-4012-7141-1 dccomics.com